DEMOCRACY and EDUCATION

DEMOCRACY AND EDUCATION

FREEDOM AND CULTURE

By John Dewey

ISBN 1934568511

Frederick Ellis, Publisher
6015 S. Virginia St., Suite E365
Reno, Nevada 89502

CONTENTS

4

Chapter One:

Education as a Necessity of Life

1. Renewal of Life by Transmission.

The most notable distinction between living and inanimate things is that the former maintain themselves by renewal. A stone when struck resists. If its resistance is greater than the force of the blow struck, it remains outwardly unchanged. Otherwise, it is shattered into smaller bits. Never does the stone attempt to react in such a way that it may maintain itself against the blow, much less so as to render the blow a contributing factor to its own continued action. While the living thing may easily be crushed by superior force, it none the less tries to turn the energies which act upon it into means of its own further existence. If it cannot do so, it does not just split into smaller pieces (at least in the higher forms of life), but loses its identity as a living thing.

As long as it endures, it struggles to use surrounding energies in its own behalf. It uses light, air, moisture, and the material of soil. To say that it uses them is to say that it turns them into means of its own conservation. As long as it is growing, the energy it expends in thus turning the environment to account is more than compensated for by the return it gets: it grows. Understanding the word "control" in this sense, it may be said that a living being is one that subjugates and controls for its own continued activity the energies that would otherwise use it up. Life is a self-renewing process through action upon the environment.

In all the higher forms this process cannot be kept up indefinitely. After a while they succumb; they die. The creature is not equal to the task of indefinite self-renewal. But continuity of the life process is not dependent upon the prolongation of the existence of any one individual. Reproduction of other forms of life goes on in continuous sequence. And though, as the geological record shows, not merely individuals but also species die out, the life process continues in increasingly complex forms. As some species die out, forms better adapted to utilize the obstacles against which they struggled in vain come into being. Continuity of life means continual re-adaptation of the environment to the needs of living organisms.

We have been speaking of life in its lowest terms — as a physical thing. But we use the word "Life" to denote the whole range of experience, individual and racial. When we see a book called the Life of Lincoln we do not expect to find within its covers a treatise on physiology. We look for an account of social antecedents; a description of early surroundings, of the conditions and occupation of the family; of the chief episodes in the development of character; of signal struggles and achievements; of the individual's hopes, tastes, joys and sufferings. In precisely similar fashion we speak of the life of a savage tribe, of the Athenian people, of the American nation. "Life" covers customs, institutions, beliefs, victories and defeats, recreations and occupations.

We employ the word "experience" in the same pregnant sense. And to it, as well as to life in the bare physiological sense, the principle of continuity through renewal applies. With the renewal of physical existence goes, in the case of human beings, the recreation of beliefs, ideals, hopes, happiness, misery, and practices. The continuity of any experience, through renewing of the social group, is a literal fact. Education, in its broadest sense, is the means of this social continuity of life. Every one of the constituent elements of a social group, in a modern city as in a savage tribe, is born immature, helpless, without language, beliefs, ideas, or social standards. Each individual, each unit who is the carrier of the life-experience of his group, in time passes away. Yet the life of the group goes on.

The primary ineluctable facts of the birth and death of each one of the constituent members in a social group determine the necessity of education. On one hand, there is the contrast between the immaturity of the new-born members of the group — its future sole representatives — and the maturity of the adult members who possess the knowledge and customs of the group. On the other hand, there is the necessity that these immature members be not merely physically preserved in adequate numbers, but that they be initiated into the interests, purposes, information, skill, and practices of the mature members: otherwise the group will cease its characteristic life. Even in a savage tribe, the achievements of adults are far beyond what the immature members would be capable of if left to themselves. With the growth of civilization, the gap between the original capacities of the immature and the standards and customs of the elders increases. Mere physical growing up, mere mastery of the bare necessities of subsistence will not suffice to reproduce the life of the group. Deliberate effort and the taking of thoughtful pains are required. Beings that are born not only unaware of, but quite indifferent to, the aims and habits of the social group have to be rendered cognizant of them and actively interested. Education, and education alone, spans the gap.

Society exists through a process of transmission quite as much as biological life. This transmission occurs by means of communication of habits of doing, thinking, and feeling from the older to the younger. Without this communication of ideals, hopes, expectations, standards, opinions, from those members of society who are passing out of the group life to those who are coming into it, social life could not survive. If the members who compose a society lived on continuously, they might educate the new-born members, but it would be a task directed by personal interest rather than social need. Now it is a work of necessity.

If a plague carried off the members of a society all at once, it is obvious that the group would be permanently done for. Yet the death of each of its constituent members is as certain as if an epidemic took them all at once. But the graded difference in age, the fact that some are born as some die, makes possible through transmission of ideas and practices the constant reweaving of the social fabric. Yet this renewal is not automatic. Unless pains are taken to see that genuine and thorough transmission takes place, the most civilized group will

8

relapse into barbarism and then into savagery. In fact, the human young are so immature that if they were left to themselves without the guidance and succor of others, they could not acquire the rudimentary abilities necessary for physical existence. The young of human beings compare so poorly in original efficiency with the young of many of the lower animals that even the powers needed for physical sustentation have to be acquired under tuition. How much more, then, is this the case with respect to all the technological, artistic, scientific, and moral achievements of humanity!

2. Education and Communication.

So obvious, indeed, is the necessity of teaching and learning for the continued existence of a society that we may seem to be dwelling unduly on a truism. But justification is found in the fact that such emphasis is a means of getting us away from an unduly scholastic and formal notion of education. Schools are, indeed, one important method of the transmission which forms the dispositions of the immature; but it is only one means, and, compared with other agencies, a relatively superficial means. Only as we have grasped the necessity of more fundamental and persistent modes of tuition can we make sure of placing the scholastic methods in their true context.

Society not only continues to exist by transmission, by communication, but it may fairly be said to exist in transmission, in communication. There is more than a verbal tie between the words common, community, and communication. Men live in a community in virtue of the things which they have in common; and communication is the way in which they come to possess things in common. What they must have in common in order to form a community or society are aims, beliefs, aspirations, knowledge—a common understanding — like-mindedness as the

sociologists say. Such things cannot be passed physically from one to another, like bricks; they cannot be shared as persons would share a pie by dividing it into physical pieces. The communication which insures participation in a common understanding is one which secures similar emotional and intellectual dispositions — like ways of responding to expectations and requirements.

Persons do not become a society by living in physical proximity, any more than a man ceases to be socially influenced by being so many feet or miles removed from others. A book or a letter may institute a more intimate association between human beings separated thousands of miles from each other than exists between dwellers under the same roof. Individuals do not even compose a social group because they all work for a common end. The parts of a machine work with a maximum of cooperativeness for a common result, but they do not form a community. If, however, they were all cognizant of the common end and all interested in it so that they regulated their specific activity in view of it, then they would form a community. But this would involve communication. Each would have to know what the other was about and would have to have some way of keeping the other informed as to his own purpose and progress. Consensus demands communication.

We are thus compelled to recognize that within even the most social group there are many relations which are not as yet social. A large number of human relationships in any social group are still upon the machine-like plane. Individuals use one another so as to get desired results, without reference to the emotional and intellectual disposition and consent of those used. Such uses express physical superiority, or superiority of position, skill, technical ability, and command of tools, mechanical or fiscal. So far as the relations of parent and child, teacher and pupil, employer and employee, governor and governed, remain upon this level, they form no true social group, no matter how closely their respective activities touch one another. Giving and taking of orders modifies action and results, but does not of itself effect a sharing of purposes, a communication of interests.

Not only is social life identical with communication, but all communication (and hence all genuine social life) is educative. To be a recipient of a communication is to have an enlarged and changed experience. One shares in what another has thought and felt and in so far, meagrely or amply, has his own attitude modified. Nor is the one who communicates left unaffected. Try the experiment of communicating, with fullness and accuracy, some experience to another, especially if it be somewhat complicated, and you will find your own attitude toward your experience changing; otherwise you resort to expletives and ejaculations. The experience has to be formulated in order to be communicated. To formulate requires getting outside of it, seeing it as another would see it, considering what points of contact it has with the life of another so that it may be got into such form that he can appreciate its meaning. Except in dealing with commonplaces and catch phrases one has to assimilate, imaginatively, something of another's experience in order to tell him intelligently of one's own experience. All communication is like art. It may fairly be said, therefore, that any social arrangement that remains vitally social, or vitally shared, is educative to those who participate in it. Only when it becomes cast in a mold and runs in a routine way does it lose its educative power.

In final account, then, not only does social life demand teaching and learning for its own permanence, but the very process of living together educates. It enlarges and enlightens experience; it stimulates and enriches imagination; it creates responsibility for accuracy and vividness of statement and thought. A man really living alone (alone mentally as well as physically) would have little or no occasion to reflect upon his past experience to extract its net meaning. The inequality of achievement between the mature and the immature not only necessitates teaching the young, but the necessity of this teaching gives an immense stimulus to reducing experience to that order and form which will render it most easily communicable and hence most usable.

3. The Place of Formal Education.

There is, accordingly, a marked difference between the education which every one gets from living with others, as long as he really lives instead of just continuing to subsist, and the deliberate educating of the young. In the former case the education is incidental; it is natural and important, but it is not the express reason of the association. While it may be said, without exaggeration, that the measure of the worth of any social institution, economic, domestic, political, legal, religious, is its effect in enlarging and improving experience; yet this effect is not a part of its original motive, which is limited and more immediately practical. Religious associations began, for example, in the desire to secure the favor of overruling powers and to ward off evil influences; family life in the desire to gratify appetites and secure family perpetuity; systematic labor, for the most part, because of enslavement to others, etc. Only gradually was the by-product of the institution, its effect upon the quality and extent of conscious life, noted, and only more gradually still was this effect considered as a directive factor in the conduct of the institution. Even today, in our industrial life, apart from certain values of industriousness and thrift, the intellectual and emotional reaction of the forms of human association under which the world's work is carried on receives little attention as compared with physical output.

But in dealing with the young, the fact of association itself as an immediate human fact, gains in importance. While it is easy to ignore in our contact with them the effect of our acts upon their disposition, or to subordinate that educative effect to some external and tangible result, it is not as easy as in dealing with adults. The need of training is too evident; the pressure to accomplish a change in their attitude and habits is too urgent to leave these consequences wholly out of account. Since our chief business with them is to enable them to share in a common life we cannot help considering whether or no we are forming the powers which will secure this ability. If humanity has made some headway in realizing that the ultimate value of every institution is its distinctively human effect — its effect upon conscious experience — we may well believe that this lesson has been learned largely through dealings with the young.

We are thus led to distinguish, within the broad educational process which we have been so far considering, a more formal kind of education — that of direct tuition or schooling. In undeveloped social groups, we find very little formal teaching and training. Savage groups mainly rely for instilling needed dispositions into the young upon the same sort of association which keeps adults loyal to their group. They have no special devices, material, or institutions for teaching save in connection with initiation ceremonies by which the youth are inducted into full social membership. For the most part, they depend upon children learning the customs of the adults, acquiring their emotional set and stock of ideas, by sharing in what the elders are doing. In part, this sharing is direct, taking part in the occupations of adults and thus serving an apprenticeship; in part, it is indirect, through the dramatic plays in which children reproduce the actions of grown-ups and thus learn to know what they are like. To savages it would seem preposterous to seek out a place where nothing but learning was going on in order that one might learn.

But as civilization advances, the gap between the capacities of the young and the concerns of adults widens. Learning by direct sharing in the pursuits of grown-ups becomes increasingly difficult except in the case of the less advanced occupations. Much of what adults do is so remote in space and in meaning that playful imitation is less and less adequate to reproduce its spirit. Ability to share effectively in adult activities thus depends upon a prior training given with this end in view. Intentional agencies — schools—and explicit material — studies — are devised. The task of teaching certain things is delegated to a special group of persons.

Without such formal education, it is not possible to transmit all the resources and achievements of a complex society. It also opens a way to a kind of experience which would not be accessible to the young, if they were left to pick up their training in informal association with others, since books and the symbols of knowledge are mastered.

But there are conspicuous dangers attendant upon the transition from indirect to formal education. Sharing in actual pursuit, whether directly or vicariously in play, is at least personal and vital. These qualities compensate, in some measure, for the narrowness of available opportunities. Formal instruction, on the contrary, easily becomes remote and dead — abstract and bookish, to use the ordinary words of depreciation. What accumulated knowledge exists in low grade societies is at least put into practice; it is transmuted into character; it exists with the depth of meaning that attaches to its coming within urgent daily interests.

But in an advanced culture much which has to be learned is stored in symbols. It is far from translation into familiar acts and objects. Such material is relatively technical and superficial. Taking the ordinary standard of reality as a measure, it is artificial. For this measure is connection with practical concerns. Such material exists in a world by itself, unassimilated to ordinary customs of thought and expression. There is the standing danger that the material of formal instruction will be merely the subject matter of the schools, isolated from the subject matter of life- experience. The permanent social interests are likely to be lost from view. Those which have not been carried over into the structure of social life, but which remain largely matters of technical information expressed in symbols, are made conspicuous in schools. Thus we reach the ordinary notion of education: the notion which ignores its social necessity and its identity with all human association that affects conscious life, and which identifies it with imparting information about remote matters and the conveying of learning through verbal signs: the acquisition of literacy.

Hence one of the weightiest problems with which the philosophy of education has to cope is the method of keeping a proper balance between the informal and the formal, the incidental and the intentional, modes of education. When the acquiring of information and of technical intellectual skill do not influence the formation of a social disposition, ordinary vital experience fails to gain in meaning, while schooling, in so far, creates only "sharps" in learning — that is, egoistic specialists. To avoid a split between what men consciously know because they are aware of having learned it by a specific job of learning, and what they unconsciously know because they have absorbed it in the formation of their characters by intercourse with others, becomes an increasingly delicate task with every development of special schooling.

Summary. It is the very nature of life to strive to continue in being. Since this continuance can be secured only by constant renewals, life is a self-renewing process. What nutrition and reproduction are to physiological life, education is to social life. This education consists primarily in transmission through communication. Communication is a process of sharing experience till it becomes a common possession. It modifies the disposition of both the parties who partake in it. That the ulterior significance of every mode of human association lies in the contribution which it makes to the improvement of the quality of experience is a fact most easily recognized in dealing with the immature. That is to say, while every social arrangement is educative in effect, the educative effect first becomes an important part of the purpose of the association in connection with the association of the older with the younger. As societies become more complex in structure and resources, the need of formal or intentional teaching and learning increases. As formal teaching and training grow in extent, there is the danger of creating an undesirable split between the experience gained in more direct associations and what is acquired in school. This danger was never greater than at the present time, on account of the rapid growth in the last few centuries of knowledge and technical modes of skill.

Chapter Two:

Education as a Social Function

1. The Nature and Meaning of Environment.

We have seen that a community or social group sustains itself through continuous self-renewal, and that this renewal takes place by means of the educational growth of the immature members of the group. By various agencies, unintentional and designed, a society transforms uninitiated and seemingly alien beings into robust trustees of its own resources and ideals. Education is thus a fostering, a nurturing, a cultivating, process. All of these words mean that it implies attention to the conditions of growth. We also speak of rearing, raising, bringing up — words which express the difference of level which education aims to cover. Etymologically, the word education means just a process of leading or bringing up. When we have the outcome of the process in mind, we speak of education as shaping, forming, molding activity — that is, a shaping into the standard form of social activity. In this chapter we are concerned with the general features of the way in which a social group brings up its immature members into its own social form.

Since what is required is a transformation of the quality of experience till it partakes in the interests, purposes, and ideas current in the social group, the problem is evidently not one of mere physical forming. Things can be physically transported in space; they may be bodily conveyed. Beliefs and aspirations cannot be physically extracted and inserted. How then are they communicated? Given the impossibility of direct contagion or literal inculcation, our problem is to discover the method by which the young assimilate the point of view of the old, or the older bring the young into like-mindedness with themselves. The answer, in general formulation, is: By means of the action of the environment in calling out certain responses. The required beliefs cannot be hammered in; the needed attitudes cannot be plastered on. But the particular medium in which an individual exists leads him to see and feel one thing rather than another; it leads him to have certain plans in order that he may act successfully with others; it strengthens some beliefs and weakens others as a condition of winning the approval of others. Thus it gradually produces in him a certain system of behavior, a certain disposition of action. The words "environment," "medium" denote something more than surroundings which encompass an individual. They denote the specific continuity of the surroundings with his own active tendencies. An inanimate being is, of course, continuous with its surroundings; but the environing circumstances do not, save metaphorically, constitute an environment. For the inorganic being is not concerned in the influences which affect it. On the other hand, some things which are remote in space and time from a living creature, especially a human creature, may form his environment even more truly than some of the things close to him. The things with which a man varies are his genuine environment. Thus the activities of the astronomer vary with the stars at which he gazes or about which he calculates. Of his immediate surroundings, his telescope is most intimately his environment. The environment of an antiquarian, as an antiquarian, consists of the remote epoch of human life with which he is concerned, and the relics, inscriptions, etc., by which he establishes connections with that period.

In brief, the environment consists of those conditions that promote or hinder, stimulate or inhibit the characteristic activities of a living being. Water is the environment of a fish because it is necessary to the fish's activities — to its life. The north pole is a significant element in the environment of an arctic explorer, whether he succeeds in reaching it or not, because it defines his activities, makes them what they distinctively are. Just because life signifies not bare passive existence (supposing there is such a thing), but a way of acting, environment or medium signifies what enters into this activity as a sustaining or frustrating condition.

2. The Social Environment.

A being whose activities are associated with others has a social environment. What he does and what he can do depend upon the expectations, demands, approvals, and condemnations of others. A being connected with other beings cannot perform his own activities without taking the activities of others into account. For they are the indispensable conditions of the realization of his tendencies. When he moves he stirs them and reciprocally. We might as well try to imagine a business man doing business, buying and selling, all by himself, as to conceive it possible to define the activities of an individual in terms of his isolated actions. The manufacturer moreover is as truly socially guided in his activities when he is laying plans in the privacy of his own counting house as when he is buying his raw material or selling his finished goods. Thinking and feeling that have to do with action in association with others is as much a social mode of behavior as is the most overt cooperative or hostile act.

What we have more especially to indicate is how the social medium nurtures its immature members. There is no great difficulty in seeing how it shapes the external habits of action. Even dogs and horses have their actions modified by association with human beings; they form different habits because human beings are concerned with what they do. Human beings control animals by controlling the natural stimuli which influence them; by creating a certain environment in other words. Food, bits and bridles, noises, vehicles, are used to direct the ways in which the natural or instinctive responses of horses occur. By operating steadily to call out certain acts, habits are formed which function with the same uniformity as the original stimuli. If a rat is put in a maze and finds food only by making a given number of turns in a given sequence, his activity is gradually modified till he habitually takes that course rather than another when he is hungry.

Human actions are modified in a like fashion. A burnt child dreads the fire; if a parent arranged conditions so that every time a child touched a certain toy he got burned, the child would learn to avoid that toy as automatically as he avoids touching fire. So far, however, we are dealing with what may be called training in distinction from educative teaching. The changes considered are in outer action rather than in mental and emotional dispositions of behavior. The distinction is not, however, a sharp one. The child might conceivably generate in time a violent antipathy, not only to that particular toy, but to the class of toys resembling it. The aversion might even persist after he had forgotten about the original burns; later on he might even invent some reason to account for his seemingly irrational antipathy. In some cases, altering the external habit of action by changing the environment to affect the stimuli to action will also alter the mental disposition concerned in the action. Yet this does not always happen; a person trained to dodge a threatening blow, dodges automatically with no corresponding thought or emotion. We have to find, then, some differentia of training from education.

A clew may be found in the fact that the horse does not really share in the social use to which his action is put. Some one else uses the horse to secure a result which is advantageous by making it advantageous to the horse to perform the act — he gets food, etc. But the horse, presumably, does not get any new interest. He remains interested in food, not in the service he is rendering. He is not a partner in a shared activity. Were he to become a co-partner, he would, in engaging in the conjoint activity, have the same interest in its accomplishment which others have. He would share their ideas and emotions.

Now in many cases — too many cases — the activity of the immature human being is simply played upon to secure habits which are useful. He is trained like an animal rather than educated like a human being. His instincts remain attached to their original objects of pain or pleasure. But to get happiness or to avoid the pain of failure he has to act in a way agreeable to others. In other cases, he really shares or participates in the common activity. In this case, his original impulse is modified. He not merely acts in a way agreeing with the actions of others, but, in so acting, the same ideas and emotions are aroused in him that animate the others. A tribe, let us say, is warlike. The successes for which it strives, the achievements upon which it sets store, are connected with fighting and victory. The presence of this medium incites bellicose exhibitions in a boy, first in games, then in fact when he is strong enough. As he fights he wins approval and advancement; as he refrains, he is disliked, ridiculed, shut out from favorable recognition. It is not surprising that his original belligerent tendencies and emotions are strengthened at the expense of others, and that his ideas turn to things connected with war. Only in this way can he become fully a recognized member of his group. Thus his mental habitudes are gradually assimilated to those of his group.

If we formulate the principle involved in this illustration, we shall perceive that the social medium neither implants certain desires and ideas directly, nor yet merely establishes certain purely muscular habits of action, like "instinctively" winking or dodging a blow. Setting up conditions which stimulate certain visible and tangible ways of acting is the first step. Making the individual a sharer or partner in the associated activity so that he feels its success as his success, its failure as his failure, is the completing step. As soon as he is possessed by the emotional attitude of the group, he will be alert to recognize the special ends at which it aims and the means employed to secure success. His beliefs and ideas, in other words, will take a form similar to those of others in the group. He will also achieve pretty much the same stock of knowledge since that knowledge is an ingredient of his habitual pursuits.

The importance of language in gaining knowledge is doubtless the chief cause of the common notion that knowledge may be passed directly from one to another. It almost seems as if all we have to do to convey an idea into the mind of another is to convey a sound into his ear. Thus imparting knowledge gets assimilated to a purely physical process. But learning from language will be found, when analyzed, to confirm the principle just laid down. It would probably be admitted with little hesitation that a child gets the idea of, say, a hat by using it as other persons do; by covering the head with it, giving it to others to wear, having it put on by others when going out, etc. But it may be asked how this principle of shared activity applies to getting through speech or reading the idea of, say, a Greek helmet, where no direct use of any kind enters in. What shared activity is there in learning from books about the discovery of America?

Since language tends to become the chief instrument of learning about many things, let us see how it works. The baby begins of course with mere sounds, noises, and tones having no meaning, expressing, that is, no idea. Sounds are just one kind of stimulus to direct response, some having a soothing effect, others tending to make one jump, and so on. The sound h-a-t would remain as meaningless as a sound in Choctaw, a seemingly inarticulate grunt, if it were not uttered in connection with an action which is participated in by a number of people. When the mother is taking the infant out of doors, she says "hat" as she puts something on the baby's head. Being taken out becomes an interest to the child; mother and child not only go out with each other physically, but both are concerned in the going out; they enjoy it in common. By conjunction with the other factors in activity the sound "hat" soon gets the same meaning for the child that it has for the parent; it becomes a sign of the activity into which it enters. The bare fact that language consists of sounds which are mutually intelligible is enough of itself to show that its meaning depends upon connection with a shared experience.

In short, the sound h-a-t gains meaning in precisely the same way that the thing "hat" gains it, by being used in a given way. And they acquire the same meaning with the child which they have with the adult because they are used in a common experience by both. The guarantee for the same manner of use is found in the fact that the thing and the sound are first employed in a joint activity, as a means of setting up an active connection between the child and a grownup. Similar ideas or meanings spring up because both persons are engaged as partners in an action where what each does depends upon and influences what the other does. If two savages were engaged in a joint hunt for game, and a certain signal meant "move to the right" to the one who uttered it, and "move to the left" to the one who heard it, they obviously could not successfully carry on their hunt together. Understanding one another means that objects, including sounds, have the same value for both with respect to carrying on a common pursuit.

After sounds have got meaning through connection with other things employed in a joint undertaking, they can be used in connection with other like sounds to develop new meanings, precisely as the things for which they stand are combined. Thus the words in which a child learns about, say, the Greek helmet originally got a meaning (or were understood) by use in an action having a common interest and end. They now arouse a new meaning by inciting the one who hears or reads to rehearse imaginatively the activities in which the helmet has its use. For the time being, the one who understands the words "Greek helmet" becomes mentally a partner with those who used the helmet. He engages, through his imagination, in a shared activity. It is not easy to get the full meaning of words. Most persons probably stop with the idea that "helmet" denotes a queer kind of headgear a people called the Greeks once wore. We conclude, accordingly, that the use of language to convey and acquire ideas is an extension and refinement of the principle that things gain meaning by being used in a shared experience or joint action; in no sense does it contravene that principle. When words do not enter as factors into a shared situation, either overtly or imaginatively, they operate as pure physical stimuli, not as having a meaning or intellectual value. They set activity running in a given groove, but there is no accompanying conscious purpose or meaning. Thus, for example, the plus sign may be a stimulus to perform the act of writing one number under another and adding the numbers, but the person performing the act will operate much as an automaton would unless he realizes the meaning of what he does.

3. The Social Medium as Educative.

Our net result thus far is that social environment forms the mental and emotional disposition of behavior in individuals by engaging them in activities that arouse and strengthen certain impulses that have certain purposes and entail certain consequences. A child growing up in a family of musicians will inevitably have whatever capacities he has in music stimulated, and, relatively, stimulated more than other impulses which might have been awakened in another environment. Save as he takes an interest in music and gains a certain competency in it, he is "out of it"; he is unable to share in the life of the group to which he belongs. Some kinds of participation in the life of those with whom the individual is connected are inevitable; with respect to them, the social environment exercises an educative or formative influence unconsciously and apart from any set purpose.

In savage and barbarian communities, such direct participation (constituting the indirect or incidental education of which we have spoken) furnishes almost the sole influence for rearing the young into the practices and beliefs of the group. Even in present-day societies, it furnishes the basic nurture of even the most insistently schooled youth. In accord with the interests and occupations of the group, certain things become objects of high esteem; others of aversion. Association does not create impulses or affection and dislike, but it furnishes the objects to which they attach themselves. The way our group or class does things tends to determine the proper objects of attention, and thus to prescribe the directions and limits of observation and memory. What is strange or foreign (that is to say outside the activities of the groups) tends to be morally forbidden and intellectually suspect. It seems almost incredible to us, for example, that things which we know very well could have escaped recognition in past ages. We incline to account for it by attributing congenital stupidity to our forerunners and by assuming superior native intelligence on our own part. But the explanation is that their modes of life did not call for attention to such facts, but held their minds riveted to other things. Just as the senses require sensible objects to stimulate them, so our powers of observation, recollection, and imagination do not work spontaneously, but are set in motion by the demands set up by current social occupations. The main texture of disposition is formed, independently of schooling, by such influences. What conscious, deliberate teaching can do is at most to free the capacities thus formed for fuller exercise, to purge them of some of their grossness, and to furnish objects which make their activity more productive of meaning.

While this "unconscious influence of the environment" is so subtle and pervasive that it affects every fiber of character and mind, it may be worth while to specify a few directions in which its effect is most marked. First, the habits of language. Fundamental modes of speech, the bulk of the vocabulary, are formed in the ordinary intercourse of life, carried on not as a set means of instruction but as a social necessity. The babe acquires, as we well say, the mother tongue. While speech habits thus contracted may be corrected or even displaced by conscious teaching, yet, in times of excitement, intentionally acquired modes of speech often fall away, and individuals relapse into their really native tongue. Secondly, manners. Example is notoriously more potent than precept. Good manners come, as we say, from good breeding or rather are good breeding; and breeding is acquired by habitual action, in response to habitual stimuli, not by conveying information. Despite the never ending play of conscious correction and instruction, the surrounding atmosphere and spirit is in the end the chief agent in forming manners. And manners are but minor morals. Moreover, in major morals, conscious instruction is likely to be efficacious only in the degree in which it falls in with the general "walk and conversation" of those who constitute the child's social environment. Thirdly, good taste and esthetic appreciation. If the eye is constantly greeted by harmonious objects, having elegance of form and color, a standard of taste naturally grows up. The effect of a tawdry, unarranged, and over-decorated environment works for the deterioration of taste, just as meager and barren surroundings starve out the desire for beauty. Against such odds, conscious teaching can hardly do more than convey second-hand information as to what others think. Such taste never becomes spontaneous and personally engrained, but remains a labored reminder of what those think to whom one has been taught to look up. To say that the deeper standards of judgments of value are framed by the situations into which a person habitually enters is not so much to mention a fourth point, as it is to point out a fusion of those already mentioned. We rarely recognize the extent in which our conscious estimates of what is worth while and what is not, are due to standards of which we are not conscious at all. But in general it may be said that the things which we take for granted without inquiry or reflection are just the things which determine our conscious thinking and decide our conclusions. And these habitudes which lie below the level of reflection are just those which have been formed in the constant give and take of relationship with others.

4. The School as a Special Environment.

The chief importance of this foregoing statement of the educative process which goes on willy-nilly is to lead us to note that the only way in which adults consciously control the kind of education which the immature get is by controlling the environment in which they act, and hence think and feel. We never educate directly, but indirectly by means of the environment. Whether we permit chance environments to do the work, or whether we design environments for the purpose makes a great difference. And any environment is a chance environment so far as its educative influence is concerned unless it has been deliberately regulated with reference to its educative effect. An intelligent home differs from an unintelligent one chiefly in that the habits of life and intercourse which prevail are chosen, or at least colored, by the thought of their bearing upon the development of children. But schools remain, of course, the typical instance of environments framed with express reference to influencing the mental and moral disposition of their members.

Roughly speaking, they come into existence when social traditions are so complex that a considerable part of the social store is committed to writing and transmitted through written symbols. Written symbols are even more artificial or conventional than spoken; they cannot be picked up in accidental intercourse with others. In addition, the written form tends to select and record matters which are comparatively foreign to everyday life. The achievements accumulated from generation to generation are deposited in it even though some of them have fallen temporarily out of use. Consequently as soon as a community depends to any considerable extent upon what lies beyond its own territory and its own immediate generation, it must rely upon the set agency of schools to insure adequate transmission of all its resources. To take an obvious illustration: The life of the ancient Greeks and Romans has profoundly influenced our own, and yet the ways in which they affect us do not present themselves on the surface of our ordinary experiences. In similar fashion, peoples still existing, but remote in space, British, Germans, Italians, directly concern our own social affairs, but the nature of the interaction cannot be understood without explicit statement and attention. In precisely similar fashion, our daily associations cannot be trusted to make clear to the young the part played in our activities by remote physical energies, and by invisible structures. Hence a special mode of social intercourse is instituted, the school, to care for such matters.

This mode of association has three functions sufficiently specific, as compared with ordinary associations of life, to be noted. First, a complex civilization is too complex to be assimilated in toto. It has to be broken up into portions, as it were, and assimilated piecemeal, in a gradual and graded way. The relationships of our present social life are so numerous and so interwoven that a child placed in the most favorable position could not readily share in many of the most important of them. Not sharing in them, their meaning would not be communicated to him, would not become a part of his own mental disposition. There would be no seeing the trees because of the forest. Business, politics, art, science, religion, would make all at once a clamor for attention; confusion would be the outcome. The first office of the social organ we call the school is to provide a simplified environment. It selects the features which are fairly fundamental and capable of being responded to by the young. Then it establishes a progressive order, using the factors first acquired as means of gaining insight into what is more complicated.

In the second place, it is the business of the school environment to eliminate, so far as possible, the unworthy features of the existing environment from influence upon mental habitudes. It establishes a purified medium of action. Selection aims not only at simplifying but at weeding out what is undesirable. Every society gets encumbered with what is trivial, with dead wood from the past, and with what is positively perverse. The school has the duty of omitting such things from the environment which it supplies, and thereby doing what it can to counteract their influence in the ordinary social environment. By selecting the best for its exclusive use, it strives to reinforce the power of this best. As a society becomes more enlightened, it realizes that it is responsible not to transmit and conserve the whole of its existing achievements, but only such as make for a better future society. The school is its chief agency for the accomplishment of this end.

In the third place, it is the office of the school environment to balance the various elements in the social environment, and to see to it that each individual gets an opportunity to escape from the limitations of the social group in which he was born, and to come into living contact with a broader environment. Such words as "society" and "community" are likely to be misleading, for they have a tendency to make us think there is a single thing corresponding to the single word. As a matter of fact, a modern society is many societies more or less loosely connected. Each household with its immediate extension of friends makes a society; the village or street group of playmates is a community; each business group, each club, is another. Passing beyond these more intimate groups, there is in a country like our own a variety of races, religious affiliations, economic divisions. Inside the modern city, in spite of its nominal political unity, there are probably more communities, more differing customs, traditions, aspirations, and forms of government or control, than existed in an entire continent at an earlier epoch.

Each such group exercises a formative influence on the active dispositions of its members. A clique, a club, a gang, a Fagin's household of thieves, the prisoners in a jail, provide educative environments for those who enter into their collective or conjoint activities, as truly as a church, a labor union, a business partnership, or a political party. Each of them is a mode of associated or community life, quite as much as is a family, a town, or a state. There are also communities whose members have little or no direct contact with one another, like the guild of artists, the republic of letters, the members of the professional learned class scattered over the face of the earth. For they have aims in common, and the activity of each member is directly modified by knowledge of what others are doing.

In the olden times, the diversity of groups was largely a geographical matter. There were many societies, but each, within its own territory, was comparatively homogeneous. But with the development of commerce, transportation, intercommunication, and emigration, countries like the United States are composed of a combination of different groups with different traditional customs. It is this situation which has, perhaps more than any other one cause, forced the demand for an educational institution which shall provide something like a homogeneous and balanced environment for the young. Only in this way can the centrifugal forces set up by juxtaposition of different groups within one and the same political unit be counteracted. The intermingling in the school of youth of different races, differing religions, and unlike customs creates for all a new and broader environment. Common subject matter accustoms all to a unity of outlook upon a broader horizon than is visible to the members of any group while it is isolated. The assimilative force of the American public school is eloquent testimony to the efficacy of the common and balanced appeal.

The school has the function also of coordinating within the disposition of each individual the diverse influences of the various social environments into which he enters. One code prevails in the family; another, on the street; a third, in the workshop or store; a fourth, in the religious association. As a person passes from one of the environments to another, he is subjected to antagonistic pulls, and is in danger of being split into a being having different standards of judgment and emotion for different occasions. This danger imposes upon the school a steadying and integrating office.

Summary.

The development within the young of the attitudes and dispositions necessary to the continuous and progressive life of a society cannot take place by direct conveyance of beliefs, emotions, and knowledge. It takes place through the intermediary of the environment. The environment consists of the sum total of conditions which are concerned in the execution of the activity characteristic of a living being. The social environment consists of all the activities of fellow beings that are bound up in the carrying on of the activities of any one of its members. It is truly educative in its effect in the degree in which an individual shares or participates in some conjoint activity. By doing his share in the associated activity, the individual appropriates the purpose which actuates it, becomes familiar with its methods and subject matters, acquires needed skill, and is saturated with its emotional spirit.

The deeper and more intimate educative formation of disposition comes, without conscious intent, as the young gradually partake of the activities of the various groups to which they may belong. As a society becomes more complex, however, it is found necessary to provide a special social environment which shall especially look after nurturing the capacities of the immature. Three of the more important functions of this special environment are: simplifying and ordering the factors of the disposition it is wished to develop; purifying and idealizing the existing social customs; creating a wider and better balanced environment than that by which the young would be likely, if left to themselves, to be influenced.

Chapter Three:

Education as Direction

1. The Environment as Directive.

We now pass to one of the special forms which the general function of education assumes: namely, that of direction, control, or guidance. Of these three words, direction, control, and guidance, the last best conveys the idea of assisting through cooperation the natural capacities of the individuals guided; control conveys rather the notion of an energy brought to bear from without and meeting some resistance from the one controlled; direction is a more neutral term and suggests the fact that the active tendencies of those directed are led in a certain continuous course, instead of dispersing aimlessly. Direction expresses the basic function, which tends at one extreme to become a guiding assistance and at another, a regulation or ruling. But in any case, we must carefully avoid a meaning sometimes read into the term "control." It is sometimes assumed, explicitly or unconsciously, that an individual's tendencies are naturally purely individualistic or egoistic, and thus antisocial. Control then denotes the process by which he is brought to subordinate his natural impulses to public or common ends. Since, by conception, his own nature is quite alien to this process and opposes it rather than helps it, control has in this view a flavor of coercion or compulsion about it. Systems of government and theories of the state have been built upon this notion, and it has seriously affected educational ideas and practices. But there is no ground for any such view. Individuals are certainly interested, at times, in having their own way, and their own way may go contrary to the ways of others. But they are also interested, and chiefly interested upon the whole, in entering into the activities of others and taking part in conjoint and cooperative doings. Otherwise, no such thing as a community would be possible. And there would not even be any one interested in furnishing the policeman to keep a semblance of harmony unless he thought that thereby he could gain some personal advantage. Control, in truth, means only an emphatic form of direction of powers, and covers the regulation gained by an individual through his own efforts quite as much as that brought about when others take the lead.

In general, every stimulus directs activity. It does not simply excite it or stir it up, but directs it toward an object. Put the other way around, a response is not just a re-action, a protest, as it were, against being disturbed; it is, as the word indicates, an answer. It meets the stimulus, and corresponds with it. There is an adaptation of the stimulus and response to each other. A light is the stimulus to the eye to see something, and the business of the eye is to see. If the eyes are open and there is light, seeing occurs; the stimulus is but a condition of the fulfillment of the proper function of the organ, not an outside interruption. To some extent, then, all direction or control is a guiding of activity to its own end; it is an assistance in doing fully what some organ is already tending to do.

This general statement needs, however, to be qualified in two respects. In the first place, except in the case of a small number of instincts, the stimuli to which an immature human being is subject are not sufficiently definite to call out, in the beginning, specific responses. There is always a great deal of superfluous energy aroused. This energy may be wasted, going aside from the point; it may also go against the successful performance of an act. It does harm by getting in the way. Compare the behavior of a beginner in riding a bicycle with that of the expert. There is little axis of direction in the energies put forth; they are largely dispersive and centrifugal. Direction involves a focusing and fixating of action in order that it may be truly a response, and this requires an elimination of unnecessary and confusing movements. In the second place, although no activity can be produced in which the person does not cooperate to some extent, yet a response may be of a kind which does not fit into the sequence and continuity of action. A person boxing may dodge a particular blow successfully, but in such a way as to expose himself the next instant to a still harder blow. Adequate control means that the successive acts are brought into a continuous order; each act not only meets its immediate stimulus but helps the acts which follow.

In short, direction is both simultaneous and successive. At a given time, it requires that, from all the tendencies that are partially called out, those be selected which center energy upon the point of need. Successively, it requires that each act be balanced with those which precede and come after, so that order of activity is achieved. Focusing and ordering are thus the two aspects of direction, one spatial, the other temporal. The first insures hitting the mark; the second keeps the balance required for further action. Obviously, it is not possible to separate them in practice as we have distinguished them in idea. Activity must be centered at a given time in such a way as to prepare for what comes next. The problem of the immediate response is complicated by one's having to be on the lookout for future occurrences.

Two conclusions emerge from these general statements. On the one hand, purely external direction is impossible. The environment can at most only supply stimuli to call out responses. These responses proceed from tendencies already possessed by the individual. Even when a person is frightened by threats into doing something, the threats work only because the person has an instinct of fear. If he has not, or if, though having it, it is under his own control, the threat has no more influence upon him than light has in causing a person to see who has no eyes. While the customs and rules of adults furnish stimuli which direct as well as evoke the activities of the young, the young, after all, participate in the direction which their actions finally take. In the strict sense, nothing can be forced upon them or into them. To overlook this fact means to distort and pervert human nature. To take into account the contribution made by the existing instincts and habits of those directed is to direct them economically and wisely. Speaking accurately, all direction is but re-direction; it shifts the activities already going on into another channel. Unless one is cognizant of the energies which are already in operation, one's attempts at direction will almost surely go amiss.

On the other hand, the control afforded by the customs and regulations of others may be short-sighted. It may accomplish its immediate effect, but at the expense of throwing the subsequent action of the person out of balance. A threat may, for example, prevent a person from doing something to which he is naturally inclined by arousing fear of disagreeable consequences if he persists. But he may be left in the position which exposes him later on to influences which will lead him to do even worse things. His instincts of cunning and slyness may be aroused, so that things henceforth appeal to him on the side of evasion and trickery more than would otherwise have been the case. Those engaged in directing the actions of others are always in danger of overlooking the importance of the sequential development of those they direct.

2. Modes of Social Direction.

Adults are naturally most conscious of directing the conduct of others when they are immediately aiming so to do. As a rule, they have such an aim consciously when they find themselves resisted; when others are doing things they do not wish them to do. But the more permanent and influential modes of control are those which operate from moment to moment continuously without such deliberate intention on our part.

1. When others are not doing what we would like them to or are threatening disobedience, we are most conscious of the need of controlling them and of the influences by which they are controlled. In such cases, our control becomes most direct, and at this point we are most likely to make the mistakes just spoken of. We are even likely to take the influence of superior force for control, forgetting that while we may lead a horse to water we cannot make him drink; and that while we can shut a man up in a penitentiary we cannot make him penitent. In all such cases of immediate action upon others, we need to discriminate between physical results and moral results. A person may be in such a condition that forcible feeding or enforced confinement is necessary for his own good. A child may have to be snatched with roughness away from a fire so that he shall not be burnt. But no improvement of disposition, no educative effect, need follow. A harsh and commanding tone may be effectual in keeping a child away from the fire, and the same desirable physical effect will follow as if he had been snatched away. But there may be no more obedience of a moral sort in one case than in the other. A man can be prevented from breaking into other persons' houses by shutting him up, but shutting him up may not alter his disposition to commit burglary. When we confuse a physical with an educative result, we always lose the chance of enlisting the person's own participating disposition in getting the result desired, and thereby of developing within him an intrinsic and persisting direction in the right way.

In general, the occasion for the more conscious acts of control should be limited to acts which are so instinctive or impulsive that the one performing them has no means of foreseeing their outcome. If a person cannot foresee the consequences of his act, and is not capable of understanding what he is told about its outcome by those with more experience, it is impossible for him to guide his act intelligently. In such a state, every act is alike to him. Whatever moves him does move him, and that is all there is to it. In some cases, it is well to permit him to experiment, and to discover the consequences for himself in order that he may act intelligently next time under similar circumstances. But some courses of action are too discommoding and obnoxious to others to allow of this course being pursued. Direct disapproval is now resorted to. Shaming, ridicule, disfavor, rebuke, and punishment are used. Or contrary tendencies in the child are appealed to to divert him from his troublesome line of behavior. His sensitiveness to approbation, his hope of winning favor by an agreeable act, are made use of to induce action in another direction.

2. These methods of control are so obvious (because so intentionally employed) that it would hardly be worth while to mention them if it were not that notice may now be taken, by way of contrast, of the other more important and permanent mode of control. This other method resides in the ways in which persons, with whom the immature being is associated, use things; the instrumentalities with which they accomplish their own ends. The very existence of the social medium in which an individual lives, moves, and has his being is the standing effective agency of directing his activity.

This fact makes it necessary for us to examine in greater detail what is meant by the social environment. We are given to separating from each other the physical and social environments in which we live. The separation is responsible on one hand for an exaggeration of the moral importance of the more direct or personal modes of control of which we have been speaking; and on the other hand for an exaggeration, in current psychology and philosophy, of the intellectual possibilities of contact with a purely physical environment. There is not, in fact, any such thing as the direct influence of one human being on another apart from use of the physical environment as an intermediary. A smile, a frown, a rebuke, a word of warning or encouragement, all involve some physical change. Otherwise, the attitude of one would not get over to alter the attitude of another. Comparatively speaking, such modes of influence may be regarded as personal. The physical medium is reduced to a mere means of personal contact. In contrast with such direct modes of mutual influence, stand associations in common pursuits involving the use of things as means and as measures of results. Even if the mother never told her daughter to help her, or never rebuked her for not helping, the child would be subjected to direction in her activities by the mere fact that she was engaged, along with the parent, in the household life. Imitation, emulation, the need of working together, enforce control.

If the mother hands the child something needed, the latter must reach the thing in order to get it. Where there is giving there must be taking. The way the child handles the thing after it is got, the use to which it is put, is surely influenced by the fact that the child has watched the mother. When the child sees the parent looking for something, it is as natural for it also to look for the object and to give it over when it finds it, as it was, under other circumstances, to receive it. Multiply such an instance by the thousand details of daily intercourse, and one has a picture of the most permanent and enduring method of giving direction to the activities of the young.

In saying this, we are only repeating what was said previously about participating in a joint activity as the chief way of forming disposition. We have explicitly added, however, the recognition of the part played in the joint activity by the use of things. The philosophy of learning has been unduly dominated by a false psychology. It is frequently stated that a person learns by merely having the qualities of things impressed upon his mind through the gateway of the senses. Having received a store of sensory impressions, association or some power of mental synthesis is supposed to combine them into ideas—into things with a meaning. An object, stone, orange, tree, chair, is supposed to convey different impressions of color, shape, size, hardness, smell, taste, etc., which aggregated together constitute the characteristic meaning of each thing. But as matter of fact, it is the characteristic use to which the thing is put, because of its specific qualities, which supplies the meaning with which it is identified. A chair is a thing which is put to one use; a table, a thing which is employed for another purpose; an orange is a thing which costs so much, which is grown in warm climes, which is eaten, and when eaten has an agreeable odor and refreshing taste, etc.

The difference between an adjustment to a physical stimulus and a mental act is that the latter involves response to a thing in its meaning; the former does not. A noise may make me jump without my mind being implicated. When I hear a noise and run and get water and put out a blaze, I respond intelligently; the sound meant fire, and fire meant need of being extinguished. I bump into a stone, and kick it to one side purely physically. I put it to one side for fear some one will stumble upon it, intelligently; I respond to a meaning which the thing has. I am startled by a thunderclap whether I recognize it or not — more likely, if I do not recognize it. But if I say, either out loud or to myself, that is thunder, I respond to the disturbance as a meaning. My behavior has a mental quality. When things have a meaning for us, we mean (intend, propose) what we do: when they do not, we act blindly, unconsciously, unintelligently.

In both kinds of responsive adjustment, our activities are directed or controlled. But in the merely blind response, direction is also blind. There may be training, but there is no education. Repeated responses to recurrent stimuli may fix a habit of acting in a certain way. All of us have many habits of whose import we are quite unaware, since they were formed without our knowing what we were about. Consequently they possess us, rather than we them. They move us; they control us. Unless we become aware of what they accomplish, and pass judgment upon the worth of the result, we do not control them. A child might be made to bow every time he met a certain person by pressure on his neck muscles, and bowing would finally become automatic. It would not, however, be an act of recognition or deference on his part, till he did it with a certain end in view — as having a certain meaning. And not till he knew what he was about and performed the act for the sake of its meaning could he be said to be "brought up" or educated to act in a certain way. To have an idea of a thing is thus not just to get certain sensations from it. It is to be able to respond to the thing in view of its place in an inclusive scheme of action; it is to foresee the drift and probable consequence of the action of the thing upon us and of our action upon it. To have the same ideas about things which others have, to be like-minded with them, and thus to be really members of a social group, is therefore to attach the same meanings to things and to acts which others attach. Otherwise, there is no common understanding, and no community life. But in a shared activity, each person refers what he is doing to what the other is doing and vice-versa. That is, the activity of each is placed in the same inclusive situation. To pull at a rope at which others happen to be pulling is not a shared or conjoint activity, unless the pulling is done with knowledge that others are pulling and for the sake of either helping or hindering what they are doing. A pin may pass in the course of its manufacture through the hands of many persons. But each may do his part without knowledge of what others do or without any reference to what they do; each may operate simply for the sake of a separate result—his own pay. There is, in this case, no common consequence to which the several acts are referred, and hence no genuine intercourse or association, in spite of juxtaposition, and in spite of the fact that their respective doings contribute to a single outcome. But if each views the consequences of his own acts as having a bearing upon what others are doing and takes into account the consequences of their behavior upon himself, then there is a common mind; a common intent in behavior. There is an understanding set up between the different contributors; and this common understanding controls the action of each. Suppose that conditions were so arranged that one person automatically caught a ball and then threw it to another person who caught and automatically returned it; and that each so acted without knowing where the ball came from or went to. Clearly, such action would be without point or meaning. It might be physically controlled, but it would not be socially directed. But suppose that each becomes aware of what the other is doing, and becomes interested in the other's action and thereby interested in what he is doing himself as connected with the action of the other. The behavior of each would then be intelligent; and socially intelligent and guided. Take one more example of a less imaginary kind. An infant is hungry, and cries while food is prepared in his presence. If he does not connect his own state with what others are doing, nor what they are doing with his own satisfaction, he simply reacts with increasing impatience to his own increasing discomfort. He is physically controlled by his own organic state. But when he makes a back and forth reference, his whole attitude changes. He takes an interest, as we say; he takes note and watches what others are doing. He no longer reacts just to his own hunger, but behaves in the light of what others are doing for its prospective satisfaction. In that way, he also no longer just gives way to hunger without knowing it, but he notes, or recognizes, or identifies his own state. It becomes an object for him. His attitude toward it becomes in some degree intelligent. And in such noting of the meaning of the actions of others and of his own state, he is socially directed.

It will be recalled that our main proposition had two sides. One of them has now been dealt with: namely, that physical things do not influence mind (or form ideas and beliefs) except as they are implicated in action for prospective consequences. The other point is persons modify one another's dispositions only through the special use they make of physical conditions. Consider first the case of so-called expressive movements to which others are sensitive; blushing, smiling, frowning, clinching of fists, natural gestures of all kinds. In themselves, these are not expressive. They are organic parts of a person's attitude. One does not blush to show modesty or embarrassment to others, but because the capillary circulation alters in response to stimuli. But others use the blush, or a slightly perceptible tightening of the muscles of a person with whom they are associated, as a sign of the state in which that person finds himself, and as an indication of what course to pursue. The frown signifies an imminent rebuke for which one must prepare, or an uncertainty and hesitation which one must, if possible, remove by saying or doing something to restore confidence. A man at some distance is waving his arms wildly. One has only to preserve an attitude of detached indifference, and the motions of the other person will be on the level of any remote physical change which we happen to note. If we have no concern or interest, the waving of the arms is as meaningless to us as the gyrations of the arms of a windmill. But if interest is aroused, we begin to participate. We refer his action to something we are doing ourselves or that we should do. We have to judge the meaning of his act in order to decide what to do. Is he beckoning for help? Is he warning us of an explosion to be set off, against which we should guard ourselves? In one case, his action means to run toward him; in the other case, to run away. In any case, it is the change he effects in the physical environment which is a sign to us of how we should conduct ourselves. Our action is socially controlled because we endeavor to refer what we are to do to the same situation in which he is acting.

Language is, as we have already seen (ante, p. 15) a case of this joint reference of our own action and that of another to a common situation. Hence its unrivaled significance as a means of social direction. But language would not be this efficacious instrument were it not that it takes place upon a background of coarser and more tangible use of physical means to accomplish results. A child sees persons with whom he lives using chairs, hats, tables, spades, saws, plows, horses, money in certain ways. If he has any share at all in what they are doing, he is led thereby to use things in the same way, or to use other things in a way which will fit in. If a chair is drawn up to a table, it is a sign that he is to sit in it; if a person extends his right hand, he is to extend his; and so on in a never ending stream of detail. The prevailing habits of using the products of human art and the raw materials of nature constitute by all odds the deepest and most pervasive mode of social control. When children go to school, they already have "minds" — they have knowledge and dispositions of judgment which may be appealed to through the use of language. But these "minds" are the organized habits of intelligent response which they have previously required by putting things to use in connection with the way other persons use things. The control is inescapable; it saturates disposition. The net outcome of the discussion is that the fundamental means of control is not personal but intellectual. It is not "moral" in the sense that a person is moved by direct personal appeal from others, important as is this method at critical junctures. It consists in the habits of understanding, which are set up in using objects in correspondence with others, whether by way of cooperation and assistance or rivalry and competition. Mind as a concrete thing is precisely the power to understand things in terms of the use made of them; a socialized mind is the power to understand them in terms of the use to which they are turned in joint or shared situations. And mind in this sense is the method of social control.

3. Imitation and Social Psychology.

We have already noted the defects of a psychology of learning which places the individual mind naked, as it were, in contact with physical objects, and which believes that knowledge, ideas, and beliefs accrue from their interaction. Only comparatively recently has the predominating influence of association with fellow beings in the formation of mental and moral disposition been perceived. Even now it is usually treated as a kind of adjunct to an alleged method of learning by direct contact with things, and as merely supplementing knowledge of the physical world with knowledge of persons. The purport of our discussion is that such a view makes an absurd and impossible separation between persons and things. Interaction with things may form habits of external adjustment. But it leads to activity having a meaning and conscious intent only when things are used to produce a result. And the only way one person can modify the mind of another is by using physical conditions, crude or artificial, so as to evoke some answering activity from him. Such are our two main conclusions. It is desirable to amplify and enforce them by placing them in contrast with the theory which uses a psychology of supposed direct relationships of human beings to one another as an adjunct to the psychology of the supposed direct relation of an individual to physical objects. In substance, this so-called social psychology has been built upon the notion of imitation. Consequently, we shall discuss the nature and role of imitation in the formation of mental disposition.

According to this theory, social control of individuals rests upon the instinctive tendency of individuals to imitate or copy the actions of others. The latter serve as models. The imitative instinct is so strong that the young devote themselves to conforming to the patterns set by others and reproducing them in their own scheme of behavior. According to our theory, what is here called imitation is a misleading name for partaking with others in a use of things which leads to consequences of common interest. The basic error in the current notion of imitation is that it puts the cart before the horse. It takes an effect for the cause of the effect. There can be no doubt that individuals in forming a social group are like-minded; they understand one another. They tend to act with the same controlling ideas, beliefs, and intentions, given similar circumstances. Looked at from without, they might be said to be engaged in "imitating" one another. In the sense that they are doing much the same sort of thing in much the same sort of way, this would be true enough. But "imitation" throws no light upon why they so act; it repeats the fact as an explanation of itself. It is an explanation of the same order as the famous saying that opium puts men to sleep because of its dormitive power.

Objective likeness of acts and the mental satisfaction found in being in conformity with others are baptized by the name imitation. This social fact is then taken for a psychological force, which produced the likeness. A considerable portion of what is called imitation is simply the fact that persons being alike in structure respond in the same way to like stimuli. Quite independently of imitation, men on being insulted get angry and attack the insulter. This statement may be met by citing the undoubted fact that response to an insult takes place in different ways in groups having different customs. In one group, it may be met by recourse to fisticuffs, in another by a challenge to a duel, in a third by an exhibition of contemptuous disregard. This happens, so it is said, because the model set for imitation is different. But there is no need to appeal to imitation. The mere fact that customs are different means that the actual stimuli to behavior are different. Conscious instruction plays a part; prior approvals and disapprovals have a large influence. Still more effective is the fact that unless an individual acts in the way current in his group, he is literally out of it. He can associate with others on intimate and equal terms only by behaving in the way in which they behave. The pressure that comes from the fact that one is let into the group action by acting in one way and shut out by acting in another way is unremitting. What is called the effect of imitation is mainly the product of conscious instruction and of the selective influence exercised by the unconscious confirmations and ratifications of those with whom one associates.

Suppose that some one rolls a ball to a child; he catches it and rolls it back, and the game goes on. Here the stimulus is not just the sight of the ball, or the sight of the other rolling it. It is the situation — the game which is playing. The response is not merely rolling the ball back; it is rolling it back so that the other one may catch and return it, — that the game may continue. The "pattern" or model is not the action of the other person. The whole situation requires that each should adapt his action in view of what the other person has done and is to do. Imitation may come in but its role is subordinate. The child has an interest on his own account; he wants to keep it going. He may then note how the other person catches and holds the ball in order to improve his own acts. He imitates the means of doing, not the end or thing to be done. And he imitates the means because he wishes, on his own behalf, as part of his own initiative, to take an effective part in the game. One has only to consider how completely the child is dependent from his earliest days for successful execution of his purposes upon fitting his acts into those of others to see what a premium is put upon behaving as others behave, and of developing an understanding of them in order that he may so behave. The pressure for like-mindedness in action from this source is so great that it is quite superfluous to appeal to imitation. As matter of fact, imitation of ends, as distinct from imitation of means which help to reach ends, is a superficial and transitory affair which leaves little effect upon disposition. Idiots are especially apt at this kind of imitation; it affects outward acts but not the meaning of their performance. When we find children engaging in this sort of mimicry, instead of encouraging them (as we would do if it were an important means of social control) we are more likely to rebuke them as apes, monkeys, parrots, or copy cats. Imitation of means of accomplishment is, on the other hand, an intelligent act. It involves close observation, and judicious selection of what will enable one to do better something which he already is trying to do. Used for a purpose, the imitative instinct may, like any other instinct, become a factor in the development of effective action.

This excursus should, accordingly, have the effect of reinforcing the conclusion that genuine social control means the formation of a certain mental disposition; a way of understanding objects, events, and acts which enables one to participate effectively in associated activities. Only the friction engendered by meeting resistance from others leads to the view that it takes place by forcing a line of action contrary to natural inclinations. Only failure to take account of the situations in which persons are mutually concerned (or interested in acting responsively to one another) leads to treating imitation as the chief agent in promoting social control.

4. Some Applications to Education.

Why does a savage group perpetuate savagery, and a civilized group civilization? Doubtless the first answer to occur to mind is because savages are savages; being of low-grade intelligence and perhaps defective moral sense. But careful study has made it doubtful whether their native capacities are appreciably inferior to those of civilized man. It has made it certain that native differences are not sufficient to account for the difference in culture. In a sense the mind of savage peoples is an effect, rather than a cause, of their backward institutions. Their social activities are such as to restrict their objects of attention and interest, and hence to limit the stimuli to mental development. Even as regards the objects that come within the scope of attention, primitive social customs tend to arrest observation and imagination upon qualities which do not fructify in the mind. Lack of control of natural forces means that a scant number of natural objects enter into associated behavior. Only a small number of natural resources are utilized and they are not worked for what they are worth. The advance of civilization means that a larger number of natural forces and objects have been transformed into instrumentalities of action, into means for securing ends. We start not so much with superior capacities as with superior stimuli for evocation and direction of our capacities. The savage deals largely with crude stimuli; we have weighted stimuli. Prior human efforts have made over natural conditions. As they originally existed they were indifferent to human endeavors. Every domesticated plant and animal, every tool, every utensil, every appliance, every manufactured article, every esthetic decoration, every work of art means a transformation of conditions once hostile or indifferent to characteristic human activities into friendly and favoring conditions. Because the activities of children today are controlled by these selected and charged stimuli, children are able to traverse in a short lifetime what the race has needed slow, tortured ages to attain. The dice have been loaded by all the successes which have preceded.

Stimuli conducive to economical and effective response, such as our system of roads and means of transportation, our ready command of heat, light, and electricity, our ready-made machines and apparatus for every purpose, do not, by themselves or in their aggregate, constitute a civilization. But the uses to which they are put are civilization, and without the things the uses would be impossible. Time otherwise necessarily devoted to wresting a livelihood from a grudging environment and securing a precarious protection against its inclemencies is freed. A body of knowledge is transmitted, the legitimacy of which is guaranteed by the fact that the physical equipment in which it is incarnated leads to results that square with the other facts of nature. Thus these appliances of art supply a protection, perhaps our chief protection, against a recrudescence of these superstitious beliefs, those fanciful myths and infertile imaginings about nature in which so much of the best intellectual power of the past has been spent. If we add one other factor, namely, that such appliances be not only used, but used in the interests of a truly shared or associated life, then the appliances become the positive resources of civilization. If Greece, with a scant tithe of our material resources, achieved a worthy and noble intellectual and artistic career, it is because Greece operated for social ends such resources as it had. But whatever the situation, whether one of barbarism or civilization, whether one of stinted control of physical forces, or of partial enslavement to a mechanism not yet made tributary to a shared experience, things as they enter into action furnish the educative conditions of daily life and direct the formation of mental and moral disposition.

Intentional education signifies, as we have already seen, a specially selected environment, the selection being made on the basis of materials and method specifically promoting growth in the desired direction. Since language represents the physical conditions that have been subjected to the maximum transformation in the interests of social life — physical things which have lost their original quality in becoming social tools — it is appropriate that language should play a large part compared with other appliances. By it we are led to share vicariously in past human experience, thus widening and enriching the experience of the present. We are enabled, symbolically and imaginatively, to anticipate situations. In countless ways, language condenses meanings that record social outcomes and presage social outlooks. So significant is it of a liberal share in what is worth while in life that unlettered and uneducated have become almost synonymous.

The emphasis in school upon this particular tool has, however, its dangers — dangers which are not theoretical but exhibited in practice. Why is it, in spite of the fact that teaching by pouring in, learning by a passive absorption, are universally condemned, that they are still so entrenched in practice? That education is not an affair of "telling" and being told, but an active and constructive process, is a principle almost as generally violated in practice as conceded in theory. Is not this deplorable situation due to the fact that the doctrine is itself merely told? It is preached; it is lectured; it is written about. But its enactment into practice requires that the school environment be equipped with agencies for doing, with tools and physical materials, to an extent rarely attained. It requires that methods of instruction and administration be modified to allow and to secure direct and continuous occupations with things. Not that the use of language as an educational resource should lessen; but that its use should be more vital and fruitful by having its normal connection with shared activities. "These things ought ye to have done, and not to have left the others undone." And for the school "these things" mean equipment with the instrumentalities of cooperative or joint activity.

For when the schools depart from the educational conditions effective in the out-of-school environment, they necessarily substitute a bookish, a pseudo-intellectual spirit for a social spirit. Children doubtless go to school to learn, but it has yet to be proved that learning occurs most adequately when it is made a separate conscious business. When treating it as a business of this sort tends to preclude the social sense which comes from sharing in an activity of common concern and value, the effort at isolated intellectual learning contradicts its own aim. We may secure motor activity and sensory excitation by keeping an individual by himself, but we cannot thereby get him to understand the meaning which things have in the life of which he is a part. We may secure technical specialized ability in algebra, Latin, or botany, but not the kind of intelligence which directs ability to useful ends. Only by engaging in a joint activity, where one person's use of material and tools is consciously referred to the use other persons are making of their capacities and appliances, is a social direction of disposition attained.

Summary. The natural or native impulses of the young do not agree with the life-customs of the group into which they are born. Consequently they have to be directed or guided. This control is not the same thing as physical compulsion; it consists in centering the impulses acting at any one time upon some specific end and in introducing an order of continuity into the sequence of acts. The action of others is always influenced by deciding what stimuli shall call out their actions. But in some cases as in commands, prohibitions, approvals, and disapprovals, the stimuli proceed from persons with a direct view to influencing action. Since in such cases we are most conscious of controlling the action of others, we are likely to exaggerate the importance of this sort of control at the expense of a more permanent and effective method. The basic control resides in the nature of the situations in which the young take part. In social situations the young have to refer their way of acting to what others are doing and make it fit in. This directs their action to a common result, and gives an understanding common to the participants. For all mean the same thing, even when performing different acts. This common understanding of the means and ends of action is the essence of social control. It is indirect, or emotional and intellectual, not direct or personal. Moreover it is intrinsic to the disposition of the person, not external and coercive. To achieve this internal control through identity of interest and understanding is the business of education. While books and conversation can do much, these agencies are usually relied upon too exclusively. Schools require for their full efficiency more opportunity for conjoint activities in which those instructed take part, so that they may acquire a social sense of their own powers and of the materials and appliances used.

Chapter Four:

Education as Growth

1. The Conditions of Growth.

In directing the activities of the young, society determines its own future in determining that of the young. Since the young at a given time will at some later date compose the society of that period, the latter's nature will largely turn upon the direction children's activities were given at an earlier period. This cumulative movement of action toward a later result is what is meant by growth.

The primary condition of growth is immaturity. This may seem to be a mere truism — saying that a being can develop only in some point in which he is undeveloped. But the prefix "im" of the word immaturity means something positive, not a mere void or lack. It is noteworthy that the terms "capacity" and "potentiality" have a double meaning, one sense being negative, the other positive. Capacity may denote mere receptivity, like the capacity of a quart measure. We may mean by potentiality a merely dormant or quiescent state — a capacity to become something different under external influences. But we also mean by capacity an ability, a power; and by potentiality potency, force. Now when we say that immaturity means the possibility of growth, we are not referring to absence of powers which may exist at a later time; we express a force positively present — the ability to develop.

Our tendency to take immaturity as mere lack, and growth as something which fills up the gap between the immature and the mature is due to regarding childhood comparatively, instead of intrinsically. We treat it simply as a privation because we are measuring it by adulthood as a fixed standard. This fixes attention upon what the child has not, and will not have till he becomes a man. This comparative standpoint is legitimate enough for some purposes, but if we make it final, the question arises whether we are not guilty of an overweening presumption. Children, if they could express themselves articulately and sincerely, would tell a different tale; and there is excellent adult authority for the conviction that for certain moral and intellectual purposes adults must become as little children. The seriousness of the assumption of the negative quality of the possibilities of immaturity is apparent when we reflect that it sets up as an ideal and standard a static end. The fulfillment of growing is taken to mean an accomplished growth: that is to say, an Ungrowth, something which is no longer growing. The futility of the assumption is seen in the fact that every adult resents the imputation of having no further possibilities of growth; and so far as he finds that they are closed to him mourns the fact as evidence of loss, instead of falling back on the achieved as adequate manifestation of power. Why an unequal measure for child and man?

Taken absolutely, instead of comparatively, immaturity designates a positive force or ability, — the pouter to grow. We do not have to draw out or educe positive activities from a child, as some educational doctrines would have it. Where there is life, there are already eager and impassioned activities. Growth is not something done to them; it is something they do. The positive and constructive aspect of possibility gives the key to understanding the two chief traits of immaturity, dependence and plasticity.

(1) It sounds absurd to hear dependence spoken of as something positive, still more absurd as a power. Yet if helplessness were all there were in dependence, no development could ever take place. A merely impotent being has to be carried, forever, by others. The fact that dependence is accompanied by growth in ability, not by an ever increasing lapse into parasitism, suggests that it is already something constructive. Being merely sheltered by others would not promote growth. For

(2) it would only build a wall around impotence. With reference to the physical world, the child is helpless. He lacks at birth and for a long time thereafter power to make his way physically, to make his own living. If he had to do that by himself, he would hardly survive an hour. On this side his helplessness is almost complete. The young of the brutes are immeasurably his superiors. He is physically weak and not able to turn the strength which he possesses to coping with the physical environment.

1. The thoroughgoing character of this helplessness suggests, however, some compensating power. The relative ability of the young of brute animals to adapt themselves fairly well to physical conditions from an early period suggests the fact that their life is not intimately bound up with the life of those about them. They are compelled, so to speak, to have physical gifts because they are lacking in social gifts. Human infants, on the other hand, can get along with physical incapacity just because of their social capacity. We sometimes talk and think as if they simply happened to be physically in a social environment; as if social forces exclusively existed in the adults who take care of them, they being passive recipients. If it were said that children are themselves marvelously endowed with power to enlist the cooperative attention of others, this would be thought to be a backhanded way of saying that others are marvelously attentive to the needs of children. But observation shows that children are gifted with an equipment of the first order for social intercourse. Few grown-up persons retain all of the flexible and sensitive ability of children to vibrate sympathetically with the attitudes and doings of those about them. Inattention to physical things (going with incapacity to control them) is accompanied by a corresponding intensification of interest and attention as to the doings of people. The native mechanism of the child and his impulses all tend to facile social responsiveness. The statement that children, before adolescence, are egotistically self-centered, even if it were true, would not contradict the truth of this statement. It would simply indicate that their social responsiveness is employed on their own behalf, not that it does not exist. But the statement is not true as matter of fact. The facts which are cited in support of the alleged pure egoism of children really show the intensity and directness with which they go to their mark. If the ends which form the mark seem narrow and selfish to adults, it is only because adults (by means of a similar engrossment in their day) have mastered these ends, which have consequently ceased to interest them. Most of the remainder of

children's alleged native egoism is simply an egoism which runs counter to an adult's egoism. To a grown-up person who is too absorbed in his own affairs to take an interest in children's affairs, children doubtless seem unreasonably engrossed in their own affairs.

From a social standpoint, dependence denotes a power rather than a weakness; it involves interdependence. There is always a danger that increased personal independence will decrease the social capacity of an individual. In making him more self-reliant, it may make him more self-sufficient; it may lead to aloofness and indifference. It often makes an individual so insensitive in his relations to others as to develop an illusion of being really able to stand and act alone — an unnamed form of insanity which is responsible for a large part of the remediable suffering of the world.

2. The specific adaptability of an immature creature for growth constitutes his plasticity. This is something quite different from the plasticity of putty or wax. It is not a capacity to take on change of form in accord with external pressure. It lies near the pliable elasticity by which some persons take on the color of their surroundings while retaining their own bent. But it is something deeper than this. It is essentially the ability to learn from experience; the power to retain from one experience something which is of avail in coping with the difficulties of a later situation. This means power to modify actions on the basis of the results of prior experiences, the power to develop dispositions. Without it, the acquisition of habits is impossible.

It is a familiar fact that the young of the higher animals, and especially the human young, have to learn to utilize their instinctive reactions. The human being is born with a greater number of instinctive tendencies than other animals. But the instincts of the lower animals perfect themselves for appropriate action at an early period after birth, while most of those of the human infant are of little account just as they stand. An original specialized power of adjustment secures immediate efficiency, but, like a railway ticket, it is good for one route only. A being who, in order to use his eyes, ears, hands, and legs, has to experiment in making varied combinations of their reactions, achieves a control that is flexible and varied. A chick, for example, pecks accurately at a bit of food in a few hours after hatching. This means that definite coordinations of activities of the eyes in seeing and of the body and head in striking are perfected in a few trials. An infant requires about six months to be able to gauge with approximate accuracy the action in reaching which will coordinate with his visual activities; to be able, that is, to tell whether he can reach a seen object and just how to execute the reaching. As a result, the chick is limited by the relative perfection of its original endowment. The infant has the advantage of the multitude of instinctive tentative reactions and of the experiences that accompany them, even though he is at a temporary disadvantage because they cross one another. In learning an action, instead of having it given ready-made, one of necessity learns to vary its factors, to make varied combinations of them, according to change of circumstances. A possibility of continuing progress is opened up by the fact that in learning one act, methods are developed good for use in other situations. Still more important is the fact that the human being acquires a habit of learning. He learns to learn.

The importance for human life of the two facts of dependence and variable control has been summed up in the doctrine of the significance of prolonged infancy. 1 This prolongation is significant from the standpoint of the adult members of the group as well as from that of the young. The presence of dependent and learning beings is a stimulus to nurture and affection. The need for constant continued care was probably a chief means in transforming temporary cohabitations into permanent unions. It certainly was a chief influence in forming habits of affectionate and sympathetic watchfulness; that constructive interest in the well-being of others which is essential to associated life. Intellectually, this moral development meant the introduction of many new objects of attention; it stimulated foresight and planning for the future. Thus there is a reciprocal influence. Increasing complexity of social life requires a longer period of infancy in which to acquire the needed powers; this prolongation of dependence means prolongation of plasticity, or power of acquiring variable and novel modes of control. Hence it provides a further push to social progress.

2. Habits as Expressions of Growth.

We have already noted that plasticity is the capacity to retain and carry over from prior experience factors which modify subsequent activities. This signifies the capacity to acquire habits, or develop definite dispositions. We have now to consider the salient features of habits. In the first place, a habit is a form of executive skill, of efficiency in doing. A habit means an ability to use natural conditions as means to ends. It is an active control of the environment through control of the organs of action. We are perhaps apt to emphasize the control of the body at the expense of control of the environment. We think of walking, talking, playing the piano, the specialized skills characteristic of the etcher, the surgeon, the bridge-builder, as if they were simply ease, deftness, and accuracy on the part of the organism. They are that, of course; but the measure of the value of these qualities lies in the economical and effective control of the environment which they secure. To be able to walk is to have certain properties of nature at our disposal—and so with all other habits.

Education is not infrequently defined as consisting in the acquisition of those habits that effect an adjustment of an individual and his environment. The definition expresses an essential phase of growth. But it is essential that adjustment be understood in its active sense of control of means for achieving ends. If we think of a habit simply as a change wrought in the organism, ignoring the fact that this change consists in ability to effect subsequent changes in the environment, we shall be led to think of "adjustment" as a conformity to environment as wax conforms to the seal which impresses it. The environment is thought of as something fixed, providing in its fixity the end and standard of changes taking place in the organism; adjustment is just fitting ourselves to this fixity of external conditions. 2 Habit as habituation is indeed something relatively passive; we get used to our surroundings — to our clothing, our shoes, and gloves; to the atmosphere as long as it is fairly equable; to our daily associates, etc. Conformity to the environment, a change wrought in the organism without reference to ability to modify surroundings, is a marked trait of such habituations. Aside from the fact that we are not entitled to carry over the traits of such adjustments (which might well be called accommodations, to mark them off from active adjustments) into habits of active use of our surroundings, two features of habituations are worth notice. In the first place, we get used to things by first using them.

Consider getting used to a strange city. At first, there is excessive stimulation and excessive and ill-adapted response. Gradually certain stimuli are selected because of their relevancy, and others are degraded. We can say either that we do not respond to them any longer, or more truly that we have effected a persistent response to them — an equilibrium of adjustment. This means, in the second place, that this enduring adjustment supplies the background upon which are made specific adjustments, as occasion arises. We are never interested in changing the whole environment; there is much that we take for granted and accept just as it already is. Upon this background our activities focus at certain points in an endeavor to introduce needed changes. Habituation is thus our adjustment to an environment which at the time we are not concerned with modifying, and which supplies a leverage to our active habits. Adaptation, in fine, is quite as much adaptation of the environment to our own activities as of our activities to the environment. A savage tribe manages to live on a desert plain. It adapts itself. But its adaptation involves a maximum of accepting, tolerating, putting up with things as they are, a maximum of passive acquiescence, and a minimum of active control, of subjection to use. A civilized people enters upon the scene. It also adapts itself. It introduces irrigation; it searches the world for plants and animals that will flourish under such conditions; it improves, by careful selection, those which are growing there. As a consequence, the wilderness blossoms as a rose. The savage is merely habituated; the civilized man has habits which transform the environment.

The significance of habit is not exhausted, however, in its executive and motor phase. It means formation of intellectual and emotional disposition as well as an increase in ease, economy, and efficiency of action. Any habit marks an inclination — an active preference and choice for the conditions involved in its exercise. A habit does not wait, Micawber-like, for a stimulus to turn up so that it may get busy; it actively seeks for occasions to pass into full operation. If its expression is unduly blocked, inclination shows itself in uneasiness and intense craving. A habit also marks an intellectual disposition. Where there is a habit, there is acquaintance with the materials and equipment to which action is applied. There is a definite way of understanding the situations in which the habit operates. Modes of thought, of observation and reflection, enter as forms of skill and of desire into the habits that make a man an engineer, an architect, a physician, or a merchant. In unskilled forms of labor, the intellectual factors are at minimum precisely because the habits involved are not of a high grade. But there are habits of judging and reasoning as truly as of handling a tool, painting a picture, or conducting an experiment. Such statements are, however, understatements. The habits of mind involved in habits of the eye and hand supply the latter with their significance. Above all, the intellectual element in a habit fixes the relation of the habit to varied and elastic use, and hence to continued growth. We speak of fixed habits. Well, the phrase may mean powers so well established that their possessor always has them as resources when needed. But the phrase is also used to mean ruts, routine ways, with loss of freshness, open- mindedness, and originality. Fixity of habit may mean that something has a fixed hold upon us, instead of our having a free hold upon things. This fact explains two points in a common notion about habits: their identification with mechanical and external modes of action to the neglect of mental and moral attitudes, and the tendency to give them a bad meaning, an identification with "bad habits." Many a person would feel surprised to have his aptitude in his chosen profession called a habit, and would naturally think of his use of tobacco, liquor, or profane language as typical of the meaning of habit. A habit is to him something which has a hold on him, something not easily thrown off even though judgment condemn it.

Habits reduce themselves to routine ways of acting, or degenerate into ways of action to which we are enslaved just in the degree in which intelligence is disconnected from them. Routine habits are unthinking habits: "bad" habits are habits so severed from reason that they are opposed to the conclusions of conscious deliberation and decision. As we have seen, the acquiring of habits is due to an original plasticity of our natures: to our ability to vary responses till we find an appropriate and efficient way of acting. Routine habits, and habits that possess us instead of our possessing them, are habits which put an end to plasticity. They mark the close of power to vary. There can be no doubt of the tendency of organic plasticity, of the physiological basis, to lessen with growing years. The instinctively mobile and eagerly varying action of childhood, the love of new stimuli and new developments, too easily passes into a "settling down," which means aversion to change and a resting on past achievements. Only an environment which secures the full use of intelligence in the process of forming habits can counteract this tendency. Of course, the same hardening of the organic conditions affects the physiological structures which are involved in thinking. But this fact only indicates the need of persistent care to see to it that the function of intelligence is invoked to its maximum possibility. The short-sighted method which falls back on mechanical routine and repetition to secure external efficiency of habit, motor skill without accompanying thought, marks a deliberate closing in of surroundings upon growth.

3. The Educational Bearings of the Conception of Development.

We have had so far but little to say in this chapter about education. We have been occupied with the conditions and implications of growth. If our conclusions are justified, they carry with them, however, definite educational consequences. When it is said that education is development, everything depends upon how development is conceived. Our net conclusion is that life is development, and that developing, growing, is life. Translated into its educational equivalents, that means (i) that the educational process has no end beyond itself; it is its own end; and that (ii) the educational process is one of continual reorganizing, reconstructing, transforming.

1. Development when it is interpreted in comparative terms, that is, with respect to the special traits of child and adult life, means the direction of power into special channels: the formation of habits involving executive skill, definiteness of interest, and specific objects of observation and thought. But the comparative view is not final. The child has specific powers; to ignore that fact is to stunt or distort the organs upon which his growth depends. The adult uses his powers to transform his environment, thereby occasioning new stimuli which redirect his powers and keep them developing. Ignoring this fact means arrested development, a passive accommodation. Normal child and normal adult alike, in other words, are engaged in growing. The difference between them is not the difference between growth and no growth, but between the modes of growth appropriate to different conditions. With respect to the development of powers devoted to coping with specific scientific and economic problems we may say the child should be growing in manhood. With respect to sympathetic curiosity, unbiased responsiveness, and openness of mind, we may say that the adult should be growing in childlikeness. One statement is as true as the other.

Three ideas which have been criticized, namely, the merely privative nature of immaturity, static adjustment to a fixed environment, and rigidity of habit, are all connected with a false idea of growth or development, — that it is a movement toward a fixed goal. Growth is regarded as having an end, instead of being an end. The educational counterparts of the three fallacious ideas are first, failure to take account of the instinctive or native powers of the young; secondly, failure to develop initiative in coping with novel situations; thirdly, an undue emphasis upon drill and other devices which secure automatic skill at the expense of personal perception. In all cases, the adult environment is accepted as a standard for the child. He is to be brought up to it.

Natural instincts are either disregarded or treated as nuisances — as obnoxious traits to be suppressed, or at all events to be brought into conformity with external standards. Since conformity is the aim, what is distinctively individual in a young person is brushed aside, or regarded as a source of mischief or anarchy. Conformity is made equivalent to uniformity. Consequently, there are induced lack of interest in the novel, aversion to progress, and dread of the uncertain and the unknown. Since the end of growth is outside of and beyond the process of growing, external agents have to be resorted to to induce movement toward it. Whenever a method of education is stigmatized as mechanical, we may be sure that external pressure is brought to bear to reach an external end.

2. Since in reality there is nothing to which growth is relative save more growth, there is nothing to which education is subordinate save more education. It is a commonplace to say that education should not cease when one leaves school. The point of this commonplace is that the purpose of school education is to insure the continuance of education by organizing the powers that insure

growth. The inclination to learn from life itself and to make the conditions of life such that all will learn in the process of living is the finest product of schooling.

When we abandon the attempt to define immaturity by means of fixed comparison with adult accomplishments, we are compelled to give up thinking of it as denoting lack of desired traits. Abandoning this notion, we are also forced to surrender our habit of thinking of instruction as a method of supplying this lack by pouring knowledge into a mental and moral hole which awaits filling. Since life means growth, a living creature lives as truly and positively at one stage as at another, with the same intrinsic fullness and the same absolute claims. Hence education means the enterprise of supplying the conditions which insure growth, or adequacy of life, irrespective of age. We first look with impatience upon immaturity, regarding it as something to be got over as rapidly as possible. Then the adult formed by such educative methods looks back with impatient regret upon childhood and youth as a scene of lost opportunities and wasted powers. This ironical situation will endure till it is recognized that living has its own intrinsic quality and that the business of education is with that quality. Realization that life is growth protects us from that so-called idealizing of childhood which in effect is nothing but lazy indulgence. Life is not to be identified with every superficial act and interest. Even though it is not always easy to tell whether what appears to be mere surface fooling is a sign of some nascent as yet untrained power, we must remember that manifestations are not to be accepted as ends in themselves. They are signs of possible growth. They are to be turned into means of development, of carrying power forward, not indulged or cultivated for their own sake. Excessive attention to surface phenomena (even in the way of rebuke as well as of encouragement) may lead to their fixation and thus to arrested development. What impulses are moving toward, not what they have been, is the important thing for parent and teacher. The true principle of respect for immaturity cannot be better put than in the words of Emerson: "Respect the child. Be not too much his parent. Trespass not on his solitude. But I hear the outcry which replies to this suggestion: Would you verily throw up the reins of public and private discipline; would you leave the young child to the mad career of his own passions and whimsies, and call this anarchy a respect for the child's nature? I answer, — Respect the child, respect him to the end, but also respect yourself.... The two points in a boy's training are, to keep his nature and train off all but that; to keep his nature, but stop off his uproar, fooling, and horseplay; keep his nature and arm it with knowledge in the very direction in which it points." And as Emerson goes on to show this reverence for childhood and youth instead of opening up an easy and easy-going path to the instructors, "involves at once, immense claims on the time, the thought, on the life of the teacher. It requires time, use, insight, event, all the great lessons and assistances of God; and only to think of using it implies character and profoundness."

Summary. Power to grow depends upon need for others and plasticity. Both of these conditions are at their height in childhood and youth. Plasticity or the power to learn from experience means the formation of habits. Habits give control over the environment, power to utilize it for human purposes. Habits take the form both of habituation, or a general and persistent balance of organic activities with the surroundings, and of active capacities to readjust activity to meet new conditions. The former furnishes the background of growth; the latter constitute growing. Active habits involve thought, invention, and initiative in applying capacities to new aims. They are opposed to routine which marks an arrest of growth. Since growth is the characteristic of life, education is all one with growing; it has no end beyond itself. The criterion of the value of school education is the extent in which it creates a desire for continued growth and supplies means for making the desire effective in fact.

1 Intimations of its significance are found in a number of writers, but John Fiske, in his Excursions of an Evolutionist, is accredited with its first systematic exposition.

2 This conception is, of course, a logical correlate of the conceptions of the external relation of stimulus and response, considered in the last chapter, and of the negative conceptions of immaturity and plasticity noted in this chapter.

Chapter Five:

Preparation, Unfolding, and Formal Discipline

1. Education as Preparation.

We have laid it down that the educative process is a continuous process of growth, having as its aim at every stage an added capacity of growth. This conception contrasts sharply with other ideas which have influenced practice. By making the contrast explicit, the meaning of the conception will be brought more clearly to light. The first contrast is with the idea that education is a process of preparation or getting ready. What is to be prepared for is, of course, the responsibilities and privileges of adult life. Children are not regarded as social members in full and regular standing. They are looked upon as candidates; they are placed on the waiting list. The conception is only carried a little farther when the life of adults is considered as not having meaning on its own account, but as a preparatory probation for "another life." The idea is but another form of the notion of the negative and privative character of growth already criticized; hence we shall not repeat the criticisms, but pass on to the evil consequences which flow from putting education on this basis. In the first place, it involves loss of impetus. Motive power is not utilized. Children proverbially live in the present; that is not only a fact not to be evaded, but it is an excellence. The future just as future lacks urgency and body. To get ready for something, one knows not what nor why, is to throw away the leverage that exists, and to seek for motive power in a vague chance. Under such circumstances, there is, in the second place, a premium put on shilly-shallying and procrastination. The future prepared for is a long way off; plenty of time will intervene before it becomes a present. Why be in a hurry about getting ready for it? The temptation to postpone is much increased because the present offers so many wonderful opportunities and proffers such invitations to adventure. Naturally attention and energy go to them; education accrues naturally as an outcome, but a lesser education than if the full stress of effort had been put upon making conditions as educative as possible. A third undesirable result is the substitution of a conventional average standard of expectation and requirement for a standard which concerns the specific powers of the individual under instruction. For a severe and definite judgment based upon the strong and weak points of the individual is substituted a vague and wavering opinion concerning what youth may be expected, upon the average, to become in some more or less remote future; say, at the end of the year, when promotions are to take place, or by the time they are ready to go to college or to enter upon what, in contrast with the probationary stage, is regarded as the serious business of life. It is impossible to overestimate the loss which results from the deflection of attention from the strategic point to a comparatively unproductive point. It fails most just where it thinks it is succeeding — in getting a preparation for the future.

Finally, the principle of preparation makes necessary recourse on a large scale to the use of adventitious motives of pleasure and pain. The future having no stimulating and directing power when severed from the possibilities of the present, something must be hitched on to it to make it work. Promises of reward and threats of pain are employed. Healthy work, done for present reasons and as a factor in living, is largely unconscious. The stimulus resides in the situation with which one is actually confronted. But when this situation is ignored, pupils have to be told that if they do not follow the prescribed course penalties will accrue; while if they do, they may expect, some time in the future, rewards for their present sacrifices. Everybody knows how largely systems of punishment have had to be resorted to by educational systems which neglect present possibilities in behalf of preparation for a future. Then, in disgust with the harshness and impotency of this method, the pendulum swings to the opposite extreme, and the dose of information required against some later day is sugar-coated, so that pupils may be fooled into taking something which they do not care for.

It is not of course a question whether education should prepare for the future. If education is growth, it must progressively realize present possibilities, and thus make individuals better fitted to cope with later requirements. Growing is not something which is completed in odd moments; it is a continuous leading into the future. If the environment, in school and out, supplies conditions which utilize adequately the present capacities of the immature, the future which grows out of the present is surely taken care of. The mistake is not in attaching importance to preparation for future need, but in making it the mainspring of present effort. Because the need of preparation for a continually developing life is great, it is imperative that every energy should be bent to making the present experience as rich and significant as possible. Then as the present merges insensibly into the future, the future is taken care of.

2. Education as Unfolding.

There is a conception of education which professes to be based upon the idea of development. But it takes back with one hand what it proffers with the other. Development is conceived not as continuous growing, but as the unfolding of latent powers toward a definite goal. The goal is conceived of as completion, -perfection. Life at any stage short of attainment of this goal is merely an unfolding toward it. Logically the doctrine is only a variant of the preparation theory. Practically the two differ in that the adherents of the latter make much of the practical and professional duties for which one is preparing, while the developmental doctrine speaks of the ideal and spiritual qualities of the principle which is unfolding.

The conception that growth and progress are just approximations to a final unchanging goal is the last infirmity of the mind in its transition from a static to a dynamic understanding of life. It simulates the style of the latter. It pays the tribute of speaking much of development, process, progress. But all of these operations are conceived to be merely transitional; they lack meaning on their own account. They possess significance only as movements toward something away from what is now going on. Since growth is just a movement toward a completed being, the final ideal is immobile. An abstract and indefinite future is in control with all which that connotes in depreciation of present power and opportunity.

Since the goal of perfection, the standard of development, is very far away, it is so beyond us that, strictly speaking, it is unattainable. Consequently, in order to be available for present guidance it must be translated into something which stands for it. Otherwise we should be compelled to regard any and every manifestation of the child as an unfolding from within, and hence sacred. Unless we set up some definite criterion representing the ideal end by which to judge whether a given attitude or act is approximating or moving away, our sole alternative is to withdraw all influences of the environment lest they interfere with proper development. Since that is not practicable, a working substitute is set up. Usually, of course, this is some idea which an adult would like to have a child acquire. Consequently, by "suggestive questioning" or some other pedagogical device, the teacher proceeds to "draw out" from the pupil what is desired. If what is desired is obtained, that is evidence that the child is unfolding properly. But as the pupil generally has no initiative of his own in this direction, the result is a random groping after what is wanted, and the formation of habits of dependence upon the cues furnished by others. Just because such methods simulate a true principle and claim to have its sanction they may do more harm than would outright "telling," where, at least, it remains with the child how much will stick.

Within the sphere of philosophic thought there have been two typical attempts to provide a working representative of the absolute goal. Both start from the conception of a whole — an absolute — which is "immanent" in human life. The perfect or complete ideal is not a mere ideal; it is operative here and now. But it is present only implicitly, "potentially," or in an enfolded condition. What is termed development is the gradual making explicit and outward of what is thus wrapped up. Froebel and Hegel, the authors of the two philosophic schemes referred to, have different ideas of the path by which the progressive realization of manifestation of the complete principle is effected. According to Hegel, it is worked out through a series of historical institutions which embody the different factors in the Absolute. According to Froebel, the actuating force is the presentation of symbols, largely mathematical, corresponding to the essential traits of the Absolute. When these are presented to the child, the Whole, or perfection, sleeping within him, is awakened. A single example may indicate the method. Every one familiar with the kindergarten is acquainted with the circle in which the children gather. It is not enough that the circle is a convenient way of grouping the children. It must be used "because it is a symbol of the collective life of mankind in general." Froebel's recognition of the significance of the native capacities of children, his loving attention to them, and his influence in inducing others to study them, represent perhaps the most effective single force in modern educational theory in effecting widespread acknowledgment of the idea of growth. But his formulation of the notion of development and his organization of devices for promoting it were badly hampered by the fact that he conceived development to be the unfolding of a ready-made latent principle. He failed to see that growing is growth, developing is development, and consequently placed the emphasis upon the completed product. Thus he set up a goal which meant the arrest of growth, and a criterion which is not applicable to immediate guidance of powers, save through translation into abstract and symbolic formulae.

A remote goal of complete unfoldedness is, in technical philosophic language, transcendental. That is, it is something apart from direct experience and perception. So far as experience is concerned, it is empty; it represents a vague sentimental aspiration rather than anything which can be intelligently grasped and stated. This vagueness must be compensated for by some a priori formula. Froebel made the connection between the concrete facts of experience and the transcendental ideal of development by regarding the former as symbols of the latter. To regard known things as symbols, according to some arbitrary a priori formula — and every a priori conception must be arbitrary — is an invitation to romantic fancy to seize upon any analogies which appeal to it and treat them as laws. After the scheme of symbolism has been settled upon, some definite technique must be invented by which the inner meaning of the sensible symbols used may be brought home to children. Adults being the formulators of the symbolism are naturally the authors and controllers of the technique. The result was that Froebel's love of abstract symbolism often got the better of his sympathetic insight; and there was substituted for development as arbitrary and externally imposed a scheme of dictation as the history of instruction has ever seen.

With Hegel the necessity of finding some working concrete counterpart of the inaccessible Absolute took an institutional, rather than symbolic, form. His philosophy, like Froebel's, marks in one direction an indispensable contribution to a valid conception of the process of life. The weaknesses of an abstract individualistic philosophy were evident to him; he saw the impossibility of making a clean sweep of historical institutions, of treating them as despotisms begot in artifice and nurtured in fraud. In his philosophy of history and society culminated the efforts of a whole series of German writers — Lessing, Herder, Kant, Schiller, Goethe — to appreciate the nurturing influence of the great collective institutional products of humanity. For those who learned the lesson of this movement, it was henceforth impossible to conceive of institutions or of culture as artificial. It destroyed completely — in idea, not in fact — the psychology that regarded "mind" as a ready-made possession of a naked individual by showing the significance of "objective mind" — language, government, art, religion — in the formation of individual minds. But since Hegel was haunted by the conception of an absolute goal, he was obliged to arrange institutions as they concretely exist, on a stepladder of ascending approximations. Each in its time and place is absolutely necessary, because a stage in the self-realizing process of the absolute mind. Taken as such a step or stage, its existence is proof of its complete rationality, for it is an integral element in the total, which is Reason. Against institutions as they are, individuals have no spiritual rights; personal development, and nurture, consist in obedient assimilation of the spirit of existing institutions. Conformity, not transformation, is the essence of education. Institutions change as history shows; but their change, the rise and fall of states, is the work of the "world-spirit." Individuals, save the great "heroes" who are the chosen organs of the world-spirit, have no share or lot in it. In the later nineteenth century, this type of idealism was amalgamated with the doctrine of biological evolution.

"Evolution" was a force working itself out to its own end. As against it, or as compared with it, the conscious ideas and preference of individuals are impotent. Or, rather, they are but the means by which it works itself out. Social progress is an "organic growth," not an experimental selection. Reason is all powerful, but only Absolute Reason has any power.

The recognition (or rediscovery, for the idea was familiar to the Greeks) that great historic institutions are active factors in the intellectual nurture of mind was a great contribution to educational philosophy. It indicated a genuine advance beyond Rousseau, who had marred his assertion that education must be a natural development and not something forced or grafted upon individuals from without, by the notion that social conditions are not natural. But in its notion of a complete and all-inclusive end of development, the Hegelian theory swallowed up concrete individualities, though magnifying The Individual in the abstract. Some of Hegel's followers sought to reconcile the claims of the Whole and of individuality by the conception of society as an organic whole, or organism. That social organization is presupposed in the adequate exercise of individual capacity is not to be doubted. But the social organism, interpreted after the relation of the organs of the body to each other and to the whole body, means that each individual has a certain limited place and function, requiring to be supplemented by the place and functions of the other organs. As one portion of the bodily tissue is differentiated so that it can be the hand and the hand only, another, the eye, and so on, all taken together making the organism, so one individual is supposed to be differentiated for the exercise of the mechanical operations of society, another for those of a statesman, another for those of a scholar, and so on. The notion of "organism" is thus used to give a philosophic sanction to class distinctions in social organization—a notion which in its educational application again means external dictation instead of growth.

3. Education as Training of Faculties. A theory which has had great vogue and which came into existence before the notion of growth had much influence is known as the theory of "formal discipline." It has in view a correct ideal; one outcome of education should be the creation of specific powers of accomplishment. A trained person is one who can do the chief things which it is important for him to do better than he could without training: "better" signifying greater ease, efficiency, economy, promptness, etc. That this is an outcome of education was indicated in what was said about habits as the product of educative development. But the theory in question takes, as it were, a short cut; it regards some powers (to be presently named) as the direct and conscious aims of instruction, and not simply as the results of growth. There is a definite number of powers to be trained, as one might enumerate the kinds of

strokes which a golfer has to master. Consequently education should get directly at the business of training them. But this implies that they are already there in some untrained form; otherwise their creation would have to be an indirect product of other activities and agencies. Being there already in some crude form, all that remains is to exercise them in constant and graded repetitions, and they will inevitably be refined and perfected. In the phrase "formal discipline" as applied to this conception, "discipline" refers both to the outcome of trained power and to the method of training through repeated exercise.

The forms of powers in question are such things as the faculties of perceiving, retaining, recalling, associating, attending, willing, feeling, imagining, thinking, etc., which are then shaped by exercise upon material presented. In its classic form, this theory was expressed by Locke. On the one hand, the outer world presents the material or content of knowledge through passively received sensations. On the other hand, the mind has certain ready powers, attention, observation, retention, comparison, abstraction, compounding, etc. Knowledge results if the mind discriminates and combines things as they are united and divided in nature itself. But the important thing for education is the exercise or practice of the faculties of the mind till they become thoroughly established habitudes. The analogy constantly employed is that of a billiard player or gymnast, who by repeated use of certain muscles in a uniform way at last secures automatic skill. Even the faculty of thinking was to be formed into a trained habit by repeated exercises in making and combining simple distinctions, for which, Locke thought, mathematics affords unrivaled opportunity.

Locke's statements fitted well into the dualism of his day. It seemed to do justice to both mind and matter, the individual and the world. One of the two supplied the matter of knowledge and the object upon which mind should work. The other supplied definite mental powers, which were few in number and which might be trained by specific exercises. The scheme appeared to give due weight to the subject matter of knowledge, and yet it insisted that the end of education is not the bare reception and storage of information, but the formation of personal powers of attention, memory, observation, abstraction, and generalization. It was realistic in its emphatic assertion that all material whatever is received from without; it was idealistic in that final stress fell upon the formation of intellectual powers. It was objective and impersonal in its assertion that the individual cannot possess or generate any true ideas on his own account; it was individualistic in placing the end of education in the perfecting of certain faculties possessed at the outset by the individual. This kind of distribution of values expressed with nicety the state of opinion in the generations following upon Locke. It became, without explicit reference to Locke, a common-place of educational theory and of psychology. Practically, it seemed to provide the educator with definite, instead of vague, tasks. It made the elaboration of a technique of instruction relatively easy. All that was necessary was to provide for sufficient practice of each of the powers. This practice consists in repeated acts of attending, observing, memorizing, etc. By grading the difficulty of the acts, making each set of repetitions somewhat more difficult than the set which preceded it, a complete scheme of instruction is evolved. There are various ways, equally conclusive, of criticizing this conception, in both its alleged foundations and in its educational application. (1) Perhaps the most direct mode of attack consists in pointing out that the supposed original faculties of observation, recollection, willing, thinking, etc., are purely mythological. There are no such ready-made powers waiting to be exercised and thereby trained. There are, indeed, a great number of original native tendencies, instinctive modes of action, based on the original connections of neurones in the central nervous system. There are impulsive tendencies of the eyes to follow and fixate light; of the neck muscles to turn toward light and sound; of the hands to reach and grasp; and turn and twist and thump; of the vocal apparatus to make sounds; of the mouth to spew out unpleasant substances; to gag and to curl the lip, and so on in almost indefinite number. But these tendencies (a) instead of being a small number sharply marked off from one another, are of an indefinite variety, interweaving with one another in all kinds of subtle ways. (b) Instead of being latent intellectual powers, requiring only exercise for their perfecting, they are tendencies to respond in certain ways to changes in the environment so as to bring about other changes. Something in the throat makes one cough; the tendency is to eject the obnoxious particle and thus modify the subsequent stimulus. The hand touches a hot thing; it is impulsively, wholly unintellectually, snatched away. But the withdrawal alters the stimuli operating, and tends to make them more consonant with the needs of the organism. It is by such specific changes of organic activities in response to specific changes in the medium that that control of the environment of which we have spoken (see ante, p. 24) is effected. Now all of our first seeings and hearings and touchings and smellings and tastings are of this kind. In any legitimate sense of the words mental or intellectual or cognitive, they are lacking in these qualities, and no amount of repetitious exercise could bestow any intellectual properties of observation, judgment, or intentional action (volition) upon them.

(2) Consequently the training of our original impulsive activities is not a refinement and perfecting achieved by "exercise" as one might strengthen a muscle by practice. It consists rather (a) in selecting from the diffused responses which are evoked at a given time those which are especially adapted to the utilization of the stimulus. That is to say, among the reactions of the body in general occur upon stimulation of the eye by light, all except those which are specifically adapted to reaching, grasping, and manipulating the object effectively are gradually eliminated—or else no training occurs. As we have already noted, the primary reactions, with a very few exceptions are too diffused and general to be practically of much use in the case of the human infant. Hence the identity of training with selective response. (Compare p. 25.) (b) Equally important is the specific coordination of different factors of response which takes place. There is not merely a selection of the hand reactions which effect grasping, but of the particular visual stimuli which call out just these reactions and no others, and an establishment of connection between the two. But the coordinating does not

stop here. Characteristic temperature reactions may take place when the object is grasped. These will also be brought in; later, the temperature reaction may be connected directly with the optical stimulus, the hand reaction being suppressed—as a bright flame, independent of close contact, may steer one away. Or the child in handling the object pounds with it, or crumples it, and a sound issues. The ear response is then brought into the system of response. If a certain sound (the conventional name) is made by others and accompanies the activity, response of both ear and the vocal apparatus connected with auditory stimulation will also become an associated factor in the complex response. 2

(3) The more specialized the adjustment of response and stimulus to each other (for, taking the sequence of activities into account, the stimuli are adapted to reactions as well as reactions to stimuli) the more rigid and the less generally available is the training secured. In equivalent language, less intellectual or educative quality attaches to the training. The usual way of stating this fact is that the more specialized the reaction, the less is the skill acquired in practicing and perfecting it transferable to other modes of behavior. According to the orthodox theory of formal discipline, a pupil in studying his spelling lesson acquires, besides ability to spell those particular words, an increase of power of observation, attention, and recollection which may be employed whenever these powers are needed. As matter of fact, the more he confines himself to noticing and fixating the forms of words, irrespective of connection with other things (such as the meaning of the words, the context in which they are habitually used, the derivation and classification of the verbal form, etc.) the less likely is he to acquire an ability which can be used for anything except the mere noting of verbal visual forms. He may not even be increasing his ability to make accurate distinctions among geometrical forms, to say nothing of ability to observe in general. He is merely selecting the stimuli supplied by the forms of the letters and the motor reactions of oral or written reproduction. The scope of coordination (to use our prior terminology) is extremely limited. The connections which are employed in other observations and recollections (or reproductions) are deliberately eliminated when the pupil is exercised merely upon forms of letters and words. Having been excluded, they cannot be restored when needed. The ability secured to observe and to recall verbal forms is not available for perceiving and recalling other things. In the ordinary phraseology, it is not transferable. But the wider the context—that is to say, the more varied the stimuli and responses coordinated—the more the ability acquired is available for the effective performance of other acts; not, strictly speaking, because there is any "transfer," but because the wide range of factors employed in the specific act is equivalent to a broad range of activity, to a flexible, instead of to a narrow and rigid, coordination. (4) Going to the root of the matter, the fundamental fallacy of the theory is its dualism; that is to say, its separation of activities and capacities from subject matter. There is no such thing as an ability to see or hear or remember in general; there is only the ability to see or hear or remember something. To talk about training a power, mental or physical, in general, apart from the subject matter involved in its exercise, is nonsense. Exercise may react

upon circulation, breathing, and nutrition so as to develop vigor or strength, but this reservoir is available for specific ends only by use in connection with the material means which accomplish them. Vigor will enable a man to play tennis or golf or to sail a boat better than he would if he were weak. But only by employing ball and racket, ball and club, sail and tiller, in definite ways does he become expert in any one of them; and expertness in one secures expertness in another only so far as it is either a sign of aptitude for fine muscular coordinations or as the same kind of coordination is involved in all of them. Moreover, the difference between the training of ability to spell which comes from taking visual forms in a narrow context and one which takes them in connection with the activities required to grasp meaning, such as context, affiliations of descent, etc., may be compared to the difference between exercises in the gymnasium with pulley weights to "develop" certain muscles, and a game or sport. The former is uniform and mechanical; it is rigidly specialized. The latter is varied from moment to moment; no two acts are quite alike; novel emergencies have to be met; the coordinations forming have to be kept flexible and elastic. Consequently, the training is much more "general"; that is to say, it covers a wider territory and includes more factors. Exactly the same thing holds of special and general education of the mind.

A monotonously uniform exercise may by practice give great skill in one special act; but the skill is limited to that act, be it bookkeeping or calculations in logarithms or experiments in hydrocarbons. One may be an authority in a particular field and yet of more than usually poor judgment in matters not closely allied, unless the training in the special field has been of a kind to ramify into the subject matter of the other fields. (5) Consequently, such powers as observation, recollection, judgment, esthetic taste, represent organized results of the occupation of native active tendencies with certain subject matters. A man does not observe closely and fully by pressing a button for the observing faculty to get to work (in other words by "willing" to observe); but if he has something to do which can be accomplished successfully only through intensive and extensive use of eye and hand, he naturally observes. Observation is an outcome, a consequence, of the interaction of sense organ and subject matter. It will vary, accordingly, with the subject matter employed.

It is consequently futile to set up even the ulterior development of faculties of observation, memory, etc., unless we have first determined what sort of subject matter we wish the pupil to become expert in observing and recalling and for what purpose. And it is only repeating in another form what has already been said, to declare that the criterion here must be social. We want the person to note and recall and judge those things which make him an effective competent member of the group in which he is associated with others. Otherwise we might as well set the pupil to observing carefully cracks on the wall and set him to memorizing meaningless lists of words in an unknown tongue—which is about what we do in fact when we give way to the doctrine of formal discipline. If the observing habits of a botanist or chemist or engineer are better habits than those which are thus formed, it is because they deal with subject matter which is more significant in life. In concluding this portion of the discussion, we note that the distinction between special and general education has nothing to do with the transferability of function or power. In the literal sense, any transfer is miraculous and impossible. But some activities are broad; they involve a coordination of many factors. Their development demands continuous alternation and readjustment. As conditions change, certain factors are subordinated, and others which had been of minor importance come to the front. There is constant redistribution of the focus of the action, as is seen in the illustration of a game as over against pulling a fixed weight by a series of uniform motions. Thus there is practice in prompt making of new combinations with the focus of activity shifted to meet change in subject matter. Wherever an activity is broad in scope (that is, involves the coordinating of a large variety of sub-activities), and is constantly and unexpectedly obliged to change direction in its progressive development, general education is bound to result. For this is what "general" means; broad and flexible. In practice, education meets these conditions, and hence is general, in the degree in which it takes account of social relationships. A person may become expert in technical philosophy, or philology, or mathematics or engineering or financiering, and be inept and ill-advised in his action and judgment outside of his specialty. If however his concern with these technical subject matters has been connected with human activities having social breadth, the range of active responses called into play and flexibly integrated is much wider. Isolation of subject matter from a social context is the chief obstruction in current practice to securing a general training of mind. Literature, art, religion, when thus dissociated, are just as narrowing as the technical things which the professional upholders of general education strenuously oppose.

Summary.

The conception that the result of the educative process is capacity for further education stands in contrast with some other ideas which have profoundly influenced practice. The first contrasting conception considered is that of preparing or getting ready for some future duty or privilege. Specific evil effects were pointed out which result from the fact that this aim diverts attention of both teacher and taught from the only point to which it may be fruitfully directed — namely, taking advantage of the needs and possibilities of the immediate present. Consequently it defeats its own professed purpose. The notion that education is an unfolding from within appears to have more likeness to the conception of growth which has been set forth. But as worked out in the theories of Froebel and Hegel, it involves ignoring the interaction of present organic tendencies with the present environment, just as much as the notion of preparation. Some implicit whole is regarded as given ready-made and the significance of growth is merely transitory; it is not an end in itself, but simply a means of making explicit what is already implicit. Since that which is not explicit cannot be made definite use of, something has to be found to represent it. According to Froebel, the mystic symbolic value of certain objects and acts (largely mathematical) stand for the Absolute Whole which is in process of unfolding. According to Hegel, existing institutions are its effective actual representatives. Emphasis upon symbols and institutions tends to divert perception from the direct growth of experience in richness of meaning. Another influential but defective theory is that which conceives that mind has, at birth, certain mental faculties or powers, such as perceiving, remembering, willing, judging, generalizing, attending, etc., and that education is the training of these faculties through repeated exercise. This theory treats subject matter as comparatively external and indifferent, its value residing simply in the fact that it may occasion exercise of the general powers. Criticism was directed upon this separation of the alleged powers from one another and from the material upon which they act. The outcome of the theory in practice was shown to be an undue emphasis upon the training of narrow specialized modes of skill at the expense of initiative, inventiveness, and readaptability — qualities which depend upon the broad and consecutive interaction of specific activities with one another. 1 As matter of fact, the interconnection is so great, there are so many paths of construction, that every stimulus brings about some change in all of the organs of response. We are accustomed however to ignore most of these modifications of the total organic activity, concentrating upon that one which is most specifically adapted to the most urgent stimulus of the moment. 2 This statement should be compared with what was said earlier about the sequential ordering of responses (p. 25). It is merely a more explicit statement of the way in which that consecutive arrangement occurs.

Chapter Six:

Education as Conservative and Progressive

1. Education as Formation.

We now come to a type of theory which denies the existence of faculties and emphasizes the unique role of subject matter in the development of mental and moral disposition. According to it, education is neither a process of unfolding from within nor is it a training of faculties resident in mind itself. It is rather the formation of mind by setting up certain associations or connections of content by means of a subject matter presented from without. Education proceeds by instruction taken in a strictly literal sense, a building into the mind from without. That education is formative of mind is not questioned; it is the conception already propounded. But formation here has a technical meaning dependent upon the idea of something operating from without. Herbart is the best historical representative of this type of theory. He denies absolutely the existence of innate faculties. The mind is simply endowed with the power of producing various qualities in reaction to the various realities which act upon it. These qualitatively different reactions are called presentations (Vorstellungen). Every presentation once called into being persists; it may be driven below the "threshold" of consciousness by new and stronger presentations, produced by the reaction of the soul to new material, but its activity continues by its own inherent momentum, below the surface of consciousness. What are termed faculties — attention, memory, thinking, perception, even the sentiments, are arrangements, associations, and complications, formed by the interaction of these submerged presentations with one another and with new presentations. Perception, for example, is the complication of presentations which result from the rise of old presentations to greet and combine with new ones; memory is the evoking of an old presentation above the threshold of consciousness by getting entangled with another presentation, etc. Pleasure is the result of reinforcement among the independent activities of presentations; pain of their pulling different ways, etc.

The concrete character of mind consists, then, wholly of the various arrangements formed by the various presentations in their different qualities. The "furniture" of the mind is the mind. Mind is wholly a matter of "contents." The educational implications of this doctrine are threefold.

(1) This or that kind of mind is formed by the use of objects which evoke this or that kind of reaction and which produce this or that arrangement among the reactions called out. The formation of mind is wholly a matter of the presentation of the proper educational materials.

(2) Since the earlier presentations constitute the "apperceiving organs" which control the assimilation of new presentations, their character is all important. The effect of new presentations is to reinforce groupings previously formed. The business of the educator is, first, to select the proper material in order to fix the nature of the original reactions, and, secondly, to arrange the sequence of

subsequent presentations on the basis of the store of ideas secured by prior transactions. The control is from behind, from the past, instead of, as in the unfolding conception, in the ultimate goal.

(3) Certain formal steps of all method in teaching may be laid down. Presentation of new subject matter is obviously the central thing, but since knowing consists in the way in which this interacts with the contents already submerged below consciousness, the first thing is the step of "preparation," — that is, calling into special activity and getting above the floor of consciousness those older presentations which are to assimilate the new one. Then after the presentation, follow the processes of interaction of new and old; then comes the application of the newly formed content to the performance of some task. Everything must go through this course; consequently there is a perfectly uniform method in instruction in all subjects for all pupils of all ages.

Herbart's great service lay in taking the work of teaching out of the region of routine and accident. He brought it into the sphere of conscious method; it became a conscious business with a definite aim and procedure, instead of being a compound of casual inspiration and subservience to tradition. Moreover, everything in teaching and discipline could be specified, instead of our having to be content with vague and more or less mystic generalities about ultimate ideals and speculative spiritual symbols. He abolished the notion of ready-made faculties, which might be trained by exercise upon any sort of material, and made attention to concrete subject matter, to the content, all-important. Herbart undoubtedly has had a greater influence in bringing to the front questions connected with the material of study than any other educational philosopher. He stated problems of method from the standpoint of their connection with subject matter: method having to do with the manner and sequence of presenting new subject matter to insure its proper interaction with old.

The fundamental theoretical defect of this view lies in ignoring the existence in a living being of active and specific functions which are developed in the redirection and combination which occur as they are occupied with their environment. The theory represents the Schoolmaster come to his own. This fact expresses at once its strength and its weakness. The conception that the mind consists of what has been taught, and that the importance of what has been taught consists in its availability for further teaching, reflects the pedagogue's view of life. The philosophy is eloquent about the duty of the teacher in instructing pupils; it is almost silent regarding his privilege of learning. It emphasizes the influence of intellectual environment upon the mind; it slurs over the fact that the environment involves a personal sharing in common experiences. It exaggerates beyond reason the possibilities of consciously formulated and used methods, and underestimates the role of vital, unconscious, attitudes. It insists upon the old, the past, and passes lightly over the operation of the genuinely novel and unforeseeable. It takes, in brief, everything educational into account save its essence, — vital energy seeking opportunity for effective exercise. All education forms character, mental and moral, but formation consists in the selection and coordination of native activities so that they may utilize the subject matter of the social environment. Moreover, the formation is not only a formation of native activities, but it takes place through them. It is a process of reconstruction, reorganization.

2. Education as Recapitulation and Retrospection.

A peculiar combination of the ideas of development and formation from without has given rise to the recapitulation theory of education, biological and cultural. The individual develops, but his proper development consists in repeating in orderly stages the past evolution of animal life and human history. The former recapitulation occurs physiologically; the latter should be made to occur by means of education. The alleged biological truth that the individual in his growth from the simple embryo to maturity repeats the history of the evolution of animal life in the progress of forms from the simplest to the most complex (or expressed technically, that ontogenesis parallels phylogenesis) does not concern us, save as it is supposed to afford scientific foundation for cultural recapitulation of the past. Cultural recapitulation says, first, that children at a certain age are in the mental and moral condition of savagery; their instincts are vagrant and predatory because their ancestors at one time lived such a life. Consequently (so it is concluded) the proper subject matter of their education at this time is the material — especially the literary material of myths, folk-tale, and song — produced by humanity in the analogous stage. Then the child passes on to something corresponding, say, to the pastoral stage, and so on till at the time when he is ready to take part in contemporary life, he arrives at the present epoch of culture.

In this detailed and consistent form, the theory, outside of a small school in Germany (followers of Herbart for the most part), has had little currency. But the idea which underlies it is that education is essentially retrospective; that it looks primarily to the past and especially to the literary products of the past, and that mind is adequately formed in the degree in which it is patterned upon the spiritual heritage of the past. This idea has had such immense influence upon higher instruction especially, that it is worth examination in its extreme formulation.

In the first place, its biological basis is fallacious. Embyronic growth of the human infant preserves, without doubt, some of the traits of lower forms of life. But in no respect is it a strict traversing of past stages. If there were any strict "law" of repetition, evolutionary development would clearly not have taken place. Each new generation would simply have repeated its predecessors' existence. Development, in short, has taken place by the entrance of shortcuts and alterations in the prior scheme of growth. And this suggests that the aim of education is to facilitate such short-circuited growth. The great advantage of immaturity, educationally speaking, is that it enables us to emancipate the young from the need of dwelling in an outgrown past. The business of education is rather to liberate the young from reviving and retraversing the past than to lead them to a recapitulation of it. The social environment of the young is constituted by the presence and action of the habits of thinking and feeling of civilized men. To ignore the directive influence of this present environment upon the young is simply to abdicate the educational function. A biologist has said: "The history of development in different animals...offers to us...a series of ingenious, determined, varied but more or less unsuccessful efforts to escape from the necessity of recapitulating, and to substitute for the ancestral method a more direct method." Surely it would be foolish if education did not deliberately attempt to facilitate similar efforts in conscious experience so that they become increasingly successful.

The two factors of truth in the conception may easily be disentangled from association with the false context which perverts them. On the biological side we have simply the fact that any infant starts with precisely the assortment of impulsive activities with which he does start, they being blind, and many of them conflicting with one another, casual, sporadic, and unadapted to their immediate environment. The other point is that it is a part of wisdom to utilize the products of past history so far as they are of help for the future. Since they represent the results of prior experience, their value for future experience may, of course, be indefinitely great. Literatures produced in the past are, so far as men are now in possession and use of them, a part of the present environment of individuals; but there is an enormous difference between availing ourselves of them as present resources and taking them as standards and patterns in their retrospective character.

(1) The distortion of the first point usually comes about through misuse of the idea of heredity. It is assumed that heredity means that past life has somehow predetermined the main traits of an individual, and that they are so fixed that little serious change can be introduced into them. Thus taken, the influence of heredity is opposed to that of the environment, and the efficacy of the latter belittled. But for educational purposes heredity means neither more nor less than the original endowment of an individual. Education must take the being as he is; that a particular individual has just such and such an equipment of native activities is a basic fact. That they were produced in such and such a way, or that they are derived from one's ancestry, is not especially important for the educator, however it may be with the biologist, as compared with the fact that they now exist. Suppose one had to advise or direct a person regarding his inheritance of property. The fallacy of assuming that the fact it is an inheritance, predetermines its future use, is obvious. The advisor is concerned with making the best use of what is there — putting it at work under the most favorable conditions. Obviously he cannot utilize what is not there; neither can the educator. In this sense, heredity is a limit of education. Recognition of this fact prevents the waste of energy and the irritation that ensue from the too prevalent habit of trying to make by instruction something out of an individual which he is not naturally fitted to become. But the doctrine does not determine what use shall be made of the capacities which exist. And, except in the case of the imbecile, these original capacities are much more varied and potential, even in the case of the more stupid, than we as yet know properly how to utilize. Consequently, while a careful study of the native aptitudes and deficiencies of an individual is always a preliminary necessity, the subsequent and important step is

to furnish an environment which will adequately function whatever activities are present. The relation of heredity and environment is well expressed in the case of language. If a being had no vocal organs from which issue articulate sounds, if he had no auditory or other sense- receptors and no connections between the two sets of apparatus, it would be a sheer waste of time to try to teach him to converse. He is born short in that respect, and education must accept the limitation. But if he has this native equipment, its possession in no way guarantees that he will ever talk any language or what language he will talk. The environment in which his activities occur and by which they are carried into execution settles these things. If he lived in a dumb unsocial environment where men refused to talk to one another and used only that minimum of gestures without which they could not get along, vocal language would be as unachieved by him as if he had no vocal organs. If the sounds which he makes occur in a medium of persons speaking the Chinese language, the activities which make like sounds will be selected and coordinated. This illustration may be applied to the entire range of the educability of any individual. It places the heritage from the past in its right connection with the demands and opportunities of the present.

(2) The theory that the proper subject matter of instruction is found in the culture-products of past ages (either in general, or more specifically in the particular literatures which were produced in the culture epoch which is supposed to correspond with the stage of development of those taught) affords another instance of that divorce between the process and product of growth which has been criticized. To keep the process alive, to keep it alive in ways which make it easier to keep it alive in the future, is the function of educational subject matter. But an individual can live only in the present. The present is not just something which comes after the past; much less something produced by it. It is what life is in leaving the past behind it. The study of past products will not help us understand the present, because the present is not due to the products, but to the life of which they were the products. A knowledge of the past and its heritage is of great significance when it enters into the present, but not otherwise. And the mistake of making the records and remains of the past the main material of education is that it cuts the vital connection of present and past, and tends to make the past a rival of the present and the present a more or less futile imitation of the past. Under such circumstances, culture becomes an ornament and solace; a refuge and an asylum. Men escape from the crudities of the present to live in its imagined refinements, instead of using what the past offers as an agency for ripening these crudities. The present, in short, generates the problems which lead us to search the past for suggestion, and which supplies meaning to what we find when we search. The past is the past precisely because it does not include what is characteristic in the present. The moving present includes the past on condition that it uses the past to direct its own movement. The past is a great resource for the imagination; it adds a new dimension to life, but OD condition that it be seen as the past of the present, and not as another and disconnected world. The principle which makes little of the present act of

living and operation of growing, the only thing always present, naturally looks to the past because the future goal which it sets up is remote and empty. But having turned its back upon the present, it has no way of returning to it laden with the spoils of the past. A mind that is adequately sensitive to the needs and occasions of the present actuality will have the liveliest of motives for interest in the background of the present, and will never have to hunt for a way back because it will never have lost connection.

3. Education as Reconstruction.

In its contrast with the ideas both of unfolding of latent powers from within, and of the formation from without, whether by physical nature or by the cultural products of the past, the ideal of growth results in the conception that education is a constant reorganizing or reconstructing of experience. It has all the time an immediate end, and so far as activity is educative, it reaches that end — the direct transformation of the quality of experience. Infancy, youth, adult life, — all stand on the same educative level in the sense that what is really learned at any and every stage of experience constitutes the value of that experience, and in the sense that it is the chief business of life at every point to make living thus contribute to an enrichment of its own perceptible meaning.

We thus reach a technical definition of education: It is that reconstruction or reorganization of experience which adds to the meaning of experience, and which increases ability to direct the course of subsequent experience. (1) The increment of meaning corresponds to the increased perception of the connections and continuities of the activities in which we are engaged. The activity begins in an impulsive form; that is, it is blind. It does not know what it is about; that is to say, what are its interactions with other activities. An activity which brings education or instruction with it makes one aware of some of the connections which had been imperceptible. To recur to our simple example, a child who reaches for a bright light gets burned. Henceforth he knows that a certain act of touching in connection with a certain act of vision (and vice-versa) means heat and pain; or, a certain light means a source of heat. The acts by which a scientific man in his laboratory learns more about flame differ no whit in principle. By doing certain things, he makes perceptible certain connections of heat with other things, which had been previously ignored. Thus his acts in relation to these things get more meaning; he knows better what he is doing or "is about" when he has to do with them; he can intend consequences instead of just letting them happen — all synonymous ways of saying the same thing. At the same stroke, the flame has gained in meaning; all that is known about combustion, oxidation, about light and temperature, may become an intrinsic part of its intellectual content.

(2) The other side of an educative experience is an added power of subsequent direction or control. To say that one knows what he is about, or can intend certain consequences, is to say, of course, that he can better anticipate what is going to happen; that he can, therefore, get ready or prepare in advance so as to secure beneficial consequences and avert undesirable ones. A genuinely educative experience, then, one in which instruction is conveyed and ability

increased, is contradistinguished from a routine activity on one hand, and a capricious activity on the other. (a) In the latter one "does not care what happens"; one just lets himself go and avoids connecting the consequences of one's act (the evidences of its connections with other things) with the act. It is customary to frown upon such aimless random activity, treating it as willful mischief or carelessness or lawlessness. But there is a tendency to seek the cause of such aimless activities in the youth's own disposition, isolated from everything else. But in fact such activity is explosive, and due to maladjustment with surroundings. Individuals act capriciously whenever they act under external dictation, or from being told, without having a purpose of their own or perceiving the bearing of the deed upon other acts. One may learn by doing something which he does not understand; even in the most intelligent action, we do much which we do not mean, because the largest portion of the connections of the act we consciously intend are not perceived or anticipated. But we learn only because after the act is performed we note results which we had not noted before. But much work in school consists in setting up rules by which pupils are to act of such a sort that even after pupils have acted, they are not led to see the connection between the result — say the answer — and the method pursued. So far as they are concerned, the whole thing is a trick and a kind of miracle. Such action is essentially capricious, and leads to capricious habits. (b) Routine action, action which is automatic, may increase skill to do a particular thing. In so far, it might be said to have an educative effect. But it does not lead to new perceptions of bearings and connections; it limits rather than widens the meaning-horizon. And since the environment changes and our way of acting has to be modified in order successfully to keep a balanced connection with things, an isolated uniform way of acting becomes disastrous at some critical moment. The vaunted "skill" turns out gross ineptitude.

The essential contrast of the idea of education as continuous reconstruction with the other one-sided conceptions which have been criticized in this and the previous chapter is that it identifies the end (the result) and the process. This is verbally self-contradictory, but only verbally. It means that experience as an active process occupies time and that its later period completes its earlier portion; it brings to light connections involved, but hitherto unperceived. The later outcome thus reveals the meaning of the earlier, while the experience as a whole establishes a bent or disposition toward the things possessing this meaning. Every such continuous experience or activity is educative, and all education resides in having such experiences.

It remains only to point out (what will receive more ample attention later) that the reconstruction of experience may be social as well as personal. For purposes of simplification we have spoken in the earlier chapters somewhat as if the education of the immature which fills them with the spirit of the social group to which they belong, were a sort of catching up of the child with the aptitudes and resources of the adult group. In static societies, societies which make the maintenance of established custom their measure of value, this conception applies in the main. But not in progressive communities. They endeavor to shape the experiences of the young so that instead of reproducing current habits, better habits shall be formed, and thus the future adult society be an improvement on their own. Men have long had some intimation of the extent to which education may be consciously used to eliminate obvious social evils through starting the young on paths which shall not produce these ills, and some idea of the extent in which education may be made an instrument of realizing the better hopes of men. But we are doubtless far from realizing the potential efficacy of education as a constructive agency of improving society, from realizing that it represents not only a development of children and youth but also of the future society of which they will be the constituents.

Summary. Education may be conceived either retrospectively or prospectively. That is to say, it may be treated as process of accommodating the future to the past, or as an utilization of the past for a resource in a developing future. The former finds its standards and patterns in what has gone before. The mind may be regarded as a group of contents resulting from having certain things presented. In this case, the earlier presentations constitute the material to which the later are to be assimilated. Emphasis upon the value of the early experiences of immature beings is most important, especially because of the tendency to regard them as of little account. But these experiences do not consist of externally presented material, but of interaction of native activities with the environment which progressively modifies both the activities and the environment. The defect of the Herbartian theory of formation through presentations consists in slighting this constant interaction and change. The same principle of criticism applies to theories which find the primary subject matter of study in the cultural products — especially the literary products — of man's history. Isolated from their connection with the present environment in which individuals have to act, they become a kind of rival and distracting environment. Their value lies in their use to increase the meaning of the things with which we have actively to do at the present time. The idea of education advanced in these chapters is formally summed up in the idea of continuous reconstruction of experience, an idea which is marked off from education as preparation for a remote future, as unfolding, as external formation, and as recapitulation of the past.

Chapter Seven:

The Democratic Conception in Education

For the most part, save incidentally, we have hitherto been concerned with education as it may exist in any social group. We have now to make explicit the differences in the spirit, material, and method of education as it operates in different types of community life. To say that education is a social function, securing direction and development in the immature through their participation in the life of the group to which they belong, is to say in effect that education will vary with the quality of life which prevails in a group. Particularly is it true that a society which not only changes but-which has the ideal of such change as will improve it, will have different standards and methods of education from one which aims simply at the perpetuation of its own customs. To make the general ideas set forth applicable to our own educational practice, it is, therefore, necessary to come to closer quarters with the nature of present social life.

1. The Implications of Human Association.

Society is one word, but many things. Men associate together in all kinds of ways and for all kinds of purposes. One man is concerned in a multitude of diverse groups, in which his associates may be quite different. It often seems as if they had nothing in common except that they are modes of associated life. Within every larger social organization there are numerous minor groups: not only political subdivisions, but industrial, scientific, religious, associations. There are political parties with differing aims, social sets, cliques, gangs, corporations, partnerships, groups bound closely together by ties of blood, and so on in endless variety. In many modern states and in some ancient, there is great diversity of populations, of varying languages, religions, moral codes, and traditions. From this standpoint, many a minor political unit, one of our large cities, for example, is a congeries of loosely associated societies, rather than an inclusive and permeating community of action and thought. (See ante, p. 20.)

The terms society, community, are thus ambiguous. They have both a eulogistic or normative sense, and a descriptive sense; a meaning de jure and a meaning de facto. In social philosophy, the former connotation is almost always uppermost. Society is conceived as one by its very nature. The qualities which accompany this unity, praiseworthy community of purpose and welfare, loyalty to public ends, mutuality of sympathy, are emphasized. But when we look at the facts which the term denotes instead of confining our attention to its intrinsic connotation, we find not unity, but a plurality of societies, good and bad. Men banded together in a criminal conspiracy, business aggregations that prey upon the public while serving it, political machines held together by the interest of plunder, are included. If it is said that such organizations are not societies because they do not meet the ideal requirements of the notion of society, the answer, in part, is that the conception of society is then made so "ideal" as to be of no use, having no reference to facts; and in part, that each of these organizations, no matter how opposed to the interests of other groups, has something of the praiseworthy qualities of "Society" which hold it together. There is honor among thieves, and a band of robbers has a common interest as respects its members. Gangs are marked by fraternal feeling, and narrow cliques by intense loyalty to their own codes. Family life may be marked by exclusiveness, suspicion, and jealousy as to those without, and yet be a model of amity and mutual aid within. Any education given by a group tends to socialize its members, but the quality and value of the socialization depends upon the habits and aims of the group. Hence, once more, the need of a measure for the worth of any given mode of social life. In seeking this measure, we have to avoid two extremes. We cannot set up, out of our heads, something we regard as an ideal society. We must base our conception upon societies which actually exist, in order to have any assurance that our ideal is a practicable one. But, as we have just seen, the ideal cannot simply repeat the traits which are actually found. The problem is to extract the desirable traits of forms of community life which actually exist, and employ them to criticize undesirable features and suggest improvement. Now in any social group whatever, even in a gang of thieves, we find some interest held in common, and we find a certain amount of interaction and cooperative intercourse with other groups. From these two traits we derive our standard. How numerous and varied are the interests which are consciously shared? How full and free is the interplay with other forms of association? If we apply these considerations to, say, a criminal band, we find that the ties which consciously hold the members together are few in number, reducible almost to a common interest in plunder; and that they are of such a nature as to isolate the group from other groups with respect to give and take of the values of life. Hence, the education such a society gives is partial and distorted. If we take, on the other hand, the kind of family life which illustrates the standard, we find that there are material, intellectual, aesthetic interests in which all participate and that the progress of one member has worth for the experience of other members — it is readily communicable — and that the family is not an isolated whole, but enters intimately into relationships with business groups, with schools, with all the agencies of culture, as well as with other similar groups, and that it plays a due part in the political organization and in return receives support from it. In short, there are many interests consciously communicated and shared; and there are varied and free points of contact with other modes of association.

I. Let us apply the first element in this criterion to a despotically governed state. It is not true there is no common interest in such an organization between governed and governors. The authorities in command must make some appeal to the native activities of the subjects, must call some of their powers into play. Talleyrand said that a government could do everything with bayonets except sit on them. This cynical declaration is at least a recognition that the bond of union is not merely one of coercive force. It may be said, however, that the activities appealed to are themselves unworthy and degrading — that such a government calls into functioning activity simply capacity for fear. In a way, this statement is true. But it overlooks the fact that fear need not be an undesirable factor in experience. Caution, circumspection, prudence, desire to foresee future events so as to avert what is harmful, these desirable traits are as much a product of calling the impulse of fear into play as is cowardice and abject submission. The real difficulty is that the appeal to fear is isolated. In evoking dread and hope of specific tangible reward — say comfort and ease — many other capacities are left untouched. Or rather, they are affected, but in such a way as to pervert them. Instead of operating on their own account they are reduced to mere servants of attaining pleasure and avoiding pain.

This is equivalent to saying that there is no extensive number of common interests; there is no free play back and forth among the members of the social group. Stimulation and response are exceedingly one-sided. In order to have a large number of values in common, all the members of the group must have an equable opportunity to receive and to take from others. There must be a large variety of shared undertakings and experiences. Otherwise, the influences which educate some into masters, educate others into slaves. And the experience of each party loses in meaning, when the free interchange of varying modes of life-experience is arrested. A separation into a privileged and a subject-class prevents social endosmosis. The evils thereby affecting the superior class are less material and less perceptible, but equally real. Their culture tends to be sterile, to be turned back to feed on itself; their art becomes a showy display and artificial; their wealth luxurious; their knowledge overspecialized; their manners fastidious rather than humane.

Lack of the free and equitable intercourse which springs from a variety of shared interests makes intellectual stimulation unbalanced. Diversity of stimulation means novelty, and novelty means challenge to thought. The more activity is restricted to a few definite lines — as it is when there are rigid class lines preventing adequate interplay of experiences — the more action tends to become routine on the part of the class at a disadvantage, and capricious, aimless, and explosive on the part of the class having the materially fortunate position. Plato defined a slave as one who accepts from another the purposes which control his conduct. This condition obtains even where there is no slavery in the legal sense. It is found wherever men are engaged in activity which is socially serviceable, but whose service they do not understand and have no personal interest in. Much is said about scientific management of work. It is a narrow view which restricts the science which secures efficiency of operation to movements of the muscles. The chief opportunity for science is the discovery of the relations of a man to his work—including his relations to others who take part — which will enlist his intelligent interest in what he is doing. Efficiency in production often demands division of labor. But it is reduced to a mechanical routine unless workers see the technical, intellectual, and social relationships involved in what they do, and engage in their work because of the motivation furnished by such perceptions. The tendency to reduce such things as efficiency of activity and scientific management to purely technical externals is evidence of the one-sided stimulation of thought given to those in control of industry — those who supply its aims. Because of their lack of all-round and well-balanced social interest, there is not sufficient stimulus for attention to the human factors and relationships in industry. Intelligence is narrowed to the factors concerned with technical production and marketing of goods. No doubt, a very acute and intense intelligence in these narrow lines can be developed, but the failure to take into account the significant social factors means none the less an absence of mind, and a corresponding distortion of emotional life. II. This illustration (whose point is to be extended to all associations lacking reciprocity of interest) brings us to our second point. The isolation and exclusiveness of a gang or clique brings its antisocial spirit into relief. But this same spirit is found wherever one group has interests "of its own" which shut it out from full interaction with other groups, so that its prevailing purpose is the protection of what it has got, instead of reorganization and progress through wider relationships. It marks nations in their isolation from one another; families which seclude their domestic concerns as if they had no connection with a larger life; schools when separated from the interest of home and community; the divisions of rich and poor; learned and unlearned. The essential point is that isolation makes for rigidity and formal institutionalizing of life, for static and selfish ideals within the group. That savage tribes regard aliens and enemies as synonymous is not accidental. It springs from the fact that they have identified their experience with rigid adherence to their past customs. On such a basis it is wholly logical to fear intercourse with others, for such contact might dissolve custom. It would certainly occasion reconstruction. It is a commonplace that an alert and expanding mental life depends upon an enlarging range of contact with the physical environment. But the principle applies even more significantly to the field where we are apt to ignore it — the sphere of social contacts. Every expansive era in the history of mankind has coincided with the operation of factors which have tended to eliminate distance between peoples and classes previously hemmed off from one another. Even the alleged benefits of war, so far as more than alleged, spring from the fact that conflict of peoples at least enforces intercourse between them and thus accidentally enables them to learn from one another, and thereby to expand their horizons. Travel, economic and commercial tendencies, have at present gone far to break down external barriers; to bring peoples and classes into closer and more perceptible connection with one another. It remains for the most part to secure the intellectual and emotional significance of this physical annihilation of space.

2. The Democratic Ideal.

The two elements in our criterion both point to democracy. The first signifies not only more numerous and more varied points of shared common interest, but greater reliance upon the recognition of mutual interests as a factor in social control. The second means not only freer interaction between social groups (once isolated so far as intention could keep up a separation) but change in social habit — its continuous readjustment through meeting the new situations produced by varied intercourse. And these two traits are precisely what characterize the democratically constituted society.

Upon the educational side, we note first that the realization of a form of social life in which interests are mutually interpenetrating, and where progress, or readjustment, is an important consideration, makes a democratic community more interested than other communities have cause to be in deliberate and systematic education. The devotion of democracy to education is a familiar fact. The superficial explanation is that a government resting upon popular suffrage cannot be successful unless those who elect and who obey their governors are educated. Since a democratic society repudiates the principle of external authority, it must find a substitute in voluntary disposition and interest; these can be created only by education. But there is a deeper explanation. A democracy is more than a form of government; it is primarily a mode of associated living, of conjoint communicated experience. The extension in space of the number of individuals who participate in an interest so that each has to refer his own action to that of others, and to consider the action of others to give point and direction to his own, is equivalent to the breaking down of those barriers of class, race, and national territory which kept men from perceiving the full import of their activity. These more numerous and more varied points of contact denote a greater diversity of stimuli to which an individual has to respond; they consequently put a premium on variation in his action. They secure a liberation of powers which remain suppressed as long as the incitations to action are partial, as they must be in a group which in its exclusiveness shuts out many interests.

The widening of the area of shared concerns, and the liberation of a greater diversity of personal capacities which characterize a democracy, are not of course the product of deliberation and conscious effort. On the contrary, they were caused by the development of modes of manufacture and commerce, travel, migration, and intercommunication which flowed from the command of science over natural energy. But after greater individualization on one hand, and a broader community of interest on the other have come into existence, it is a matter of deliberate effort to sustain and extend them. Obviously a society to which stratification into separate classes would be fatal, must see to it that intellectual opportunities are accessible to all on equable and easy terms. A society marked off into classes need be specially attentive only to the education of its ruling elements. A society which is mobile, which is full of channels for the distribution of a change occurring anywhere, must see to it that its members are educated to personal initiative and adaptability. Otherwise, they will be overwhelmed by the changes in which they are caught and whose significance or connections they do not perceive. The result will be a confusion in which a few will appropriate to themselves the results of the blind and externally directed activities of others.

3. The Platonic Educational Philosophy.

Subsequent chapters will be devoted to making explicit the implications of the democratic ideas in education. In the remaining portions of this chapter, we shall consider the educational theories which have been evolved in three epochs when the social import of education was especially conspicuous. The first one to be considered is that of Plato. No one could better express than did he the fact that a society is stably organized when each individual is doing that for which he has aptitude by nature in such a way as to be useful to others (or to contribute to the whole to which he belongs); and that it is the business of education to discover these aptitudes and progressively to train them for social use. Much which has been said so far is borrowed from what Plato first consciously taught the world. But conditions which he could not intellectually control led him to restrict these ideas in their application. He never got any conception of the indefinite plurality of activities which may characterize an individual and a social group, and consequently limited his view to a limited number of classes of capacities and of social arrangements. Plato's starting point is that the organization of society depends ultimately upon knowledge of the end of existence. If we do not know its end, we shall be at the mercy of accident and caprice. Unless we know the end, the good, we shall have no criterion for rationally deciding what the possibilities are which should be promoted, nor how social arrangements are to be ordered. We shall have no conception of the proper limits and distribution of activities — what he called justice — as a trait of both individual and social organization. But how is the knowledge of the final and permanent good to be achieved? In dealing with this question we come upon the seemingly insuperable obstacle that such knowledge is not possible save in a just and harmonious social order. Everywhere else the mind is distracted and misled by false valuations and false perspectives. A disorganized and factional society sets up a number of different models and standards. Under such conditions it is impossible for the individual to attain consistency of mind. Only a complete whole is fully self-consistent. A society which rests upon the supremacy of some factor over another irrespective of its rational or proportionate claims, inevitably leads thought astray. It puts a premium on certain things and slurs over others, and creates a mind whose seeming unity is forced and distorted. Education proceeds ultimately from the patterns furnished by institutions, customs, and laws. Only in a just state will these be such as to give the right education; and only those who have rightly trained minds will be able to recognize the end, and ordering principle of things. We seem to be caught in a hopeless circle. However, Plato suggested a way out. A few men, philosophers or lovers of wisdom — or truth — may by study learn at least in outline the proper patterns of true existence. If a powerful ruler should form a state after these patterns, then its regulations could be preserved. An education could be given which would sift individuals, discovering what they were good for, and supplying a method of assigning each to the work in life for which his nature fits him. Each doing his own part, and never transgressing, the order and unity of the whole would be maintained.

It would be impossible to find in any scheme of philosophic thought a more adequate recognition on one hand of the educational significance of social arrangements and, on the other, of the dependence of those arrangements upon the means used to educate the young. It would be impossible to find a deeper sense of the function of education in discovering and developing personal capacities, and training them so that they would connect with the activities of others. Yet the society in which the theory was propounded was so undemocratic that Plato could not work out a solution for the problem whose terms he clearly saw.

While he affirmed with emphasis that the place of the individual in society should not be determined by birth or wealth or any conventional status, but by his own nature as discovered in the process of education, he had no perception of the uniqueness of individuals. For him they fall by nature into classes, and into a very small number of classes at that. Consequently the testing and sifting function of education only shows to which one of three classes an individual belongs. There being no recognition that each individual constitutes his own class, there could be no recognition of the infinite diversity of active tendencies and combinations of tendencies of which an individual is capable. There were only three types of faculties or powers in the individual's constitution. Hence education would soon reach a static limit in each class, for only diversity makes change and progress.

In some individuals, appetites naturally dominate; they are assigned to the laboring and trading class, which expresses and supplies human wants. Others reveal, upon education, that over and above appetites, they have a generous, outgoing, assertively courageous disposition. They become the citizen-subjects of the state; its defenders in war; its internal guardians in peace. But their limit is fixed by their lack of reason, which is a capacity to grasp the universal. Those who possess this are capable of the highest kind of education, and become in time the legislators of the state — for laws are the universals which control the particulars of experience. Thus it is not true that in intent, Plato subordinated the individual to the social whole. But it is true that lacking the perception of the uniqueness of every individual, his incommensurability with others, and consequently not recognizing that a society might change and yet be stable, his doctrine of limited powers and classes came in net effect to the idea of the subordination of individuality. We cannot better Plato's conviction that an individual is happy and society well organized when each individual engages in those activities for which he has a natural equipment, nor his conviction that it is the primary office of education to discover this equipment to its possessor and train him for its effective use. But progress in knowledge has made us aware of the superficiality of Plato's lumping of individuals and their original powers into a few sharply marked-off classes; it has taught us that original capacities are indefinitely numerous and variable. It is but the other side of this fact to say that in the degree in which society has become democratic, social organization means utilization of the specific and variable qualities of individuals, not stratification by classes. Although his educational philosophy was revolutionary, it was none the less in bondage to static ideals. He thought that change or alteration was evidence of lawless flux; that true reality was unchangeable. Hence while he would radically change the existing state of society, his aim was to construct a state in which change would subsequently have no place. The final end of life is fixed; given a state framed with this end in view, not even minor details are to be altered. Though they might not be inherently important, yet if permitted they would inure the minds of men to the idea of change, and hence be dissolving and anarchic. The breakdown of his philosophy is made apparent in the fact that he could not trust to gradual improvements in education to bring about a better society which should then improve education, and so on indefinitely. Correct education could not come into existence until an ideal state existed, and after that education would be devoted simply to its conservation. For the existence of this state he was obliged to trust to some happy accident by which philosophic wisdom should happen to coincide with possession of ruling power in the state.

4. The "Individualistic" Ideal of the Eighteenth Century.

In the eighteenth-century philosophy we find ourselves in a very different circle of ideas. "Nature" still means something antithetical to existing social organization; Plato exercised a great influence upon Rousseau. But the voice of nature now speaks for the diversity of individual talent and for the need of free development of individuality in all its variety. Education in accord with nature furnishes the goal and the method of instruction and discipline. Moreover, the native or original endowment was conceived, in extreme cases, as nonsocial or even as antisocial. Social arrangements were thought of as mere external expedients by which these nonsocial individuals might secure a greater amount of private happiness for themselves. Nevertheless, these statements convey only an inadequate idea of the true significance of the movement. In reality its chief interest was in progress and in social progress. The seeming antisocial philosophy was a somewhat transparent mask for an impetus toward a wider and freer society — toward cosmopolitanism. The positive ideal was humanity. In membership in humanity, as distinct from a state, man's capacities would be liberated; while in existing political organizations his powers were hampered and distorted to meet the requirements and selfish interests of the rulers of the state. The doctrine of extreme individualism was but the counterpart, the obverse, of ideals of the indefinite perfectibility of man and of a social organization having a scope as wide as humanity. The emancipated individual was to become the organ and agent of a comprehensive and progressive society.

The heralds of this gospel were acutely conscious of the evils of the social estate in which they found themselves. They attributed these evils to the limitations imposed upon the free powers of man. Such limitation was both distorting and corrupting. Their impassioned devotion to emancipation of life from external restrictions which operated to the exclusive advantage of the class to whom a past feudal system consigned power, found intellectual formulation in a worship of nature. To give "nature" full swing was to replace an artificial, corrupt, and inequitable social order by a new and better kingdom of humanity. Unrestrained faith in Nature as both a model and a working power was strengthened by the advances of natural science. Inquiry freed from prejudice and artificial restraints of church and state had revealed that the world is a scene of law. The Newtonian solar system, which expressed the reign of natural law, was a scene of wonderful harmony, where every force balanced with every other. Natural law would accomplish the same result in human relations, if men would only get rid of the artificial man-imposed coercive restrictions.

Education in accord with nature was thought to be the first step in insuring this more social society. It was plainly seen that economic and political limitations were ultimately dependent upon limitations of thought and feeling. The first step in freeing men from external chains was to emancipate them from the internal chains of false beliefs and ideals. What was called social life, existing institutions, were too false and corrupt to be intrusted with this work. How could it be expected to undertake it when the undertaking meant its own destruction? "Nature" must then be the power to which the enterprise was to be left. Even the extreme sensationalistic theory of knowledge which was current derived itself from this conception. To insist that mind is originally passive and empty was one way of glorifying the possibilities of education. If the mind was a wax tablet to be written upon by objects, there were no limits to the possibility of education by means of the natural environment. And since the natural world of objects is a scene of harmonious "truth," this education would infallibly produce minds filled with the truth.

5. Education as National and as Social.

As soon as the first enthusiasm for freedom waned, the weakness of the theory upon the constructive side became obvious. Merely to leave everything to nature was, after all, but to negate the very idea of education; it was to trust to the accidents of circumstance. Not only was some method required but also some positive organ, some administrative agency for carrying on the process of instruction. The "complete and harmonious development of all powers," having as its social counterpart an enlightened and progressive humanity, required definite organization for its realization. Private individuals here and there could proclaim the gospel; they could not execute the work. A Pestalozzi could try experiments and exhort philanthropically inclined persons having wealth and power to follow his example. But even Pestalozzi saw that any effective pursuit of the new educational ideal required the support of the state. The realization of the new education destined to produce a new society was, after all, dependent upon the activities of existing states. The movement for the democratic idea inevitably became a movement for publicly conducted and administered schools.

So far as Europe was concerned, the historic situation identified the movement for a state-supported education with the nationalistic movement in political life — a fact of incalculable significance for subsequent movements. Under the influence of German thought in particular, education became a civic function and the civic function was identified with the realization of the ideal of the national state. The "state" was substituted for humanity; cosmopolitanism gave way to nationalism. To form the citizen, not the "man," became the aim of education. 1 The historic situation to which reference is made is the after-effects of the Napoleonic conquests, especially in Germany. The German states felt (and subsequent events demonstrate the correctness of the belief) that systematic attention to education was the best means of recovering and maintaining their political integrity and power. Externally they were weak and divided. Under the leadership of Prussian statesmen they made this condition a stimulus to the development of an extensive and thoroughly grounded system of public education.

This change in practice necessarily brought about a change in theory. The individualistic theory receded into the background. The state furnished not only the instrumentalities of public education but also its goal. When the actual practice was such that the school system, from the elementary grades through the university faculties, supplied the patriotic citizen and soldier and the future state official and administrator and furnished the means for military, industrial, and political defense and expansion, it was impossible for theory not to emphasize the aim of social efficiency. And with the immense importance attached to the nationalistic state, surrounded by other competing and more or less hostile states, it was equally impossible to interpret social efficiency in terms of a vague cosmopolitan humanitarianism. Since the maintenance of a particular national sovereignty required subordination of individuals to the superior interests of the state both in military defense and in struggles for international supremacy in commerce, social efficiency was understood to imply a like subordination. The educational process was taken to be one of disciplinary training rather than of personal development. Since, however, the ideal of culture as complete development of personality persisted, educational philosophy attempted a reconciliation of the two ideas. The reconciliation took the form of the conception of the "organic" character of the state. The individual in his isolation is nothing; only in and through an absorption of the aims and meaning of organized institutions does he attain true personality. What appears to be his subordination to political authority and the demand for sacrifice of himself to the commands of his superiors is in reality but making his own the objective reason manifested in the state — the only way in which he can become truly rational. The notion of development which we have seen to be characteristic of institutional idealism (as in the Hegelian philosophy) was just such a deliberate effort to combine the two ideas of complete realization of personality and thoroughgoing "disciplinary" subordination to existing institutions. The extent of the transformation of educational philosophy which occurred in Germany in the generation occupied by the struggle against Napoleon for national independence, may be gathered from Kant, who well expresses the earlier individual-cosmopolitan ideal. In his treatise on Pedagogics, consisting of lectures given in the later years of the eighteenth century, he defines education as the process by which man becomes man. Mankind begins its history submerged in nature — not as Man who is a creature of reason, while nature furnishes only instinct and appetite. Nature offers simply the germs which education is to develop and perfect. The peculiarity of truly human life is that man has to create himself by his own voluntary efforts; he has to make himself a truly moral, rational, and free being. This creative effort is carried on by the educational activities of slow generations. Its acceleration depends upon men consciously striving to educate their successors not for the existing state of affairs but so as to make possible a future better humanity. But there is the great difficulty. Each generation is inclined to educate its young so as to get along in the present world instead of with a view to the proper end of education: the promotion of the best possible realization of humanity as humanity. Parents educate their children so that they may get on; princes educate their subjects as instruments of their own purposes.

Who, then, shall conduct education so that humanity may improve? We must depend upon the efforts of enlightened men in their private capacity. "All culture begins with private men and spreads outward from them. Simply through the efforts of persons of enlarged inclinations, who are capable of grasping the ideal of a future better condition, is the gradual approximation of human nature to its end possible. Rulers are simply interested in such training as will make their subjects better tools for their own intentions." Even the subsidy by rulers of privately conducted schools must be carefully safeguarded. For the rulers' interest in the welfare of their own nation instead of in what is best for humanity, will make them, if they give money for the schools, wish to draw their plans. We have in this view an express statement of the points characteristic of the eighteenth century individualistic cosmopolitanism. The full development of private personality is identified with the aims of humanity as a whole and with the idea of progress. In addition we have an explicit fear of the hampering influence of a state-conducted and state-regulated education upon the attainment of these ideas. But in less than two decades after this time, Kant's philosophic successors, Fichte and Hegel, elaborated the idea that the chief function of the state is educational; that in particular the regeneration of Germany is to be accomplished by an education carried on in the interests of the state, and that the private individual is of necessity an egoistic, irrational being, enslaved to his appetites and to circumstances unless he submits voluntarily to the educative discipline of state institutions and laws. In this spirit, Germany was the first country to undertake a public, universal, and compulsory system of education extending from the primary school through the university, and to submit to jealous state regulation and supervision all private educational enterprises. Two results should stand out from this brief historical survey. The first is that such terms as the individual and the social conceptions of education are quite meaningless taken at large, or apart from their context. Plato had the ideal of an education which should equate individual realization and social coherency and stability. His situation forced his ideal into the notion of a society organized in stratified classes, losing the individual in the class. The eighteenth century educational philosophy was highly individualistic in form, but this form was inspired by a noble and generous social ideal: that of a society organized to include humanity, and providing for the indefinite perfectibility of mankind. The idealistic philosophy of Germany in the early nineteenth century endeavored again to equate the ideals of a free and complete development of cultured personality with social discipline and political subordination. It made the national state an intermediary between the realization of private personality on one side and of humanity on the other. Consequently, it is equally possible to state its animating principle with equal truth either in the classic terms of "harmonious development of all the powers of personality" or in the more recent terminology of "social efficiency." All this reinforces the statement which opens this chapter: The conception of education as a social process and function has no definite meaning until we define the kind of society we have in mind. These considerations pave the way for our second conclusion. One of the fundamental problems of education in and for a democratic society is set by the conflict of a nationalistic and a wider social aim. The earlier cosmopolitan and "humanitarian" conception suffered both from vagueness and from lack of definite organs of execution and agencies of administration. In Europe, in the Continental states particularly, the new idea of the importance of education for human welfare and progress was captured by national interests and harnessed to do a work whose social aim was definitely narrow and exclusive. The social aim of education and its national aim were identified, and the result was a marked obscuring of the meaning of a social aim.

This confusion corresponds to the existing situation of human intercourse. On the one hand, science, commerce, and art transcend national boundaries. They are largely international in quality and method. They involve interdependencies and cooperation among the peoples inhabiting different countries. At the same time, the idea of national sovereignty has never been as accentuated in politics as it is at the present time. Each nation lives in a state of suppressed hostility and incipient war with its neighbors. Each is supposed to be the supreme judge of its own interests, and it is assumed as matter of course that each has interests which are exclusively its own. To question this is to question the very idea of national sovereignty which is assumed to be basic to political practice and political science. This contradiction (for it is nothing less) between the wider sphere of associated and mutually helpful social life and the narrower sphere of exclusive and hence potentially hostile pursuits and purposes, exacts of educational theory a clearer conception of the meaning of "social" as a function and test of education than has yet been attained. Is it possible for an educational system to be conducted by a national state and yet the full social ends of the educative process not be restricted, constrained, and corrupted? Internally, the question has to face the tendencies, due to present economic conditions, which split society into classes some of which are made merely tools for the higher culture of others. Externally, the question is concerned with the reconciliation of national loyalty, of patriotism, with superior devotion to the things which unite men in common ends, irrespective of national political boundaries. Neither phase of the problem can be worked out by merely negative means. It is not enough to see to it that education is not actively used as an instrument to make easier the exploitation of one class by another. School facilities must be secured of such amplitude and efficiency as will in fact and not simply in name discount the effects of economic inequalities, and secure to all the wards of the nation equality of equipment for their future careers. Accomplishment of this end demands not only adequate administrative provision of school facilities, and such supplementation of family resources as will enable youth to take advantage of them, but also such modification of traditional ideals of culture, traditional subjects of study and traditional methods of teaching and discipline as will retain all the youth under educational influences until they are equipped to be masters of their own economic and social careers. The ideal may seem remote of execution, but the democratic ideal of education is a farcical yet tragic delusion except as the ideal more and more dominates our public system of education. The same principle has application on the side of the considerations which concern the relations of one nation to another. It is not enough to teach the horrors of war and to avoid everything which would stimulate international jealousy and animosity. The emphasis must be put upon whatever binds people together in cooperative human pursuits and results, apart from geographical limitations. The secondary and provisional character of national sovereignty in respect to the fuller, freer, and more fruitful association and intercourse of all human beings with one another must be instilled as a working disposition of mind. If these applications seem to be remote from a consideration of the philosophy of education, the impression shows that the meaning of the idea of education previously developed has not been adequately grasped. This conclusion is bound up with the very idea of education as a freeing of individual capacity in a progressive growth directed to social aims. Otherwise a democratic criterion of education can only be inconsistently applied.

Summary. Since education is a social process, and there are many kinds of societies, a criterion for educational criticism and construction implies a particular social ideal. The two points selected by which to measure the worth of a form of social life are the extent in which the interests of a group are shared by all its members, and the fullness and freedom with which it interacts with other groups. An undesirable society, in other words, is one which internally and externally sets up barriers to free intercourse and communication of experience. A society which makes provision for participation in its good of all its members on equal terms and which secures flexible readjustment of its institutions through interaction of the different forms of associated life is in so far democratic. Such a society must have a type of education which gives individuals a personal interest in social relationships and control, and the habits of mind which secure social changes without introducing disorder. Three typical historic philosophies of education were considered from this point of view. The Platonic was found to have an ideal formally quite similar to that stated, but which was compromised in its working out by making a class rather than an individual the social unit. The so-called individualism of the eighteenth- century enlightenment was found to involve the notion of a society as broad as humanity, of whose progress the individual was to be the organ. But it lacked any agency for securing the development of its ideal as was evidenced in its falling back upon Nature. The institutional idealistic philosophies of the nineteenth century supplied this lack by making the national state the agency, but in so doing narrowed the conception of the social aim to those who were members of the same political unit, and reintroduced the idea of the subordination of the individual to the institution. 1 There is a much neglected strain in Rousseau tending intellectually in this direction. He opposed the existing state of affairs on the ground that it formed neither the citizen nor the man. Under existing conditions, he preferred to try for the latter rather than for the former. But there are many sayings of his which point to the formation of the citizen as ideally the higher, and which indicate that his own endeavor, as embodied in the Emile, was simply the best makeshift the corruption of the times permitted him to sketch.

Chapter Eight:

Aims in Education

1. The Nature of an Aim.

The account of education given in our earlier chapters virtually anticipated the results reached in a discussion of the purport of education in a democratic community. For it assumed that the aim of education is to enable individuals to continue their education — or that the object and reward of learning is continued capacity for growth. Now this idea cannot be applied to all the members of a society except where intercourse of man with man is mutual, and except where there is adequate provision for the reconstruction of social habits and institutions by means of wide stimulation arising from equitably distributed interests. And this means a democratic society. In our search for aims in education, we are not concerned, therefore, with finding an end outside of the educative process to which education is subordinate. Our whole conception forbids. We are rather concerned with the contrast which exists when aims belong within the process in which they operate and when they are set up from without. And the latter state of affairs must obtain when social relationships are not equitably balanced. For in that case, some portions of the whole social group will find their aims determined by an external dictation; their aims will not arise from the free growth of their own experience, and their nominal aims will be means to more ulterior ends of others rather than truly their own.

Our first question is to define the nature of an aim so far as it falls within an activity, instead of being furnished from without. We approach the definition by a contrast of mere results with ends. Any exhibition of energy has results. The wind blows about the sands of the desert; the position of the grains is changed. Here is a result, an effect, but not an end. For there is nothing in the outcome which completes or fulfills what went before it. There is mere spatial redistribution. One state of affairs is just as good as any other. Consequently there is no basis upon which to select an earlier state of affairs as a beginning, a later as an end, and to consider what intervenes as a process of transformation and realization.

Consider for example the activities of bees in contrast with the changes in the sands when the wind blows them about. The results of the bees' actions may be called ends not because they are designed or consciously intended, but because they are true terminations or completions of what has preceded. When the bees gather pollen and make wax and build cells, each step prepares the way for the next. When cells are built, the queen lays eggs in them; when eggs are laid, they are sealed and bees brood them and keep them at a temperature required to hatch them. When they are hatched, bees feed the young till they can take care of themselves. Now we are so familiar with such facts, that we are apt to dismiss them on the ground that life and instinct are a kind of miraculous thing anyway. Thus we fail to note what the essential characteristic of the event is; namely, the significance of the temporal place and order of each element; the way each prior event leads into its successor while the successor takes up what is furnished and utilizes it for some other stage, until we arrive at the end, which, as it were, summarizes and finishes off the process. Since aims relate always to results, the first thing to look to when it is a question of aims, is whether the work assigned possesses intrinsic continuity. Or is it a mere serial aggregate of acts, first doing one thing and then another? To talk about an educational aim when approximately each act of a pupil is dictated by the teacher, when the only order in the sequence of his acts is that which comes from the assignment of lessons and the giving of directions by another, is to talk nonsense. It is equally fatal to an aim to permit capricious or discontinuous action in the name of spontaneous self- expression. An aim implies an orderly and ordered activity, one in which the order consists in the progressive completing of a process. Given an activity having a time span and cumulative growth within the time succession, an aim means foresight in advance of the end or possible termination. If bees anticipated the consequences of their activity, if they perceived their end in imaginative foresight, they would have the primary element in an aim. Hence it is nonsense to talk about the aim of education—or any other undertaking—where conditions do not permit of foresight of results, and do not stimulate a person to look ahead to see what the outcome of a given activity is to be. In the next place the aim as a foreseen end gives direction to the activity; it is not an idle view of a mere spectator, but influences the steps taken to reach the end. The foresight functions in three ways. In the first place, it involves careful observation of the given conditions to see what are the means available for reaching the end, and to discover the hindrances in the way. In the second place, it suggests the proper order or sequence in the use of means. It facilitates an economical selection and arrangement. In the third place, it makes choice of alternatives possible. If we can predict the outcome of acting this way or that, we can then compare the value of the two courses of action; we can pass judgment upon their relative desirability. If we know that stagnant water breeds mosquitoes and that they are likely to carry disease, we can, disliking that anticipated result, take steps to avert it. Since we do not anticipate results as mere intellectual onlookers, but as persons concerned in the outcome, we are partakers in the process which produces the result. We intervene to bring about this result or that.

Of course these three points are closely connected with one another. We can definitely foresee results only as we make careful scrutiny of present conditions, and the importance of the outcome supplies the motive for observations. The more adequate our observations, the more varied is the scene of conditions and obstructions that presents itself, and the more numerous are the alternatives between which choice may be made. In turn, the more numerous the recognized possibilities of the situation, or alternatives of action, the more meaning does the chosen activity possess, and the more flexibly controllable is it. Where only a single outcome has been thought of, the mind has nothing else to think of; the meaning attaching to the act is limited. One only steams ahead toward the mark. Sometimes such a narrow course may be effective. But if unexpected difficulties offer themselves, one has not as many resources at command as if he had chosen the same line of action after a broader survey of the possibilities of the field. He cannot make needed readjustments readily.

The net conclusion is that acting with an aim is all one with acting intelligently. To foresee a terminus of an act is to have a basis upon which to observe, to select, and to order objects and our own capacities. To do these things means to have a mind — for mind is precisely intentional purposeful activity controlled by perception of facts and their relationships to one another. To have a mind to do a thing is to foresee a future possibility; it is to have a plan for its accomplishment; it is to note the means which make the plan capable of execution and the obstructions in the way, — or, if it is really a mind to do the thing and not a vague aspiration — it is to have a plan which takes account of resources and difficulties. Mind is capacity to refer present conditions to future results, and future consequences to present conditions. And these traits are just what is meant by having an aim or a purpose. A man is stupid or blind or unintelligent — lacking in mind — just in the degree in which in any activity he does not know what he is about, namely, the probable consequences of his acts. A man is imperfectly intelligent when he contents himself with looser guesses about the outcome than is needful, just taking a chance with his luck, or when he forms plans apart from study of the actual conditions, including his own capacities. Such relative absence of mind means to make our feelings the measure of what is to happen. To be intelligent we must "stop, look, listen" in making the plan of an activity.

To identify acting with an aim and intelligent activity is enough to show its value — its function in experience. We are only too given to making an entity out of the abstract noun "consciousness." We forget that it comes from the adjective "conscious." To be conscious is to be aware of what we are about; conscious signifies the deliberate, observant, planning traits of activity. Consciousness is nothing which we have which gazes idly on the scene around one or which has impressions made upon it by physical things; it is a name for the purposeful quality of an activity, for the fact that it is directed by an aim. Put the other way about, to have an aim is to act with meaning, not like an automatic machine; it is to mean to do something and to perceive the meaning of things in the light of that intent.

2. The Criteria of Good Aims.

We may apply the results of our discussion to a consideration of the criteria involved in a correct establishing of aims.

(1) The aim set up must be an outgrowth of existing conditions. It must be based upon a consideration of what is already going on; upon the resources and difficulties of the situation. Theories about the proper end of our activities — educational and moral theories — often violate this principle. They assume ends lying outside our activities; ends foreign to the concrete makeup of the situation; ends which issue from some outside source. Then the problem is to bring our activities to bear upon the realization of these externally supplied ends. They are something for which we ought to act. In any case such "aims" limit intelligence;

they are not the expression of mind in foresight, observation, and choice of the better among alternative possibilities. They limit intelligence because, given ready-made, they must be imposed by some authority external to intelligence, leaving to the latter nothing but a mechanical choice of means.

(2) We have spoken as if aims could be completely formed prior to the attempt to realize them. This impression must now be qualified. The aim as it first emerges is a mere tentative sketch. The act of striving to realize it tests its worth. If it suffices to direct activity successfully, nothing more is required, since its whole function is to set a mark in advance; and at times a mere hint may suffice. But usually — at least in complicated situations — acting upon it brings to light conditions which had been overlooked. This calls for revision of the original aim; it has to be added to and subtracted from. An aim must, then, be flexible; it must be capable of alteration to meet circumstances. An end established externally to the process of action is always rigid. Being inserted or imposed from without, it is not supposed to have a working relationship to the concrete conditions of the situation. What happens in the course of action neither confirms, refutes, nor alters it. Such an end can only be insisted upon. The failure that results from its lack of adaptation is attributed simply to the perverseness of conditions, not to the fact that the end is not reasonable under the circumstances. The value of a legitimate aim, on the contrary, lies in the fact that we can use it to change conditions. It is a method for dealing with conditions so as to effect desirable alterations in them. A farmer who should passively accept things just as he finds them would make as great a mistake as he who framed his plans in complete disregard of what soil, climate, etc., permit. One of the evils of an abstract or remote external aim in education is that its very inapplicability in practice is likely to react into a haphazard snatching at immediate conditions. A good aim surveys the present state of experience of pupils, and forming a tentative plan of treatment, keeps the plan constantly in view and yet modifies it as conditions develop. The aim, in short, is experimental, and hence constantly growing as it is tested in action.

(3) The aim must always represent a freeing of activities. The term end in view is suggestive, for it puts before the mind the termination or conclusion of some process. The only way in which we can define an activity is by putting before ourselves the objects in which it terminates — as one's aim in shooting is the target. But we must remember that the object is only a mark or sign by which the mind specifies the activity one desires to carry out. Strictly speaking, not the target but hitting the target is the end in view; one takes aim by means of the target, but also by the sight on the gun. The different objects which are thought of are means of directing the activity. Thus one aims at, say, a rabbit; what he wants is to shoot straight: a certain kind of activity. Or, if it is the rabbit he wants, it is not rabbit apart from his activity, but as a factor in activity; he wants to eat the rabbit, or to show it as evidence of his marksmanship — he wants to do something with it. The doing with the thing, not the thing in isolation, is his end. The object is but a phase of the active end, — continuing

the activity successfully. This is what is meant by the phrase, used above, "freeing activity."

In contrast with fulfilling some process in order that activity may go on, stands the static character of an end which is imposed from without the activity. It is always conceived of as fixed; it is something to be attained and possessed. When one has such a notion, activity is a mere unavoidable means to something else; it is not significant or important on its own account. As compared with the end it is but a necessary evil; something which must be gone through before one can reach the object which is alone worth while. In other words, the external idea of the aim leads to a separation of means from end, while an end which grows up within an activity as plan for its direction is always both ends and means, the distinction being only one of convenience. Every means is a temporary end until we have attained it. Every end becomes a means of carrying activity further as soon as it is achieved. We call it end when it marks off the future direction of the activity in which we are engaged; means when it marks off the present direction. Every divorce of end from means diminishes by that much the significance of the activity and tends to reduce it to a drudgery from which one would escape if he could. A farmer has to use plants and animals to carry on his farming activities. It certainly makes a great difference to his life whether he is fond of them, or whether he regards them merely as means which he has to employ to get something else in which alone he is interested. In the former case, his entire course of activity is significant; each phase of it has its own value. He has the experience of realizing his end at every stage; the postponed aim, or end in view, being merely a sight ahead by which to keep his activity going fully and freely. For if he does not look ahead, he is more likely to find himself blocked. The aim is as definitely a means of action as is any other portion of an activity.

3. Applications in Education.

There is nothing peculiar about educational aims. They are just like aims in any directed occupation. The educator, like the farmer, has certain things to do, certain resources with which to do, and certain obstacles with which to contend. The conditions with which the farmer deals, whether as obstacles or resources, have their own structure and operation independently of any purpose of his. Seeds sprout, rain falls, the sun shines, insects devour, blight comes, the seasons change. His aim is simply to utilize these various conditions; to make his activities and their energies work together, instead of against one another. It would be absurd if the farmer set up a purpose of farming, without any reference to these conditions of soil, climate, characteristic of plant growth, etc. His purpose is simply a foresight of the consequences of his energies connected with those of the things about him, a foresight used to direct his movements from day to day. Foresight of possible consequences leads to more careful and extensive observation of the nature and performances of the things he had to do with, and to laying out a plan — that is, of a certain order in the acts to be performed.

It is the same with the educator, whether parent or teacher. It is as absurd for the latter to set up his "own" aims as the proper objects of the growth of the children as it would be for the farmer to set up an ideal of farming irrespective of conditions. Aims mean acceptance of responsibility for the observations, anticipations, and arrangements required in carrying on a function — whether farming or educating. Any aim is of value so far as it assists observation, choice, and planning in carrying on activity from moment to moment and hour to hour; if it gets in the way of the individual's own common sense (as it will surely do if imposed from without or accepted on authority) it does harm.

And it is well to remind ourselves that education as such has no aims. Only persons, parents, and teachers, etc., have aims, not an abstract idea like education. And consequently their purposes are indefinitely varied, differing with different children, changing as children grow and with the growth of experience on the part of the one who teaches. Even the most valid aims which can be put in words will, as words, do more harm than good unless one recognizes that they are not aims, but rather suggestions to educators as to how to observe, how to look ahead, and how to choose in liberating and directing the energies of the concrete situations in which they find themselves. As a recent writer has said: "To lead this boy to read Scott's novels instead of old Sleuth's stories; to teach this girl to sew; to root out the habit of bullying from John's make-up; to prepare this class to study medicine, — these are samples of the millions of aims we have actually before us in the concrete work of education." Bearing these qualifications in mind, we shall proceed to state some of the characteristics found in all good educational aims.

(1) An educational aim must be founded upon the intrinsic activities and needs (including original instincts and acquired habits) of the given individual to be educated. The tendency of such an aim as preparation is, as we have seen, to omit existing powers, and find the aim in some remote accomplishment or responsibility. In general, there is a disposition to take considerations which are dear to the hearts of adults and set them up as ends irrespective of the capacities of those educated. There is also an inclination to propound aims which are so uniform as to neglect the specific powers and requirements of an individual, forgetting that all learning is something which happens to an individual at a given time and place. The larger range of perception of the adult is of great value in observing the abilities and weaknesses of the young, in deciding what they may amount to. Thus the artistic capacities of the adult exhibit what certain tendencies of the child are capable of; if we did not have the adult achievements we should be without assurance as to the significance of the drawing, reproducing, modeling, coloring activities of childhood. So if it were not for adult language, we should not be able to see the import of the babbling impulses of infancy. But it is one thing to use adult accomplishments as a context in which to place and survey the doings of childhood and youth; it is quite another to set them up as a fixed aim without regard to the concrete activities of those educated.

(2) An aim must be capable of translation into a method of cooperating with the activities of those undergoing instruction. It must suggest the kind of environment needed to liberate and to organize their capacities. Unless it lends itself to the construction of specific procedures, and unless these procedures test, correct, and amplify the aim, the latter is worthless. Instead of helping the specific task of teaching, it prevents the use of ordinary judgment in observing and sizing up the situation. It operates to exclude recognition of everything except what squares up with the fixed end in view. Every rigid aim just because it is rigidly given seems to render it unnecessary to give careful attention to concrete conditions. Since it must apply anyhow, what is the use of noting details which do not count?

The vice of externally imposed ends has deep roots. Teachers receive them from superior authorities; these authorities accept them from what is current in the community. The teachers impose them upon children. As a first consequence, the intelligence of the teacher is not free; it is confined to receiving the aims laid down from above. Too rarely is the individual teacher so free from the dictation of authoritative supervisor, textbook on methods, prescribed course of study, etc., that he can let his mind come to close quarters with the pupil's mind and the subject matter. This distrust of the teacher's experience is then reflected in lack of confidence in the responses of pupils. The latter receive their aims through a double or treble external imposition, and are constantly confused by the conflict between the aims which are natural to their own experience at the time and those in which they are taught to acquiesce. Until the democratic criterion of the intrinsic significance of every growing experience is recognized, we shall be intellectually confused by the demand for adaptation to external aims.

(3) Educators have to be on their guard against ends that are alleged to be general and ultimate. Every activity, however specific, is, of course, general in its ramified connections, for it leads out indefinitely into other things. So far as a general idea makes us more alive to these connections, it cannot be too general. But "general" also means "abstract," or detached from all specific context. And such abstractness means remoteness, and throws us back, once more, upon teaching and learning as mere means of getting ready for an end disconnected from the means. That education is literally and all the time its own reward means that no alleged study or discipline is educative unless it is worth while in its own immediate having. A truly general aim broadens the outlook; it stimulates one to take more consequences (connections) into account. This means a wider and more flexible observation of means. The more interacting forces, for example, the farmer takes into account, the more varied will be his immediate resources. He will see a greater number of possible starting places, and a greater number of ways of getting at what he wants to do. The fuller one's conception of possible future achievements, the less his present activity is tied down to a small number of alternatives. If one knew enough, one could start almost anywhere and sustain his activities continuously and fruitfully.

Understanding then the term general or comprehensive aim simply in the sense of a broad survey of the field of present activities, we shall take up some of the larger ends which have currency in the educational theories of the day, and consider what light they throw upon the immediate concrete and diversified aims which are always the educator's real concern. We premise (as indeed immediately follows from what has been said) that there is no need of making a choice among them or regarding them as competitors. When we come to act in a tangible way we have to select or choose a particular act at a particular time, but any number of comprehensive ends may exist without competition, since they mean simply different ways of looking at the same scene. One cannot climb a number of different mountains simultaneously, but the views had when different mountains are ascended supplement one another: they do not set up incompatible, competing worlds. Or, putting the matter in a slightly different way, one statement of an end may suggest certain questions and observations, and another statement another set of questions, calling for other observations. Then the more general ends we have, the better. One statement will emphasize what another slurs over. What a plurality of hypotheses does for the scientific investigator, a plurality of stated aims may do for the instructor.

Summary. An aim denotes the result of any natural process brought to consciousness and made a factor in determining present observation and choice of ways of acting. It signifies that an activity has become intelligent. Specifically it means foresight of the alternative consequences attendant upon acting in a given situation in different ways, and the use of what is anticipated to direct observation and experiment. A true aim is thus opposed at every point to an aim which is imposed upon a process of action from without. The latter is fixed and rigid; it is not a stimulus to intelligence in the given situation, but is an externally dictated order to do such and such things. Instead of connecting directly with present activities, it is remote, divorced from the means by which it is to be reached. Instead of suggesting a freer and better balanced activity, it is a limit set to activity. In education, the currency of these externally imposed aims is responsible for the emphasis put upon the notion of preparation for a remote future and for rendering the work of both teacher and pupil mechanical and slavish.

Chapter Nine:

Natural Development and Social Efficiency as Aims

1. Nature as Supplying the Aim.

We have just pointed out the futility of trying to establish the aim of education—some one final aim which subordinates all others to itself. We have indicated that since general aims are but prospective points of view from which to survey the existing conditions and estimate their possibilities, we might have any number of them, all consistent with one another. As matter of fact, a large number have been stated at different times, all having great local value. For the statement of aim is a matter of emphasis at a given time. And we do not emphasize things which do not require emphasis—that is, such things as are taking care of themselves fairly well. We tend rather to frame our statement on the basis of the defects and needs of the contemporary situation; we take for granted, without explicit statement which would be of no use, whatever is right or approximately so. We frame our explicit aims in terms of some alteration to be brought about. It is, then, DO paradox requiring explanation that a given epoch or generation tends to emphasize in its conscious projections just the things which it has least of in actual fact. A time of domination by authority will call out as response the desirability of great individual freedom; one of disorganized individual activities the need of social control as an educational aim.

The actual and implicit practice and the conscious or stated aim thus balance each other. At different times such aims as complete living, better methods of language study, substitution of things for words, social efficiency, personal culture, social service, complete development of personality, encyclopedic knowledge, discipline, a esthetic contemplation, utility, etc., have served. The following discussion takes up three statements of recent influence; certain others have been incidentally discussed in the previous chapters, and others will be considered later in a discussion of knowledge and of the values of studies. We begin with a consideration that education is a process of development in accordance with nature, taking Rousseau's statement, which opposed natural to social (See ante, p. 91); and then pass over to the antithetical conception of social efficiency, which often opposes social to natural.

(1) Educational reformers disgusted with the conventionality and artificiality of the scholastic methods they find about them are prone to resort to nature as a standard. Nature is supposed to furnish the law and the end of development; ours it is to follow and conform to her ways. The positive value of this conception lies in the forcible way in which it calls attention to the wrongness of aims which do not have regard to the natural endowment of those educated. Its weakness is the ease with which natural in the sense of normal is confused with the physical. The constructive use of intelligence in foresight, and contriving, is then discounted; we are just to get out of the way and allow nature to do the

work. Since no one has stated in the doctrine both its truth and falsity better than Rousseau, we shall turn to him.

"Education," he says, "we receive from three sources—Nature, men, and things. The spontaneous development of our organs and capacities constitutes the education of Nature. The use to which we are taught to put this development constitutes that education given us by Men. The acquirement of personal experience from surrounding objects constitutes that of things. Only when these three kinds of education are consonant and make for the same end, does a man tend towards his true goal. If we are asked what is this end, the answer is that of Nature. For since the concurrence of the three kinds of education is necessary to their completeness, the kind which is entirely independent of our control must necessarily regulate us in determining the other two." Then he defines Nature to mean the capacities and dispositions which are inborn, "as they exist prior to the modification due to constraining habits and the influence of the opinion of others."

The wording of Rousseau will repay careful study. It contains as fundamental truths as have been uttered about education in conjunction with a curious twist. It would be impossible to say better what is said in the first sentences. The three factors of educative development are (a) the native structure of our bodily organs and their functional activities; (b) the uses to which the activities of these organs are put under the influence of other persons; (c) their direct interaction with the environment. This statement certainly covers the ground. His other two propositions are equally sound; namely, (a) that only when the three factors of education are consonant and cooperative does adequate development of the individual occur, and (b) that the native activities of the organs, being original, are basic in conceiving consonance. But it requires but little reading between the lines, supplemented by other statements of Rousseau, to perceive that instead of regarding these three things as factors which must work together to some extent in order that any one of them may proceed educatively, he regards them as separate and independent operations. Especially does he believe that there is an independent and, as he says, "spontaneous" development of the native organs and faculties. He thinks that this development can go on irrespective of the use to which they are put. And it is to this separate development that education coming from social contact is to be subordinated. Now there is an immense difference between a use of native activities in accord with those activities themselves — as distinct from forcing them and perverting them — and supposing that they have a normal development apart from any use, which development furnishes the standard and norm of all learning by use. To recur to our previous illustration, the process of acquiring language is a practically perfect model of proper educative growth. The start is from native activities of the vocal apparatus, organs of hearing, etc. But it is absurd to suppose that these have an independent growth of their own, which left to itself would evolve a perfect speech. Taken literally, Rousseau's principle would mean that adults should accept and repeat the babblings and noises of children not merely as the beginnings of the development of articulate speech —

which they are — but as furnishing language itself — the standard for all teaching of language.

The point may be summarized by saying that Rousseau was right, introducing a much-needed reform into education, in holding that the structure and activities of the organs furnish the conditions of all teaching of the use of the organs; but profoundly wrong in intimating that they supply not only the conditions but also the ends of their development. As matter of fact, the native activities develop, in contrast with random and capricious exercise, through the uses to which they are put. And the office of the social medium is, as we have seen, to direct growth through putting powers to the best possible use. The instinctive activities may be called, metaphorically, spontaneous, in the sense that the organs give a strong bias for a certain sort of operation, — a bias so strong that we cannot go contrary to it, though by trying to go contrary we may pervert, stunt, and corrupt them. But the notion of a spontaneous normal development of these activities is pure mythology. The natural, or native, powers furnish the initiating and limiting forces in all education; they do not furnish its ends or aims. There is no learning except from a beginning in unlearned powers, but learning is not a matter of the spontaneous overflow of the unlearned powers. Rousseau's contrary opinion is doubtless due to the fact that he identified God with Nature; to him the original powers are wholly good, coming directly from a wise and good creator. To paraphrase the old saying about the country and the town, God made the original human organs and faculties, man makes the uses to which they are put. Consequently the development of the former furnishes the standard to which the latter must be subordinated. When men attempt to determine the uses to which the original activities shall be put, they interfere with a divine plan. The interference by social arrangements with Nature, God's work, is the primary source of corruption in individuals.

Rousseau's passionate assertion of the intrinsic goodness of all natural tendencies was a reaction against the prevalent notion of the total depravity of innate human nature, and has had a powerful influence in modifying the attitude towards children's interests. But it is hardly necessary to say that primitive impulses are of themselves neither good nor evil, but become one or the other according to the objects for which they are employed. That neglect, suppression, and premature forcing of some instincts at the expense of others, are responsible for many avoidable ills, there can be no doubt. But the moral is not to leave them alone to follow their own "spontaneous development," but to provide an environment which shall organize them.

Returning to the elements of truth contained in Rousseau's statements, we find that natural development, as an aim, enables him to point the means of correcting many evils in current practices, and to indicate a number of desirable specific aims.

(1) Natural development as an aim fixes attention upon the bodily organs and the need of health and vigor. The aim of natural development says to parents and teachers: Make health an aim; normal development cannot be had without regard to the vigor of the body—an obvious enough fact and yet one

whose due recognition in practice would almost automatically revolutionize many of our educational practices. "Nature" is indeed a vague and metaphorical term, but one thing that "Nature" may be said to utter is that there are conditions of educational efficiency, and that till we have learned what these conditions are and have learned to make our practices accord with them, the noblest and most ideal of our aims are doomed to suffer — are verbal and sentimental rather than efficacious.

(2) The aim of natural development translates into the aim of respect for physical mobility. In Rousseau's words: "Children are always in motion; a sedentary life is injurious." When he says that "Nature's intention is to strengthen the body before exercising the mind" he hardly states the fact fairly. But if he had said that nature's "intention" (to adopt his poetical form of speech) is to develop the mind especially by exercise of the muscles of the body he would have stated a positive fact. In other words, the aim of following nature means, in the concrete, regard for the actual part played by use of the bodily organs in explorations, in handling of materials, in plays and games. (3) The general aim translates into the aim of regard for individual differences among children. Nobody can take the principle of consideration of native powers into account without being struck by the fact that these powers differ in different individuals. The difference applies not merely to their intensity, but even more to their quality and arrangement. As Rouseau said: "Each individual is born with a distinctive temperament. We indiscriminately employ children of different bents on the same exercises; their education destroys the special bent and leaves a dull uniformity. Therefore after we have wasted our efforts in stunting the true gifts of nature we see the short-lived and illusory brilliance we have substituted die away, while the natural abilities we have crushed do not revive."

Lastly, the aim of following nature means to note the origin, the waxing, and waning, of preferences and interests. Capacities bud and bloom irregularly; there is no even four-abreast development. We must strike while the iron is hot. Especially precious are the first dawnings of power. More than we imagine, the ways in which the tendencies of early childhood are treated fix fundamental dispositions and condition the turn taken by powers that show themselves later. Educational concern with the early years of life — as distinct from inculcation of useful arts — dates almost entirely from the time of the emphasis by Pestalozzi and Froebel, following Rousseau, of natural principles of growth. The irregularity of growth and its significance is indicated in the following passage of a student of the growth of the nervous system. "While growth continues, things bodily and mental are lopsided, for growth is never general, but is accentuated now at one spot, now at another. The methods which shall recognize in the presence of these enormous differences of endowment the dynamic values of natural inequalities of growth, and utilize them, preferring irregularity to the rounding out gained by pruning will most closely follow that which takes place in the body and thus prove most effective." 1 Observation of natural tendencies is difficult under conditions of restraint. They show themselves most readily in a child's spontaneous sayings and doings, — that is, in those he engages in when not put at set tasks and when not aware of being under observation. It does not follow that these tendencies are all desirable because they are natural; but it does follow that since they are there, they are operative and must be taken account of. We must see to it that the desirable ones have an environment which keeps them active, and that their activity shall control the direction the others take and thereby induce the disuse of the latter because they lead to nothing. Many tendencies that trouble parents when they appear are likely to be transitory, and sometimes too much direct attention to them only fixes a child's attention upon them. At all events, adults too easily assume their own habits and wishes as standards, and regard all deviations of children's impulses as evils to be eliminated. That artificiality against which the conception of following nature is so largely a protest, is the outcome of attempts to force children directly into the mold of grown-up standards.

In conclusion, we note that the early history of the idea of following nature combined two factors which had no inherent connection with one another. Before the time of Rousseau educational reformers had been inclined to urge the importance of education by ascribing practically unlimited power to it. All the differences between peoples and between classes and persons among the same people were said to be due to differences of training, of exercise, and practice. Originally, mind, reason, understanding is, for all practical purposes, the same in all. This essential identity of mind means the essential equality of all and the possibility of bringing them all to the same level. As a protest against this view, the doctrine of accord with nature meant a much less formal and abstract view of mind and its powers. It substituted specific instincts and impulses and physiological capacities, differing from individual to individual (just as they differ, as Rousseau pointed out, even in dogs of the same litter), for abstract faculties of discernment, memory, and generalization. Upon this side, the doctrine of educative accord with nature has been reinforced by the development of modern biology, physiology, and psychology. It means, in effect, that great as is the significance of nurture, of modification, and transformation through direct educational effort, nature, or unlearned capacities, affords the foundation and ultimate resources for such nurture. On the other hand, the doctrine of following nature was a political dogma. It meant a rebellion against existing social institutions, customs, and ideals (See ante, p. 91). Rousseau's statement that everything is good as it comes from the hands of the Creator has its signification only in its contrast with the concluding part of the same sentence: "Everything degenerates in the hands of man." And again he says: "Natural man has an absolute value; he is a numerical unit, a complete integer and has no relation save to himself and to his fellow man. Civilized man is only a relative unit, the numerator of a fraction whose value depends upon its dominator, its relation to the integral body of society. Good political institutions are those which make a man unnatural." It is upon this conception of the artificial and harmful character of organized social life as it now exists 2 that he rested the notion that nature not merely furnishes prime forces which initiate growth but also its plan and goal. That evil institutions and customs work almost automatically to give a wrong education which the most careful schooling cannot offset is true enough; but the conclusion is not to education apart from the environment, but to provide an environment in which native powers will be put to better uses.

2. Social Efficiency as Aim.

A conception which made nature supply the end of a true education and society the end of an evil one, could hardly fail to call out a protest. The opposing emphasis took the form of a doctrine that the business of education is to supply precisely what nature fails to secure; namely, habituation of an individual to social control; subordination of natural powers to social rules. It is not surprising to find that the value in the idea of social efficiency resides largely in its protest against the points at which the doctrine of natural development went astray; while its misuse comes when it is employed to slur over the truth in that conception. It is a fact that we must look to the activities and achievements of associated life to find what the development of power — that is to say, efficiency — means. The error is in implying that we must adopt measures of subordination rather than of utilization to secure efficiency. The doctrine is rendered adequate when we recognize that social efficiency is attained not by negative constraint but by positive use of native individual capacities in occupations having a social meaning.

(1) Translated into specific aims, social efficiency indicates the importance of industrial competency. Persons cannot live without means of subsistence; the ways in which these means are employed and consumed have a profound influence upon all the relationships of persons to one another. If an individual is not able to earn his own living and that of the children dependent upon him, he is a drag or parasite upon the activities of others. He misses for himself one of the most educative experiences of life. If he is not trained in the right use of the products of industry, there is grave danger that he may deprave himself and injure others in his possession of wealth. No scheme of education can afford to neglect such basic considerations. Yet in the name of higher and more spiritual ideals, the arrangements for higher education have often not only neglected them, but looked at them with scorn as beneath the level of educative concern. With the change from an oligarchical to a democratic society, it is natural that the significance of an education which should have as a result ability to make one's way economically in the world, and to manage economic resources usefully instead of for mere display and luxury, should receive emphasis.

There is, however, grave danger that in insisting upon this end, existing economic conditions and standards will be accepted as final. A democratic criterion requires us to develop capacity to the point of competency to choose and make its own career. This principle is violated when the attempt is made to fit individuals in advance for definite industrial callings, selected not on the basis of trained original capacities, but on that of the wealth or social status of parents. As a matter of fact, industry at the present time undergoes rapid and abrupt changes through the evolution of new inventions. New industries spring up, and old ones are revolutionized. Consequently an attempt to train for too specific a mode of efficiency defeats its own purpose. When the occupation changes its methods, such individuals are left behind with even less ability to readjust themselves than if they had a less definite training. But, most of all, the present industrial constitution of society is, like every society which has ever existed, full of inequities. It is the aim of progressive education to take part in correcting unfair privilege and unfair deprivation, not to perpetuate them. Wherever social control means subordination of individual activities to class authority, there is danger that industrial education will be dominated by acceptance of the status quo. Differences of economic opportunity then dictate what the future callings of individuals are to be. We have an unconscious revival of the defects of the Platonic scheme (ante, p. 89) without its enlightened method of selection.

(2) Civic efficiency, or good citizenship. It is, of course, arbitrary to separate industrial competency from capacity in good citizenship. But the latter term may be used to indicate a number of qualifications which are vaguer than vocational ability. These traits run from whatever make an individual a more agreeable companion to citizenship in the political sense: it denotes ability to judge men and measures wisely and to take a determining part in making as well as obeying laws. The aim of civic efficiency has at least the merit of protecting us from the notion of a training of mental power at large. It calls attention to the fact that power must be relative to doing something, and to the fact that the things which most need to be done are things which involve one's relationships with others.

Here again we have to be on guard against understanding the aim too narrowly. An over-definite interpretation would at certain periods have excluded scientific discoveries, in spite of the fact that in the last analysis security of social progress depends upon them. For scientific men would have been thought to be mere theoretical dreamers, totally lacking in social efficiency. It must be borne in mind that ultimately social efficiency means neither more nor less than capacity to share in a give and take of experience. It covers all that makes one's own experience more worth while to others, and all that enables one to participate more richly in the worthwhile experiences of others. Ability to produce and to enjoy art, capacity for recreation, the significant utilization of leisure, are more important elements in it than elements conventionally associated oftentimes with citizenship. In the broadest sense, social efficiency is nothing less than that socialization of mind which is actively concerned in making experiences more communicable; in breaking down the barriers of social stratification which make individuals impervious to the interests of others. When social efficiency is confined to the service rendered by overt acts, its chief constituent (because its only guarantee) is omitted, — intelligent sympathy or good will. For sympathy as a desirable quality is something more than mere feeling; it is a cultivated imagination for what men have in common and a rebellion at whatever unnecessarily divides them. What is sometimes called a benevolent interest in others may be but an unwitting mask for an attempt to dictate to them what their good shall be, instead of an endeavor to free them so that they may seek and find the good of their own choice. Social efficiency, even social service, are hard and metallic things when severed from an active acknowledgment of the diversity of goods which life may afford to different persons, and from faith in the social utility of encouraging every individual to make his own choice intelligent.

3. Culture as Aim.

Whether or not social efficiency is an aim which is consistent with culture turns upon these considerations. Culture means at least something cultivated, something ripened; it is opposed to the raw and crude. When the "natural" is identified with this rawness, culture is opposed to what is called natural development. Culture is also something personal; it is cultivation with respect to appreciation of ideas and art and broad human interests. When efficiency is identified with a narrow range of acts, instead of with the spirit and meaning of activity, culture is opposed to efficiency. Whether called culture or complete development of personality, the outcome is identical with the true meaning of social efficiency whenever attention is given to what is unique in an individual— and he would not be an individual if there were not something incommensurable about him. Its opposite is the mediocre, the average. Whenever distinctive quality is developed, distinction of personality results, and with it greater promise for a social service which goes beyond the supply in quantity of material commodities. For how can there be a society really worth serving unless it is constituted of individuals of significant personal qualities?

The fact is that the opposition of high worth of personality to social efficiency is a product of a feudally organized society with its rigid division of inferior and superior. The latter are supposed to have time and opportunity to develop themselves as human beings; the former are confined to providing external products. When social efficiency as measured by product or output is urged as an ideal in a would-be democratic society, it means that the depreciatory estimate of the masses characteristic of an aristocratic community is accepted and carried over. But if democracy has a moral and ideal meaning, it is that a social return be demanded from all and that opportunity for development of distinctive capacities be afforded all. The separation of the two aims in education is fatal to democracy; the adoption of the narrower meaning of efficiency deprives it of its essential justification.

The aim of efficiency (like any educational aim) must be included within the process of experience. When it is measured by tangible external products, and not by the achieving of a distinctively valuable experience, it becomes materialistic. Results in the way of commodities which may be the outgrowth of an efficient personality are, in the strictest sense, by-products of education: by-products which are inevitable and important, but nevertheless by-products. To set up an external aim strengthens by reaction the false conception of culture which identifies it with something purely "inner." And the idea of perfecting an "inner" personality is a sure sign of social divisions. What is called inner is simply that which does not connect with others — which is not capable of free and full communication. What is termed spiritual culture has usually been futile, with something rotten about it, just because it has been conceived as a thing which a man might have internally — and therefore exclusively. What one is as a person is what one is as associated with others, in a free give and take of intercourse. This transcends both the efficiency which consists in supplying products to others and the culture which is an exclusive refinement and polish.

Any individual has missed his calling, farmer, physician, teacher, student, who does not find that the accomplishments of results of value to others is an accompaniment of a process of experience inherently worth while. Why then should it be thought that one must take his choice between sacrificing himself to doing useful things for others, or sacrificing them to pursuit of his own exclusive ends, whether the saving of his own soul or the building of an inner spiritual life and personality? What happens is that since neither of these things is persistently possible, we get a compromise and an alternation. One tries each course by turns. There is no greater tragedy than that so much of the professedly spiritual and religious thought of the world has emphasized the two ideals of self-sacrifice and spiritual self-perfecting instead of throwing its weight against this dualism of life. The dualism is too deeply established to be easily overthrown; for that reason, it is the particular task of education at the present time to struggle in behalf of an aim in which social efficiency and personal culture are synonyms instead of antagonists.

Summary.

General or comprehensive aims are points of view for surveying the specific problems of education. Consequently it is a test of the value of the manner in which any large end is stated to see if it will translate readily and consistently into the procedures which are suggested by another. We have applied this test to three general aims: Development according to nature, social efficiency, and culture or personal mental enrichment. In each case we have seen that the aims when partially stated come into conflict with each other. The partial statement of natural development takes the primitive powers in an alleged spontaneous development as the end-all. From this point of view training which renders them useful to others is an abnormal constraint; one which profoundly modifies them through deliberate nurture is corrupting. But when we recognize that natural activities mean native activities which develop only through the uses in which they are nurtured, the conflict disappears. Similarly a social efficiency which is defined in terms of rendering external service to others is of necessity opposed to the aim of enriching the meaning of experience, while a culture which is taken to consist in an internal refinement of a mind is opposed to a socialized disposition. But social efficiency as an educational purpose should mean cultivation of power to join freely and fully in shared or common activities. This is impossible without culture, while it brings a reward in culture, because one cannot share in intercourse with others without learning — without getting a broader point of view and perceiving things of which one would otherwise be ignorant. And there is perhaps no better definition of culture than that it is the capacity for constantly expanding the range and accuracy of one's perception of meanings.

1 Donaldson, Growth of Brain, p. 356.

2 We must not forget that Rousseau had the idea of a radically different sort of society, a fraternal society whose end should be identical with the good of all its members, which he thought to be as much better than existing states as these are worse than the state of nature.

Chapter Ten:

Interest and Discipline

1. The Meaning of the Terms.

We have already noticed the difference in the attitude of a spectator and of an agent or participant. The former is indifferent to what is going on; one result is just as good as another, since each is just something to look at. The latter is bound up with what is going on; its outcome makes a difference to him. His fortunes are more or less at stake in the issue of events. Consequently he does whatever he can to influence the direction present occurrences take. One is like a man in a prison cell watching the rain out of the window; it is all the same to him. The other is like a man who has planned an outing for the next day which continuing rain will frustrate. He cannot, to be sure, by his present reactions affect to-morrow's weather, but he may take some steps which will influence future happenings, if only to postpone the proposed picnic. If a man sees a carriage coming which may run over him, if he cannot stop its movement, he can at least get out of the way if he foresees the consequence in time. In many instances, he can intervene even more directly. The attitude of a participant in the course of affairs is thus a double one: there is solicitude, anxiety concerning future consequences, and a tendency to act to assure better, and avert worse, consequences. There are words which denote this attitude: concern, interest. These words suggest that a person is bound up with the possibilities inhering in objects; that he is accordingly on the lookout for what they are likely to do to him; and that, on the basis of his expectation or foresight, he is eager to act so as to give things one turn rather than another. Interest and aims, concern and purpose, are necessarily connected. Such words as aim, intent, end, emphasize the results which are wanted and striven for; they take for granted the personal attitude of solicitude and attentive eagerness. Such words as interest, affection, concern, motivation, emphasize the bearing of what is foreseen upon the individual's fortunes, and his active desire to act to secure a possible result. They take for granted the objective changes. But the difference is but one of emphasis; the meaning that is shaded in one set of words is illuminated in the other. What is anticipated is objective and impersonal; to-morrow's rain; the possibility of being run over. But for an active being, a being who partakes of the consequences instead of standing aloof from them, there is at the same time a personal response. The difference imaginatively foreseen makes a present difference, which finds expression in solicitude and effort. While such words as affection, concern, and motive indicate an attitude of personal preference, they are always attitudes toward objects — toward what is foreseen. We may call the phase of objective foresight intellectual, and the phase of personal concern emotional and volitional, but there is no separation in the facts of the situation.

Such a separation could exist only if the personal attitudes ran their course in a world by themselves. But they are always responses to what is going on in the situation of which they are a part, and their successful or unsuccessful expression depends upon their interaction with other changes. Life activities flourish and fail only in connection with changes of the environment. They are literally bound up with these changes; our desires, emotions, and affections are but various ways in which our doings are tied up with the doings of things and persons about us. Instead of marking a purely personal or subjective realm, separated from the objective and impersonal, they indicate the non-existence of such a separate world. They afford convincing evidence that changes in things are not alien to the activities of a self, and that the career and welfare of the self are bound up with the movement of persons and things. Interest, concern, mean that self and world are engaged with each other in a developing situation.

The word interest, in its ordinary usage, expresses (i) the whole state of active development, (ii) the objective results that are foreseen and wanted, and (iii) the personal emotional inclination.

(i) An occupation, employment, pursuit, business is often referred to as an interest. Thus we say that a man's interest is politics, or journalism, or philanthropy, or archaeology, or collecting Japanese prints, or banking.

(ii) By an interest we also mean the point at which an object touches or engages a man; the point where it influences him. In some legal transactions a man has to prove "interest" in order to have a standing at court. He has to show that some proposed step concerns his affairs. A silent partner has an interest in a business, although he takes no active part in its conduct because its prosperity or decline affects his profits and liabilities.

(iii) When we speak of a man as interested in this or that the emphasis falls directly upon his personal attitude. To be interested is to be absorbed in, wrapped up in, carried away by, some object. To take an interest is to be on the alert, to care about, to be attentive. We say of an interested person both that he has lost himself in some affair and that he has found himself in it. Both terms express the engrossment of the self in an object.

When the place of interest in education is spoken of in a depreciatory way, it will be found that the second of the meanings mentioned is first exaggerated and then isolated. Interest is taken to mean merely the effect of an object upon personal advantage or disadvantage, success or failure. Separated from any objective development of affairs, these are reduced to mere personal states of pleasure or pain. Educationally, it then follows that to attach importance to interest means to attach some feature of seductiveness to material otherwise indifferent; to secure attention and effort by offering a bribe of pleasure. This procedure is properly stigmatized as "soft" pedagogy; as a "soup-kitchen" theory of education.

But the objection is based upon the fact — or assumption — that the forms of skill to be acquired and the subject matter to be appropriated have no interest on their own account: in other words, they are supposed to be irrelevant to the normal activities of the pupils. The remedy is not in finding fault with the doctrine of interest, any more than it is to search for some pleasant bait that may be hitched to the alien material. It is to discover objects and modes of action, which are connected with present powers. The function of this material in engaging activity and carrying it on consistently and continuously is its interest. If the material operates in this way, there is no call either to hunt for devices which will make it interesting or to appeal to arbitrary, semi-coerced effort.

The word interest suggests, etymologically, what is between, — that which connects two things otherwise distant. In education, the distance covered may be looked at as temporal. The fact that a process takes time to mature is so obvious a fact that we rarely make it explicit. We overlook the fact that in growth there is ground to be covered between an initial stage of process and the completing period; that there is something intervening. In learning, the present powers of the pupil are the initial stage; the aim of the teacher represents the remote limit. Between the two lie means — that is middle conditions: — acts to be performed; difficulties to be overcome; appliances to be used. Only through them, in the literal time sense, will the initial activities reach a satisfactory consummation.

These intermediate conditions are of interest precisely because the development of existing activities into the foreseen and desired end depends upon them. To be means for the achieving of present tendencies, to be "between" the agent and his end, to be of interest, are different names for the same thing. When material has to be made interesting, it signifies that as presented, it lacks connection with purposes and present power: or that if the connection be there, it is not perceived. To make it interesting by leading one to realize the connection that exists is simply good sense; to make it interesting by extraneous and artificial inducements deserves all the bad names which have been applied to the doctrine of interest in education.

So much for the meaning of the term interest. Now for that of discipline. Where an activity takes time, where many means and obstacles lie between its initiation and completion, deliberation and persistence are required. It is obvious that a very large part of the everyday meaning of will is precisely the deliberate or conscious disposition to persist and endure in a planned course of action in spite of difficulties and contrary solicitations. A man of strong will, in the popular usage of the words, is a man who is neither fickle nor half-hearted in achieving chosen ends. His ability is executive; that is, he persistently and energetically strives to execute or carry out his aims. A weak will is unstable as water.

Clearly there are two factors in will. One has to do with the foresight of results, the other with the depth of hold the foreseen outcome has upon the person.

(i) Obstinacy is persistence but it is not strength of volition. Obstinacy may be mere animal inertia and insensitiveness. A man keeps on doing a thing just because he has got started, not because of any clearly thought-out purpose. In fact, the obstinate man generally declines (although he may not be quite aware of his refusal) to make clear to himself what his proposed end is; he has a feeling that if he allowed himself to get a clear and full idea of it, it might not be worth while. Stubbornness shows itself even more in reluctance to criticize ends which present themselves than it does in persistence and energy in use of means to achieve the end. The really executive man is a man who ponders his ends, who makes his ideas of the results of his actions as clear and full as possible. The people we called weak-willed or self-indulgent always deceive themselves as to the consequences of their acts. They pick out some feature which is agreeable and neglect all attendant circumstances. When they begin to act, the disagreeable results they ignored begin to show themselves. They are discouraged, or complain of being thwarted in their good purpose by a hard fate, and shift to some other line of action. That the primary difference between strong and feeble volition is intellectual, consisting in the degree of persistent firmness and fullness with which consequences are thought out, cannot be over-emphasized.

(ii) There is, of course, such a thing as a speculative tracing out of results. Ends are then foreseen, but they do not lay deep hold of a person. They are something to look at and for curiosity to play with rather than something to achieve. There is no such thing as over-intellectuality, but there is such a thing as a one-sided intellectuality. A person "takes it out" as we say in considering the consequences of proposed lines of action. A certain flabbiness of fiber prevents the contemplated object from gripping him and engaging him in action. And most persons are naturally diverted from a proposed course of action by unusual, unforeseen obstacles, or by presentation of inducements to an action that is directly more agreeable.

A person who is trained to consider his actions, to undertake them deliberately, is in so far forth disciplined. Add to this ability a power to endure in an intelligently chosen course in face of distraction, confusion, and difficulty, and you have the essence of discipline. Discipline means power at command; mastery of the resources available for carrying through the action undertaken. To know what one is to do and to move to do it promptly and by use of the requisite means is to be disciplined, whether we are thinking of an army or a mind. Discipline is positive. To cow the spirit, to subdue inclination, to compel obedience, to mortify the flesh, to make a subordinate perform an uncongenial task — these things are or are not disciplinary according as they do or do not tend to the development of power to recognize what one is about and to persistence in accomplishment.

It is hardly necessary to press the point that interest and discipline are connected, not opposed.

(i) Even the more purely intellectual phase of trained power — apprehension of what one is doing as exhibited in consequences — is not possible without interest. Deliberation will be perfunctory and superficial where there is no interest. Parents and teachers often complain — and correctly — that children "do not want to hear, or want to understand." Their minds are not upon the subject precisely because it does not touch them; it does not enter into their concerns. This is a state of things that needs to be remedied, but the remedy is not in the use of methods which increase indifference and aversion. Even punishing a child for inattention is one way of trying to make him realize that the matter is not a thing of complete unconcern; it is one way of arousing "interest," or bringing about a sense of connection. In the long run, its value is measured by whether it supplies a mere physical excitation to act in the way desired by the adult or whether it leads the child "to think"—that is, to reflect upon his acts and impregnate them with aims.

(ii) That interest is requisite for executive persistence is even more obvious. Employers do not advertise for workmen who are not interested in what they are doing. If one were engaging a lawyer or a doctor, it would never occur to one to reason that the person engaged would stick to his work more conscientiously if it was so uncongenial to him that he did it merely from a sense of obligation. Interest measures — or rather is — the depth of the grip which the foreseen end has upon one, moving one to act for its realization.

2. The Importance of the Idea of Interest in Education.

Interest represents the moving force of objects — whether perceived or presented in imagination — in any experience having a purpose. In the concrete, the value of recognizing the dynamic place of interest in an educative development is that it leads to considering individual children in their specific capabilities, needs, and preferences. One who recognizes the importance of interest will not assume that all minds work in the same way because they happen to have the same teacher and textbook. Attitudes and methods of approach and response vary with the specific appeal the same material makes, this appeal itself varying with difference of natural aptitude, of past experience, of plan of life, and so on. But the facts of interest also supply considerations of general value to the philosophy of education. Rightly understood, they put us on our guard against certain conceptions of mind and of subject matter which have had great vogue in philosophic thought in the past, and which exercise a serious hampering influence upon the conduct of instruction and discipline. Too frequently mind is set over the world of things and facts to be known; it is regarded as something existing in isolation, with mental states and operations that exist independently. Knowledge is then regarded as an external application of purely mental existences to the things to be known, or else as a result of the impressions which this outside subject matter makes on mind, or as a combination of the two. Subject matter is then regarded as something complete in itself; it is just something to be learned or known, either by the voluntary application of mind to it or through the impressions it makes on mind.

The facts of interest show that these conceptions are mythical. Mind appears in experience as ability to respond to present stimuli on the basis of anticipation of future possible consequences, and with a view to controlling the kind of consequences that are to take place. The things, the subject matter known, consist of whatever is recognized as having a bearing upon the anticipated course of events, whether assisting or retarding it. These statements are too formal to be very intelligible. An illustration may clear up their significance. You are engaged in a certain occupation, say writing with a typewriter. If you are an expert, your formed habits take care of the physical movements and leave your thoughts free to consider your topic. Suppose, however, you are not skilled, or that, even if you are, the machine does not work well. You then have to use intelligence. You do not wish to strike the keys at random and let the consequences be what they may; you wish to record certain words in a given order so as to make sense. You attend to the keys, to what you have written, to your movements, to the ribbon or the mechanism of the machine. Your attention is not distributed indifferently and miscellaneously to any and every detail. It is centered upon whatever has a bearing upon the effective pursuit of your occupation. Your look is ahead, and you are concerned to note the existing facts because and in so far as they are factors in the achievement of the result intended. You have to find out what your resources are, what conditions are at command, and what the difficulties and obstacles are. This foresight and this survey with reference to what is foreseen constitute mind. Action that does not involve such a forecast of results and such an examination of means and hindrances is either a matter of habit or else it is blind. In neither case is it intelligent. To be vague and uncertain as to what is intended and careless in observation of conditions of its realization is to be, in that degree, stupid or partially intelligent.

If we recur to the case where mind is not concerned with the physical manipulation of the instruments but with what one intends to write, the case is the same. There is an activity in process; one is taken up with the development of a theme. Unless one writes as a phonograph talks, this means intelligence; namely, alertness in foreseeing the various conclusions to which present data and considerations are tending, together with continually renewed observation and recollection to get hold of the subject matter which bears upon the conclusions to be reached. The whole attitude is one of concern with what is to be, and with what is so far as the latter enters into the movement toward the end. Leave out the direction which depends upon foresight of possible future results, and there is no intelligence in present behavior. Let there be imaginative forecast but no attention to the conditions upon which its attainment depends, and there is self-deception or idle dreaming — abortive intelligence.

If this illustration is typical, mind is not a name for something complete by itself; it is a name for a course of action in so far as that is intelligently directed; in so far, that is to say, as aims, ends, enter into it, with selection of means to further the attainment of aims. Intelligence is not a peculiar possession which a person owns; but a person is intelligent in so far as the activities in which he plays a part have the qualities mentioned. Nor are the activities in which a person engages, whether intelligently or not, exclusive properties of himself; they are something in which he engages and partakes. Other things, the independent changes of other things and persons, cooperate and hinder. The individual's act may be initial in a course of events, but the outcome depends upon the interaction of his response with energies supplied by other agencies. Conceive mind as anything but one factor partaking along with others in the production of consequences, and it becomes meaningless.

The problem of instruction is thus that of finding material which will engage a person in specific activities having an aim or purpose of moment or interest to him, and dealing with things not as gymnastic appliances but as conditions for the attainment of ends. The remedy for the evils attending the doctrine of formal discipline previously spoken of, is not to be found by substituting a doctrine of specialized disciplines, but by reforming the notion of mind and its training. Discovery of typical modes of activity, whether play or useful occupations, in which individuals are concerned, in whose outcome they recognize they have something at stake, and which cannot be carried through without reflection and use of judgment to select material of observation and recollection, is the remedy. In short, the root of the error long prevalent in the conception of training of mind consists in leaving out of account movements of things to future results in which an individual shares, and in the direction of which observation, imagination, and memory are enlisted. It consists in regarding mind as complete in itself, ready to be directly applied to a present material.

In historic practice the error has cut two ways. On one hand, it has screened and protected traditional studies and methods of teaching from intelligent criticism and needed revisions. To say that they are "disciplinary" has safeguarded them from all inquiry. It has not been enough to show that they were of no use in life or that they did not really contribute to the cultivation of the self. That they were "disciplinary" stifled every question, subdued every doubt, and removed the subject from the realm of rational discussion. By its nature, the allegation could not be checked up. Even when discipline did not accrue as matter of fact, when the pupil even grew in laxity of application and lost power of intelligent self-direction, the fault lay with him, not with the study or the methods of teaching. His failure was but proof that he needed more discipline, and thus afforded a reason for retaining the old methods. The responsibility was transferred from the educator to the pupil because the material did not have to meet specific tests; it did not have to be shown that it fulfilled any particular need or served any specific end. It was designed to discipline in general, and if it failed, it was because the individual was unwilling to be disciplined. In the other direction, the tendency was towards a negative conception of discipline, instead of an identification of it with growth in constructive power of achievement. As we have already seen, will means an attitude toward the future, toward the production of possible consequences, an attitude involving effort to foresee clearly and comprehensively the probable results of ways of acting, and an active identification with some anticipated consequences. Identification of will, or effort, with mere strain, results when a mind is set up, endowed with powers that are only to be applied to existing material. A person just either will or will not apply himself to the matter in hand. The more indifferent the subject matter, the less concern it has for the habits and preferences of the individual, the more demand there is for an effort to bring the mind to bear upon it—and hence the more discipline of will. To attend to material because there is something to be done in which the person is concerned is not disciplinary in this view; not even if it results in a desirable increase of constructive power. Application just for the sake of application, for the sake of training, is alone disciplinary. This is more likely to occur if the subject matter presented is uncongenial, for then there is no motive (so it is supposed) except the acknowledgment of duty or the value of discipline. The logical result is expressed with literal truth in the words of an American humorist: "It makes no difference what you teach a boy so long as he doesn't like it."

The counterpart of the isolation of mind from activities dealing with objects to accomplish ends is isolation of the subject matter to be learned. In the traditional schemes of education, subject matter means so much material to be studied. Various branches of study represent so many independent branches, each having its principles of arrangement complete within itself. History is one such group of facts; algebra another; geography another, and so on till we have run through the entire curriculum. Having a ready- made existence on their own account, their relation to mind is exhausted in what they furnish it to acquire. This idea corresponds to the conventional practice in which the program of school work, for the day, month, and successive years, consists of "studies" all marked off from one another, and each supposed to be complete by itself — for educational purposes at least.

Later on a chapter is devoted to the special consideration of the meaning of the subject matter of instruction. At this point, we need only to say that, in contrast with the traditional theory, anything which intelligence studies represents things in the part which they play in the carrying forward of active lines of interest. Just as one "studies" his typewriter as part of the operation of putting it to use to effect results, so with any fact or truth. It becomes an object of study — that is, of inquiry and reflection — when it figures as a factor to be reckoned with in the completion of a course of events in which one is engaged and by whose outcome one is affected. Numbers are not objects of study just because they are numbers already constituting a branch of learning called mathematics, but because they represent qualities and relations of the world in which our action goes on, because they are factors upon which the accomplishment of our purposes depends. Stated thus broadly, the formula may appear abstract. Translated into details, it means that the act of learning or studying is artificial and ineffective in the degree in which pupils are merely presented with a lesson to be learned. Study is effectual in the degree in which the pupil realizes the place of the numerical truth he is dealing with in carrying to fruition activities in which he is concerned. This connection of an object and a topic with the promotion of an activity having a purpose is the first and the last word of a genuine theory of interest in education.

3. Some Social Aspects of the Question.

While the theoretical errors of which we have been speaking have their expressions in the conduct of schools, they are themselves the outcome of conditions of social life. A change confined to the theoretical conviction of educators will not remove the difficulties, though it should render more effective efforts to modify social conditions. Men's fundamental attitudes toward the world are fixed by the scope and qualities of the activities in which they partake. The ideal of interest is exemplified in the artistic attitude. Art is neither merely internal nor merely external; merely mental nor merely physical. Like every mode of action, it brings about changes in the world. The changes made by some actions (those which by contrast may be called mechanical) are external; they are shifting things about. No ideal reward, no enrichment of emotion and intellect, accompanies them. Others contribute to the maintenance of life, and to its external adornment and display. Many of our existing social activities, industrial and political, fall in these two classes. Neither the people who engage in them, nor those who are directly affected by them, are capable of full and free interest in their work. Because of the lack of any purpose in the work for the one doing it, or because of the restricted character of its aim, intelligence is not adequately engaged. The same conditions force many people back upon themselves. They take refuge in an inner play of sentiment and fancies. They are aesthetic but not artistic, since their feelings and ideas are turned upon themselves, instead of being methods in acts which modify conditions. Their mental life is sentimental; an enjoyment of an inner landscape. Even the pursuit of science may become an asylum of refuge from the hard conditions of life — not a temporary retreat for the sake of recuperation and clarification in future dealings with the world. The very word art may become associated not with specific transformation of things, making them more significant for mind, but with stimulations of eccentric fancy and with emotional indulgences. The separation and mutual contempt of the "practical" man and the man of theory or culture, the divorce of fine and industrial arts, are indications of this situation. Thus interest and mind are either narrowed, or else made perverse. Compare what was said in an earlier chapter about the one-sided meanings which have come to attach to the ideas of efficiency and of culture.

This state of affairs must exist so far as society is organized on a basis of division between laboring classes and leisure classes. The intelligence of those who do things becomes hard in the unremitting struggle with things; that of those freed from the discipline of occupation becomes luxurious and effeminate. Moreover, the majority of human beings still lack economic freedom. Their pursuits are fixed by accident and necessity of circumstance; they are not the normal expression of their own powers interacting with the needs and resources of the environment. Our economic conditions still relegate many men to a servile status. As a consequence, the intelligence of those in control of the practical situation is not liberal. Instead of playing freely upon the subjugation of the world for human ends, it is devoted to the manipulation of other men for ends that are non-human in so far as they are exclusive.

This state of affairs explains many things in our historic educational traditions. It throws light upon the clash of aims manifested in different portions of the school system; the narrowly utilitarian character of most elementary education, and the narrowly disciplinary or cultural character of most higher education. It accounts for the tendency to isolate intellectual matters till knowledge is scholastic, academic, and professionally technical, and for the widespread conviction that liberal education is opposed to the requirements of an education which shall count in the vocations of life. But it also helps define the peculiar problem of present education. The school cannot immediately escape from the ideals set by prior social conditions. But it should contribute through the type of intellectual and emotional disposition which it forms to the improvement of those conditions. And just here the true conceptions of interest and discipline are full of significance. Persons whose interests have been enlarged and intelligence trained by dealing with things and facts in active occupations having a purpose (whether in play or work) will be those most likely to escape the alternatives of an academic and aloof knowledge and a hard, narrow, and merely "practical" practice. To organize education so that natural active tendencies shall be fully enlisted in doing something, while seeing to it that the doing requires observation, the acquisition of information, and the use of a constructive imagination, is what most needs to be done to improve social conditions. To oscillate between drill exercises that strive to attain efficiency in outward doing without the use of intelligence, and an accumulation of knowledge that is supposed to be an ultimate end in itself, means that education accepts the present social conditions as final, and thereby takes upon itself the responsibility for perpetuating them. A reorganization of education so that learning takes place in connection with the intelligent carrying forward of purposeful activities is a slow work. It can only be accomplished piecemeal, a step at a time. But this is not a reason for nominally accepting one educational philosophy and accommodating ourselves in practice to another. It is a challenge to undertake the task of reorganization courageously and to keep at it persistently.

Summary.

Interest and discipline are correlative aspects of activity having an aim. Interest means that one is identified with the objects which define the activity and which furnish the means and obstacles to its realization. Any activity with an aim implies a distinction between an earlier incomplete phase and later completing phase; it implies also intermediate steps. To have an interest is to take things as entering into such a continuously developing situation, instead of taking them in isolation. The time difference between the given incomplete state of affairs and the desired fulfillment exacts effort in transformation, it demands continuity of attention and endurance. This attitude is what is practically meant by will. Discipline or development of power of continuous attention is its fruit. The significance of this doctrine for the theory of education is twofold. On the one hand it protects us from the notion that mind and mental states are something complete in themselves, which then happen to be applied to some ready-made objects and topics so that knowledge results. It shows that mind and intelligent or purposeful engagement in a course of action into which things enter are identical. Hence to develop and train mind is to provide an environment which induces such activity. On the other side, it protects us from the notion that subject matter on its side is something isolated and independent. It shows that subject matter of learning is identical with all the objects, ideas, and principles which enter as resources or obstacles into the continuous intentional pursuit of a course of action. The developing course of action, whose end and conditions are perceived, is the unity which holds together what are often divided into an independent mind on one side and an independent world of objects and facts on the other.

Chapter Eleven:

Experience and Thinking

1. The Nature of Experience.

The nature of experience can be understood only by noting that it includes an active and a passive element peculiarly combined. On the active hand, experience is trying — a meaning which is made explicit in the connected term experiment. On the passive, it is undergoing. When we experience something we act upon it, we do something with it; then we suffer or undergo the consequences. We do something to the thing and then it does something to us in return: such is the peculiar combination. The connection of these two phases of experience measures the fruitfulness or value of the experience. Mere activity does not constitute experience. It is dispersive, centrifugal, dissipating. Experience as trying involves change, but change is meaningless transition unless it is consciously connected with the return wave of consequences which flow from it. When an activity is continued into the undergoing of consequences, when the change made by action is reflected back into a change made in us, the mere flux is loaded with significance. We learn something. It is not experience when a child merely sticks his finger into a flame; it is experience when the movement is connected with the pain which he undergoes in consequence. Henceforth the sticking of the finger into flame means a burn. Being burned is a mere physical change, like the burning of a stick of wood, if it is not perceived as a consequence of some other action. Blind and capricious impulses hurry us on heedlessly from one thing to another. So far as this happens, everything is writ in water. There is none of that cumulative growth which makes an experience in any vital sense of that term. On the other hand, many things happen to us in the way of pleasure and pain which we do not connect with any prior activity of our own. They are mere accidents so far as we are concerned. There is no before or after to such experience; no retrospect nor outlook, and consequently no meaning. We get nothing which may be carried over to foresee what is likely to happen next, and no gain in ability to adjust ourselves to what is coming—no added control. Only by courtesy can such an experience be called experience. To "learn from experience" is to make a backward and forward connection between what we do to things and what we enjoy or suffer from things in consequence. Under such conditions, doing becomes a trying; an experiment with the world to find out what it is like; the undergoing becomes instruction—discovery of the connection of things.

Two conclusions important for education follow. (1) Experience is primarily an active-passive affair; it is not primarily cognitive. But (2) the measure of the value of an experience lies in the perception of relationships or continuities to which it leads up. It includes cognition in the degree in which it is cumulative or amounts to something, or has meaning. In schools, those under instruction are too customarily looked upon as acquiring knowledge as theoretical spectators, minds which appropriate knowledge by direct energy of intellect. The very word pupil has almost come to mean one who is engaged not in having fruitful experiences but in absorbing knowledge directly. Something which is called mind or consciousness is severed from the physical organs of activity. The former is then thought to be purely intellectual and cognitive; the latter to be an irrelevant and intruding physical factor. The intimate union of activity and undergoing its consequences which leads to recognition of meaning is broken; instead we have two fragments: mere bodily action on one side, and meaning directly grasped by "spiritual" activity on the other.

It would be impossible to state adequately the evil results which have flowed from this dualism of mind and body, much less to exaggerate them. Some of the more striking effects, may, however, be enumerated.

(a) In part bodily activity becomes an intruder. Having nothing, so it is thought, to do with mental activity, it becomes a distraction, an evil to be contended with. For the pupil has a body, and brings it to school along with his mind. And the body is, of necessity, a wellspring of energy; it has to do something. But its activities, not being utilized in occupation with things which yield significant results, have to be frowned upon. They lead the pupil away from the lesson with which his "mind" ought to be occupied; they are sources of mischief. The chief source of the "problem of discipline" in schools is that the teacher has often to spend the larger part of the time in suppressing the bodily activities which take the mind away from its material. A premium is put on physical quietude; on silence, on rigid uniformity of posture and movement; upon a machine-like simulation of the attitudes of intelligent interest. The teachers' business is to hold the pupils up to these requirements and to punish the inevitable deviations which occur.

The nervous strain and fatigue which result with both teacher and pupil are a necessary consequence of the abnormality of the situation in which bodily activity is divorced from the perception of meaning. Callous indifference and explosions from strain alternate. The neglected body, having no organized fruitful channels of activity, breaks forth, without knowing why or how, into meaningless boisterousness, or settles into equally meaningless fooling — both very different from the normal play of children. Physically active children become restless and unruly; the more quiescent, so-called conscientious ones spend what energy they have in the negative task of keeping their instincts and active tendencies suppressed, instead of in a positive one of constructive planning and execution; they are thus educated not into responsibility for the significant and graceful use of bodily powers, but into an enforced duty not to give them free play. It may be seriously asserted that a chief cause for the remarkable achievements of Greek education was that it was never misled by false notions into an attempted separation of mind and body.

(b) Even, however, with respect to the lessons which have to be learned by the application of "mind," some bodily activities have to be used. The senses — especially the eye and ear — have to be employed to take in what the book, the map, the blackboard, and the teacher say. The lips and vocal organs, and the hands, have to be used to reproduce in speech and writing what has been stowed away. The senses are then regarded as a kind of mysterious conduit through which information is conducted from the external world into the mind; they are spoken of as gateways and avenues of knowledge. To keep the eyes on the book and the ears open to the teacher's words is a mysterious source of intellectual grace. Moreover, reading, writing, and figuring — important school arts — demand muscular or motor training. The muscles of eye, hand, and vocal organs accordingly have to be trained to act as pipes for carrying knowledge back out of the mind into external action. For it happens that using the muscles repeatedly in the same way fixes in them an automatic tendency to repeat.

The obvious result is a mechanical use of the bodily activities which (in spite of the generally obtrusive and interfering character of the body in mental action) have to be employed more or less. For the senses and muscles are used not as organic participants in having an instructive experience, but as external inlets and outlets of mind. Before the child goes to school, he learns with his hand, eye, and ear, because they are organs of the process of doing something from which meaning results. The boy flying a kite has to keep his eye on the kite, and has to note the various pressures of the string on his hand. His senses are avenues of knowledge not because external facts are somehow "conveyed" to the brain, but because they are used in doing something with a purpose. The qualities of seen and touched things have a bearing on what is done, and are alertly perceived; they have a meaning. But when pupils are expected to use their eyes to note the form of words, irrespective of their meaning, in order to reproduce them in spelling or reading, the resulting training is simply of isolated sense organs and muscles. It is such isolation of an act from a purpose which makes it mechanical. It is customary for teachers to urge children to read with expression, so as to bring out the meaning. But if they originally learned the sensory- motor technique of reading — the ability to identify forms and to reproduce the sounds they stand for — by methods which did not call for attention to meaning, a mechanical habit was established which makes it difficult to read subsequently with intelligence. The vocal organs have been trained to go their own way automatically in isolation; and meaning cannot be tied on at will. Drawing, singing, and writing may be taught in the same mechanical way; for, we repeat, any way is mechanical which narrows down the bodily activity so that a separation of body from mind — that is, from recognition of meaning — is set up. Mathematics, even in its higher branches, when undue emphasis is put upon the technique of calculation, and science, when laboratory exercises are given for their own sake, suffer from the same evil.

(c) On the intellectual side, the separation of "mind" from direct occupation with things throws emphasis on things at the expense of relations or connections. It is altogether too common to separate perceptions and even ideas from judgments. The latter are thought to come after the former in order to compare them. It is alleged that the mind perceives things apart from relations; that it forms ideas of them in isolation from their connections — with what goes before and comes after. Then judgment or thought is called upon to combine the separated items of "knowledge" so that their resemblance or causal connection shall be brought out. As matter of fact, every perception and every idea is a sense of the bearings, use, and cause, of a thing. We do not really know a chair or have an idea of it by inventorying and enumerating its various isolated qualities, but only by bringing these qualities into connection with something else — the purpose which makes it a chair and not a table; or its difference from the kind of chair we are accustomed to, or the "period" which it represents, and so on. A wagon is not perceived when all its parts are summed up; it is the characteristic connection of the parts which makes it a wagon. And these connections are not those of mere physical juxtaposition; they involve connection with the animals that draw it, the things that are carried on it, and so on. Judgment is employed in the perception; otherwise the perception is mere sensory excitation or else a recognition of the result of a prior judgment, as in the case of familiar objects.

Words, the counters for ideals, are, however, easily taken for ideas. And in just the degree in which mental activity is separated from active concern with the world, from doing something and connecting the doing with what is undergone, words, symbols, come to take the place of ideas. The substitution is the more subtle because some meaning is recognized. But we are very easily trained to be content with a minimum of meaning, and to fail to note how restricted is our perception of the relations which confer significance. We get so thoroughly used to a kind of pseudo-idea, a half perception, that we are not aware how half-dead our mental action is, and how much keener and more extensive our observations and ideas would be if we formed them under conditions of a vital experience which required us to use judgment: to hunt for the connections of the thing dealt with. There is no difference of opinion as to the theory of the matter. All authorities agree that that discernment of relationships is the genuinely intellectual matter; hence, the educative matter. The failure arises in supposing that relationships can become perceptible without experience — without that conjoint trying and undergoing of which we have spoken. It is assumed that "mind" can grasp them if it will only give attention, and that this attention may be given at will irrespective of the situation. Hence the deluge of half-observations, of verbal ideas, and unassimilated "knowledge" which afflicts the world. An ounce of experience is better than a ton of theory simply because it is only in experience that any theory has vital and verifiable significance. An experience, a very humble experience, is capable of generating and carrying any amount of theory (or intellectual content), but a theory apart from an experience cannot be definitely grasped even as theory. It tends to become a mere verbal formula, a set of catchwords used to render thinking, or genuine theorizing, unnecessary and impossible. Because of our education we use words, thinking they are ideas, to dispose of questions, the disposal being in reality simply such an obscuring of perception as prevents us from seeing any longer the difficulty.

2. Reflection in Experience.

Thought or reflection, as we have already seen virtually if not explicitly, is the discernment of the relation between what we try to do and what happens in consequence. No experience having a meaning is possible without some element of thought. But we may contrast two types of experience according to the proportion of reflection found in them. All our experiences have a phase of "cut and try" in them — what psychologists call the method of trial and error. We simply do something, and when it fails, we do something else, and keep on trying till we hit upon something which works, and then we adopt that method as a rule of thumb measure in subsequent procedure. Some experiences have very little else in them than this hit and miss or succeed process. We see that a certain way of acting and a certain consequence are connected, but we do not see how they are. We do not see the details of the connection; the links are missing. Our discernment is very gross. In other cases we push our observation farther. We analyze to see just what lies between so as to bind together cause and effect, activity and consequence. This extension of our insight makes foresight more accurate and comprehensive. The action which rests simply upon the trial and error method is at the mercy of circumstances; they may change so that the act performed does not operate in the way it was expected to. But if we know in detail upon what the result depends, we can look to see whether the required conditions are there. The method extends our practical control. For if some of the conditions are missing, we may, if we know what the needed antecedents for an effect are, set to work to supply them; or, if they are such as to produce undesirable effects as well, we may eliminate some of the superfluous causes and economize effort.

In discovery of the detailed connections of our activities and what happens in consequence, the thought implied in cut and try experience is made explicit. Its quantity increases so that its proportionate value is very different. Hence the quality of the experience changes; the change is so significant that we may call this type of experience reflective — that is, reflective par excellence. The deliberate cultivation of this phase of thought constitutes thinking as a distinctive experience. Thinking, in other words, is the intentional endeavor to discover specific connections between something which we do and the consequences which result, so that the two become continuous. Their isolation, and consequently their purely arbitrary going together, is canceled; a unified developing situation takes its place. The occurrence is now understood; it is explained; it is reasonable, as we say, that the thing should happen as it does.

Thinking is thus equivalent to an explicit rendering of the intelligent element in our experience. It makes it possible to act with an end in view. It is the condition of our having aims. As soon as an infant begins to expect he begins to use something which is now going on as a sign of something to follow; he is, in however simple a fashion, judging. For he takes one thing as evidence of something else, and so recognizes a relationship. Any future development, however elaborate it may be, is only an extending and a refining of this simple act of inference. All that the wisest man can do is to observe what is going on more widely and more minutely and then select more carefully from what is noted just those factors which point to something to happen. The opposites, once more, to thoughtful action are routine and capricious behavior. The former accepts what has been customary as a full measure of possibility and omits to take into account the connections of the particular things done. The latter makes the momentary act a measure of value, and ignores the connections of our personal action with the energies of the environment. It says, virtually, "things are to be just as I happen to like them at this instant," as routine says in effect "let things continue just as I have found them in the past." Both refuse to acknowledge responsibility for the future consequences which flow from present action. Reflection is the acceptance of such responsibility.

The starting point of any process of thinking is something going on, something which just as it stands is incomplete or unfulfilled. Its point, its meaning lies literally in what it is going to be, in how it is going to turn out. As this is written, the world is filled with the clang of contending armies. For an active participant in the war, it is clear that the momentous thing is the issue, the future consequences, of this and that happening. He is identified, for the time at least, with the issue; his fate hangs upon the course things are taking. But even for an onlooker in a neutral country, the significance of every move made, of every advance here and retreat there, lies in what it portends. To think upon the news as it comes to us is to attempt to see what is indicated as probable or possible regarding an outcome. To fill our heads, like a scrapbook, with this and that item as a finished and done-for thing, is not to think. It is to turn ourselves into a piece of registering apparatus. To consider the bearing of the occurrence upon what may be, but is not yet, is to think. Nor will the reflective experience be different in kind if we substitute distance in time for separation in space. Imagine the war done with, and a future historian giving an account of it. The episode is, by assumption, past. But he cannot give a thoughtful account of the war save as he preserves the time sequence; the meaning of each occurrence, as he deals with it, lies in what was future for it, though not for the historian. To take it by itself as a complete existence is to take it unreflectively. Reflection also implies concern with the issue — a certain sympathetic identification of our own destiny, if only dramatic, with the outcome of the course of events. For the general in the war, or a common soldier, or a citizen of one of the contending nations, the stimulus to thinking is direct and urgent. For neutrals, it is indirect and dependent upon imagination. But the flagrant partisanship of human nature is evidence of the intensity of the tendency to identify ourselves with one possible course of events, and to reject the other as foreign. If we cannot take sides in overt action, and throw in our little weight to help determine the final balance, we take sides emotionally and imaginatively. We desire this or that outcome. One wholly indifferent to the outcome does not follow or think about what is happening at all. From this dependence of the act of thinking upon a sense of sharing in the consequences of what goes on, flows one of the chief paradoxes of thought. Born in partiality, in order to accomplish its tasks it must achieve a certain detached impartiality. The general who allows his hopes and desires to affect his observations and interpretations of the existing situation will surely make a mistake in calculation. While hopes and fears may be the chief motive for a thoughtful following of the war on the part of an onlooker in a neutral country, he too will think ineffectively in the degree in which his preferences modify the stuff of his observations and reasonings. There is, however, no incompatibility between the fact that the occasion of reflection lies in a personal sharing in what is going on and the fact that the value of the reflection lies upon keeping one's self out of the data. The almost insurmountable difficulty of achieving this detachment is evidence that thinking originates in situations where the course of thinking is an actual part of the course of events and is designed to influence the result. Only gradually and with a widening of the area of vision through a growth of social sympathies does thinking develop to include what lies beyond our direct interests: a fact of great significance for education.

To say that thinking occurs with reference to situations which are still going on, and incomplete, is to say that thinking occurs when things are uncertain or doubtful or problematic. Only what is finished, completed, is wholly assured. Where there is reflection there is suspense. The object of thinking is to help reach a conclusion, to project a possible termination on the basis of what is already given. Certain other facts about thinking accompany this feature. Since the situation in which thinking occurs is a doubtful one, thinking is a process of inquiry, of looking into things, of investigating. Acquiring is always secondary, and instrumental to the act of inquiring. It is seeking, a quest, for something that is not at hand. We sometimes talk as if "original research" were a peculiar prerogative of scientists or at least of advanced students. But all thinking is research, and all research is native, original, with him who carries it on, even if everybody else in the world already is sure of what he is still looking for.

It also follows that all thinking involves a risk. Certainty cannot be guaranteed in advance. The invasion of the unknown is of the nature of an adventure; we cannot be sure in advance. The conclusions of thinking, till confirmed by the event, are, accordingly, more or less tentative or hypothetical. Their dogmatic assertion as final is unwarranted, short of the issue, in fact. The Greeks acutely raised the question: How can we learn? For either we know already what we are after, or else we do not know. In neither case is learning possible; on the first alternative because we know already; on the second, because we do not know what to look for, nor if, by chance, we find it can we tell that it is what we were after. The dilemma makes no provision for coming to know, for learning; it assumes either complete knowledge or complete ignorance. Nevertheless the twilight zone of inquiry, of thinking, exists. The possibility of hypothetical conclusions, of tentative results, is the fact which the Greek dilemma overlooked. The perplexities of the situation suggest certain ways out. We try these ways, and either push our way out, in which case we know we have found what we were looking for, or the situation gets darker and more confused—in which case, we know we are still ignorant. Tentative means trying out, feeling one's way along provisionally. Taken by itself, the Greek argument is a nice piece of formal logic. But it is also true that as long as men kept a sharp disjunction between knowledge and ignorance, science made only slow and accidental advance. Systematic advance in invention and discovery began when men recognized that they could utilize doubt for purposes of inquiry by forming conjectures to guide action in tentative explorations, whose development would confirm, refute, or modify the guiding conjecture. While the Greeks made knowledge more than learning, modern science makes conserved knowledge only a means to learning, to discovery. To recur to our illustration. A commanding general cannot base his actions upon either absolute certainty or absolute ignorance. He has a certain amount of information at hand which is, we will assume, reasonably trustworthy. He then infers certain prospective movements, thus assigning meaning to the bare facts of the given situation. His inference is more or less dubious and hypothetical. But he acts upon it. He develops a plan of procedure, a method of dealing with the situation. The consequences which directly follow from his acting this way rather than that test and reveal the worth of his reflections. What he already knows functions and has value in what he learns. But will this account apply in the case of the one in a neutral country who is thoughtfully following as best he can the progress of events? In form, yes, though not of course in content. It is self-evident that his guesses about the future indicated by present facts, guesses by which he attempts to supply meaning to a multitude of disconnected data, cannot be the basis of a method which shall take effect in the campaign. That is not his problem. But in the degree in which he is actively thinking, and not merely passively following the course of events, his tentative inferences will take effect in a method of procedure appropriate to his situation. He will anticipate certain future moves, and will be on the alert to see whether they happen or not. In the degree in which he is intellectually concerned, or thoughtful, he will be actively on the lookout; he will take steps which although they do not affect the campaign, modify in some degree his subsequent actions. Otherwise his later "I told you so" has no intellectual quality at all; it does not mark any testing or verification of prior thinking, but only a coincidence that yields emotional satisfaction — and includes a large factor of self-deception. The case is comparable to that of an astronomer who from given data has been led to foresee (infer) a future eclipse. No matter how great the mathematical probability, the inference is hypothetical — a matter of probability. 1 The hypothesis as to the date and position of the anticipated eclipse becomes the material of forming a method of future conduct. Apparatus is arranged; possibly an expedition is made to some far part of the globe. In any case, some active steps are taken which actually change some physical conditions. And apart from such steps and the consequent modification of the situation, there is no completion of the act of thinking. It remains suspended. Knowledge, already attained knowledge, controls thinking and makes it fruitful.

So much for the general features of a reflective experience. They are (i) perplexity, confusion, doubt, due to the fact that one is implicated in an incomplete situation whose full character is not yet determined; (ii) a conjectural anticipation — a tentative interpretation of the given elements, attributing to them a tendency to effect certain consequences; (iii) a careful survey (examination, inspection, exploration, analysis) of all attainable consideration which will define and clarify the problem in hand; (iv) a consequent elaboration of the tentative hypothesis to make it more precise and more consistent, because squaring with a wider range of facts; (v) taking one stand upon the projected hypothesis as a plan of action which is applied to the existing state of affairs: doing something overtly to bring about the anticipated result, and thereby testing the hypothesis. It is the extent and accuracy of steps three and four which mark off a distinctive reflective experience from one on the trial and error plane. They make thinking itself into an experience. Nevertheless, we never get wholly beyond the trial and error situation. Our most elaborate and rationally consistent thought has to be tried in the world and thereby tried out. And since it can never take into account all the connections, it can never cover with perfect accuracy all the consequences. Yet a thoughtful survey of conditions is so careful, and the guessing at results so controlled, that we have a right to mark off the reflective experience from the grosser trial and error forms of action.

Summary.

In determining the place of thinking in experience we first noted that experience involves a connection of doing or trying with something which is undergone in consequence. A separation of the active doing phase from the passive undergoing phase destroys the vital meaning of an experience. Thinking is the accurate and deliberate instituting of connections between what is done and its consequences. It notes not only that they are connected, but the details of the connection. It makes connecting links explicit in the form of relationships. The stimulus to thinking is found when we wish to determine the significance of some act, performed or to be performed. Then we anticipate consequences. This implies that the situation as it stands is, either in fact or to us, incomplete and hence indeterminate. The projection of consequences means a proposed or tentative solution. To perfect this hypothesis, existing conditions have to be carefully scrutinized and the implications of the hypothesis developed — an operation called reasoning. Then the suggested solution — the idea or theory — has to be tested by acting upon it. If it brings about certain consequences, certain determinate changes, in the world, it is accepted as valid. Otherwise it is modified, and another trial made. Thinking includes all of these steps, — the sense of a problem, the observation of conditions, the formation and rational elaboration of a suggested conclusion, and the active experimental testing. While all thinking results in knowledge, ultimately the value of knowledge is subordinate to its use in thinking. For we live not in a settled and finished world, but in one which is going on, and where our main task is prospective, and where retrospect — and all knowledge as distinct from thought is retrospect — is of value in the solidity, security, and fertility it affords our dealings with the future.

1 It is most important for the practice of science that men in many cases can calculate the degree of probability and the amount of probable error involved, but that does alter the features of the situation as described. It refines them.

Chapter Twelve:

Thinking in Education

1. The Essentials of Method.

No one doubts, theoretically, the importance of fostering in school good habits of thinking. But apart from the fact that the acknowledgment is not so great in practice as in theory, there is not adequate theoretical recognition that all which the school can or need do for pupils, so far as their minds are concerned (that is, leaving out certain specialized muscular abilities), is to develop their ability to think. The parceling out of instruction among various ends such as acquisition of skill (in reading, spelling, writing, drawing, reciting); acquiring information (in history and geography), and training of thinking is a measure of the ineffective way in which we accomplish all three. Thinking which is not connected with increase of efficiency in action, and with learning more about ourselves and the world in which we live, has something the matter with it just as thought (See ante, p. 147). And skill obtained apart from thinking is not connected with any sense of the purposes for which it is to be used. It consequently leaves a man at the mercy of his routine habits and of the authoritative control of others, who know what they are about and who are not especially scrupulous as to their means of achievement. And information severed from thoughtful action is dead, a mind-crushing load. Since it simulates knowledge and thereby develops the poison of conceit, it is a most powerful obstacle to further growth in the grace of intelligence. The sole direct path to enduring improvement in the methods of instruction and learning consists in centering upon the conditions which exact, promote, and test thinking. Thinking is the method of intelligent learning, of learning that employs and rewards mind. We speak, legitimately enough, about the method of thinking, but the important thing to bear in mind about method is that thinking is method, the method of intelligent experience in the course which it takes.

I. The initial stage of that developing experience which is called thinking is experience. This remark may sound like a silly truism. It ought to be one; but unfortunately it is not. On the contrary, thinking is often regarded both in philosophic theory and in educational practice as something cut off from experience, and capable of being cultivated in isolation. In fact, the inherent limitations of experience are often urged as the sufficient ground for attention to thinking. Experience is then thought to be confined to the senses and appetites; to a mere material world, while thinking proceeds from a higher faculty (of reason), and is occupied with spiritual or at least literary things. So, oftentimes, a sharp distinction is made between pure mathematics as a peculiarly fit subject matter of thought (since it has nothing to do with physical existences) and applied mathematics, which has utilitarian but not mental value.

Speaking generally, the fundamental fallacy in methods of instruction lies in supposing that experience on the part of pupils may be assumed. What is here insisted upon is the necessity of an actual empirical situation as the initiating phase of thought. Experience is here taken as previously defined: trying to do something and having the thing perceptibly do something to one in return. The fallacy consists in supposing that we can begin with ready-made subject matter of arithmetic, or geography, or whatever, irrespective of some direct personal experience of a situation. Even the kindergarten and Montessori techniques are so anxious to get at intellectual distinctions, without "waste of time," that they tend to ignore — or reduce — the immediate crude handling of the familiar material of experience, and to introduce pupils at once to material which expresses the intellectual distinctions which adults have made. But the first stage of contact with any new material, at whatever age of maturity, must inevitably be of the trial and error sort. An individual must actually try, in play or work, to do something with material in carrying out his own impulsive activity, and then note the interaction of his energy and that of the material employed. This is what happens when a child at first begins to build with blocks, and it is equally what happens when a scientific man in his laboratory begins to experiment with unfamiliar objects.

Hence the first approach to any subject in school, if thought is to be aroused and not words acquired, should be as unscholastic as possible. To realize what an experience, or empirical situation, means, we have to call to mind the sort of situation that presents itself outside of school; the sort of occupations that interest and engage activity in ordinary life. And careful inspection of methods which are permanently successful in formal education, whether in arithmetic or learning to read, or studying geography, or learning physics or a foreign language, will reveal that they depend for their efficiency upon the fact that they go back to the type of the situation which causes reflection out of school in ordinary life. They give the pupils something to do, not something to learn; and the doing is of such a nature as to demand thinking, or the intentional noting of connections; learning naturally results.

That the situation should be of such a nature as to arouse thinking means of course that it should suggest something to do which is not either routine or capricious—something, in other words, presenting what is new (and hence uncertain or problematic) and yet sufficiently connected with existing habits to call out an effective response. An effective response means one which accomplishes a perceptible result, in distinction from a purely haphazard activity, where the consequences cannot be mentally connected with what is done. The most significant question which can be asked, accordingly, about any situation or experience proposed to induce learning is what quality of problem it involves.

At first thought, it might seem as if usual school methods measured well up to the standard here set. The giving of problems, the putting of questions, the assigning of tasks, the magnifying of difficulties, is a large part of school work. But it is indispensable to discriminate between genuine and simulated or mock problems. The following questions may aid in making such discrimination. (a) Is there anything but a problem? Does the question naturally suggest itself within some situation or personal experience? Or is it an aloof thing, a problem only for the purposes of conveying instruction in some school topic? Is it the sort of trying that would arouse observation and engage experimentation outside of school? (b) Is it the pupil's own problem, or is it the teacher's or textbook's problem, made a problem for the pupil only because he cannot get the required mark or be promoted or win the teacher's approval, unless he deals with it? Obviously, these two questions overlap. They are two ways of getting at the same point: Is the experience a personal thing of such a nature as inherently to stimulate and direct observation of the connections involved, and to lead to inference and its testing? Or is it imposed from without, and is the pupil's problem simply to meet the external requirement? Such questions may give us pause in deciding upon the extent to which current practices are adapted to develop reflective habits. The physical equipment and arrangements of the average schoolroom are hostile to the existence of real situations of experience. What is there similar to the conditions of everyday life which will generate difficulties? Almost everything testifies to the great premium put upon listening, reading, and the reproduction of what is told and read. It is hardly possible to overstate the contrast between such conditions and the situations of active contact with things and persons in the home, on the playground, in fulfilling of ordinary responsibilities of life. Much of it is not even comparable with the questions which may arise in the mind of a boy or girl in conversing with others or in reading books outside of the school. No one has ever explained why children are so full of questions outside of the school (so that they pester grown-up persons if they get any encouragement), and the conspicuous absence of display of curiosity about the subject matter of school lessons. Reflection on this striking contrast will throw light upon the question of how far customary school conditions supply a context of experience in which problems naturally suggest themselves. No amount of improvement in the personal technique of the instructor will wholly remedy this state of things. There must be more actual material, more stuff, more appliances, and more opportunities for doing things, before the gap can be overcome. And where children are engaged in doing things and in discussing what arises in the course of their doing, it is found, even with comparatively indifferent modes of instruction, that children's inquiries are spontaneous and numerous, and the proposals of solution advanced, varied, and ingenious.

As a consequence of the absence of the materials and occupations which generate real problems, the pupil's problems are not his; or, rather, they are his only as a pupil, not as a human being. Hence the lamentable waste in carrying over such expertness as is achieved in dealing with them to the affairs of life beyond the schoolroom. A pupil has a problem, but it is the problem of meeting the peculiar requirements set by the teacher. His problem becomes that of finding out what the teacher wants, what will satisfy the teacher in recitation and examination and outward deportment. Relationship to subject matter is no longer direct. The occasions and material of thought are not found in the arithmetic or the history or geography itself, but in skillfully adapting that material to the teacher's requirements. The pupil studies, but unconsciously to himself the objects of his study are the conventions and standards of the school system and school authority, not the nominal "studies." The thinking thus evoked is artificially one-sided at the best. At its worst, the problem of the pupil is not how to meet the requirements of school life, but how to seem to meet them — or, how to come near enough to meeting them to slide along without an undue amount of friction. The type of judgment formed by these devices is not a desirable addition to character. If these statements give too highly colored a picture of usual school methods, the exaggeration may at least serve to illustrate the point: the need of active pursuits, involving the use of material to accomplish purposes, if there are to be situations which normally generate problems occasioning thoughtful inquiry.

II. There must be data at command to supply the considerations required in dealing with the specific difficulty which has presented itself. Teachers following a "developing" method sometimes tell children to think things out for themselves as if they could spin them out of their own heads. The material of thinking is not thoughts, but actions, facts, events, and the relations of things. In other words, to think effectively one must have had, or now have, experiences which will furnish him resources for coping with the difficulty at hand. A difficulty is an indispensable stimulus to thinking, but not all difficulties call out thinking. Sometimes they overwhelm and submerge and discourage. The perplexing situation must be sufficiently like situations which have already been dealt with so that pupils will have some control of the meanings of handling it. A large part of the art of instruction lies in making the difficulty of new problems large enough to challenge thought, and small enough so that, in addition to the confusion naturally attending the novel elements, there shall be luminous familiar spots from which helpful suggestions may spring.

In one sense, it is a matter of indifference by what psychological means the subject matter for reflection is provided. Memory, observation, reading, communication, are all avenues for supplying data. The relative proportion to be obtained from each is a matter of the specific features of the particular problem in hand. It is foolish to insist upon observation of objects presented to the senses if the student is so familiar with the objects that he could just as well recall the facts independently. It is possible to induce undue and crippling dependence upon sense-presentations. No one can carry around with him a museum of all the things whose properties will assist the conduct of thought. A well-trained mind is one that has a maximum of resources behind it, so to speak, and that is accustomed to go over its past experiences to see what they yield. On the other hand, a quality or relation of even a familiar object may previously have been passed over, and be just the fact that is helpful in dealing with the question. In this case direct observation is called for. The same principle applies to the use to be made of observation on one hand and of reading and "telling" on the other. Direct observation is naturally more vivid and vital. But it has its limitations; and in any case it is a necessary part of education that one should acquire the ability to supplement the narrowness of his immediately personal experiences by utilizing the experiences of others. Excessive reliance upon others for data (whether got from reading or listening) is to be depreciated. Most objectionable of all is the probability that others, the book or the teacher, will supply solutions ready-made, instead of giving material that the student has to adapt and apply to the question in hand for himself.

There is no inconsistency in saying that in schools there is usually both too much and too little information supplied by others. The accumulation and acquisition of information for purposes of reproduction in recitation and examination is made too much of. "Knowledge," in the sense of information, means the working capital, the indispensable resources, of further inquiry; of finding out, or learning, more things. Frequently it is treated as an end itself, and then the goal becomes to heap it up and display it when called for. This static, cold-storage ideal of knowledge is inimical to educative development. It not only lets occasions for thinking go unused, but it swamps thinking. No one could construct a house on ground cluttered with miscellaneous junk. Pupils who have stored their "minds" with all kinds of material which they have never put to intellectual uses are sure to be hampered when they try to think. They have no practice in selecting what is appropriate, and no criterion to go by; everything is on the same dead static level. On the other hand, it is quite open to question whether, if information actually functioned in experience through use in application to the student's own purposes, there would not be need of more varied resources in books, pictures, and talks than are usually at command.

III. The correlate in thinking of facts, data, knowledge already acquired, is suggestions, inferences, conjectured meanings, suppositions, tentative explanations:—ideas, in short. Careful observation and recollection determine what is given, what is already there, and hence assured. They cannot furnish what is lacking. They define, clarify, and locate the question; they cannot supply its answer. Projection, invention, ingenuity, devising come in for that purpose. The data arouse suggestions, and only by reference to the specific data can we pass upon the appropriateness of the suggestions. But the suggestions run beyond what is, as yet, actually given in experience. They forecast possible results, things to do, not facts (things already done). Inference is always an invasion of the unknown, a leap from the known.

In this sense, a thought (what a thing suggests but is not as it is presented) is creative, — an incursion into the novel. It involves some inventiveness. What is suggested must, indeed, be familiar in some context; the novelty, the inventive devising, clings to the new light in which it is seen, the different use to which it is put. When Newton thought of his theory of gravitation, the creative aspect of his thought was not found in its materials. They were familiar; many of them commonplaces — sun, moon, planets, weight, distance, mass, square of numbers. These were not original ideas; they were established facts. His originality lay in the use to which these familiar acquaintances were put by introduction into an unfamiliar context. The same is true of every striking scientific discovery, every great invention, every admirable artistic production. Only silly folk identify creative originality with the extraordinary and fanciful; others recognize that its measure lies in putting everyday things to uses which had not occurred to others. The operation is novel, not the materials out of which it is constructed.

The educational conclusion which follows is that all thinking is original in a projection of considerations which have not been previously apprehended. The child of three who discovers what can be done with blocks, or of six who finds out what he can make by putting five cents and five cents together, is really a discoverer, even though everybody else in the world knows it. There is a genuine increment of experience; not another item mechanically added on, but enrichment by a new quality. The charm which the spontaneity of little children has for sympathetic observers is due to perception of this intellectual originality. The joy which children themselves experience is the joy of intellectual constructiveness — of creativeness, if the word may be used without misunderstanding. The educational moral I am chiefly concerned to draw is not, however, that teachers would find their own work less of a grind and strain if school conditions favored learning in the sense of discovery and not in that of storing away what others pour into them; nor that it would be possible to give even children and youth the delights of personal intellectual productiveness — true and important as are these things. It is that no thought, no idea, can possibly be conveyed as an idea from one person to another. When it is told, it is, to the one to whom it is told, another given fact, not an idea. The communication may stimulate the other person to realize the question for himself and to think out a like idea, or it may smother his intellectual interest and suppress his dawning effort at thought. But what he directly gets cannot be an idea. Only by wrestling with the conditions of the problem at first hand, seeking and finding his own way out, does he think. When the parent or teacher has provided the conditions which stimulate thinking and has taken a sympathetic attitude toward the activities of the learner by entering into a common or conjoint experience, all has been done which a second party can do to instigate learning. The rest lies with the one directly concerned. If he cannot devise his own solution (not of course in isolation, but in correspondence with the teacher and other pupils) and find his own way out he will not learn, not even if he can recite some correct answer with one hundred per cent accuracy. We can and do supply ready-made "ideas" by the thousand; we do not usually take much pains to see that the one learning engages in significant situations where his own activities generate, support, and clinch ideas — that is, perceived meanings or connections. This does not mean that the teacher is to stand off and look on; the alternative to furnishing ready-made subject matter and listening to the accuracy with which it is reproduced is not quiescence, but participation, sharing, in an activity. In such shared activity, the teacher is a learner, and the learner is, without knowing it, a teacher — and upon the whole, the less consciousness there is, on either side, of either giving or receiving instruction, the better. IV. Ideas, as we have seen, whether they be humble guesses or dignified theories, are anticipations of possible solutions. They are anticipations of some continuity or connection of an activity and a consequence which has not as yet shown itself. They are therefore tested by the operation of acting upon them. They are to guide and organize further observations, recollections, and experiments. They are intermediate in learning, not final. All educational reformers, as we have had occasion to remark, are given to attacking the passivity of traditional education. They have opposed pouring in from without, and absorbing like a sponge; they have attacked drilling in material as into hard and resisting rock. But it is not easy to secure conditions which will make the getting of an idea identical with having an experience which widens and makes more precise our contact with the environment. Activity, even self-activity, is too easily thought of as something merely mental, cooped up within the head, or finding expression only through the vocal organs.

While the need of application of ideas gained in study is acknowledged by all the more successful methods of instruction, the exercises in application are sometimes treated as devices for fixing what has already been learned and for getting greater practical skill in its manipulation. These results are genuine and not to be despised. But practice in applying what has been gained in study ought primarily to have an intellectual quality. As we have already seen, thoughts just as thoughts are incomplete. At best they are tentative; they are suggestions, indications. They are standpoints and methods for dealing with situations of experience. Till they are applied in these situations they lack full point and reality. Only application tests them, and only testing confers full meaning and a sense of their reality. Short of use made of them, they tend to segregate into a peculiar world of their own. It may be seriously questioned whether the philosophies (to which reference has been made in section 2 of chapter X) which isolate mind and set it over against the world did not have their origin in the fact that the reflective or theoretical class of men elaborated a large stock of ideas which social conditions did not allow them to act upon and test. Consequently men were thrown back into their own thoughts as ends in themselves.

However this may be, there can be no doubt that a peculiar artificiality attaches to much of what is learned in schools. It can hardly be said that many students consciously think of the subject matter as unreal; but it assuredly does not possess for them the kind of reality which the subject matter of their vital experiences possesses. They learn not to expect that sort of reality of it; they become habituated to treating it as having reality for the purposes of recitations, lessons, and examinations. That it should remain inert for the experiences of daily life is more or less a matter of course. The bad effects are twofold. Ordinary experience does not receive the enrichment which it should; it is not fertilized by school learning. And the attitudes which spring from getting used to and accepting half-understood and ill-digested material weaken vigor and efficiency of thought.

If we have dwelt especially on the negative side, it is for the sake of suggesting positive measures adapted to the effectual development of thought. Where schools are equipped with laboratories, shops, and gardens, where dramatizations, plays, and games are freely used, opportunities exist for reproducing situations of life, and for acquiring and applying information and ideas in the carrying forward of progressive experiences. Ideas are not segregated, they do not form an isolated island. They animate and enrich the ordinary course of life. Information is vitalized by its function; by the place it occupies in direction of action. The phrase "opportunities exist" is used purposely. They may not be taken advantage of; it is possible to employ manual and constructive activities in a physical way, as means of getting just bodily skill; or they may be used almost exclusively for "utilitarian," i.e., pecuniary, ends. But the disposition on the part of upholders of "cultural" education to assume that such activities are merely physical or professional in quality, is itself a product of the philosophies which isolate mind from direction of the course of experience and hence from action upon and with things. When the "mental" is regarded as a self-contained separate realm, a counterpart fate befalls bodily activity and movements. They are regarded as at the best mere external annexes to mind. They may be necessary for the satisfaction of bodily needs and the attainment of external decency and comfort, but they do not occupy a necessary place in mind nor enact an indispensable role in the completion of thought. Hence they have no place in a liberal education—i.e., one which is concerned with the interests of intelligence. If they come in at all, it is as a concession to the material needs of the masses. That they should be allowed to invade the education of the elite is unspeakable. This conclusion follows irresistibly from the isolated conception of mind, but by the same logic it disappears when we perceive what mind really is — namely, the purposive and directive factor in the development of experience. While it is desirable that all educational institutions should be equipped so as to give students an opportunity for acquiring and testing ideas and information in active pursuits typifying important social situations, it will, doubtless, be a long time before all of them are thus furnished. But this state of affairs does not afford instructors an excuse for folding their hands and persisting in methods which segregate school knowledge. Every recitation in every subject gives an opportunity for establishing cross connections between the subject matter of the lesson and the wider and more direct experiences of everyday life. Classroom instruction falls into three kinds. The least desirable treats each lesson as an independent whole. It does not put upon the student the responsibility of finding points of contact between it and other lessons in the same subject, or other subjects of study. Wiser teachers see to it that the student is systematically led to utilize his earlier lessons to help understand the present one, and also to use the present to throw additional light upon what has already been acquired. Results are better, but school subject matter is still isolated. Save by accident, out-of-school experience is left in its crude and comparatively irreflective state. It is not subject to the refining and expanding influences of the more accurate and comprehensive material of direct instruction. The latter is not motivated and impregnated with a sense of reality by being intermingled with the realities of everyday life. The best type of teaching bears in mind the desirability of affecting this interconnection. It puts the student in the habitual attitude of finding points of contact and mutual bearings.

124

Summary.

Processes of instruction are unified in the degree in which they center in the production of good habits of thinking. While we may speak, without error, of the method of thought, the important thing is that thinking is the method of an educative experience. The essentials of method are therefore identical with the essentials of reflection. They are first that the pupil have a genuine situation of experience — that there be a continuous activity in which he is interested for its own sake; secondly, that a genuine problem develop within this situation as a stimulus to thought; third, that he possess the information and make the observations needed to deal with it; fourth, that suggested solutions occur to him which he shall be responsible for developing in an orderly way; fifth, that he have opportunity and occasion to test his ideas by application, to make their meaning clear and to discover for himself their validity.

Chapter Thirteen:

The Nature of Method

1. The Unity of Subject Matter and Method.

The trinity of school topics is subject matter, methods, and administration or government. We have been concerned with the two former in recent chapters. It remains to disentangle them from the context in which they have been referred to, and discuss explicitly their nature. We shall begin with the topic of method, since that lies closest to the considerations of the last chapter. Before taking it up, it may be well, however, to call express attention to one implication of our theory; the connection of subject matter and method with each other. The idea that mind and the world of things and persons are two separate and independent realms — a theory which philosophically is known as dualism — carries with it the conclusion that method and subject matter of instruction are separate affairs. Subject matter then becomes a ready-made systematized classification of the facts and principles of the world of nature and man. Method then has for its province a consideration of the ways in which this antecedent subject matter may be best presented to and impressed upon the mind; or, a consideration of the ways in which the mind may be externally brought to bear upon the matter so as to facilitate its acquisition and possession. In theory, at least, one might deduce from a science of the mind as something existing by itself a complete theory of methods of learning, with no knowledge of the subjects to which the methods are to be applied. Since many who are actually most proficient in various branches of subject matter are wholly innocent of these methods, this state of affairs gives opportunity for the retort that pedagogy, as an alleged science of methods of the mind in learning, is futile; — a mere screen for concealing the necessity a teacher is under of profound and accurate acquaintance with the subject in hand.

But since thinking is a directed movement of subject matter to a completing issue, and since mind is the deliberate and intentional phase of the process, the notion of any such split is radically false. The fact that the material of a science is organized is evidence that it has already been subjected to intelligence; it has been methodized, so to say. Zoology as a systematic branch of knowledge represents crude, scattered facts of our ordinary acquaintance with animals after they have been subjected to careful examination, to deliberate supplementation, and to arrangement to bring out connections which assist observation, memory, and further inquiry. Instead of furnishing a starting point for learning, they mark out a consummation. Method means that arrangement of subject matter which makes it most effective in use. Never is method something outside of the material.

How about method from the standpoint of an individual who is dealing with subject matter? Again, it is not something external. It is simply an effective treatment of material — efficiency meaning such treatment as utilizes the material (puts it to a purpose) with a minimum of waste of time and energy. We can distinguish a way of acting, and discuss it by itself; but the way exists only as way-of-dealing-with-material. Method is not antithetical to subject matter; it is the effective direction of subject matter to desired results. It is antithetical to random and ill-considered action, — ill-considered signifying ill-adapted.

The statement that method means directed movement of subject matter towards ends is formal. An illustration may give it content. Every artist must have a method, a technique, in doing his work. Piano playing is not hitting the keys at random. It is an orderly way of using them, and the order is not something which exists ready- made in the musician's hands or brain prior to an activity dealing with the piano. Order is found in the disposition of acts which use the piano and the hands and brain so as to achieve the result intended. It is the action of the piano directed to accomplish the purpose of the piano as a musical instrument. It is the same with "pedagogical" method. The only difference is that the piano is a mechanism constructed in advance for a single end; while the material of study is capable of indefinite uses. But even in this regard the illustration may apply if we consider the infinite variety of kinds of music which a piano may produce, and the variations in technique required in the different musical results secured. Method in any case is but an effective way of employing some material for some end.

These considerations may be generalized by going back to the conception of experience. Experience as the perception of the connection between something tried and something undergone in consequence is a process. Apart from effort to control the course which the process takes, there is no distinction of subject matter and method. There is simply an activity which includes both what an individual does and what the environment does. A piano player who had perfect mastery of his instrument would have no occasion to distinguish between his contribution and that of the piano. In well-formed, smooth-running functions of any sort, — skating, conversing, hearing music, enjoying a landscape, — there is no consciousness of separation of the method of the person and of the subject matter. In whole-hearted play and work there is the same phenomenon.

When we reflect upon an experience instead of just having it, we inevitably distinguish between our own attitude and the objects toward which we sustain the attitude. When a man is eating, he is eating food. He does not divide his act into eating and food. But if he makes a scientific investigation of the act, such a discrimination is the first thing he would effect. He would examine on the one hand the properties of the nutritive material, and on the other hand the acts of the organism in appropriating and digesting. Such reflection upon experience gives rise to a distinction of what we experience (the experienced) and the experiencing — the how. When we give names to this distinction we have subject matter and method as our terms. There is the thing seen, heard, loved, hated, imagined, and there is the act of seeing, hearing, loving, hating, imagining, etc.

This distinction is so natural and so important for certain purposes, that we are only too apt to regard it as a separation in existence and not as a distinction in thought. Then we make a division between a self and the environment or world. This separation is the root of the dualism of method and subject matter. That is, we assume that knowing, feeling, willing, etc., are things which belong to the self or mind in its isolation, and which then may be brought to bear upon an independent subject matter. We assume that the things which belong in isolation to the self or mind have their own laws of operation irrespective of the modes of active energy of the object. These laws are supposed to furnish method. It would be no less absurd to suppose that men can eat without eating something, or that the structure and movements of the jaws, throat muscles, the digestive activities of stomach, etc., are not what they are because of the material with which their activity is engaged. Just as the organs of the organism are a continuous part of the very world in which food materials exist, so the capacities of seeing, hearing, loving, imagining are intrinsically connected with the subject matter of the world. They are more truly ways in which the environment enters into experience and functions there than they are independent acts brought to bear upon things. Experience, in short, is not a combination of mind and world, subject and object, method and subject matter, but is a single continuous interaction of a great diversity (literally countless in number) of energies.

For the purpose of controlling the course or direction which the moving unity of experience takes we draw a mental distinction between the how and the what. While there is no way of walking or of eating or of learning over and above the actual walking, eating, and studying, there are certain elements in the act which give the key to its more effective control. Special attention to these elements makes them more obvious to perception (letting other factors recede for the time being from conspicuous recognition). Getting an idea of how the experience proceeds indicates to us what factors must be secured or modified in order that it may go on more successfully. This is only a somewhat elaborate way of saying that if a man watches carefully the growth of several plants, some of which do well and some of which amount to little or nothing, he may be able to detect the special conditions upon which the prosperous development of a plant depends. These conditions, stated in an orderly sequence, would constitute the method or way or manner of its growth. There is no difference between the growth of a plant and the prosperous development of an experience. It is not easy, in either case, to seize upon just the factors which make for its best movement. But study of cases of success and failure and minute and extensive comparison, helps to seize upon causes. When we have arranged these causes in order, we have a method of procedure or a technique.

A consideration of some evils in education that flow from the isolation of method from subject matter will make the point more definite.

(i) In the first place, there is the neglect (of which we have spoken) of concrete situations of experience. There can be no discovery of a method without cases to be studied. The method is derived from observation of what actually happens, with a view to seeing that it happen better next time. But in instruction and discipline, there is rarely sufficient opportunity for children and youth to have the direct normal experiences from which educators might derive an idea of method or order of best development. Experiences are had under conditions of such constraint that they throw little or no light upon the normal course of an experience to its fruition. "Methods" have then to be authoritatively recommended to teachers, instead of being an expression of their own intelligent observations. Under such circumstances, they have a mechanical uniformity, assumed to be alike for all minds. Where flexible personal experiences are promoted by providing an environment which calls out directed occupations in work and play, the methods ascertained will vary with individuals — for it is certain that each individual has something characteristic in his way of going at things.

(ii) In the second place, the notion of methods isolated from subject matter is responsible for the false conceptions of discipline and interest already noted. When the effective way of managing material is treated as something ready-made apart from material, there are just three possible ways in which to establish a relationship lacking by assumption. One is to utilize excitement, shock of pleasure, tickling the palate. Another is to make the consequences of not attending painful; we may use the menace of harm to motivate concern with the alien subject matter. Or a direct appeal may be made to the person to put forth effort without any reason. We may rely upon immediate strain of "will." In practice, however, the latter method is effectual only when instigated by fear of unpleasant results. (iii) In the third place, the act of learning is made a direct and conscious end in itself. Under normal conditions, learning is a product and reward of occupation with subject matter. Children do not set out, consciously, to learn walking or talking. One sets out to give his impulses for communication and for fuller intercourse with others a show. He learns in consequence of his direct activities. The better methods of teaching a child, say, to read, follow the same road. They do not fix his attention upon the fact that he has to learn something and so make his attitude self-conscious and constrained. They engage his activities, and in the process of engagement he learns: the same is true of the more successful methods in dealing with number or whatever. But when the subject matter is not used in carrying forward impulses and habits to significant results, it is just something to be learned. The pupil's attitude to it is just that of having to learn it. Conditions more unfavorable to an alert and concentrated response would be hard to devise. Frontal attacks are even more wasteful in learning than in war. This does not mean, however, that students are to be seduced unaware into preoccupation with lessons. It means that they shall be occupied with them for real reasons or ends, and not just as something to be learned. This is accomplished whenever the pupil perceives the place occupied by the subject matter in the fulfilling of some experience.

(iv) In the fourth place, under the influence of the conception of the separation of mind and material, method tends to be reduced to a cut and dried routine, to following mechanically prescribed steps. No one can tell in how many schoolrooms children reciting in arithmetic or grammar are compelled to go through, under the alleged sanction of method, certain preordained verbal formulae. Instead of being encouraged to attack their topics directly, experimenting with methods that seem promising and learning to discriminate by the consequences that accrue, it is assumed that there is one fixed method to be followed. It is also naively assumed that if the pupils make their statements and explanations in a certain form of "analysis," their mental habits will in time conform. Nothing has brought pedagogical theory into greater disrepute than the belief that it is identified with handing out to teachers recipes and models to be followed in teaching. Flexibility and initiative in dealing with problems are characteristic of any conception to which method is a way of managing material to develop a conclusion. Mechanical rigid woodenness is an inevitable corollary of any theory which separates mind from activity motivated by a purpose.

2. Method as General and as Individual.

In brief, the method of teaching is the method of an art, of action intelligently directed by ends. But the practice of a fine art is far from being a matter of extemporized inspirations. Study of the operations and results of those in the past who have greatly succeeded is essential. There is always a tradition, or schools of art, definite enough to impress beginners, and often to take them captive. Methods of artists in every branch depend upon thorough acquaintance with materials and tools; the painter must know canvas, pigments, brushes, and the technique of manipulation of all his appliances. Attainment of this knowledge requires persistent and concentrated attention to objective materials. The artist studies the progress of his own attempts to see what succeeds and what fails. The assumption that there are no alternatives between following ready-made rules and trusting to native gifts, the inspiration of the moment and undirected "hard work," is contradicted by the procedures of every art.

Such matters as knowledge of the past, of current technique, of materials, of the ways in which one's own best results are assured, supply the material for what may be called general method. There exists a cumulative body of fairly stable methods for reaching results, a body authorized by past experience and by intellectual analysis, which an individual ignores at his peril. As was pointed out in the discussion of habit-forming (ante, p. 49), there is always a danger that these methods will become mechanized and rigid, mastering an agent instead of being powers at command for his own ends. But it is also true that the innovator who achieves anything enduring, whose work is more than a passing sensation, utilizes classic methods more than may appear to himself or to his critics. He devotes them to new uses, and in so far transforms them.

Education also has its general methods. And if the application of this remark is more obvious in the case of the teacher than of the pupil, it is equally real in the case of the latter. Part of his learning, a very important part, consists in becoming master of the methods which the experience of others has shown to be more efficient in like cases of getting knowledge. 1[1] These general methods are in no way opposed to individual initiative and originality — to personal ways of doing things. On the contrary they are reinforcements of them. For there is

---

[1] 1 This point is developed below in a discussion of what are termed psychological and logical methods respectively.

radical difference between even the most general method and a prescribed rule. The latter is a direct guide to action; the former operates indirectly through the enlightenment it supplies as to ends and means. It operates, that is to say, through intelligence, and not through conformity to orders externally imposed. Ability to use even in a masterly way an established technique gives no warranty of artistic work, for the latter also depends upon an animating idea.

If knowledge of methods used by others does not directly tell us what to do, or furnish ready-made models, how does it operate? What is meant by calling a method intellectual? Take the case of a physician. No mode of behavior more imperiously demands knowledge of established modes of diagnosis and treatment than does his. But after all, cases are like, not identical. To be used intelligently, existing practices, however authorized they may be, have to be adapted to the exigencies of particular cases. Accordingly, recognized procedures indicate to the physician what inquiries to set on foot for himself, what measures to try. They are standpoints from which to carry on investigations; they economize a survey of the features of the particular case by suggesting the things to be especially looked into. The physician's own personal attitudes, his own ways (individual methods) of dealing with the situation in which he is concerned, are not subordinated to the general principles of procedure, but are facilitated and directed by the latter. The instance may serve to point out the value to the teacher of a knowledge of the psychological methods and the empirical devices found useful in the past. When they get in the way of his own common sense, when they come between him and the situation in which he has to act, they are worse than useless. But if he has acquired them as intellectual aids in sizing up the needs, resources, and difficulties of the unique experiences in which he engages, they are of constructive value. In the last resort, just because everything depends upon his own methods of response, much depends upon how far he can utilize, in making his own response, the knowledge which has accrued in the experience of others. As already intimated, every word of this account is directly applicable also to the method of the pupil, the way of learning. To suppose that students, whether in the primary school or in the university, can be supplied with models of method to be followed in acquiring and expounding a subject is to fall into a self-deception that has lamentable consequences. (See ante, p. 169.) One must make his own reaction in any case. Indications of the standardized or general methods used in like cases by others—particularly by those who are already experts—are of worth or of harm according as they make his personal reaction more intelligent or as they induce a person to dispense with exercise of his own judgment. If what was said earlier (See p. 159) about originality of thought seemed overstrained, demanding more of education than the capacities of average human nature permit, the difficulty is that we lie under the incubus of a superstition. We have set up the notion of mind at large, of intellectual method that is the same for all. Then we regard individuals as differing in the quantity of mind with which they are charged. Ordinary persons are then expected to be ordinary. Only the exceptional are allowed to have originality. The measure of difference between the average student and the genius is a measure of the absence of originality in the former. But this notion of mind in general is a fiction. How one person's abilities compare in quantity with those of another is none of the teacher's business. It is irrelevant to his work. What is required is that every individual shall have opportunities to employ his own powers in activities that have meaning. Mind, individual method, originality (these are convertible terms) signify the quality of purposive or directed action. If we act upon this conviction, we shall secure more originality even by the conventional standard than now develops. Imposing an alleged uniform general method upon everybody breeds mediocrity in all but the very exceptional. And measuring originality by deviation from the mass breeds eccentricity in them. Thus we stifle the distinctive quality of the many, and save in rare instances (like, say, that of Darwin) infect the rare geniuses with an unwholesome quality.

3. The Traits of Individual Method.

The most general features of the method of knowing have been given in our chapter on thinking. They are the features of the reflective situation: Problem, collection and analysis of data, projection and elaboration of suggestions or ideas, experimental application and testing; the resulting conclusion or judgment. The specific elements of an individual's method or way of attack upon a problem are found ultimately in his native tendencies and his acquired habits and interests. The method of one will vary from that of another (and properly vary) as his original instinctive capacities vary, as his past experiences and his preferences vary. Those who have already studied these matters are in possession of information which will help teachers in understanding the responses different pupils make, and help them in guiding these responses to greater efficiency. Child-study, psychology, and a knowledge of social environment supplement the personal acquaintance gained by the teacher. But methods remain the personal concern, approach, and attack of an individual, and no catalogue can ever exhaust their diversity of form and tint.

Some attitudes may be named, however,-which are central in effective intellectual ways of dealing with subject matter. Among the most important are directness, open-mindedness, single-mindedness (or whole-heartedness), and responsibility.

1. It is easier to indicate what is meant by directness through negative terms than in positive ones. Self-consciousness, embarrassment, and constraint are its menacing foes. They indicate that a person is not immediately concerned with subject matter. Something has come between which deflects concern to side issues. A self-conscious person is partly thinking about his problem and partly about what others think of his performances. Diverted energy means loss of power and confusion of ideas. Taking an attitude is by no means identical with being conscious of one's attitude. The former is spontaneous, naive, and simple. It is a sign of whole-souled relationship between a person and what he is dealing with. The latter is not of necessity abnormal. It is sometimes the easiest way of correcting a false method of approach, and of improving the effectiveness of the means one is employing, — as golf players, piano players, public speakers, etc., have occasionally to give especial attention to their position and movements. But

this need is occasional and temporary. When it is effectual a person thinks of himself in terms of what is to be done, as one means among others of the realization of an end — as in the case of a tennis player practicing to get the "feel" of a stroke. In abnormal cases, one thinks of himself not as part of the agencies of execution, but as a separate object — as when the player strikes an attitude thinking of the impression it will make upon spectators, or is worried because of the impression he fears his movements give rise to.

Confidence is a good name for what is intended by the term directness. It should not be confused, however, with self-confidence which may be a form of self-consciousness—or of "cheek." Confidence is not a name for what one thinks or feels about his attitude it is not reflex. It denotes the straightforwardness with which one goes at what he has to do. It denotes not conscious trust in the efficacy of one's powers but unconscious faith in the possibilities of the situation. It signifies rising to the needs of the situation. We have already pointed out (See p. 169) the objections to making students emphatically aware of the fact that they are studying or learning. Just in the degree in which they are induced by the conditions to be so aware, they are not studying and learning. They are in a divided and complicated attitude. Whatever methods of a teacher call a pupil's attention off from what he has to do and transfer it to his own attitude towards what he is doing impair directness of concern and action. Persisted in, the pupil acquires a permanent tendency to fumble, to gaze about aimlessly, to look for some clew of action beside that which the subject matter supplies. Dependence upon extraneous suggestions and directions, a state of foggy confusion, take the place of that sureness with which children (and grown-up people who have not been sophisticated by "education") confront the situations of life.

2. Open-mindedness. Partiality is, as we have seen, an accompaniment of the existence of interest, since this means sharing, partaking, taking sides in some movement. All the more reason, therefore, for an attitude of mind which actively welcomes suggestions and relevant information from all sides. In the chapter on Aims it was shown that foreseen ends are factors in the development of a changing situation. They are the means by which the direction of action is controlled. They are subordinate to the situation, therefore, not the situation to them. They are not ends in the sense of finalities to which everything must be bent and sacrificed. They are, as foreseen, means of guiding the development of a situation. A target is not the future goal of shooting; it is the centering factor in a present shooting. Openness of mind means accessibility of mind to any and every consideration that will throw light upon the situation that needs to be cleared up, and that will help determine the consequences of acting this way or that. Efficiency in accomplishing ends which have been settled upon as unalterable can coexist with a narrowly opened mind. But intellectual growth means constant expansion of horizons and consequent formation of new purposes and new responses. These are impossible without an active disposition to welcome points of view hitherto alien; an active desire to entertain considerations which modify existing purposes. Retention of capacity to grow is

the reward of such intellectual hospitality. The worst thing about stubbornness of mind, about prejudices, is that they arrest development; they shut the mind off from new stimuli. Open-mindedness means retention of the childlike attitude; closed-mindedness means premature intellectual old age.

Exorbitant desire for uniformity of procedure and for prompt external results are the chief foes which the open-minded attitude meets in school. The teacher who does not permit and encourage diversity of operation in dealing with questions is imposing intellectual blinders upon pupils — restricting their vision to the one path the teacher's mind happens to approve. Probably the chief cause of devotion to rigidity of method is, however, that it seems to promise speedy, accurately measurable, correct results. The zeal for "answers" is the explanation of much of the zeal for rigid and mechanical methods. Forcing and overpressure have the same origin, and the same result upon alert and varied intellectual interest.

Open-mindedness is not the same as empty-mindedness. To hang out a sign saying "Come right in; there is no one at home" is not the equivalent of hospitality. But there is a kind of passivity, willingness to let experiences accumulate and sink in and ripen, which is an essential of development. Results (external answers or solutions) may be hurried; processes may not be forced. They take their own time to mature. Were all instructors to realize that the quality of mental process, not the production of correct answers, is the measure of educative growth something hardly less than a revolution in teaching would be worked.

3. Single-mindedness. So far as the word is concerned, much that was said under the head of "directness" is applicable. But what the word is here intended to convey is completeness of interest, unity of purpose; the absence of suppressed but effectual ulterior aims for which the professed aim is but a mask. It is equivalent to mental integrity. Absorption, engrossment, full concern with subject matter for its own sake, nurture it. Divided interest and evasion destroy it.

Intellectual integrity, honesty, and sincerity are at bottom not matters of conscious purpose but of quality of active response. Their acquisition is fostered of course by conscious intent, but self-deception is very easy. Desires are urgent. When the demands and wishes of others forbid their direct expression they are easily driven into subterranean and deep channels. Entire surrender, and wholehearted adoption of the course of action demanded by others are almost impossible. Deliberate revolt or deliberate attempts to deceive others may result. But the more frequent outcome is a confused and divided state of interest in which one is fooled as to one's own real intent. One tries to serve two masters at once. Social instincts, the strong desire to please others and get their approval, social training, the general sense of duty and of authority, apprehension of penalty, all lead to a half-hearted effort to conform, to "pay attention to the lesson," or whatever the requirement is. Amiable individuals want to do what they are expected to do. Consciously the pupil thinks he is doing this. But his own desires are not abolished. Only their evident exhibition is suppressed. Strain of attention to what is hostile to desire is irksome; in spite of one's conscious wish, the underlying desires determine the main course of thought, the deeper emotional responses. The mind wanders from the nominal subject and devotes itself to what is intrinsically more desirable. A systematized divided attention expressing the duplicity of the state of desire is the result. One has only to recall his own experiences in school or at the present time when outwardly employed in actions which do not engage one's desires and purposes, to realize how prevalent is this attitude of divided attention — double-mindedness. We are so used to it that we take it for granted that a considerable amount of it is necessary. It may be; if so, it is the more important to face its bad intellectual effects. Obvious is the loss of energy of thought immediately available when one is consciously trying (or trying to seem to try) to attend to one matter, while unconsciously one's imagination is spontaneously going out to more congenial affairs. More subtle and more permanently crippling to efficiency of intellectual activity is a fostering of habitual self-deception, with the confused sense of reality which accompanies it. A double standard of reality, one for our own private and more or less concealed interests, and another for public and acknowledged concerns, hampers, in most of us, integrity and completeness of mental action. Equally serious is the fact that a split is set up between conscious thought and attention and impulsive blind affection and desire. Reflective dealings with the material of instruction is constrained and half-hearted; attention wanders. The topics to which it wanders are unavowed and hence intellectually illicit; transactions with them are furtive. The discipline that comes from regulating response by deliberate inquiry having a purpose fails; worse than that, the deepest concern and most congenial enterprises of the imagination (since they center about the things dearest to desire) are casual, concealed. They enter into action in ways which are unacknowledged. Not subject to rectification by consideration of consequences, they are demoralizing.

School conditions favorable to this division of mind between avowed, public, and socially responsible undertakings, and private, ill-regulated, and suppressed indulgences of thought are not hard to find. What is sometimes called "stern discipline," i.e., external coercive pressure, has this tendency. Motivation through rewards extraneous to the thing to be done has a like effect. Everything that makes schooling merely preparatory (See ante, p. 55) works in this direction. Ends being beyond the pupil's present grasp, other agencies have to be found to procure immediate attention to assigned tasks. Some responses are secured, but desires and affections not enlisted must find other outlets. Not less serious is exaggerated emphasis upon drill exercises designed to produce skill in action, independent of any engagement of thought — exercises have no purpose but the production of automatic skill. Nature abhors a mental vacuum. What do teachers imagine is happening to thought and emotion when the latter get no outlet in the things of immediate activity? Were they merely kept in temporary abeyance, or even only calloused, it would not be a matter of so much moment. But they are not abolished; they are not suspended; they are not suppressed—save with reference to the task in question. They follow their own chaotic and undisciplined course. What is native, spontaneous, and vital in mental reaction goes unused and untested, and the habits formed are such that these qualities become less and less available for public and avowed ends.

4. Responsibility.

By responsibility as an element in intellectual attitude is meant the disposition to consider in advance the probable consequences of any projected step and deliberately to accept them: to accept them in the sense of taking them into account, acknowledging them in action, not yielding a mere verbal assent. Ideas, as we have seen, are intrinsically standpoints and methods for bringing about a solution of a perplexing situation; forecasts calculated to influence responses. It is only too easy to think that one accepts a statement or believes a suggested truth when one has not considered its implications; when one has made but a cursory and superficial survey of what further things one is committed to by acceptance. Observation and recognition, belief and assent, then become names for lazy acquiescence in what is externally presented.

It would be much better to have fewer facts and truths in instruction — that is, fewer things supposedly accepted, — if a smaller number of situations could be intellectually worked out to the point where conviction meant something real — some identification of the self with the type of conduct demanded by facts and foresight of results. The most permanent bad results of undue complication of school subjects and congestion of school studies and lessons are not the worry, nervous strain, and superficial acquaintance that follow (serious as these are), but the failure to make clear what is involved in really knowing and believing a thing. Intellectual responsibility means severe standards in this regard. These standards can be built up only through practice in following up and acting upon the meaning of what is acquired.

Intellectual thoroughness is thus another name for the attitude we are considering. There is a kind of thoroughness which is almost purely physical: the kind that signifies mechanical and exhausting drill upon all the details of a subject. Intellectual thoroughness is seeing a thing through. It depends upon a unity of purpose to which details are subordinated, not upon presenting a multitude of disconnected details. It is manifested in the firmness with which the full meaning of the purpose is developed, not in attention, however "conscientious" it may be, to the steps of action externally imposed and directed.

Summary.

Method is a statement of the way the subject matter of an experience develops most effectively and fruitfully. It is derived, accordingly, from observation of the course of experiences where there is no conscious distinction of personal attitude and manner from material dealt with. The assumption that method is something separate is connected with the notion of the isolation of mind and self from the world of things. It makes instruction and learning formal, mechanical, constrained. While methods are individualized, certain features of the normal course of an experience to its fruition may be discriminated, because of the fund of wisdom derived from prior experiences and because of general similarities in the materials dealt with from time to time. Expressed in terms of the attitude of the individual the traits of good method are straightforwardness, flexible intellectual interest or open-minded will to learn, integrity of purpose, and acceptance of responsibility for the consequences of one's activity including thought.

Chapter Fourteen:

The Nature of Subject Matter

1. Subject Matter of Educator and of Learner.

So far as the nature of subject matter in principle is concerned, there is nothing to add to what has been said (See ante, p. 134). It consists of the facts observed, recalled, read, and talked about, and the ideas suggested, in course of a development of a situation having a purpose. This statement needs to be rendered more specific by connecting it with the materials of school instruction, the studies which make up the curriculum. What is the significance of our definition in application to reading, writing, mathematics, history, nature study, drawing, singing, physics, chemistry, modern and foreign languages, and so on? Let us recur to two of the points made earlier in our discussion. The educator's part in the enterprise of education is to furnish the environment which stimulates responses and directs the learner's course. In last analysis, all that the educator can do is modify stimuli so that response will as surely as is possible result in the formation of desirable intellectual and emotional dispositions. Obviously studies or the subject matter of the curriculum have intimately to do with this business of supplying an environment. The other point is the necessity of a social environment to give meaning to habits formed. In what we have termed informal education, subject matter is carried directly in the matrix of social intercourse. It is what the persons with whom an individual associates do and say. This fact gives a clew to the understanding of the subject matter of formal or deliberate instruction. A connecting link is found in the stories, traditions, songs, and liturgies which accompany the doings and rites of a primitive social group. They represent the stock of meanings which have been precipitated out of previous experience, which are so prized by the group as to be identified with their conception of their own collective life. Not being obviously a part of the skill exhibited in the daily occupations of eating, hunting, making war and peace, constructing rugs, pottery, and baskets, etc., they are consciously impressed upon the young; often, as in the initiation ceremonies, with intense emotional fervor. Even more pains are consciously taken to perpetuate the myths, legends, and sacred verbal formulae of the group than to transmit the directly useful customs of the group just because they cannot be picked up, as the latter can be in the ordinary processes of association.

As the social group grows more complex, involving a greater number of acquired skills which are dependent, either in fact or in the belief of the group, upon standard ideas deposited from past experience, the content of social life gets more definitely formulated for purposes of instruction. As we have previously noted, probably the chief motive for consciously dwelling upon the group life, extracting the meanings which are regarded as most important and systematizing them in a coherent arrangement, is just the need of instructing the young so as to perpetuate group life. Once started on this road of selection, formulation, and organization, no definite limit exists. The invention of writing and of printing gives the operation an immense impetus. Finally, the bonds which connect the subject matter of school study with the habits and ideals of the social group are disguised and covered up. The ties are so loosened that it often appears as if there were none; as if subject matter existed simply as knowledge on its own independent behoof, and as if study were the mere act of mastering it for its own sake, irrespective of any social values. Since it is highly important for practical reasons to counter-act this tendency (See ante, p. 8) the chief purposes of our theoretical discussion are to make clear the connection which is so readily lost from sight, and to show in some detail the social content and function of the chief constituents of the course of study.

The points need to be considered from the standpoint of instructor and of student. To the former, the significance of a knowledge of subject matter, going far beyond the present knowledge of pupils, is to supply definite standards and to reveal to him the possibilities of the crude activities of the immature. (i) The material of school studies translates into concrete and detailed terms the meanings of current social life which it is desirable to transmit. It puts clearly before the instructor the essential ingredients of the culture to be perpetuated, in such an organized form as to protect him from the haphazard efforts he would be likely to indulge in if the meanings had not been standardized. (ii) A knowledge of the ideas which have been achieved in the past as the outcome of activity places the educator in a position to perceive the meaning of the seeming impulsive and aimless reactions of the young, and to provide the stimuli needed to direct them so that they will amount to something. The more the educator knows of music the more he can perceive the possibilities of the inchoate musical impulses of a child. Organized subject matter represents the ripe fruitage of experiences like theirs, experiences involving the same world, and powers and needs similar to theirs. It does not represent perfection or infallible wisdom; but it is the best at command to further new experiences which may, in some respects at least, surpass the achievements embodied in existing knowledge and works of art.

From the standpoint of the educator, in other words, the various studies represent working resources, available capital. Their remoteness from the experience of the young is not, however, seeming; it is real. The subject matter of the learner is not, therefore, it cannot be, identical with the formulated, the crystallized, and systematized subject matter of the adult; the material as found in books and in works of art, etc. The latter represents the possibilities of the former; not its existing state. It enters directly into the activities of the expert and the educator, not into that of the beginner, the learner. Failure to bear in mind the difference in subject matter from the respective standpoints of teacher and student is responsible for most of the mistakes made in the use of texts and other expressions of preexistent knowledge.

The need for a knowledge of the constitution and functions, in the concrete, of human nature is great just because the teacher's attitude to subject matter is so different from that of the pupil. The teacher presents in actuality what the pupil represents only in posse. That is, the teacher already knows the things which the student is only learning. Hence the problem of the two is radically unlike. When engaged in the direct act of teaching, the instructor needs to have subject matter at his fingers' ends; his attention should be upon the attitude and response of the pupil. To understand the latter in its interplay with subject matter is his task, while the pupil's mind, naturally, should be not on itself but on the topic in hand. Or to state the same point in a somewhat different manner: the teacher should be occupied not with subject matter in itself but in its interaction with the pupils' present needs and capacities. Hence simple scholarship is not enough. In fact, there are certain features of scholarship or mastered subject matter — taken by itself — which get in the way of effective teaching unless the instructor's habitual attitude is one of concern with its interplay in the pupil's own experience. In the first place, his knowledge extends indefinitely beyond the range of the pupil's acquaintance. It involves principles which are beyond the immature pupil's understanding and interest. In and of itself, it may no more represent the living world of the pupil's experience than the astronomer's knowledge of Mars represents a baby's acquaintance with the room in which he stays. In the second place, the method of organization of the material of achieved scholarship differs from that of the beginner. It is not true that the experience of the young is unorganized — that it consists of isolated scraps. But it is organized in connection with direct practical centers of interest. The child's home is, for example, the organizing center of his geographical knowledge. His own movements about the locality, his journeys abroad, the tales of his friends, give the ties which hold his items of information together. But the geography of the geographer, of the one who has already developed the implications of these smaller experiences, is organized on the basis of the relationship which the various facts bear to one another — not the relations which they bear to his house, bodily movements, and friends. To the one who is learned, subject matter is extensive, accurately defined, and logically interrelated. To the one who is learning, it is fluid, partial, and connected through his personal occupations. 1 The problem of teaching is to keep the experience of the student moving in the direction of what the expert already knows. Hence the need that the teacher know both subject matter and the characteristic needs and capacities of the student.

2. The Development of Subject Matter in the Learner.

It is possible, without doing violence to the facts, to mark off three fairly typical stages in the growth of subject matter in the experience of the learner. In its first estate, knowledge exists as the content of intelligent ability — power to do. This kind of subject matter, or known material, is expressed in familiarity or acquaintance with things. Then this material gradually is surcharged and deepened through communicated knowledge or information. Finally, it is enlarged and worked over into rationally or logically organized material — that of the one who, relatively speaking, is expert in the subject.

I. The knowledge which comes first to persons, and that remains most deeply ingrained, is knowledge of how to do; how to walk, talk, read, write, skate, ride a bicycle, manage a machine, calculate, drive a horse, sell goods, manage people, and so on indefinitely. The popular tendency to regard instinctive acts which are adapted to an end as a sort of miraculous knowledge, while unjustifiable, is evidence of the strong tendency to identify intelligent control of the means of action with knowledge. When education, under the influence of a scholastic conception of knowledge which ignores everything but scientifically formulated facts and truths, fails to recognize that primary or initial subject matter always exists as matter of an active doing, involving the use of the body and the handling of material, the subject matter of instruction is isolated from the needs and purposes of the learner, and so becomes just a something to be memorized and reproduced upon demand. Recognition of the natural course of development, on the contrary, always sets out with situations which involve learning by doing. Arts and occupations form the initial stage of the curriculum, corresponding as they do to knowing how to go about the accomplishment of ends. Popular terms denoting knowledge have always retained the connection with ability in action lost by academic philosophies. Ken and can are allied words. Attention means caring for a thing, in the sense of both affection and of looking out for its welfare. Mind means carrying out instructions in action — as a child minds his mother — and taking care of something — as a nurse minds the baby. To be thoughtful, considerate, means to heed the claims of others. Apprehension means dread of undesirable consequences, as well as intellectual grasp. To have good sense or judgment is to know the conduct a situation calls for; discernment is not making distinctions for the sake of making them, an exercise reprobated as hair splitting, but is insight into an affair with reference to acting. Wisdom has never lost its association with the proper direction of life. Only in education, never in the life of farmer, sailor, merchant, physician, or laboratory experimenter, does knowledge mean primarily a store of information aloof from doing. Having to do with things in an intelligent way issues in acquaintance or familiarity. The things we are best acquainted with are the things we put to frequent use — such things as chairs, tables, pen, paper, clothes, food, knives and forks on the commonplace level, differentiating into more special objects according to a person's occupations in life. Knowledge of things in that intimate and emotional sense suggested by the word acquaintance is a precipitate from our employing them with a purpose. We have acted with or upon the thing so frequently that we can anticipate how it will act and react — such is the meaning of familiar acquaintance. We are ready for a familiar thing; it does not catch us napping, or play unexpected tricks with us. This attitude carries with it a sense of congeniality or friendliness, of ease and illumination; while the things with which we are not accustomed to deal are strange, foreign, cold, remote, "abstract."

II. But it is likely that elaborate statements regarding this primary stage of knowledge will darken understanding. It includes practically all of our knowledge which is not the result of deliberate technical study. Modes of purposeful doing include dealings with persons as well as things. Impulses of communication and habits of intercourse have to be adapted to maintaining successful connections with others; a large fund of social knowledge accrues. As a part of this intercommunication one learns much from others. They tell of their experiences and of the experiences which, in turn, have been told them. In so far as one is interested or concerned in these communications, their matter becomes a part of one's own experience. Active connections with others are such an intimate and vital part of our own concerns that it is impossible to draw sharp lines, such as would enable us to say, "Here my experience ends; there yours begins." In so far as we are partners in common undertakings, the things which others communicate to us as the consequences of their particular share in the enterprise blend at once into the experience resulting from our own special doings. The ear is as much an organ of experience as the eye or hand; the eye is available for reading reports of what happens beyond its horizon. Things remote in space and time affect the issue of our actions quite as much as things which we can smell and handle. They really concern us, and, consequently, any account of them which assists us in dealing with things at hand falls within personal experience.

Information is the name usually given to this kind of subject matter. The place of communication in personal doing supplies us with a criterion for estimating the value of informational material in school. Does it grow naturally out of some question with which the student is concerned? Does it fit into his more direct acquaintance so as to increase its efficacy and deepen its meaning? If it meets these two requirements, it is educative. The amount heard or read is of no importance—the more the better, provided the student has a need for it and can apply it in some situation of his own.

But it is not so easy to fulfill these requirements in actual practice as it is to lay them down in theory. The extension in modern times of the area of intercommunication; the invention of appliances for securing acquaintance with remote parts of the heavens and bygone events of history; the cheapening of devices, like printing, for recording and distributing information — genuine and alleged — have created an immense bulk of communicated subject matter. It is much easier to swamp a pupil with this than to work it into his direct experiences. All too frequently it forms another strange world which just overlies the world of personal acquaintance. The sole problem of the student is to learn, for school purposes, for purposes of recitations and promotions, the constituent parts of this strange world. Probably the most conspicuous connotation of the word knowledge for most persons to-day is just the body of facts and truths ascertained by others; the material found in the rows and rows of atlases, cyclopedias, histories, biographies, books of travel, scientific treatises, on the shelves of libraries.

The imposing stupendous bulk of this material has unconsciously influenced men's notions of the nature of knowledge itself. The statements, the propositions, in which knowledge, the issue of active concern with problems, is deposited, are taken to be themselves knowledge. The record of knowledge, independent of its place as an outcome of inquiry and a resource in further inquiry, is taken to be knowledge. The mind of man is taken captive by the spoils of its prior victories; the spoils, not the weapons and the acts of waging the battle against the unknown, are used to fix the meaning of knowledge, of fact, and truth.

If this identification of knowledge with propositions stating information has fastened itself upon logicians and philosophers, it is not surprising that the same ideal has almost dominated instruction. The "course of study" consists largely of information distributed into various branches of study, each study being subdivided into lessons presenting in serial cutoff portions of the total store. In the seventeenth century, the store was still small enough so that men set up the ideal of a complete encyclopedic mastery of it. It is now so bulky that the impossibility of any one man's coming into possession of it all is obvious. But the educational ideal has not been much affected. Acquisition of a modicum of information in each branch of learning, or at least in a selected group, remains the principle by which the curriculum, from elementary school through college, is formed; the easier portions being assigned to the earlier years, the more difficult to the later. The complaints of educators that learning does not enter into character and affect conduct; the protests against memoriter work, against cramming, against gradgrind preoccupation with "facts," against devotion to wire-drawn distinctions and ill-understood rules and principles, all follow from this state of affairs. Knowledge which is mainly second-hand, other men's knowledge, tends to become merely verbal. It is no objection to information that it is clothed in words; communication necessarily takes place through words. But in the degree in which what is communicated cannot be organized into the existing experience of the learner, it becomes mere words: that is, pure sense-stimuli, lacking in meaning. Then it operates to call out mechanical reactions, ability to use the vocal organs to repeat statements, or the hand to write or to do "sums."

To be informed is to be posted; it is to have at command the subject matter needed for an effective dealing with a problem, and for giving added significance to the search for solution and to the solution itself. Informational knowledge is the material which can be fallen back upon as given, settled, established, assured in a doubtful situation. It is a kind of bridge for mind in its passage from doubt to discovery. It has the office of an intellectual middleman. It condenses and records in available form the net results of the prior experiences of mankind, as an agency of enhancing the meaning of new experiences. When one is told that Brutus assassinated Caesar, or that the length of the year is three hundred sixty-five and one fourth days, or that the ratio of the diameter of the circle to its circumference is 3.1415...one receives what is indeed knowledge for others, but for him it is a stimulus to knowing. His acquisition of knowledge depends upon his response to what is communicated.

3. Science or Rationalized Knowledge.

Science is a name for knowledge in its most characteristic form. It represents in its degree, the perfected outcome of learning, — its consummation. What is known, in a given case, is what is sure, certain, settled, disposed of; that which we think with rather than that which we think about. In its honorable sense, knowledge is distinguished from opinion, guesswork, speculation, and mere tradition. In knowledge, things are ascertained; they are so and not dubiously otherwise. But experience makes us aware that there is difference between intellectual certainty of subject matter and our certainty. We are made, so to speak, for belief; credulity is natural. The undisciplined mind is averse to suspense and intellectual hesitation; it is prone to assertion. It likes things undisturbed, settled, and treats them as such without due warrant. Familiarity, common repute, and congeniality to desire are readily made measuring rods of truth. Ignorance gives way to opinionated and current error, — a greater foe to learning than ignorance itself. A Socrates is thus led to declare that consciousness of ignorance is the beginning of effective love of wisdom, and a Descartes to say that science is born of doubting.

We have already dwelt upon the fact that subject matter, or data, and ideas have to have their worth tested experimentally: that in themselves they are tentative and provisional. Our predilection for premature acceptance and assertion, our aversion to suspended judgment, are signs that we tend naturally to cut short the process of testing. We are satisfied with superficial and immediate short-visioned applications. If these work out with moderate satisfactoriness, we are content to suppose that our assumptions have been confirmed. Even in the case of failure, we are inclined to put the blame not on the inadequacy and incorrectness of our data and thoughts, but upon our hard luck and the hostility of circumstance. We charge the evil consequence not to the error of our schemes and our incomplete inquiry into conditions (thereby getting material for revising the former and stimulus for extending the latter) but to untoward fate. We even plume ourselves upon our firmness in clinging to our conceptions in spite of the way in which they work out.

Science represents the safeguard of the race against these natural propensities and the evils which flow from them. It consists of the special appliances and methods which the race has slowly worked out in order to conduct reflection under conditions whereby its procedures and results are tested. It is artificial (an acquired art), not spontaneous; learned, not native. To this fact is due the unique, the invaluable place of science in education, and also the dangers which threaten its right use. Without initiation into the scientific spirit one is not in possession of the best tools which humanity has so far devised for effectively directed reflection. One in that case not merely conducts inquiry and learning without the use of the best instruments, but fails to understand the full meaning of knowledge. For he does not become acquainted with the traits that mark off opinion and assent from authorized conviction. On the other hand, the fact that science marks the perfecting of knowing in highly specialized conditions of technique renders its results, taken by themselves, remote from ordinary experience — a quality of aloofness that is popularly designated by the term abstract. When this isolation appears in instruction, scientific information is even more exposed to the dangers attendant upon presenting ready-made subject matter than are other forms of information.

Science has been defined in terms of method of inquiry and testing. At first sight, this definition may seem opposed to the current conception that science is organized or systematized knowledge. The opposition, however, is only seeming, and disappears when the ordinary definition is completed. Not organization but the kind of organization effected by adequate methods of tested discovery marks off science. The knowledge of a farmer is systematized in the degree in which he is competent. It is organized on the basis of relation of means to ends — practically organized. Its organization as knowledge (that is, in the eulogistic sense of adequately tested and confirmed) is incidental to its organization with reference to securing crops, live-stock, etc. But scientific subject matter is organized with specific reference to the successful conduct of the enterprise of discovery, to knowing as a specialized undertaking. Reference to the kind of assurance attending science will shed light upon this statement. It is rational assurance, — logical warranty. The ideal of scientific organization is, therefore, that every conception and statement shall be of such a kind as to follow from others and to lead to others. Conceptions and propositions mutually imply and support one another. This double relation of 'leading to and confirming" is what is meant by the terms logical and rational. The everyday conception of water is more available for ordinary uses of drinking, washing, irrigation, etc., than the chemist's notion of it. The latter's description of it as H20 is superior from the standpoint of place and use in inquiry. It states the nature of water in a way which connects it with knowledge of other things, indicating to one who understands it how the knowledge is arrived at and its bearings upon other portions of knowledge of the structure of things. Strictly speaking, it does not indicate the objective relations of water any more than does a statement that water is transparent, fluid, without taste or odor, satisfying to thirst, etc. It is just as true that water has these relations as that it is constituted by two molecules of hydrogen in combination with one of oxygen. But for the particular purpose of conducting discovery with a view to ascertainment of fact, the latter relations are fundamental. The more one emphasizes organization as a mark of science, then, the more he is committed to a recognition of the primacy of method in the definition of science. For method defines the kind of organization in virtue of which science is science.

4. Subject Matter as Social.

Our next chapters will take up various school activities and studies and discuss them as successive stages in that evolution of knowledge which we have just been discussing. It remains to say a few words upon subject matter as social, since our prior remarks have been mainly concerned with its intellectual aspect. A difference in breadth and depth exists even in vital knowledge; even in the data and ideas which are relevant to real problems and which are motivated by purposes. For there is a difference in the social scope of purposes and the social importance of problems. With the wide range of possible material to select from, it is important that education (especially in all its phases short of the most specialized) should use a criterion of social worth. All information and systematized scientific subject matter have been worked out under the conditions of social life and have been transmitted by social means. But this does not prove that all is of equal value for the purposes of forming the disposition and supplying the equipment of members of present society. The scheme of a curriculum must take account of the adaptation of studies to the needs of the existing community life; it must select with the intention of improving the life we live in common so that the future shall be better than the past. Moreover, the curriculum must be planned with reference to placing essentials first, and refinements second. The things which are socially most fundamental, that is, which have to do with the experiences in which the widest groups share, are the essentials. The things which represent the needs of specialized groups and technical pursuits are secondary. There is truth in the saying that education must first be human and only after that professional. But those who utter the saying frequently have in mind in the term human only a highly specialized class: the class of learned men who preserve the classic traditions of the past. They forget that material is humanized in the degree in which it connects with the common interests of men as men. Democratic society is peculiarly dependent for its maintenance upon the use in forming a course of study of criteria which are broadly human. Democracy cannot flourish where the chief influences in selecting subject matter of instruction are utilitarian ends narrowly conceived for the masses, and, for the higher education of the few, the traditions of a specialized cultivated class. The notion that the "essentials" of elementary education are the three R's mechanically treated, is based upon ignorance of the essentials needed for realization of democratic ideals. Unconsciously it assumes that these ideals are unrealizable; it assumes that in the future, as in the past, getting a livelihood, "making a living," must signify for most men and women doing things which are not significant, freely chosen, and ennobling to those who do them; doing things which serve ends unrecognized by those engaged in them, carried on under the direction of others for the sake of pecuniary reward. For preparation of large numbers for a life of this sort, and only for this purpose, are mechanical efficiency in reading, writing, spelling and figuring, together with attainment of a certain amount of muscular dexterity, "essentials." Such conditions also infect the education called liberal, with illiberality. They imply a somewhat parasitic cultivation bought at the expense of not having the enlightenment and discipline which come from concern with the deepest problems of common humanity. A curriculum which acknowledges the social responsibilities of education must present situations where problems are relevant to the problems of living together, and where observation and information are calculated to develop social insight and interest.

Summary. The subject matter of education consists primarily of the meanings which supply content to existing social life. The continuity of social life means that many of these meanings are contributed to present activity by past collective experience. As social life grows more complex, these factors increase in number and import. There is need of special selection, formulation, and organization in order that they may be adequately transmitted to the new generation. But this very process tends to set up subject matter as something of value just by itself, apart from its function in promoting the realization of the meanings implied in the present experience of the immature. Especially is the educator exposed to the temptation to conceive his task in terms of the pupil's ability to appropriate and reproduce the subject matter in set statements, irrespective of its organization into his activities as a developing social member. The positive principle is maintained when the young begin with active occupations having a social origin and use, and proceed to a scientific insight in the materials and laws involved, through assimilating into their more direct experience the ideas and facts communicated by others who have had a larger experience. 1 Since the learned man should also still be a learner, it will be understood that these contrasts are relative, not absolute. But in the earlier stages of learning at least they are practically all-important.

Chapter Fifteen:

Play and Work in the Curriculum

1. The Place of Active Occupations in Education.

In consequence partly of the efforts of educational reformers, partly of increased interest in child-psychology, and partly of the direct experience of the schoolroom, the course of study has in the past generation undergone considerable modification. The desirability of starting from and with the experience and capacities of learners, a lesson enforced from all three quarters, has led to the introduction of forms of activity, in play and work, similar to those in which children and youth engage outside of school. Modern psychology has substituted for the general, ready-made faculties of older theory a complex group of instinctive and impulsive tendencies. Experience has shown that when children have a chance at physical activities which bring their natural impulses into play, going to school is a joy, management is less of a burden, and learning is easier. Sometimes, perhaps, plays, games, and constructive occupations are resorted to only for these reasons, with emphasis upon relief from the tedium and strain of "regular" school work. There is no reason, however, for using them merely as agreeable diversions. Study of mental life has made evident the fundamental worth of native tendencies to explore, to manipulate tools and materials, to construct, to give expression to joyous emotion, etc. When exercises which are prompted by these instincts are a part of the regular school program, the whole pupil is engaged, the artificial gap between life in school and out is reduced, motives are afforded for attention to a large variety of materials and processes distinctly educative in effect, and cooperative associations which give information in a social setting are provided. In short, the grounds for assigning to play and active work a definite place in the curriculum are intellectual and social, not matters of temporary expediency and momentary agreeableness. Without something of the kind, it is not possible to secure the normal estate of effective learning; namely, that knowledge-getting be an outgrowth of activities having their own end, instead of a school task. More specifically, play and work correspond, point for point, with the traits of the initial stage of knowing, which consists, as we saw in the last chapter, in learning how to do things and in acquaintance with things and processes gained in the doing. It is suggestive that among the Greeks, till the rise of conscious philosophy, the same word, techne, was used for art and science. Plato gave his account of knowledge on the basis of an analysis of the knowledge of cobblers, carpenters, players of musical instruments, etc., pointing out that their art (so far as it was not mere routine) involved an end, mastery of material or stuff worked upon, control of appliances, and a definite order of procedure—all of which had to be known in order that there be intelligent skill or art.

Doubtless the fact that children normally engage in play and work out of school has seemed to many educators a reason why they should concern themselves in school with things radically different. School time seemed too precious to spend in doing over again what children were sure to do any way. In some social conditions, this reason has weight. In pioneer times, for example, outside occupations gave a definite and valuable intellectual and moral training. Books and everything concerned with them were, on the other hand, rare and difficult of access; they were the only means of outlet from a narrow and crude environment. Wherever such conditions obtain, much may be said in favor of concentrating school activity upon books. The situation is very different, however, in most communities to-day. The kinds of work in which the young can engage, especially in cities, are largely anti-educational. That prevention of child labor is a social duty is evidence on this point. On the other hand, printed matter has been so cheapened and is in such universal circulation, and all the opportunities of intellectual culture have been so multiplied, that the older type of book work is far from having the force it used to possess.

But it must not be forgotten that an educational result is a by- product of play and work in most out-of-school conditions. It is incidental, not primary. Consequently the educative growth secured is more or less accidental. Much work shares in the defects of existing industrial society — defects next to fatal to right development. Play tends to reproduce and affirm the crudities, as well as the excellencies, of surrounding adult life. It is the business of the school to set up an environment in which play and work shall be conducted with reference to facilitating desirable mental and moral growth. It is not enough just to introduce plays and games, hand work and manual exercises. Everything depends upon the way in which they are employed.

2. Available Occupations. A

bare catalogue of the list of activities which have already found their way into schools indicates what a rich field is at hand. There is work with paper, cardboard, wood, leather, cloth, yarns, clay and sand, and the metals, with and without tools. Processes employed are folding, cutting, pricking, measuring, molding, modeling, pattern-making, heating and cooling, and the operations characteristic of such tools as the hammer, saw, file, etc. Outdoor excursions, gardening, cooking, sewing, printing, book-binding, weaving, painting, drawing, singing, dramatization, story-telling, reading and writing as active pursuits with social aims (not as mere exercises for acquiring skill for future use), in addition to a countless variety of plays and games, designate some of the modes of occupation.

The problem of the educator is to engage pupils in these activities in such ways that while manual skill and technical efficiency are gained and immediate satisfaction found in the work, together with preparation for later usefulness, these things shall be subordinated to education — that is, to intellectual results and the forming of a socialized disposition. What does this principle signify? In the first place, the principle rules out certain practices. Activities which follow definite prescription and dictation or which reproduce without modification ready-made models, may give muscular dexterity, but they do not require the perception and elaboration of ends, nor (what is the same thing in other words) do they permit the use of judgment in selecting and adapting means. Not merely manual training specifically so called but many traditional kindergarten exercises have erred here. Moreover, opportunity for making mistakes is an incidental requirement. Not because mistakes are ever desirable, but because overzeal to select material and appliances which forbid a chance for mistakes to occur, restricts initiative, reduces judgment to a minimum, and compels the use of methods which are so remote from the complex situations of life that the power gained is of little availability. It is quite true that children tend to exaggerate their powers of execution and to select projects that are beyond them. But limitation of capacity is one of the things which has to be learned; like other things, it is learned through the experience of consequences. The danger that children undertaking too complex projects will simply muddle and mess, and produce not merely crude results (which is a minor matter) but acquire crude standards (which is an important matter) is great. But it is the fault of the teacher if the pupil does not perceive in due season the inadequacy of his performances, and thereby receive a stimulus to attempt exercises which will perfect his powers. Meantime it is more important to keep alive a creative and constructive attitude than to secure an external perfection by engaging the pupil's action in too minute and too closely regulated pieces of work. Accuracy and finish of detail can be insisted upon in such portions of a complex work as are within the pupil's capacity.

Unconscious suspicion of native experience and consequent overdoing of external control are shown quite as much in the material supplied as in the matter of the teacher's orders. The fear of raw material is shown in laboratory, manual training shop, Froebelian kindergarten, and Montessori house of childhood. The demand is for materials which have already been subjected to the perfecting work of mind: a demand which shows itself in the subject matter of active occupations quite as well as in academic book learning. That such material will control the pupil's operations so as to prevent errors is true. The notion that a pupil operating with such material will somehow absorb the intelligence that went originally to its shaping is fallacious. Only by starting with crude material and subjecting it to purposeful handling will he gain the intelligence embodied in finished material. In practice, overemphasis upon formed material leads to an exaggeration of mathematical qualities, since intellect finds its profit in physical things from matters of size, form, and proportion and the relations that flow from them. But these are known only when their perception is a fruit of acting upon purposes which require attention to them. The more human the purpose, or the more it approximates the ends which appeal in daily experience, the more real the knowledge. When the purpose of the activity is restricted to ascertaining these qualities, the resulting knowledge is only technical.

To say that active occupations should be concerned primarily with wholes is another statement of the same principle. Wholes for purposes of education are not, however, physical affairs. Intellectually the existence of a whole depends upon a concern or interest; it is qualitative, the completeness of appeal made by a situation. Exaggerated devotion to formation of efficient skill irrespective of present purpose always shows itself in devising exercises isolated from a purpose. Laboratory work is made to consist of tasks of accurate measurement with a view to acquiring knowledge of the fundamental units of physics, irrespective of contact with the problems which make these units important; or of operations designed to afford facility in the manipulation of experimental apparatus. The technique is acquired independently of the purposes of discovery and testing which alone give it meaning. Kindergarten employments are calculated to give information regarding cubes, spheres, etc., and to form certain habits of manipulation of material (for everything must always be done "just so"), the absence of more vital purposes being supposedly compensated for by the alleged symbolism of the material used. Manual training is reduced to a series of ordered assignments calculated to secure the mastery of one tool after another and technical ability in the various elements of construction — like the different joints. It is argued that pupils must know how to use tools before they attack actual making, — assuming that pupils cannot learn how in the process of making. Pestalozzi's just insistence upon the active use of the senses, as a substitute for memorizing words, left behind it in practice schemes for "object lessons" intended to acquaint pupils with all the qualities of selected objects. The error is the same: in all these cases it is assumed that before objects can be intelligently used, their properties must be known. In fact, the senses are normally used in the course of intelligent (that is, purposeful) use of things, since the qualities perceived are factors to be reckoned with in accomplishment. Witness the different attitude of a boy in making, say, a kite, with respect to the grain and other properties of wood, the matter of size, angles, and proportion of parts, to the attitude of a pupil who has an object-lesson on a piece of wood, where the sole function of wood and its properties is to serve as subject matter for the lesson.

The failure to realize that the functional development of a situation alone constitutes a "whole" for the purpose of mind is the cause of the false notions which have prevailed in instruction concerning the simple and the complex. For the person approaching a subject, the simple thing is his purpose—the use he desires to make of material, tool, or technical process, no matter how complicated the process of execution may be. The unity of the purpose, with the concentration upon details which it entails, confers simplicity upon the elements which have to be reckoned with in the course of action. It furnishes each with a single meaning according to its service in carrying on the whole enterprise. After one has gone through the process, the constituent qualities and relations are elements, each possessed with a definite meaning of its own. The false notion referred to takes the standpoint of the expert, the one for whom elements exist; isolates them from purposeful action, and presents them to beginners as the "simple" things. But it is time for a positive statement. Aside from the fact that active occupations represent things to do, not studies, their educational significance consists in the fact that they may typify social situations. Men's fundamental common concerns center about food, shelter, clothing, household furnishings, and the appliances connected with production, exchange, and consumption.

Representing both the necessities of life and the adornments with which the necessities have been clothed, they tap instincts at a deep level; they are saturated with facts and principles having a social quality.

To charge that the various activities of gardening, weaving, construction in wood, manipulation of metals, cooking, etc., which carry over these fundamental human concerns into school resources, have a merely bread and butter value is to miss their point. If the mass of mankind has usually found in its industrial occupations nothing but evils which had to be endured for the sake of maintaining existence, the fault is not in the occupations, but in the conditions under which they are carried on. The continually increasing importance of economic factors in contemporary life makes it the more needed that education should reveal their scientific content and their social value. For in schools, occupations are not carried on for pecuniary gain but for their own content. Freed from extraneous associations and from the pressure of wage-earning, they supply modes of experience which are intrinsically valuable; they are truly liberalizing in quality.

Gardening, for example, need not be taught either for the sake of preparing future gardeners, or as an agreeable way of passing time. It affords an avenue of approach to knowledge of the place farming and horticulture have had in the history of the race and which they occupy in present social organization. Carried on in an environment educationally controlled, they are means for making a study of the facts of growth, the chemistry of soil, the role of light, air, and moisture, injurious and helpful animal life, etc. There is nothing in the elementary study of botany which cannot be introduced in a vital way in connection with caring for the growth of seeds. Instead of the subject matter belonging to a peculiar study called botany, it will then belong to life, and will find, moreover, its natural correlations with the facts of soil, animal life, and human relations. As students grow mature, they will perceive problems of interest which may be pursued for the sake of discovery, independent of the original direct interest in gardening — problems connected with the germination and nutrition of plants, the reproduction of fruits, etc., thus making a transition to deliberate intellectual investigations.

The illustration is intended to apply, of course, to other school occupations, — wood-working, cooking, and on through the list. It is pertinent to note that in the history of the race the sciences grew gradually out from useful social occupations. Physics developed slowly out of the use of tools and machines; the important branch of physics known as mechanics testifies in its name to its original associations. The lever, wheel, inclined plane, etc., were among the first great intellectual discoveries of mankind, and they are none the less intellectual because they occurred in the course of seeking for means of accomplishing practical ends. The great advance of electrical science in the last generation was closely associated, as effect and as cause, with application of electric agencies to means of communication, transportation, lighting of cities and houses, and more economical production of goods. These are social ends, moreover, and if they are too closely associated with notions of private profit, it is not because of anything in them, but because they have been deflected to private uses: — a fact which puts upon the school the responsibility of restoring their connection, in the mind of the coming generation, with public scientific and social interests. In like ways, chemistry grew out of processes of dying, bleaching, metal working, etc., and in recent times has found innumerable new uses in industry.

Mathematics is now a highly abstract science; geometry, however, means literally earth-measuring: the practical use of number in counting to keep track of things and in measuring is even more important to-day than in the times when it was invented for these purposes. Such considerations (which could be duplicated in the history of any science) are not arguments for a recapitulation of the history of the race or for dwelling long in the early rule of thumb stage. But they indicate the possibilities—greater to-day than ever before — of using active occupations as opportunities for scientific study. The opportunities are just as great on the social side, whether we look at the life of collective humanity in its past or in its future. The most direct road for elementary students into civics and economics is found in consideration of the place and office of industrial occupations in social life. Even for older students, the social sciences would be less abstract and formal if they were dealt with less as sciences (less as formulated bodies of knowledge) and more in their direct subject-matter as that is found in the daily life of the social groups in which the student shares.

Connection of occupations with the method of science is at least as close as with its subject matter. The ages when scientific progress was slow were the ages when learned men had contempt for the material and processes of everyday life, especially for those concerned with manual pursuits. Consequently they strove to develop knowledge out of general principles — almost out of their heads — by logical reasons. It seems as absurd that learning should come from action on and with physical things, like dropping acid on a stone to see what would happen, as that it should come from sticking an awl with waxed thread through a piece of leather. But the rise of experimental methods proved that, given control of conditions, the latter operation is more typical of the right way of knowledge than isolated logical reasonings. Experiment developed in the seventeenth and succeeding centuries and became the authorized way of knowing when men's interests were centered in the question of control of nature for human uses. The active occupations in which appliances are brought to bear upon physical things with the intention of effecting useful changes is the most vital introduction to the experimental method.

3. Work and Play.

What has been termed active occupation includes both play and work. In their intrinsic meaning, play and industry are by no means so antithetical to one another as is often assumed, any sharp contrast being due to undesirable social conditions. Both involve ends consciously entertained and the selection and adaptations of materials and processes designed to effect the desired ends. The difference between them is largely one of time-span, influencing the directness of the connection of means and ends. In play, the interest is more direct — a fact frequently indicated by saying that in play the activity is its own end, instead of its having an ulterior result. The statement is correct, but it is falsely taken, if supposed to mean that play activity is momentary, having no element of looking ahead and none of pursuit. Hunting, for example, is one of the commonest forms of adult play, but the existence of foresight and the direction of present activity by what one is watching for are obvious. When an activity is its own end in the sense that the action of the moment is complete in itself, it is purely physical; it has no meaning (See p. 77). The person is either going through motions quite blindly, perhaps purely imitatively, or else is in a state of excitement which is exhausting to mind and nerves. Both results may be seen in some types of kindergarten games where the idea of play is so highly symbolic that only the adult is conscious of it. Unless the children succeed in reading in some quite different idea of their own, they move about either as if in a hypnotic daze, or they respond to a direct excitation.

The point of these remarks is that play has an end in the sense of a directing idea which gives point to the successive acts. Persons who play are not just doing something (pure physical movement); they are trying to do or effect something, an attitude that involves anticipatory forecasts which stimulate their present responses. The anticipated result, however, is rather a subsequent action than the production of a specific change in things. Consequently play is free, plastic. Where some definite external outcome is wanted, the end has to be held to with some persistence, which increases as the contemplated result is complex and requires a fairly long series of intermediate adaptations. When the intended act is another activity, it is not necessary to look far ahead and it is possible to alter it easily and frequently. If a child is making a toy boat, he must hold on to a single end and direct a considerable number of acts by that one idea. If he is just "playing boat" he may change the material that serves as a boat almost at will, and introduce new factors as fancy suggests. The imagination makes what it will of chairs, blocks, leaves, chips, if they serve the purpose of carrying activity forward.

From a very early age, however, there is no distinction of exclusive periods of play activity and work activity, but only one of emphasis. There are definite results which even young children desire, and try to bring to pass. Their eager interest in sharing the occupations of others, if nothing else, accomplishes this. Children want to "help"; they are anxious to engage in the pursuits of adults which effect external changes: setting the table, washing dishes, helping care for animals, etc. In their plays, they like to construct their own toys and appliances. With increasing maturity, activity which does not give back results of tangible and visible achievement loses its interest. Play then changes to fooling and if habitually indulged in is demoralizing. Observable results are necessary to enable persons to get a sense and a measure of their own powers. When make-believe is recognized to be make-believe, the device of making objects in fancy alone is too easy to stimulate intense action. One has only to observe the countenance of children really playing to note that their attitude is one of serious absorption; this attitude cannot be maintained when things cease to afford adequate stimulation.

When fairly remote results of a definite character are foreseen and enlist persistent effort for their accomplishment, play passes into work. Like play, it signifies purposeful activity and differs not in that activity is subordinated to an external result, but in the fact that a longer course of activity is occasioned by the idea of a result. The demand for continuous attention is greater, and more intelligence must be shown in selecting and shaping means. To extend this account would be to repeat what has been said under the caption of aim, interest, and thinking. It is pertinent, however, to inquire why the idea is so current that work involves subordination of an activity to an ulterior material result. The extreme form of this subordination, namely drudgery, offers a clew. Activity carried on under conditions of external pressure or coercion is not carried on for any significance attached to the doing. The course of action is not intrinsically satisfying; it is a mere means for avoiding some penalty, or for gaining some reward at its conclusion. What is inherently repulsive is endured for the sake of averting something still more repulsive or of securing a gain hitched on by others. Under unfree economic conditions, this state of affairs is bound to exist. Work or industry offers little to engage the emotions and the imagination; it is a more or less mechanical series of strains. Only the hold which the completion of the work has upon a person will keep him going. But the end should be intrinsic to the action; it should be its end — a part of its own course. Then it affords a stimulus to effort very different from that arising from the thought of results which have nothing to do with the intervening action. As already mentioned, the absence of economic pressure in schools supplies an opportunity for reproducing industrial situations of mature life under conditions where the occupation can be carried on for its own sake. If in some cases, pecuniary recognition is also a result of an action, though not the chief motive for it, that fact may well increase the significance of the occupation. Where something approaching drudgery or the need of fulfilling externally imposed tasks exists, the demand for play persists, but tends to be perverted. The ordinary course of action fails to give adequate stimulus to emotion and imagination. So in leisure time, there is an imperious demand for their stimulation by any kind of means; gambling, drink, etc., may be resorted to. Or, in less extreme cases, there is recourse to idle amusement; to anything which passes time with immediate agreeableness. Recreation, as the word indicates, is recuperation of energy. No demand of human nature is more urgent or less to be escaped. The idea that the need can be suppressed is absolutely fallacious, and the Puritanic tradition which disallows the need has entailed an enormous crop of evils. If education does not afford opportunity for wholesome recreation and train capacity for seeking and finding it, the suppressed instincts find all sorts of illicit outlets, sometimes overt, sometimes confined to indulgence of the imagination. Education has no more serious responsibility than making adequate provision for enjoyment of recreative leisure; not only for the sake of immediate health, but still more if possible for the sake of its lasting effect upon habits of mind. Art is again the answer to this demand.

Summary.

In the previous chapter we found that the primary subject matter of knowing is that contained in learning how to do things of a fairly direct sort. The educational equivalent of this principle is the consistent use of simple occupations which appeal to the powers of youth and which typify general modes of social activity. Skill and information about materials, tools, and laws of energy are acquired while activities are carried on for their own sake. The fact that they are socially representative gives a quality to the skill and knowledge gained which makes them transferable to out-of-school situations. It is important not to confuse the psychological distinction between play and work with the economic distinction. Psychologically, the defining characteristic of play is not amusement nor aimlessness. It is the fact that the aim is thought of as more activity in the same line, without defining continuity of action in reference to results produced. Activities as they grow more complicated gain added meaning by greater attention to specific results achieved. Thus they pass gradually into work. Both are equally free and intrinsically motivated, apart from false economic conditions which tend to make play into idle excitement for the well to do, and work into uncongenial labor for the poor. Work is psychologically simply an activity which consciously includes regard for consequences as a part of itself; it becomes constrained labor when the consequences are outside of the activity as an end to which activity is merely a means. Work which remains permeated with the play attitude is art — in quality if not in conventional designation.

Chapter Sixteen:

The Significance of Geography and History

1. Extension of Meaning of Primary Activities.

Nothing is more striking than the difference between an activity as merely physical and the wealth of meanings which the same activity may assume. From the outside, an astronomer gazing through a telescope is like a small boy looking through the same tube. In each case, there is an arrangement of glass and metal, an eye, and a little speck of light in the distance. Yet at a critical moment, the activity of an astronomer might be concerned with the birth of a world, and have whatever is known about the starry heavens as its significant content. Physically speaking, what man has effected on this globe in his progress from savagery is a mere scratch on its surface, not perceptible at a distance which is slight in comparison with the reaches even of the solar system. Yet in meaning what has been accomplished measures just the difference of civilization from savagery. Although the activities, physically viewed, have changed somewhat, this change is slight in comparison with the development of the meanings attaching to the activities. There is no limit to the meaning which an action may come to possess. It all depends upon the context of perceived connections in which it is placed; the reach of imagination in realizing connections is inexhaustible. The advantage which the activity of man has in appropriating and finding meanings makes his education something else than the manufacture of a tool or the training of an animal. The latter increase efficiency; they do not develop significance. The final educational importance of such occupations in play and work as were considered in the last chapter is that they afford the most direct instrumentalities for such extension of meaning. Set going under adequate conditions they are magnets for gathering and retaining an indefinitely wide scope of intellectual considerations. They provide vital centers for the reception and assimilation of information. When information is purveyed in chunks simply as information to be retained for its own sake, it tends to stratify over vital experience. Entering as a factor into an activity pursued for its own sake— whether as a means or as a widening of the content of the aim—it is informing. The insight directly gained fuses with what is told. Individual experience is then capable of taking up and holding in solution the net results of the experience of the group to which he belongs—including the results of sufferings and trials over long stretches of time. And such media have no fixed saturation point where further absorption is impossible. The more that is taken in, the greater capacity there is for further assimilation. New receptiveness follows upon new curiosity, and new curiosity upon information gained.

The meanings with which activities become charged, concern nature and man. This is an obvious truism, which however gains meaning when translated into educational equivalents. So translated, it signifies that geography and history supply subject matter which gives background and outlook, intellectual perspective, to what might otherwise be narrow personal actions or mere forms of technical skill. With every increase of ability to place our own doings in their time and space connections, our doings gain in significant content. We realize that we are citizens of no mean city in discovering the scene in space of which we are denizens, and the continuous manifestation of endeavor in time of which we are heirs and continuers. Thus our ordinary daily experiences cease to be things of the moment and gain enduring substance. Of course if geography and history are taught as ready-made studies which a person studies simply because he is sent to school, it easily happens that a large number of statements about things remote and alien to everyday experience are learned. Activity is divided, and two separate worlds are built up, occupying activity at divided periods. No transmutation takes place; ordinary experience is not enlarged in meaning by getting its connections; what is studied is not animated and made real by entering into immediate activity. Ordinary experience is not even left as it was, narrow but vital. Rather, it loses something of its mobility and sensitiveness to suggestions. It is weighed down and pushed into a corner by a load of unassimilated information. It parts with its flexible responsiveness and alert eagerness for additional meaning. Mere amassing of information apart from the direct interests of life makes mind wooden; elasticity disappears.

Normally every activity engaged in for its own sake reaches out beyond its immediate self. It does not passively wait for information to be bestowed which will increase its meaning; it seeks it out. Curiosity is not an accidental isolated possession; it is a necessary consequence of the fact that an experience is a moving, changing thing, involving all kinds of connections with other things. Curiosity is but the tendency to make these conditions perceptible. It is the business of educators to supply an environment so that this reaching out of an experience may be fruitfully rewarded and kept continuously active. Within a certain kind of environment, an activity may be checked so that the only meaning which accrues is of its direct and tangible isolated outcome. One may cook, or hammer, or walk, and the resulting consequences may not take the mind any farther than the consequences of cooking, hammering, and walking in the literal — or physical — sense. But nevertheless the consequences of the act remain far-reaching. To walk involves a displacement and reaction of the resisting earth, whose thrill is felt wherever there is matter. It involves the structure of the limbs and the nervous system; the principles of mechanics. To cook is to utilize heat and moisture to change the chemical relations of food materials; it has a bearing upon the assimilation of food and the growth of the body. The utmost that the most learned men of science know in physics, chemistry, physiology is not enough to make all these consequences and connections perceptible. The task of education, once more, is to see to it that such activities are performed in such ways and under such conditions as render these conditions as perceptible as possible. To "learn geography" is to gain in power to perceive the spatial, the natural, connections of an ordinary act; to "learn history" is essentially to gain in power to recognize its human connections. For what is called geography as a formulated study is simply the body of facts and principles which have been discovered in other men's experience about the natural medium in which we live, and in connection with which the particular acts of our life have an explanation. So history as a formulated study is but the body of known facts about the activities and sufferings of the social groups with which our own lives are continuous, and through reference to which our own customs and institutions are illuminated.

2. The Complementary Nature of History and Geography.

History and geography — including in the latter, for reasons about to be mentioned, nature study — are the information studies par excellence of the schools. Examination of the materials and the method of their use will make clear that the difference between penetration of this information into living experience and its mere piling up in isolated heaps depends upon whether these studies are faithful to the interdependence of man and nature which affords these studies their justification. Nowhere, however, is there greater danger that subject matter will be accepted as appropriate educational material simply because it has become customary to teach and learn it. The idea of a philosophic reason for it, because of the function of the material in a worthy transformation of experience, is looked upon as a vain fancy, or as supplying a high-sounding phraseology in support of what is already done. The words "history" and "geography" suggest simply the matter which has been traditionally sanctioned in the schools. The mass and variety of this matter discourage an attempt to see what it really stands for, and how it can be so taught as to fulfill its mission in the experience of pupils. But unless the idea that there is a unifying and social direction in education is a farcical pretense, subjects that bulk as large in the curriculum as history and geography, must represent a general function in the development of a truly socialized and intellectualized experience. The discovery of this function must be employed as a criterion for trying and sifting the facts taught and the methods used.

The function of historical and geographical subject matter has been stated; it is to enrich and liberate the more direct and personal contacts of life by furnishing their context, their background and outlook. While geography emphasizes the physical side and history the social, these are only emphases in a common topic, namely, the associated life of men. For this associated life, with its experiments, its ways and means, its achievements and failures, does not go on in the sky nor yet in a vacuum. It takes place on the earth. This setting of nature does not bear to social activities the relation that the scenery of a theatrical performance bears to a dramatic representation; it enters into the very make-up of the social happenings that form history. Nature is the medium of social occurrences. It furnishes original stimuli; it supplies obstacles and resources. Civilization is the progressive mastery of its varied energies. When this interdependence of the study of history, representing the human emphasis, with the study of geography, representing the natural, is ignored, history sinks to a listing of dates with an appended inventory of events, labeled "important"; or else it becomes a literary phantasy — for in purely literary history the natural environment is but stage scenery.

Geography, of course, has its educative influence in a counterpart connection of natural facts with social events and their consequences. The classic definition of geography as an account of the earth as the home of man expresses the educational reality. But it is easier to give this definition than it is to present specific geographical subject matter in its vital human bearings. The residence, pursuits, successes, and failures of men are the things that give the geographic data their reason for inclusion in the material of instruction. But to hold the two together requires an informed and cultivated imagination. When the ties are broken, geography presents itself as that hodge-podge of unrelated fragments too often found. It appears as a veritable rag-bag of intellectual odds and ends: the height of a mountain here, the course of a river there, the quantity of shingles produced in this town, the tonnage of the shipping in that, the boundary of a county, the capital of a state. The earth as the home of man is humanizing and unified; the earth viewed as a miscellany of facts is scattering and imaginatively inert. Geography is a topic that originally appeals to imagination — even to the romantic imagination. It shares in the wonder and glory that attach to adventure, travel, and exploration. The variety of peoples and environments, their contrast with familiar scenes, furnishes infinite stimulation. The mind is moved from the monotony of the customary. And while local or home geography is the natural starting point in the reconstructive development of the natural environment, it is an intellectual starting point for moving out into the unknown, not an end in itself. When not treated as a basis for getting at the large world beyond, the study of the home geography becomes as deadly as do object lessons which simply summarize the properties of familiar objects. The reason is the same. The imagination is not fed, but is held down to recapitulating, cataloguing, and refining what is already known. But when the familiar fences that mark the limits of the village proprietors are signs that introduce an understanding of the boundaries of great nations, even fences are lighted with meaning. Sunlight, air, running water, inequality of earth's surface, varied industries, civil officers and their duties — all these things are found in the local environment. Treated as if their meaning began and ended in those confines, they are curious facts to be laboriously learned. As instruments for extending the limits of experience, bringing within its scope peoples and things otherwise strange and unknown, they are transfigured by the use to which they are put. Sunlight, wind, stream, commerce, political relations come from afar and lead the thoughts afar. To follow their course is to enlarge the mind not by stuffing it with additional information, but by remaking the meaning of what was previously a matter of course.

The same principle coordinates branches, or phases, of geographical study which tend to become specialized and separate. Mathematical or astronomical, physiographic, topographic, political, commercial, geography, all make their claims. How are they to be adjusted? By an external compromise that crowds in so much of each? No other method is to be found unless it be constantly borne in mind that the educational center of gravity is in the cultural or humane aspects of the subject. From this center, any material becomes relevant in so far as it is needed to help appreciate the significance of human activities and relations. The differences of civilization in cold and tropical regions, the special inventions, industrial and political, of peoples in the temperate regions, cannot be understood without appeal to the earth as a member of the solar system. Economic activities deeply influence social intercourse and political organization on one side, and reflect physical conditions on the other. The specializations of these topics are for the specialists; their interaction concerns man as a being whose experience is social.

To include nature study within geography doubtless seems forced; verbally, it is. But in educational idea there is but one reality, and it is pity that in practice we have two names: for the diversity of names tends to conceal the identity of meaning. Nature and the earth should be equivalent terms, and so should earth study and nature study. Everybody knows that nature study has suffered in schools from scrappiness of subject matter, due to dealing with a large number of isolated points. The parts of a flower have been studied, for example, apart from the flower as an organ; the flower apart from the plant; the plant apart from the soil, air, and light in which and through which it lives. The result is an inevitable deadness of topics to which attention is invited, but which are so isolated that they do not feed imagination. The lack of interest is so great that it was seriously proposed to revive animism, to clothe natural facts and events with myths in order that they might attract and hold the mind. In numberless cases, more or less silly personifications were resorted to. The method was silly, but it expressed a real need for a human atmosphere. The facts had been torn to pieces by being taken out of their context. They no longer belonged to the earth; they had no abiding place anywhere. To compensate, recourse was had to artificial and sentimental associations. The real remedy is to make nature study a study of nature, not of fragments made meaningless through complete removal from the situations in which they are produced and in which they operate. When nature is treated as a whole, like the earth in its relations, its phenomena fall into their natural relations of sympathy and association with human life, and artificial substitutes are not needed.

3. History and Present Social Life. T

he segregation which kills the vitality of history is divorce from present modes and concerns of social life. The past just as past is no longer our affair. If it were wholly gone and done with, there would be only one reasonable attitude toward it. Let the dead bury their dead. But knowledge of the past is the key to understanding the present. History deals with the past, but this past is the history of the present. An intelligent study of the discovery, explorations, colonization of America, of the pioneer movement westward, of immigration, etc., should be a study of the United States as it is to-day: of the country we now live in. Studying it in process of formation makes much that is too complex to be directly grasped open to comprehension. Genetic method was perhaps the chief scientific achievement of the latter half of the nineteenth century. Its principle is that the way to get insight into any complex product is to trace the process of its making, — to follow it through the successive stages of its growth.

To apply this method to history as if it meant only the truism that the present social state cannot be separated from its past, is one-sided. It means equally that past events cannot be separated from the living present and retain meaning. The true starting point of history is always some present situation with its problems.

This general principle may be briefly applied to a consideration of its bearing upon a number of points. The biographical method is generally recommended as the natural mode of approach to historical study. The lives of great men, of heroes and leaders, make concrete and vital historic episodes otherwise abstract and incomprehensible. They condense into vivid pictures complicated and tangled series of events spread over so much space and time that only a highly trained mind can follow and unravel them. There can be no doubt of the psychological soundness of this principle. But it is misused when employed to throw into exaggerated relief the doings of a few individuals without reference to the social situations which they represent. When a biography is related just as an account of the doings of a man isolated from the conditions that aroused him and to which his activities were a response, we do not have a study of history, for we have no study of social life, which is an affair of individuals in association. We get only a sugar coating which makes it easier to swallow certain fragments of information. Much attention has been given of late to primitive life as an introduction to learning history. Here also there is a right and a wrong way of conceiving its value. The seemingly ready-made character and the complexity of present conditions, their apparently hard and fast character, is an almost insuperable obstacle to gaining insight into their nature. Recourse to the primitive may furnish the fundamental elements of the present situation in immensely simplified form. It is like unraveling a cloth so complex and so close to the eyes that its scheme cannot be seen, until the larger coarser features of the pattern appear. We cannot simplify the present situations by deliberate experiment, but resort to primitive life presents us with the sort of results we should desire from an experiment. Social relationships and modes of organized action are reduced to their lowest terms. When this social aim is overlooked, however, the study of primitive life becomes simply a rehearsing of sensational and exciting features of savagery. Primitive history suggests industrial history. For one of the chief reasons for going to more primitive conditions to resolve the present into more easily perceived factors is that we may realize how the fundamental problems of procuring subsistence, shelter, and protection have been met; and by seeing how these were solved in the earlier days of the human race, form some conception of the long road which has had to be traveled, and of the successive inventions by which the race has been brought forward in culture. We do not need to go into disputes regarding the economic interpretation of history to realize that the industrial history of mankind gives insight into two important phases of social life in a way which no other phase of history can possibly do. It presents us with knowledge of the successive inventions by which theoretical science has been applied to the control of nature in the interests of security and prosperity of social life. It thus reveals the successive causes of social progress. Its other service is to put before us the

162

things that fundamentally concern all men in common — the occupations and values connected with getting a living. Economic history deals with the activities, the career, and fortunes of the common man as does no other branch of history. The one thing every individual must do is to live; the one thing that society must do is to secure from each individual his fair contribution to the general well being and see to it that a just return is made to him.

Economic history is more human, more democratic, and hence more liberalizing than political history. It deals not with the rise and fall of principalities and powers, but with the growth of the effective liberties, through command of nature, of the common man for whom powers and principalities exist.

Industrial history also offers a more direct avenue of approach to the realization of the intimate connection of man's struggles, successes, and failures with nature than does political history — to say nothing of the military history into which political history so easily runs when reduced to the level of youthful comprehension. For industrial history is essentially an account of the way in which man has learned to utilize natural energy from the time when men mostly exploited the muscular energies of other men to the time when, in promise if not in actuality, the resources of nature are so under command as to enable men to extend a common dominion over her. When the history of work, when the conditions of using the soil, forest, mine, of domesticating and cultivating grains and animals, of manufacture and distribution, are left out of account, history tends to become merely literary — a systematized romance of a mythical humanity living upon itself instead of upon the earth.

Perhaps the most neglected branch of history in general education is intellectual history. We are only just beginning to realize that the great heroes who have advanced human destiny are not its politicians, generals, and diplomatists, but the scientific discoverers and inventors who have put into man's hands the instrumentalities of an expanding and controlled experience, and the artists and poets who have celebrated his struggles, triumphs, and defeats in such language, pictorial, plastic, or written, that their meaning is rendered universally accessible to others. One of the advantages of industrial history as a history of man's progressive adaptation of natural forces to social uses is the opportunity which it affords for consideration of advance in the methods and results of knowledge. At present men are accustomed to eulogize intelligence and reason in general terms; their fundamental importance is urged. But pupils often come away from the conventional study of history, and think either that the human intellect is a static quantity which has not progressed by the invention of better methods, or else that intelligence, save as a display of personal shrewdness, is a negligible historic factor. Surely no better way could be devised of instilling a genuine sense of the part which mind has to play in life than a study of history which makes plain how the entire advance of humanity from savagery to civilization has been dependent upon intellectual discoveries and inventions, and the extent to which the things which ordinarily figure most largely in historical writings have been side issues, or even obstructions for intelligence to overcome.

Pursued in this fashion, history would most naturally become of ethical value in teaching. Intelligent insight into present forms of associated life is necessary for a character whose morality is more than colorless innocence. Historical knowledge helps provide such insight. It is an organ for analysis of the warp and woof of the present social fabric, of making known the forces which have woven the pattern. The use of history for cultivating a socialized intelligence constitutes its moral significance. It is possible to employ it as a kind of reservoir of anecdotes to be drawn on to inculcate special moral lessons on this virtue or that vice. But such teaching is not so much an ethical use of history as it is an effort to create moral impressions by means of more or less authentic material. At best, it produces a temporary emotional glow; at worst, callous indifference to moralizing. The assistance which may be given by history to a more intelligent sympathetic understanding of the social situations of the present in which individuals share is a permanent and constructive moral asset.

Summary.

It is the nature of an experience to have implications which go far beyond what is at first consciously noted in it. Bringing these connections or implications to consciousness enhances the meaning of the experience. Any experience, however trivial in its first appearance, is capable of assuming an indefinite richness of significance by extending its range of perceived connections. Normal communication with others is the readiest way of effecting this development, for it links up the net results of the experience of the group and even the race with the immediate experience of an individual. By normal communication is meant that in which there is a joint interest, a common interest, so that one is eager to give and the other to take. It contrasts with telling or stating things simply for the sake of impressing them upon another, merely in order to test him to see how much he has retained and can literally reproduce.

Geography and history are the two great school resources for bringing about the enlargement of the significance of a direct personal experience. The active occupations described in the previous chapter reach out in space and time with respect to both nature and man. Unless they are taught for external reasons or as mere modes of skill their chief educational value is that they provide the most direct and interesting roads out into the larger world of meanings stated in history and geography. While history makes human implications explicit and geography natural connections, these subjects are two phases of the same living whole, since the life of men in association goes on in nature, not as an accidental setting, but as the material and medium of development.

Chapter Seventeen:

Science in the Course of Study

1. The Logical and the Psychological.

By science is meant, as already stated, that knowledge which is the outcome of methods of observation, reflection, and testing which are deliberately adopted to secure a settled, assured subject matter. It involves an intelligent and persistent endeavor to revise current beliefs so as to weed out what is erroneous, to add to their accuracy, and, above all, to give them such shape that the dependencies of the various facts upon one another may be as obvious as possible. It is, like all knowledge, an outcome of activity bringing about certain changes in the environment. But in its case, the quality of the resulting knowledge is the controlling factor and not an incident of the activity. Both logically and educationally, science is the perfecting of knowing, its last stage.

Science, in short, signifies a realization of the logical implications of any knowledge. Logical order is not a form imposed upon what is known; it is the proper form of knowledge as perfected. For it means that the statement of subject matter is of a nature to exhibit to one who understands it the premises from which it follows and the conclusions to which it points (See ante, p. 190). As from a few bones the competent zoologist reconstructs an animal; so from the form of a statement in mathematics or physics the specialist in the subject can form an idea of the system of truths in which it has its place.

To the non-expert, however, this perfected form is a stumbling block. Just because the material is stated with reference to the furtherance of knowledge as an end in itself, its connections with the material of everyday life are hidden. To the layman the bones are a mere curiosity. Until he had mastered the principles of zoology, his efforts to make anything out of them would be random and blind. From the standpoint of the learner scientific form is an ideal to be achieved, not a starting point from which to set out. It is, nevertheless, a frequent practice to start in instruction with the rudiments of science somewhat simplified. The necessary consequence is an isolation of science from significant experience. The pupil learns symbols without the key to their meaning. He acquires a technical body of information without ability to trace its connections with the objects and operations with which he is familiar—often he acquires simply a peculiar vocabulary. There is a strong temptation to assume that presenting subject matter in its perfected form provides a royal road to learning. What more natural than to suppose that the immature can be saved time and energy, and be protected from needless error by commencing where competent inquirers have left off? The outcome is written large in the history of education. Pupils begin their study of science with texts in which the subject is organized into topics according to the order of the specialist. Technical concepts, with their definitions, are introduced at the outset. Laws are introduced at a very early stage, with at best a few indications of the way in which they were arrived at. The pupils learn a "science" instead of learning the scientific way of treating the familiar material of ordinary experience. The method of the advanced student dominates college teaching; the approach of the college is transferred into the high school, and so down the line, with such omissions as may make the subject easier.

The chronological method which begins with the experience of the learner and develops from that the proper modes of scientific treatment is often called the "psychological" method in distinction from the logical method of the expert or specialist. The apparent loss of time involved is more than made up for by the superior understanding and vital interest secured. What the pupil learns he at least understands. Moreover by following, in connection with problems selected from the material of ordinary acquaintance, the methods by which scientific men have reached their perfected knowledge, he gains independent power to deal with material within his range, and avoids the mental confusion and intellectual distaste attendant upon studying matter whose meaning is only symbolic. Since the mass of pupils are never going to become scientific specialists, it is much more important that they should get some insight into what scientific method means than that they should copy at long range and second hand the results which scientific men have reached. Students will not go so far, perhaps, in the "ground covered," but they will be sure and intelligent as far as they do go. And it is safe to say that the few who go on to be scientific experts will have a better preparation than if they had been swamped with a large mass of purely technical and symbolically stated information. In fact, those who do become successful men of science are those who by their own power manage to avoid the pitfalls of a traditional scholastic introduction into it.

The contrast between the expectations of the men who a generation or two ago strove, against great odds, to secure a place for science in education, and the result generally achieved is painful. Herbert Spencer, inquiring what knowledge is of most worth, concluded that from all points of view scientific knowledge is most valuable. But his argument unconsciously assumed that scientific knowledge could be communicated in a ready-made form. Passing over the methods by which the subject matter of our ordinary activities is transmuted into scientific form, it ignored the method by which alone science is science. Instruction has too often proceeded upon an analogous plan. But there is no magic attached to material stated in technically correct scientific form. When learned in this condition it remains a body of inert information. Moreover its form of statement removes it further from fruitful contact with everyday experiences than does the mode of statement proper to literature. Nevertheless that the claims made for instruction in science were unjustifiable does not follow. For material so taught is not science to the pupil.

Contact with things and laboratory exercises, while a great improvement upon textbooks arranged upon the deductive plan, do not of themselves suffice to meet the need. While they are an indispensable portion of scientific method, they do not as a matter of course constitute scientific method. Physical materials may be manipulated with scientific apparatus, but the materials may be disassociated in themselves and in the ways in which they are handled, from the materials and processes used out of school. The problems dealt with may be only problems of science: problems, that is, which would occur to one already initiated in the science of the subject. Our attention may be devoted to getting skill in technical manipulation without reference to the connection of laboratory exercises with a problem belonging to subject matter. There is sometimes a ritual of laboratory instruction as well as of heathen religion. 1 It has been mentioned, incidentally, that scientific statements, or logical form, implies the use of signs or symbols. The statement applies, of course, to all use of language. But in the vernacular, the mind proceeds directly from the symbol to the thing signified. Association with familiar material is so close that the mind does not pause upon the sign. The signs are intended only to stand for things and acts. But scientific terminology has an additional use. It is designed, as we have seen, not to stand for the things directly in their practical use in experience, but for the things placed in a cognitive system. Ultimately, of course, they denote the things of our common sense acquaintance. But immediately they do not designate them in their common context, but translated into terms of scientific inquiry. Atoms, molecules, chemical formulae, the mathematical propositions in the study of physics — all these have primarily an intellectual value and only indirectly an empirical value. They represent instruments for the carrying on of science. As in the case of other tools, their significance can be learned only by use. We cannot procure understanding of their meaning by pointing to things, but only by pointing to their work when they are employed as part of the technique of knowledge. Even the circle, square, etc., of geometry exhibit a difference from the squares and circles of familiar acquaintance, and the further one proceeds in mathematical science the greater the remoteness from the everyday empirical thing. Qualities which do not count for the pursuit of knowledge about spatial relations are left out; those which are important for this purpose are accentuated. If one carries his study far enough, he will find even the properties which are significant for spatial knowledge giving way to those which facilitate knowledge of other things — perhaps a knowledge of the general relations of number. There will be nothing in the conceptual definitions even to suggest spatial form, size, or direction. This does not mean that they are unreal mental inventions, but it indicates that direct physical qualities have been transmuted into tools for a special end—the end of intellectual organization. In every machine the primary state of material has been modified by subordinating it to use for a purpose. Not the stuff in its original form but in its adaptation to an end is important. No one would have a knowledge of a machine who could enumerate all the materials entering into its structure, but only he who knew their uses and could tell why they are employed as they are. In like fashion one has a knowledge of mathematical conceptions only when he sees the problems in which they function and their specific utility in dealing with these problems. "Knowing" the definitions, rules, formulae, etc., is like knowing the names of parts of a machine without knowing what they do. In one case, as in the other, the meaning, or intellectual content, is what the element accomplishes in the system of which it is a member.

2. Science and Social Progress.

Assuming that the development of the direct knowledge gained in occupations of social interest is carried to a perfected logical form, the question arises as to its place in experience. In general, the reply is that science marks the emancipation of mind from devotion to customary purposes and makes possible the systematic pursuit of new ends. It is the agency of progress in action. Progress is sometimes thought of as consisting in getting nearer to ends already sought. But this is a minor form of progress, for it requires only improvement of the means of action or technical advance. More important modes of progress consist in enriching prior purposes and in forming new ones. Desires are not a fixed quantity, nor does progress mean only an increased amount of satisfaction. With increased culture and new mastery of nature, new desires, demands for new qualities of satisfaction, show themselves, for intelligence perceives new possibilities of action. This projection of new possibilities leads to search for new means of execution, and progress takes place; while the discovery of objects not already used leads to suggestion of new ends.

That science is the chief means of perfecting control of means of action is witnessed by the great crop of inventions which followed intellectual command of the secrets of nature. The wonderful transformation of production and distribution known as the industrial revolution is the fruit of experimental science. Railways, steamboats, electric motors, telephone and telegraph, automobiles, aeroplanes and dirigibles are conspicuous evidences of the application of science in life. But none of them would be of much importance without the thousands of less sensational inventions by means of which natural science has been rendered tributary to our daily life.

It must be admitted that to a considerable extent the progress thus procured has been only technical: it has provided more efficient means for satisfying preexistent desires, rather than modified the quality of human purposes. There is, for example, no modern civilization which is the equal of Greek culture in all respects. Science is still too recent to have been absorbed into imaginative and emotional disposition. Men move more swiftly and surely to the realization of their ends, but their ends too largely remain what they were prior to scientific enlightenment. This fact places upon education the responsibility of using science in a way to modify the habitual attitude of imagination and feeling, not leave it just an extension of our physical arms and legs.

The advance of science has already modified men's thoughts of the purposes and goods of life to a sufficient extent to give some idea of the nature of this responsibility and the ways of meeting it. Science taking effect in human activity has broken down physical barriers which formerly separated men; it has immensely widened the area of intercourse. It has brought about interdependence of interests on an enormous scale. It has brought with it an established conviction of the possibility of control of nature in the interests of mankind and thus has led men to look to the future, instead of the past. The coincidence of the ideal of progress with the advance of science is not a mere coincidence. Before this advance men placed the golden age in remote antiquity.

Now they face the future with a firm belief that intelligence properly used can do away with evils once thought inevitable. To subjugate devastating disease is no longer a dream; the hope of abolishing poverty is not utopian. Science has familiarized men with the idea of development, taking effect practically in persistent gradual amelioration of the estate of our common humanity.

The problem of an educational use of science is then to create an intelligence pregnant with belief in the possibility of the direction of human affairs by itself. The method of science engrained through education in habit means emancipation from rule of thumb and from the routine generated by rule of thumb procedure. The word empirical in its ordinary use does not mean "connected with experiment," but rather crude and unrational. Under the influence of conditions created by the non-existence of experimental science, experience was opposed in all the ruling philosophies of the past to reason and the truly rational. Empirical knowledge meant the knowledge accumulated by a multitude of past instances without intelligent insight into the principles of any of them. To say that medicine was empirical meant that it was not scientific, but a mode of practice based upon accumulated observations of diseases and of remedies used more or less at random. Such a mode of practice is of necessity happy-go-lucky; success depends upon chance. It lends itself to deception and quackery. Industry that is "empirically" controlled forbids constructive applications of intelligence; it depends upon following in an imitative slavish manner the models set in the past. Experimental science means the possibility of using past experiences as the servant, not the master, of mind. It means that reason operates within experience, not beyond it, to give it an intelligent or reasonable quality. Science is experience becoming rational. The effect of science is thus to change men's idea of the nature and inherent possibilities of experience. By the same token, it changes the idea and the operation of reason. Instead of being something beyond experience, remote, aloof, concerned with a sublime region that has nothing to do with the experienced facts of life, it is found indigenous in experience: — the factor by which past experiences are purified and rendered into tools for discovery and advance.

The term "abstract" has a rather bad name in popular speech, being used to signify not only that which is abstruse and hard to understand, but also that which is far away from life. But abstraction is an indispensable trait in reflective direction of activity. Situations do not literally repeat themselves. Habit treats new occurrences as if they were identical with old ones; it suffices, accordingly, when the different or novel element is negligible for present purposes. But when the new element requires especial attention, random reaction is the sole recourse unless abstraction is brought into play. For abstraction deliberately selects from the subject matter of former experiences that which is thought helpful in dealing with the new. It signifies conscious transfer of a meaning embedded in past experience for use in a new one. It is the very artery of intelligence, of the intentional rendering of one experience available for guidance of another.

Science carries on this working over of prior subject matter on a large scale. It aims to free an experience from all which is purely personal and strictly immediate; it aims to detach whatever it has in common with the subject matter of other experiences, and which, being common, may be saved for further use. It is, thus, an indispensable factor in social progress. In any experience just as it occurs there is much which, while it may be of precious import to the individual implicated in the experience, is peculiar and unreduplicable. From the standpoint of science, this material is accidental, while the features which are widely shared are essential. Whatever is unique in the situation, since dependent upon the peculiarities of the individual and the coincidence of circumstance, is not available for others; so that unless what is shared is abstracted and fixed by a suitable symbol, practically all the value of the experience may perish in its passing. But abstraction and the use of terms to record what is abstracted put the net value of individual experience at the permanent disposal of mankind. No one can foresee in detail when or how it may be of further use. The man of science in developing his abstractions is like a manufacturer of tools who does not know who will use them nor when. But intellectual tools are indefinitely more flexible in their range of adaptation than other mechanical tools.

Generalization is the counterpart of abstraction. It is the functioning of an abstraction in its application to a new concrete experience, — its extension to clarify and direct new situations. Reference to these possible applications is necessary in order that the abstraction may be fruitful, instead of a barren formalism ending in itself. Generalization is essentially a social device. When men identified their interests exclusively with the concerns of a narrow group, their generalizations were correspondingly restricted. The viewpoint did not permit a wide and free survey. Men's thoughts were tied down to a contracted space and a short time, — limited to their own established customs as a measure of all possible values. Scientific abstraction and generalization are equivalent to taking the point of view of any man, whatever his location in time and space. While this emancipation from the conditions and episodes of concrete experiences accounts for the remoteness, the "abstractness," of science, it also accounts for its wide and free range of fruitful novel applications in practice. Terms and propositions record, fix, and convey what is abstracted. A meaning detached from a given experience cannot remain hanging in the air. It must acquire a local habitation. Names give abstract meanings a physical locus and body. Formulation is thus not an after-thought or by-product; it is essential to the completion of the work of thought. Persons know many things which they cannot express, but such knowledge remains practical, direct, and personal. An individual can use it for himself; he may be able to act upon it with efficiency. Artists and executives often have their knowledge in this state. But it is personal, untransferable, and, as it were, instinctive. To formulate the significance of an experience a man must take into conscious account the experiences of others. He must try to find a standpoint which includes the experience of others as well as his own. Otherwise his communication cannot be understood. He talks a language which no one else knows. While literary art furnishes the supreme successes in stating of experiences so that they are vitally significant to others, the vocabulary of science is designed, in another fashion, to express the meaning of experienced things in symbols which any one will know who studies the science. Aesthetic formulation reveals and enhances the meaning of experiences one already has; scientific formulation supplies one with tools for constructing new experiences with transformed meanings.

To sum up: Science represents the office of intelligence, in projection and control of new experiences, pursued systematically, intentionally, and on a scale due to freedom from limitations of habit. It is the sole instrumentality of conscious, as distinct from accidental, progress. And if its generality, its remoteness from individual conditions, confer upon it a certain technicality and aloofness, these qualities are very different from those of merely speculative theorizing. The latter are in permanent dislocation from practice; the former are temporarily detached for the sake of wider and freer application in later concrete action. There is a kind of idle theory which is antithetical to practice; but genuinely scientific theory falls within practice as the agency of its expansion and its direction to new possibilities.

3. Naturalism and Humanism in Education.

There exists an educational tradition which opposes science to literature and history in the curriculum. The quarrel between the representatives of the two interests is easily explicable historically. Literature and language and a literary philosophy were entrenched in all higher institutions of learning before experimental science came into being. The latter had naturally to win its way. No fortified and protected interest readily surrenders any monopoly it may possess. But the assumption, from whichever side, that language and literary products are exclusively humanistic in quality, and that science is purely physical in import, is a false notion which tends to cripple the educational use of both studies. Human life does not occur in a vacuum, nor is nature a mere stage setting for the enactment of its drama (ante, p. 211). Man's life is bound up in the processes of nature; his career, for success or defeat, depends upon the way in which nature enters it. Man's power of deliberate control of his own affairs depends upon ability to direct natural energies to use: an ability which is in turn dependent upon insight into nature's processes. Whatever natural science may be for the specialist, for educational purposes it is knowledge of the conditions of human action. To be aware of the medium in which social intercourse goes on, and of the means and obstacles to its progressive development is to be in command of a knowledge which is thoroughly humanistic in quality. One who is ignorant of the history of science is ignorant of the struggles by which mankind has passed from routine and caprice, from superstitious subjection to nature, from efforts to use it magically, to intellectual self-possession. That science may be taught as a set of formal and technical exercises is only too true. This happens whenever information about the world is made an end in itself. The failure of such instruction to procure culture is not, however, evidence of the antithesis of natural knowledge to humanistic concern, but evidence of a wrong educational attitude. Dislike to employ scientific knowledge as it functions in men's occupations is itself a survival of an aristocratic culture. The notion that "applied" knowledge is somehow less worthy than "pure" knowledge, was natural to a society in which all useful work was performed by slaves and serfs, and in which industry was controlled by the models set by custom rather than by intelligence. Science, or the highest knowing, was then identified with pure theorizing, apart from all application in the uses of life; and knowledge relating to useful arts suffered the stigma attaching to the classes who engaged in them (See below, Ch. XIX). The idea of science thus generated persisted after science had itself adopted the appliances of the arts, using them for the production of knowledge, and after the rise of democracy. Taking theory just as theory, however, that which concerns humanity is of more significance for man than that which concerns a merely physical world. In adopting the criterion of knowledge laid down by a literary culture, aloof from the practical needs of the mass of men, the educational advocates of scientific education put themselves at a strategic disadvantage. So far as they adopt the idea of science appropriate to its experimental method and to the movements of a democratic and industrial society, they have no difficulty in showing that natural science is more humanistic than an alleged humanism which bases its educational schemes upon the specialized interests of a leisure class. For, as we have already stated, humanistic studies when set in opposition to study of nature are hampered. They tend to reduce themselves to exclusively literary and linguistic studies, which in turn tend to shrink to "the classics," to languages no longer spoken. For modern languages may evidently be put to use, and hence fall under the ban. It would be hard to find anything in history more ironical than the educational practices which have identified the "humanities" exclusively with a knowledge of Greek and Latin. Greek and Roman art and institutions made such important contributions to our civilization that there should always be the amplest opportunities for making their acquaintance. But to regard them as par excellence the humane studies involves a deliberate neglect of the possibilities of the subject matter which is accessible in education to the masses, and tends to cultivate a narrow snobbery: that of a learned class whose insignia are the accidents of exclusive opportunity. Knowledge is humanistic in quality not because it is about human products in the past, but because of what it does in liberating human intelligence and human sympathy. Any subject matter which accomplishes this result is humane, and any subject matter which does not accomplish it is not even educational.

Summary.

Science represents the fruition of the cognitive factors in experience. Instead of contenting itself with a mere statement of what commends itself to personal or customary experience, it aims at a statement which will reveal the sources, grounds, and consequences of a belief. The achievement of this aim gives logical character to the statements. Educationally, it has to be noted that logical characteristics of method, since they belong to subject matter which has reached a high degree of intellectual elaboration, are different from the method of the learner—the chronological order of passing from a cruder to a more refined intellectual quality of experience. When this fact is ignored, science is treated as so much bare information, which however is less interesting and more remote than ordinary information, being stated in an unusual and technical vocabulary. The function which science has to perform in the curriculum is that which it has performed for the race: emancipation from local and temporary incidents of experience, and the opening of intellectual vistas unobscured by the accidents of personal habit and predilection. The logical traits of abstraction, generalization, and definite formulation are all associated with this function. In emancipating an idea from the particular context in which it originated and giving it a wider reference the results of the experience of any individual are put at the disposal of all men. Thus ultimately and philosophically science is the organ of general social progress. 1 Upon the positive side, the value of problems arising in work in the garden, the shop, etc., may be referred to (See p. 200). The laboratory may be treated as an additional resource to supply conditions and appliances for the better pursuit of these problems.

Chapter Eighteen:

Educational Values

The considerations involved in a discussion of educational values have already been brought out in the discussion of aims and interests.

The specific values usually discussed in educational theories coincide with aims which are usually urged. They are such things as utility, culture, information, preparation for social efficiency, mental discipline or power, and so on. The aspect of these aims in virtue of which they are valuable has been treated in our analysis of the nature of interest, and there is no difference between speaking of art as an interest or concern and referring to it as a value. It happens, however, that discussion of values has usually been centered about a consideration of the various ends subserved by specific subjects of the curriculum. It has been a part of the attempt to justify those subjects by pointing out the significant contributions to life accruing from their study. An explicit discussion of educational values thus affords an opportunity for reviewing the prior discussion of aims and interests on one hand and of the curriculum on the other, by bringing them into connection with one another.

1. The Nature of Realization or Appreciation.

Much of our experience is indirect; it is dependent upon signs which intervene between the things and ourselves, signs which stand for or represent the former. It is one thing to have been engaged in war, to have shared its dangers and hardships; it is another thing to hear or read about it. All language, all symbols, are implements of an indirect experience; in technical language the experience which is procured by their means is "mediated." It stands in contrast with an immediate, direct experience, something in which we take part vitally and at first hand, instead of through the intervention of representative media. As we have seen, the scope of personal, vitally direct experience is very limited. If it were not for the intervention of agencies for representing absent and distant affairs, our experience would remain almost on the level of that of the brutes. Every step from savagery to civilization is dependent upon the invention of media which enlarge the range of purely immediate experience and give it deepened as well as wider meaning by connecting it with things which can only be signified or symbolized. It is doubtless this fact which is the cause of the disposition to identify an uncultivated person with an illiterate person—so dependent are we on letters for effective representative or indirect experience.

At the same time (as we have also had repeated occasion to see) there is always a danger that symbols will not be truly representative; danger that instead of really calling up the absent and remote in a way to make it enter a present experience, the linguistic media of representation will become an end in themselves. Formal education is peculiarly exposed to this danger, with the result that when literacy supervenes, mere bookishness, what is popularly termed the academic, too often comes with it. In colloquial speech, the phrase a "realizing sense" is used to express the urgency, warmth, and intimacy of a direct experience in contrast with the remote, pallid, and coldly detached quality of a representative experience. The terms "mental realization" and "appreciation" (or genuine appreciation) are more elaborate names for the realizing sense of a thing. It is not possible to define these ideas except by synonyms, like "coming home to one" "really taking it in," etc., for the only way to appreciate what is meant by a direct experience of a thing is by having it. But it is the difference between reading a technical description of a picture, and seeing it; or between just seeing it and being moved by it; between learning mathematical equations about light and being carried away by some peculiarly glorious illumination of a misty landscape. We are thus met by the danger of the tendency of technique and other purely representative forms to encroach upon the sphere of direct appreciations; in other words, the tendency to assume that pupils have a foundation of direct realization of situations sufficient for the superstructure of representative experience erected by formulated school studies. This is not simply a matter of quantity or bulk. Sufficient direct experience is even more a matter of quality; it must be of a sort to connect readily and fruitfully with the symbolic material of instruction. Before teaching can safely enter upon conveying facts and ideas through the media of signs, schooling must provide genuine situations in which personal participation brings home the import of the material and the problems which it conveys. From the standpoint of the pupil, the resulting experiences are worth while on their own account; from the standpoint of the teacher they are also means of supplying subject matter required for understanding instruction involving signs, and of evoking attitudes of open-mindedness and concern as to the material symbolically conveyed.

In the outline given of the theory of educative subject matter, the demand for this background of realization or appreciation is met by the provision made for play and active occupations embodying typical situations. Nothing need be added to what has already been said except to point out that while the discussion dealt explicitly with the subject matter of primary education, where the demand for the available background of direct experience is most obvious, the principle applies to the primary or elementary phase of every subject. The first and basic function of laboratory work, for example, in a high school or college in a new field, is to familiarize the student at first hand with a certain range of facts and problems — to give him a "feeling" for them. Getting command of technique and of methods of reaching and testing generalizations is at first secondary to getting appreciation. As regards the primary school activities, it is to be borne in mind that the fundamental intent is not to amuse nor to convey information with a minimum of vexation nor yet to acquire skill, — though these results may accrue as by-products, — but to enlarge and enrich the scope of experience, and to keep alert and effective the interest in intellectual progress.

The rubric of appreciation supplies an appropriate head for bringing out three further principles: the nature of effective or real (as distinct from nominal) standards of value; the place of the imagination in appreciative realizations; and the place of the fine arts in the course of study.

1. The nature of standards of valuation. Every adult has acquired, in the course of his prior experience and education, certain measures of the worth of various sorts of experience. He has learned to look upon qualities like honesty, amiability, perseverance, loyalty, as moral goods; upon certain classics of literature, painting, music, as aesthetic values, and so on. Not only this, but he has learned certain rules for these values — the golden rule in morals; harmony, balance, etc., proportionate distribution in aesthetic goods; definition, clarity, system in intellectual accomplishments. These principles are so important as standards of judging the worth of new experiences that parents and instructors are always tending to teach them directly to the young. They overlook the danger that standards so taught will be merely symbolic; that is, largely conventional and verbal. In reality, working as distinct from professed standards depend upon what an individual has himself specifically appreciated to be deeply significant in concrete situations. An individual may have learned that certain characteristics are conventionally esteemed in music; he may be able to converse with some correctness about classic music; he may even honestly believe that these traits constitute his own musical standards. But if in his own past experience, what he has been most accustomed to and has most enjoyed is ragtime, his active or working measures of valuation are fixed on the ragtime level. The appeal actually made to him in his own personal realization fixes his attitude much more deeply than what he has been taught as the proper thing to say; his habitual disposition thus fixed forms his real "norm" of valuation in subsequent musical experiences.

Probably few would deny this statement as to musical taste. But it applies equally well in judgments of moral and intellectual worth. A youth who has had repeated experience of the full meaning of the value of kindliness toward others built into his disposition has a measure of the worth of generous treatment of others. Without this vital appreciation, the duty and virtue of unselfishness impressed upon him by others as a standard remains purely a matter of symbols which he cannot adequately translate into realities. His "knowledge" is second-handed; it is only a knowledge that others prize unselfishness as an excellence, and esteem him in the degree in which he exhibits it. Thus there grows up a split between a person's professed standards and his actual ones. A person may be aware of the results of this struggle between his inclinations and his theoretical opinions; he suffers from the conflict between doing what is really dear to him and what he has learned will win the approval of others. But of the split itself he is unaware; the result is a kind of unconscious hypocrisy, an instability of disposition. In similar fashion, a pupil who has worked through some confused intellectual situation and fought his way to clearing up obscurities in a definite outcome, appreciates the value of clarity and definition. He has a standard which can be depended upon. He may be trained externally to go through certain motions of analysis and division of subject matter and may acquire information about the value of these processes as standard logical functions, but unless it somehow comes home to him at some point as an appreciation of his own, the significance of the logical norms — so-called — remains as much an external piece of information as, say, the names of rivers in China. He may be able to recite, but the recital is a mechanical rehearsal.

It is, then, a serious mistake to regard appreciation as if it were confined to such things as literature and pictures and music. Its scope is as comprehensive as the work of education itself. The formation of habits is a purely mechanical thing unless habits are also tastes — habitual modes of preference and esteem, an effective sense of excellence. There are adequate grounds for asserting that the premium so often put in schools upon external "discipline," and upon marks and rewards, upon promotion and keeping back, are the obverse of the lack of attention given to life situations in which the meaning of facts, ideas, principles, and problems is vitally brought home.

2. Appreciative realizations are to be distinguished from symbolic or representative experiences. They are not to be distinguished from the work of the intellect or understanding. Only a personal response involving imagination can possibly procure realization even of pure "facts." The imagination is the medium of appreciation in every field. The engagement of the imagination is the only thing that makes any activity more than mechanical. Unfortunately, it is too customary to identify the imaginative with the imaginary, rather than with a warm and intimate taking in of the full scope of a situation. This leads to an exaggerated estimate of fairy tales, myths, fanciful symbols, verse, and something labeled "Fine Art," as agencies for developing imagination and appreciation; and, by neglecting imaginative vision in other matters, leads to methods which reduce much instruction to an unimaginative acquiring of specialized skill and amassing of a load of information. Theory, and — to some extent — practice, have advanced far enough to recognize that play-activity is an imaginative enterprise. But it is still usual to regard this activity as a specially marked- off stage of childish growth, and to overlook the fact that the difference between play and what is regarded as serious employment should be not a difference between the presence and absence of imagination, but a difference in the materials with which imagination is occupied. The result is an unwholesome exaggeration of the phantastic and "unreal" phases of childish play and a deadly reduction of serious occupation to a routine efficiency prized simply for its external tangible results. Achievement comes to denote the sort of thing that a well-planned machine can do better than a human being can, and the main effect of education, the achieving of a life of rich significance, drops by the wayside. Meantime mind-wandering and wayward fancy are nothing but the unsuppressible imagination cut loose from concern with what is done.

An adequate recognition of the play of imagination as the medium of realization of every kind of thing which lies beyond the scope of direct physical response is the sole way of escape from mechanical methods in teaching. The emphasis put in this book, in accord with many tendencies in contemporary education, upon activity, will be misleading if it is not recognized that the imagination is as much a normal and integral part of human activity as is muscular movement. The educative value of manual activities and of laboratory exercises, as well as of play, depends upon the extent in which they aid in bringing about a sensing of the meaning of what is going on. In effect, if not in name, they are dramatizations. Their utilitarian value in forming habits of skill to be used for tangible results is important, but not when isolated from the appreciative side. Were it not for the accompanying play of imagination, there would be no road from a direct activity to representative knowledge; for it is by imagination that symbols are translated over into a direct meaning and integrated with a narrower activity so as to expand and enrich it. When the representative creative imagination is made merely literary and mythological, symbols are rendered mere means of directing physical reactions of the organs of speech.

3. In the account previously given nothing was explicitly said about the place of literature and the fine arts in the course of study. The omission at that point was intentional. At the outset, there is no sharp demarcation of useful, or industrial, arts and fine arts. The activities mentioned in Chapter XV contain within themselves the factors later discriminated into fine and useful arts. As engaging the emotions and the imagination, they have the qualities which give the fine arts their quality. As demanding method or skill, the adaptation of tools to materials with constantly increasing perfection, they involve the element of technique indispensable to artistic production. From the standpoint of product, or the work of art, they are naturally defective, though even in this respect when they comprise genuine appreciation they often have a rudimentary charm. As experiences they have both an artistic and an esthetic quality. When they emerge into activities which are tested by their product and when the socially serviceable value of the product is emphasized, they pass into useful or industrial arts. When they develop in the direction of an enhanced appreciation of the immediate qualities which appeal to taste, they grow into fine arts.

In one of its meanings, appreciation is opposed to depreciation. It denotes an enlarged, an intensified prizing, not merely a prizing, much less — like depreciation — a lowered and degraded prizing. This enhancement of the qualities which make any ordinary experience appealing, appropriable — capable of full assimilation — and enjoyable, constitutes the prime function of literature, music, drawing, painting, etc., in education. They are not the exclusive agencies of appreciation in the most general sense of that word; but they are the chief agencies of an intensified, enhanced appreciation. As such, they are not only intrinsically and directly enjoyable, but they serve a purpose beyond themselves. They have the office, in increased degree, of all appreciation in fixing taste, in forming standards for the worth of later experiences. They arouse discontent with conditions which fall below their measure; they create a demand for surroundings coming up to their own level. They reveal a depth and range of meaning in experiences which otherwise might be mediocre and trivial. They supply, that is, organs of vision. Moreover, in their fullness they represent the concentration and consummation of elements of good which are otherwise scattered and incomplete. They select and focus the elements of enjoyable worth which make any experience directly enjoyable. They are not luxuries of education, but emphatic expressions of that which makes any education worth while.

2. The Valuation of Studies.

The theory of educational values involves not only an account of the nature of appreciation as fixing the measure of subsequent valuations, but an account of the specific directions in which these valuations occur. To value means primarily to prize, to esteem; but secondarily it means to apprise, to estimate. It means, that is, the act of cherishing something, holding it dear, and also the act of passing judgment upon the nature and amount of its value as compared with something else. To value in the latter sense is to valuate or evaluate. The distinction coincides with that sometimes made between intrinsic and instrumental values. Intrinsic values are not objects of judgment, they cannot (as intrinsic) be compared, or regarded as greater and less, better or worse. They are invaluable; and if a thing is invaluable, it is neither more nor less so than any other invaluable. But occasions present themselves when it is necessary to choose, when we must let one thing go in order to take another. This establishes an order of preference, a greater and less, better and worse. Things judged or passed upon have to be estimated in relation to some third thing, some further end. With respect to that, they are means, or instrumental values.

We may imagine a man who at one time thoroughly enjoys converse with his friends, at another the hearing of a symphony; at another the eating of his meals; at another the reading of a book; at another the earning of money, and so on. As an appreciative realization, each of these is an intrinsic value. It occupies a particular place in life; it serves its own end, which cannot be supplied by a substitute. There is no question of comparative value, and hence none of valuation. Each is the specific good which it is, and that is all that can be said. In its own place, none is a means to anything beyond itself. But there may arise a situation in which they compete or conflict, in which a choice has to be made. Now comparison comes in. Since a choice has to be made, we want to know the respective claims of each competitor. What is to be said for it? What does it offer in comparison with, as balanced over against, some other possibility? Raising these questions means that a particular good is no longer an end in itself, an intrinsic good. For if it were, its claims would be incomparable, imperative. The question is now as to its status as a means of realizing something else, which is then the invaluable of that situation. If a man has just eaten, or if he is well fed generally and the opportunity to hear music is a rarity, he will probably prefer the music to eating. In the given situation that will render the greater contribution. If he is starving, or if he is satiated with music for the time being, he will naturally judge food to have the greater worth. In the abstract or at large, apart from the needs of a particular situation in which choice has to be made, there is no such thing as degrees or order of value. Certain conclusions follow with respect to educational values. We cannot establish a hierarchy of values among studies. It is futile to attempt to arrange them in an order, beginning with one having least worth and going on to that of maximum value. In so far as any study has a unique or irreplaceable function in experience, in so far as it marks a characteristic enrichment of life, its worth is intrinsic or incomparable. Since education is not a means to living, but is identical with the operation of living a life which is fruitful and inherently significant, the only ultimate value which can be set up is just the process of living itself. And this is not an end to which studies and activities are subordinate means; it is the whole of which they are ingredients. And what has been said about appreciation means that every study in one of its aspects ought to have just such ultimate significance. It is true of arithmetic as it is of poetry that in some place and at some time it ought to be a good to be appreciated on its own account — just as an enjoyable experience, in short. If it is not, then when the time and place come for it to be used as a means or instrumentality, it will be in just that much handicapped. Never having been realized or appreciated for itself, one will miss something of its capacity as a resource for other ends.

It equally follows that when we compare studies as to their values, that is, treat them as means to something beyond themselves, that which controls their proper valuation is found in the specific situation in which they are to be used. The way to enable a student to apprehend the instrumental value of arithmetic is not to lecture him upon the benefit it will be to him in some remote and uncertain future, but to let him discover that success in something he is interested in doing depends upon ability to use number.

It also follows that the attempt to distribute distinct sorts of value among different studies is a misguided one, in spite of the amount of time recently devoted to the undertaking. Science for example may have any kind of value, depending upon the situation into which it enters as a means. To some the value of science may be military; it may be an instrument in strengthening means of offense or defense; it may be technological, a tool for engineering; or it may be commercial — an aid in the successful conduct of business; under other conditions, its worth may be philanthropic — the service it renders in relieving human suffering; or again it may be quite conventional — of value in establishing one's social status as an "educated" person. As matter of fact, science serves all these purposes, and it would be an arbitrary task to try to fix upon one of them as its "real" end. All that we can be sure of educationally is that science should be taught so as to be an end in itself in the lives of students—something worth while on account of its own unique intrinsic contribution to the experience of life. Primarily it must have "appreciation value." If we take something which seems to be at the opposite pole, like poetry, the same sort of statement applies. It may be that, at the present time, its chief value is the contribution it makes to the enjoyment of leisure. But that may represent a degenerate condition rather than anything necessary. Poetry has historically been allied with religion and morals; it has served the purpose of penetrating the mysterious depths of things. It has had an enormous patriotic value. Homer to the Greeks was a Bible, a textbook of morals, a history, and a national inspiration. In any case, it may be said that an education which does not succeed in making poetry a resource in the business of life as well as in its leisure, has something the matter with it — or else the poetry is artificial poetry.

The same considerations apply to the value of a study or a topic of a study with reference to its motivating force. Those responsible for planning and teaching the course of study should have grounds for thinking that the studies and topics included furnish both direct increments to the enriching of lives of the pupils and also materials which they can put to use in other concerns of direct interest. Since the curriculum is always getting loaded down with purely inherited traditional matter and with subjects which represent mainly the energy of some influential person or group of persons in behalf of something dear to them, it requires constant inspection, criticism, and revision to make sure it is accomplishing its purpose. Then there is always the probability that it represents the values of adults rather than those of children and youth, or those of pupils a generation ago rather than those of the present day. Hence a further need for a critical outlook and survey. But these considerations do not mean that for a subject to have motivating value to a pupil (whether intrinsic or instrumental) is the same thing as for him to be aware of the value, or to be able to tell what the study is good for.

In the first place, as long as any topic makes an immediate appeal, it is not necessary to ask what it is good for. This is a question which can be asked only about instrumental values. Some goods are not good for anything; they are just goods. Any other notion leads to an absurdity. For we cannot stop asking the question about an instrumental good, one whose value lies in its being good for something, unless there is at some point something intrinsically good, good for itself. To a hungry, healthy child, food is a good of the situation; we do not have to bring him to consciousness of the ends subserved by food in order to supply a motive to eat. The food in connection with his appetite is a motive. The same thing holds of mentally eager pupils with respect to many topics. Neither they nor the teacher could possibly foretell with any exactness the purposes learning is to accomplish in the future; nor as long as the eagerness continues is it advisable to try to specify particular goods which are to come of it. The proof of a good is found in the fact that the pupil responds; his response is use. His response to the material shows that the subject functions in his life. It is unsound to urge that, say, Latin has a value per se in the abstract, just as a study, as a sufficient justification for teaching it. But it is equally absurd to argue that unless teacher or pupil can point out some definite assignable future use to which it is to be put, it lacks justifying value. When pupils are genuinely concerned in learning Latin, that is of itself proof that it possesses value. The most which one is entitled to ask in such cases is whether in view of the shortness of time, there are not other things of intrinsic value which in addition have greater instrumental value.

This brings us to the matter of instrumental values — topics studied because of some end beyond themselves. If a child is ill and his appetite does not lead him to eat when food is presented, or if his appetite is perverted so that he prefers candy to meat and vegetables, conscious reference to results is indicated. He needs to be made conscious of consequences as a justification of the positive or negative value of certain objects. Or the state of things may be normal enough, and yet an individual not be moved by some matter because he does not grasp how his attainment of some intrinsic good depends upon active concern with what is presented. In such cases, it is obviously the part of wisdom to establish consciousness of connection. In general what is desirable is that a topic be presented in such a way that it either have an immediate value, and require no justification, or else be perceived to be a means of achieving something of intrinsic value. An instrumental value then has the intrinsic value of being a means to an end. It may be questioned whether some of the present pedagogical interest in the matter of values of studies is not either excessive or else too narrow. Sometimes it appears to be a labored effort to furnish an apologetic for topics which no longer operate to any purpose, direct or indirect, in the lives of pupils. At other times, the reaction against useless lumber seems to have gone to the extent of supposing that no subject or topic should be taught unless some quite definite future utility can be pointed out by those making the course of study or by the pupil himself, unmindful of the fact that life is its own excuse for being; and that definite utilities which can be pointed out are themselves justified only because they increase the experienced content of life itself. 3. The Segregation and Organization of Values. It is of course possible to classify in a general way the various valuable phases of life. In order to get a survey of aims sufficiently wide (See ante, p. 110) to give breadth and flexibility to the enterprise of education, there is some advantage in such a classification. But it is a great mistake to regard these values as ultimate ends to which the concrete satisfactions of experience are subordinate. They are nothing but generalizations, more or less adequate, of concrete goods. Health, wealth, efficiency, sociability, utility, culture, happiness itself are only abstract terms which sum up a multitude of particulars. To regard such things as standards for the valuation of concrete topics and process of education is to subordinate to an abstraction the concrete facts from which the abstraction is derived. They are not in any true sense standards of valuation; these are found, as we have previously seen, in the specific realizations which form tastes and habits of preference. They are, however, of significance as points of view elevated above the details of life whence to survey the field and see how its constituent details are distributed, and whether they are well proportioned. No classification can have other than a provisional validity. The following may prove of some help. We may say that the kind of experience to which the work of the schools should contribute is one marked by executive competency in the management of resources and obstacles encountered (efficiency); by sociability, or interest in the direct companionship of others; by aesthetic taste or capacity to appreciate artistic excellence in at least some of its classic forms; by trained intellectual method, or interest in some mode of scientific achievement; and by sensitiveness to the rights and claims of others — conscientiousness. And while these considerations are not standards of value, they are useful criteria for survey, criticism, and better organization of existing methods and subject matter of instruction.

The need of such general points of view is the greater because of a tendency to segregate educational values due to the isolation from one another of the various pursuits of life. The idea is prevalent that different studies represent separate kinds of values, and that the curriculum should, therefore, be constituted by gathering together various studies till a sufficient variety of independent values have been cared for. The following quotation does not use the word value, but it contains the notion of a curriculum constructed on the idea that there are a number of separate ends to be reached, and that various studies may be evaluated by referring each study to its respective end. "Memory is trained by most studies, but best by languages and history; taste is trained by the more advanced study of languages, and still better by English literature; imagination by all higher language teaching, but chiefly by Greek and Latin poetry; observation by science work in the laboratory, though some training is to be got from the earlier stages of Latin and Greek; for expression, Greek and Latin composition comes first and English composition next; for abstract reasoning, mathematics stands almost alone; for concrete reasoning, science comes first, then geometry; for social reasoning, the Greek and Roman historians and orators come first, and general history next. Hence the narrowest education which can claim to be at all complete includes Latin, one modern language, some history, some English literature, and one science." There is much in the wording of this passage which is irrelevant to our point and which must be discounted to make it clear. The phraseology betrays the particular provincial tradition within which the author is writing. There is the unquestioned assumption of "faculties" to be trained, and a dominant interest in the ancient languages; there is comparative disregard of the earth on which men happen to live and the bodies they happen to carry around with them. But with allowances made for these matters (even with their complete abandonment) we find much in contemporary educational philosophy which parallels the fundamental notion of parceling out special values to segregated studies. Even when some one end is set up as a standard of value, like social efficiency or culture, it will often be found to be but a verbal heading under which a variety of disconnected factors are comprised. And although the general tendency is to allow a greater variety of values to a given study than does the passage quoted, yet the attempt to inventory a number of values attaching to each study and to state the amount of each value which the given study possesses emphasizes an implied educational disintegration.

As matter of fact, such schemes of values of studies are largely but unconscious justifications of the curriculum with which one is familiar. One accepts, for the most part, the studies of the existing course and then assigns values to them as a sufficient reason for their being taught. Mathematics is said to have, for example, disciplinary value in habituating the pupil to accuracy of statement and closeness of reasoning; it has utilitarian value in giving command of the arts of calculation involved in trade and the arts; culture value in its enlargement of the imagination in dealing with the most general relations of things; even religious value in its concept of the infinite and allied ideas. But clearly mathematics does not accomplish such results, because it is endowed with miraculous potencies called values; it has these values if and when it accomplishes these results, and not otherwise. The statements may help a teacher to a larger vision of the possible results to be effected by instruction in mathematical topics. But unfortunately, the tendency is to treat the statement as indicating powers inherently residing in the subject, whether they operate or not, and thus to give it a rigid justification. If they do not operate, the blame is put not on the subject as taught, but on the indifference and recalcitrancy of pupils.

This attitude toward subjects is the obverse side of the conception of experience or life as a patchwork of independent interests which exist side by side and limit one another. Students of politics are familiar with a check and balance theory of the powers of government. There are supposed to be independent separate functions, like the legislative, executive, judicial, administrative, and all goes well if each of these checks all the others and thus creates an ideal balance. There is a philosophy which might well be called the check and balance theory of experience. Life presents a diversity of interests. Left to themselves, they tend to encroach on one another. The ideal is to prescribe a special territory for each till the whole ground of experience is covered, and then see to it each remains within its own boundaries. Politics, business, recreation, art, science, the learned professions, polite intercourse, leisure, represent such interests. Each of these ramifies into many branches: business into manual occupations, executive positions, bookkeeping, railroading, banking, agriculture, trade and commerce, etc., and so with each of the others. An ideal education would then supply the means of meeting these separate and pigeon-holed interests. And when we look at the schools, it is easy to get the impression that they accept this view of the nature of adult life, and set for themselves the task of meeting its demands. Each interest is acknowledged as a kind of fixed institution to which something in the course of study must correspond. The course of study must then have some civics and history politically and patriotically viewed: some utilitarian studies; some science; some art (mainly literature of course); some provision for recreation; some moral education; and so on. And it will be found that a large part of current agitation about schools is concerned with clamor and controversy about the due need of recognition to be given to each of these interests, and with struggles to secure for each its due share in the course of study; or, if this does not seem feasible in the existing school system, then to secure a new and separate kind of schooling to meet the need. In the multitude of educations education is forgotten.

The obvious outcome is congestion of the course of study, overpressure and distraction of pupils, and a narrow specialization fatal to the very idea of education. But these bad results usually lead to more of the same sort of thing as a remedy. When it is perceived that after all the requirements of a full life experience are not met, the deficiency is not laid to the isolation and narrowness of the teaching of the existing subjects, and this recognition made the basis of reorganization of the system. No, the lack is something to be made up for by the introduction of still another study, or, if necessary, another kind of school. And as a rule those who object to the resulting overcrowding and consequent superficiality and distraction usually also have recourse to a merely quantitative criterion: the remedy is to cut off a great many studies as fads and frills, and return to the good old curriculum of the three R's in elementary education and the equally good and equally old-fashioned curriculum of the classics and mathematics in higher education.

The situation has, of course, its historic explanation. Various epochs of the past have had their own characteristic struggles and interests. Each of these great epochs has left behind itself a kind of cultural deposit, like a geologic stratum. These deposits have found their way into educational institutions in the form of studies, distinct courses of study, distinct types of schools. With the rapid change of political, scientific, and economic interests in the last century, provision had to be made for new values. Though the older courses resisted, they have had at least in this country to retire their pretensions to a monopoly. They have not, however, been reorganized in content and aim; they have only been reduced in amount. The new studies, representing the new interests, have not been used to transform the method and aim of all instruction; they have been injected and added on. The result is a conglomerate, the cement of which consists in the mechanics of the school program or time table. Thence arises the scheme of values and standards of value which we have mentioned.

This situation in education represents the divisions and separations which obtain in social life. The variety of interests which should mark any rich and balanced experience have been torn asunder and deposited in separate institutions with diverse and independent purposes and methods. Business is business, science is science, art is art, politics is politics, social intercourse is social intercourse, morals is morals, recreation is recreation, and so on. Each possesses a separate and independent province with its own peculiar aims and ways of proceeding. Each contributes to the others only externally and accidentally. All of them together make up the whole of life by just apposition and addition. What does one expect from business save that it should furnish money, to be used in turn for making more money and for support of self and family, for buying books and pictures, tickets to concerts which may afford culture, and for paying taxes, charitable gifts and other things of social and ethical value? How unreasonable to expect that the pursuit of business should be itself a culture of the imagination, in breadth and refinement; that it should directly, and not through the money which it supplies, have social service for its animating principle and be conducted as an enterprise in behalf of social organization! The same thing is to be said, mutatis mutandis, of the pursuit of art or science or politics or religion. Each has become specialized not merely in its appliances and its demands upon time, but in its aim and animating spirit. Unconsciously, our course of studies and our theories of the educational values of studies reflect this division of interests. The point at issue in a theory of educational value is then the unity or integrity of experience. How shall it be full and varied without losing unity of spirit? How shall it be one and yet not narrow and monotonous in its unity? Ultimately, the question of values and a standard of values is the moral question of the organization of the interests of life. Educationally, the question concerns that organization of schools, materials, and methods which will operate to achieve breadth and richness of experience. How shall we secure breadth of outlook without sacrificing efficiency of execution? How shall we secure the diversity of interests, without paying the price of isolation? How shall the individual be rendered executive in his intelligence instead of at the cost of his intelligence? How shall art, science, and politics reinforce one another in an enriched temper of mind instead of constituting ends pursued at one another's expense? How can the interests of life and the studies which enforce them enrich the common experience of men instead of dividing men from one another? With the questions of reorganization thus suggested, we shall be concerned in the concluding chapters.

Summary.

Fundamentally, the elements involved in a discussion of value have been covered in the prior discussion of aims and interests. But since educational values are generally discussed in connection with the claims of the various studies of the curriculum, the consideration of aim and interest is here resumed from the point of view of special studies. The term "value" has two quite different meanings. On the one hand, it denotes the attitude of prizing a thing finding it worth while, for its own sake, or intrinsically. This is a name for a full or complete experience. To value in this sense is to appreciate. But to value also means a distinctively intellectual act—an operation of comparing and judging— to valuate. This occurs when direct full experience is lacking, and the question arises which of the various possibilities of a situation is to be preferred in order to reach a full realization, or vital experience.

We must not, however, divide the studies of the curriculum into the appreciative, those concerned with intrinsic value, and the instrumental, concerned with those which are of value or ends beyond themselves. The formation of proper standards in any subject depends upon a realization of the contribution which it makes to the immediate significance of experience, upon a direct appreciation. Literature and the fine arts are of peculiar value because they represent appreciation at its best—a heightened realization of meaning through selection and concentration. But every subject at some phase of its development should possess, what is for the individual concerned with it, an aesthetic quality.

Contribution to immediate intrinsic values in all their variety in experience is the only criterion for determining the worth of instrumental and derived values in studies. The tendency to assign separate values to each study and to regard the curriculum in its entirety as a kind of composite made by the aggregation of segregated values is a result of the isolation of social groups and classes. Hence it is the business of education in a democratic social group to struggle against this isolation in order that the various interests may reinforce and play into one another.

Chapter Nineteen:

Labor and Leisure

1. The Origin of the Opposition.

The isolation of aims and values which we have been considering leads to opposition between them. Probably the most deep-seated antithesis which has shown itself in educational history is that between education in preparation for useful labor and education for a life of leisure. The bare terms "useful labor" and "leisure" confirm the statement already made that the segregation and conflict of values are not self-inclosed, but reflect a division within social life. Were the two functions of gaining a livelihood by work and enjoying in a cultivated way the opportunities of leisure, distributed equally among the different members of a community, it would not occur to any one that there was any conflict of educational agencies and aims involved. It would be self-evident that the question was how education could contribute most effectively to both. And while it might be found that some materials of instruction chiefly accomplished one result and other subject matter the other, it would be evident that care must be taken to secure as much overlapping as conditions permit; that is, the education which had leisure more directly in view should indirectly reinforce as much as possible the efficiency and the enjoyment of work, while that aiming at the latter should produce habits of emotion and intellect which would procure a worthy cultivation of leisure. These general considerations are amply borne out by the historical development of educational philosophy. The separation of liberal education from professional and industrial education goes back to the time of the Greeks, and was formulated expressly on the basis of a division of classes into those who had to labor for a living and those who were relieved from this necessity. The conception that liberal education, adapted to men in the latter class, is intrinsically higher than the servile training given to the latter class reflected the fact that one class was free and the other servile in its social status. The latter class labored not only for its own subsistence, but also for the means which enabled the superior class to live without personally engaging in occupations taking almost all the time and not of a nature to engage or reward intelligence.

That a certain amount of labor must be engaged in goes without saying. Human beings have to live and it requires work to supply the resources of life. Even if we insist that the interests connected with getting a living are only material and hence intrinsically lower than those connected with enjoyment of time released from labor, and even if it were admitted that there is something engrossing and insubordinate in material interests which leads them to strive to usurp the place belonging to the higher ideal interests, this would not—barring the fact of socially divided classes — lead to neglect of the kind of education which trains men for the useful pursuits. It would rather lead to scrupulous care for them, so that men were trained to be efficient in them and yet to keep them in their place; education would see to it that we avoided the evil results which flow from their being allowed to flourish in obscure purlieus of neglect. Only when a division of these interests coincides with a division of an inferior and a superior social class will preparation for useful work be looked down upon with contempt as an unworthy thing: a fact which prepares one for the conclusion that the rigid identification of work with material interests, and leisure with ideal interests is itself a social product. The educational formulations of the social situation made over two thousand years ago have been so influential and give such a clear and logical recognition of the implications of the division into laboring and leisure classes, that they deserve especial note. According to them, man occupies the highest place in the scheme of animate existence. In part, he shares the constitution and functions of plants and animals — nutritive, reproductive, motor or practical. The distinctively human function is reason existing for the sake of beholding the spectacle of the universe. Hence the truly human end is the fullest possible of this distinctive human prerogative. The life of observation, meditation, cogitation, and speculation pursued as an end in itself is the proper life of man. From reason moreover proceeds the proper control of the lower elements of human nature — the appetites and the active, motor, impulses. In themselves greedy, insubordinate, lovers of excess, aiming only at their own satiety, they observe moderation — the law of the mean—and serve desirable ends as they are subjected to the rule of reason.

Such is the situation as an affair of theoretical psychology and as most adequately stated by Aristotle. But this state of things is reflected in the constitution of classes of men and hence in the organization of society. Only in a comparatively small number is the function of reason capable of operating as a law of life. In the mass of people, vegetative and animal functions dominate. Their energy of intelligence is so feeble and inconstant that it is constantly overpowered by bodily appetite and passion. Such persons are not truly ends in themselves, for only reason constitutes a final end. Like plants, animals and physical tools, they are means, appliances, for the attaining of ends beyond themselves, although unlike them they have enough intelligence to exercise a certain discretion in the execution of the tasks committed to them. Thus by nature, and not merely by social convention, there are those who are slaves— that is, means for the ends of others. 1 The great body of artisans are in one important respect worse off than even slaves. Like the latter they are given up to the service of ends external to themselves; but since they do not enjoy the intimate association with the free superior class experienced by domestic slaves they remain on a lower plane of excellence. Moreover, women are classed with slaves and craftsmen as factors among the animate instrumentalities of production and reproduction of the means for a free or rational life.

Individually and collectively there is a gulf between merely living and living worthily. In order that one may live worthily he must first live, and so with collective society. The time and energy spent upon mere life, upon the gaining of subsistence, detracts from that available for activities that have an inherent rational meaning; they also unfit for the latter. Means are menial, the serviceable is servile. The true life is possible only in the degree in which the physical

188

necessities are had without effort and without attention. Hence slaves, artisans, and women are employed in furnishing the means of subsistence in order that others, those adequately equipped with intelligence, may live the life of leisurely concern with things intrinsically worth while.

To these two modes of occupation, with their distinction of servile and free activities (or "arts") correspond two types of education: the base or mechanical and the liberal or intellectual. Some persons are trained by suitable practical exercises for capacity in doing things, for ability to use the mechanical tools involved in turning out physical commodities and rendering personal service. This training is a mere matter of habituation and technical skill; it operates through repetition and assiduity in application, not through awakening and nurturing thought. Liberal education aims to train intelligence for its proper office: to know. The less this knowledge has to do with practical affairs, with making or producing, the more adequately it engages intelligence. So consistently does Aristotle draw the line between menial and liberal education that he puts what are now called the "fine" arts, music, painting, sculpture, in the same class with menial arts so far as their practice is concerned. They involve physical agencies, assiduity of practice, and external results. In discussing, for example, education in music he raises the question how far the young should be practiced in the playing of instruments. His answer is that such practice and proficiency may be tolerated as conduce to appreciation; that is, to understanding and enjoyment of music when played by slaves or professionals. When professional power is aimed at, music sinks from the liberal to the professional level. One might then as well teach cooking, says Aristotle. Even a liberal concern with the works of fine art depends upon the existence of a hireling class of practitioners who have subordinated the development of their own personality to attaining skill in mechanical execution. The higher the activity the more purely mental is it; the less does it have to do with physical things or with the body. The more purely mental it is, the more independent or self-sufficing is it.

These last words remind us that Aristotle again makes a distinction of superior and inferior even within those living the life of reason. For there is a distinction in ends and in free action, according as one's life is merely accompanied by reason or as it makes reason its own medium. That is to say, the free citizen who devotes himself to the public life of his community, sharing in the management of its affairs and winning personal honor and distinction, lives a life accompanied by reason. But the thinker, the man who devotes himself to scientific inquiry and philosophic speculation, works, so to speak, in reason, not simply by *. Even the activity of the citizen in his civic relations, in other words, retains some of the taint of practice, of external or merely instrumental doing. This infection is shown by the fact that civic activity and civic excellence need the help of others; one cannot engage in public life all by himself. But all needs, all desires imply, in the philosophy of Aristotle, a material factor; they involve lack, privation; they are dependent upon something beyond themselves for completion. A purely intellectual life, however, one carries on by himself, in himself; such assistance as he may derive from others is accidental, rather than intrinsic. In knowing, in the life of theory, reason finds its own full manifestation; knowing for the sake of knowing irrespective of any application is alone independent, or self-sufficing. Hence only the education that makes for power to know as an end in itself, without reference to the practice of even civic duties, is truly liberal or free.

2. The Present Situation.

If the Aristotelian conception represented just Aristotle's personal view, it would be a more or less interesting historical curiosity. It could be dismissed as an illustration of the lack of sympathy or the amount of academic pedantry which may coexist with extraordinary intellectual gifts. But Aristotle simply described without confusion and without that insincerity always attendant upon mental confusion, the life that was before him. That the actual social situation has greatly changed since his day there is no need to say. But in spite of these changes, in spite of the abolition of legal serfdom, and the spread of democracy, with the extension of science and of general education (in books, newspapers, travel, and general intercourse as well as in schools), there remains enough of a cleavage of society into a learned and an unlearned class, a leisure and a laboring class, to make his point of view a most enlightening one from which to criticize the separation between culture and utility in present education. Behind the intellectual and abstract distinction as it figures in pedagogical discussion, there looms a social distinction between those whose pursuits involve a minimum of self-directive thought and aesthetic appreciation, and those who are concerned more directly with things of the intelligence and with the control of the activities of others.

Aristotle was certainly permanently right when he said that "any occupation or art or study deserves to be called mechanical if it renders the body or soul or intellect of free persons unfit for the exercise and practice of excellence." The force of the statement is almost infinitely increased when we hold, as we nominally do at present, that all persons, instead of a comparatively few, are free. For when the mass of men and all women were regarded as unfree by the very nature of their bodies and minds, there was neither intellectual confusion nor moral hypocrisy in giving them only the training which fitted them for mechanical skill, irrespective of its ulterior effect upon their capacity to share in a worthy life. He was permanently right also when he went on to say that "all mercenary employments as well as those which degrade the condition of the body are mechanical, since they deprive the intellect of leisure and dignity," — permanently right, that is, if gainful pursuits as matter of fact deprive the intellect of the conditions of its exercise and so of its dignity. If his statements are false, it is because they identify a phase of social custom with a natural necessity. But a different view of the relations of mind and matter, mind and body, intelligence and social service, is better than Aristotle's conception only if it helps render the old idea obsolete in fact — in the actual conduct of life and education. Aristotle was permanently right in assuming the inferiority and subordination of mere skill in performance and mere accumulation of external products to understanding, sympathy of appreciation, and the free play of ideas.

If there was an error, it lay in assuming the necessary separation of the two: in supposing that there is a natural divorce between efficiency in producing commodities and rendering service, and self-directive thought; between significant knowledge and practical achievement. We hardly better matters if we just correct his theoretical misapprehension, and tolerate the social state of affairs which generated and sanctioned his conception. We lose rather than gain in change from serfdom to free citizenship if the most prized result of the change is simply an increase in the mechanical efficiency of the human tools of production. So we lose rather than gain in coming to think of intelligence as an organ of control of nature through action, if we are content that an unintelligent, unfree state persists in those who engage directly in turning nature to use, and leave the intelligence which controls to be the exclusive possession of remote scientists and captains of industry. We are in a position honestly to criticize the division of life into separate functions and of society into separate classes only so far as we are free from responsibility for perpetuating the educational practices which train the many for pursuits involving mere skill in production, and the few for a knowledge that is an ornament and a cultural embellishment. In short, ability to transcend the Greek philosophy of life and education is not secured by a mere shifting about of the theoretical symbols meaning free, rational, and worthy. It is not secured by a change of sentiment regarding the dignity of labor, and the superiority of a life of service to that of an aloof self-sufficing independence. Important as these theoretical and emotional changes are, their importance consists in their being turned to account in the development of a truly democratic society, a society in which all share in useful service and all enjoy a worthy leisure. It is not a mere change in the concepts of culture — or a liberal mind — and social service which requires an educational reorganization; but the educational transformation is needed to give full and explicit effect to the changes implied in social life. The increased political and economic emancipation of the "masses" has shown itself in education; it has effected the development of a common school system of education, public and free. It has destroyed the idea that learning is properly a monopoly of the few who are predestined by nature to govern social affairs. But the revolution is still incomplete. The idea still prevails that a truly cultural or liberal education cannot have anything in common, directly at least, with industrial affairs, and that the education which is fit for the masses must be a useful or practical education in a sense which opposes useful and practical to nurture of appreciation and liberation of thought. As a consequence, our actual system is an inconsistent mixture. Certain studies and methods are retained on the supposition that they have the sanction of peculiar liberality, the chief content of the term liberal being uselessness for practical ends. This aspect is chiefly visible in what is termed the higher education — that of the college and of preparation for it. But is has filtered through into elementary education and largely controls its processes and aims. But, on the other hand, certain concessions have been made to the masses who must engage in getting a livelihood and to the increased role of economic activities in modern life. These concessions are exhibited in special schools and courses for the professions, for engineering, for manual training and commerce, in vocational and prevocational courses; and in the spirit in which certain elementary subjects, like the three R's, are taught. The result is a system in which both "cultural" and "utilitarian" subjects exist in an inorganic composite where the former are not by dominant purpose socially serviceable and the latter not liberative of imagination or thinking power.

In the inherited situation, there is a curious intermingling, in even the same study, of concession to usefulness and a survival of traits once exclusively attributed to preparation for leisure. The "utility" element is found in the motives assigned for the study, the "liberal" element in methods of teaching. The outcome of the mixture is perhaps less satisfactory than if either principle were adhered to in its purity. The motive popularly assigned for making the studies of the first four or five years consist almost entirely of reading, spelling, writing, and arithmetic, is, for example, that ability to read, write, and figure accurately is indispensable to getting ahead. These studies are treated as mere instruments for entering upon a gainful employment or of later progress in the pursuit of learning, according as pupils do not or do remain in school. This attitude is reflected in the emphasis put upon drill and practice for the sake of gaining automatic skill. If we turn to Greek schooling, we find that from the earliest years the acquisition of skill was subordinated as much as possible to acquisition of literary content possessed of aesthetic and moral significance. Not getting a tool for subsequent use but present subject matter was the emphasized thing. Nevertheless the isolation of these studies from practical application, their reduction to purely symbolic devices, represents a survival of the idea of a liberal training divorced from utility. A thorough adoption of the idea of utility would have led to instruction which tied up the studies to situations in which they were directly needed and where they were rendered immediately and not remotely helpful. It would be hard to find a subject in the curriculum within which there are not found evil results of a compromise between the two opposed ideals. Natural science is recommended on the ground of its practical utility, but is taught as a special accomplishment in removal from application. On the other hand, music and literature are theoretically justified on the ground of their culture value and are then taught with chief emphasis upon forming technical modes of skill.

If we had less compromise and resulting confusion, if we analyzed more carefully the respective meanings of culture and utility, we might find it easier to construct a course of study which should be useful and liberal at the same time. Only superstition makes us believe that the two are necessarily hostile so that a subject is illiberal because it is useful and cultural because it is useless. It will generally be found that instruction which, in aiming at utilitarian results, sacrifices the development of imagination, the refining of taste and the deepening of intellectual insight — surely cultural values — also in the same degree renders what is learned limited in its use. Not that it makes it wholly unavailable but that its applicability is restricted to routine activities carried on under the supervision of others. Narrow modes of skill cannot be made useful beyond themselves; any mode of skill which is achieved with deepening of knowledge and perfecting of judgment is readily put to use in new situations and is under personal control. It was not the bare fact of social and economic utility which made certain activities seem servile to the Greeks but the fact that the activities directly connected with getting a livelihood were not, in their days, the expression of a trained intelligence nor carried on because of a personal appreciation of their meaning. So far as farming and the trades were rule-of-thumb occupations and so far as they were engaged in for results external to the minds of agricultural laborers and mechanics, they were illiberal—but only so far. The intellectual and social context has now changed. The elements in industry due to mere custom and routine have become subordinate in most economic callings to elements derived from scientific inquiry. The most important occupations of today represent and depend upon applied mathematics, physics, and chemistry. The area of the human world influenced by economic production and influencing consumption has been so indefinitely widened that geographical and political considerations of an almost infinitely wide scope enter in. It was natural for Plato to deprecate the learning of geometry and arithmetic for practical ends, because as matter of fact the practical uses to which they were put were few, lacking in content and mostly mercenary in quality. But as their social uses have increased and enlarged, their liberalizing or "intellectual" value and their practical value approach the same limit.

Doubtless the factor which chiefly prevents our full recognition and employment of this identification is the conditions under which so much work is still carried on. The invention of machines has extended the amount of leisure which is possible even while one is at work. It is a commonplace that the mastery of skill in the form of established habits frees the mind for a higher order of thinking. Something of the same kind is true of the introduction of mechanically automatic operations in industry. They may release the mind for thought upon other topics. But when we confine the education of those who work with their hands to a few years of schooling devoted for the most part to acquiring the use of rudimentary symbols at the expense of training in science, literature, and history, we fail to prepare the minds of workers to take advantage of this opportunity. More fundamental is the fact that the great majority of workers have no insight into the social aims of their pursuits and no direct personal interest in them. The results actually achieved are not the ends of their actions, but only of their employers. They do what they do, not freely and intelligently, but for the sake of the wage earned. It is this fact which makes the action illiberal, and which will make any education designed simply to give skill in such undertakings illiberal and immoral. The activity is not free because not freely participated in.

Nevertheless, there is already an opportunity for an education which, keeping in mind the larger features of work, will reconcile liberal nurture with training in social serviceableness, with ability to share efficiently and happily in occupations which are productive. And such an education will of itself tend to do away with the evils of the existing economic situation. In the degree in which men have an active concern in the ends that control their activity, their activity becomes free or voluntary and loses its externally enforced and servile quality, even though the physical aspect of behavior remain the same. In what is termed politics, democratic social organization makes provision for this direct participation in control: in the economic region, control remains external and autocratic. Hence the split between inner mental action and outer physical action of which the traditional distinction between the liberal and the utilitarian is the reflex. An education which should unify the disposition of the members of society would do much to unify society itself.

Summary.

Of the segregations of educational values discussed in the last chapter, that between culture and utility is probably the most fundamental. While the distinction is often thought to be intrinsic and absolute, it is really historical and social. It originated, so far as conscious formulation is concerned, in Greece, and was based upon the fact that the truly human life was lived only by a few who subsisted upon the results of the labor of others. This fact affected the psychological doctrine of the relation of intelligence and desire, theory and practice. It was embodied in a political theory of a permanent division of human beings into those capable of a life of reason and hence having their own ends, and those capable only of desire and work, and needing to have their ends provided by others. The two distinctions, psychological and political, translated into educational terms, effected a division between a liberal education, having to do with the self-sufficing life of leisure devoted to knowing for its own sake, and a useful, practical training for mechanical occupations, devoid of intellectual and aesthetic content. While the present situation is radically diverse in theory and much changed in fact, the factors of the older historic situation still persist sufficiently to maintain the educational distinction, along with compromises which often reduce the efficacy of the educational measures. The problem of education in a democratic society is to do away with the dualism and to construct a course of studies which makes thought a guide of free practice for all and which makes leisure a reward of accepting responsibility for service, rather than a state of exemption from it.

1 Aristotle does not hold that the class of actual slaves and of natural slaves necessarily coincide.

Chapter Twenty:

Intellectual and Practical Studies

1. The Opposition of Experience and True Knowledge. A
s livelihood and leisure are opposed, so are theory and practice, intelligence
and execution, knowledge and activity. The latter set of oppositions doubtless
springs from the same social conditions which produce the former conflict; but
certain definite problems of education connected with them make it desirable to
discuss explicitly the matter of the relationship and alleged separation of
knowing and doing.

The notion that knowledge is derived from a higher source than is practical
activity, and possesses a higher and more spiritual worth, has a long history. The
history so far as conscious statement is concerned takes us back to the
conceptions of experience and of reason formulated by Plato and Aristotle.
Much as these thinkers differed in many respects, they agreed in identifying
experience with purely practical concerns; and hence with material interests as to
its purpose and with the body as to its organ. Knowledge, on the other hand,
existed for its own sake free from practical reference, and found its source and
organ in a purely immaterial mind; it had to do with spiritual or ideal interests.
Again, experience always involved lack, need, desire; it was never self-sufficing.
Rational knowing on the other hand, was complete and comprehensive within
itself. Hence the practical life was in a condition of perpetual flux, while
intellectual knowledge concerned eternal truth.

This sharp antithesis is connected with the fact that Athenian philosophy
began as a criticism of custom and tradition as standards of knowledge and
conduct. In a search for something to replace them, it hit upon reason as the
only adequate guide of belief and activity. Since custom and tradition were
identified with experience, it followed at once that reason was superior to
experience. Moreover, experience, not content with its proper position of
subordination, was the great foe to the acknowledgment of the authority of
reason. Since custom and traditionary beliefs held men in bondage, the struggle
of reason for its legitimate supremacy could be won only by showing the
inherently unstable and inadequate nature of experience. The statement of Plato
that philosophers should be kings may best be understood as a statement that
rational intelligence and not habit, appetite, impulse, and emotion should
regulate human affairs. The former secures unity, order, and law; the latter
signify multiplicity and discord, irrational fluctuations from one estate to
another.

The grounds for the identification of experience with the unsatisfactory
condition of things, the state of affairs represented by rule of mere custom, are
not far to seek. Increasing trade and travel, colonizations, migrations and wars,
had broadened the intellectual horizon. The customs and beliefs of different
communities were found to diverge sharply from one another. Civil disturbance
had become a custom in Athens; the fortunes of the city seemed given over to

strife of factions. The increase of leisure coinciding with the broadening of the horizon had brought into ken many new facts of nature and had stimulated curiosity and speculation. The situation tended to raise the question as to the existence of anything constant and universal in the realm of nature and society. Reason was the faculty by which the universal principle and essence is apprehended; while the senses were the organs of perceiving change, — the unstable and the diverse as against the permanent and uniform. The results of the work of the senses, preserved in memory and imagination, and applied in the skill given by habit, constituted experience.

Experience at its best is thus represented in the various handicrafts — the arts of peace and war. The cobbler, the flute player, the soldier, have undergone the discipline of experience to acquire the skill they have. This means that the bodily organs, particularly the senses, have had repeated contact with things and that the result of these contacts has been preserved and consolidated till ability in foresight and in practice had been secured. Such was the essential meaning of the term "empirical." It suggested a knowledge and an ability not based upon insight into principles, but expressing the result of a large number of separate trials. It expressed the idea now conveyed by "method of trial and error," with especial emphasis upon the more or less accidental character of the trials. So far as ability of control, of management, was concerned, it amounted to rule-of-thumb procedure, to routine. If new circumstances resembled the past, it might work well enough; in the degree in which they deviated, failure was likely. Even to-day to speak of a physician as an empiricist is to imply that he lacks scientific training, and that he is proceeding simply on the basis of what he happens to have got out of the chance medley of his past practice. Just because of the lack of science or reason in "experience" it is hard to keep it at its poor best. The empiric easily degenerates into the quack. He does not know where his knowledge begins or leaves off, and so when he gets beyond routine conditions he begins to pretend — to make claims for which there is no justification, and to trust to luck and to ability to impose upon others — to "bluff." Moreover, he assumes that because he has learned one thing, he knows others — as the history of Athens showed that the common craftsmen thought they could manage household affairs, education, and politics, because they had learned to do the specific things of their trades. Experience is always hovering, then, on the edge of pretense, of sham, of seeming, and appearance, in distinction from the reality upon which reason lays hold.

The philosophers soon reached certain generalizations from this state of affairs. The senses are connected with the appetites, with wants and desires. They lay hold not on the reality of things but on the relation which things have to our pleasures and pains, to the satisfaction of wants and the welfare of the body. They are important only for the life of the body, which is but a fixed substratum for a higher life. Experience thus has a definitely material character; it has to do with physical things in relation to the body. In contrast, reason, or science, lays hold of the immaterial, the ideal, the spiritual. There is something morally dangerous about experience, as such words as sensual, carnal, material, worldly, interests suggest; while pure reason and spirit connote something morally praiseworthy. Moreover, ineradicable connection with the changing, the inexplicably shifting, and with the manifold, the diverse, clings to experience. Its material is inherently variable and untrustworthy. It is anarchic, because unstable. The man who trusts to experience does not know what he depends upon, since it changes from person to person, from day to day, to say nothing of from country to country. Its connection with the "many," with various particulars, has the same effect, and also carries conflict in its train.

Only the single, the uniform, assures coherence and harmony. Out of experience come warrings, the conflict of opinions and acts within the individual and between individuals. From experience no standard of belief can issue, because it is the very nature of experience to instigate all kinds of contrary beliefs, as varieties of local custom proved. Its logical outcome is that anything is good and true to the particular individual which his experience leads him to believe true and good at a particular time and place. Finally practice falls of necessity within experience. Doing proceeds from needs and aims at change. To produce or to make is to alter something; to consume is to alter. All the obnoxious characters of change and diversity thus attach themselves to doing while knowing is as permanent as its object. To know, to grasp a thing intellectually or theoretically, is to be out of the region of vicissitude, chance, and diversity. Truth has no lack; it is untouched by the perturbations of the world of sense. It deals with the eternal and the universal. And the world of experience can be brought under control, can be steadied and ordered, only through subjection to its law of reason.

It would not do, of course, to say that all these distinctions persisted in full technical definiteness. But they all of them profoundly influenced men's subsequent thinking and their ideas about education. The contempt for physical as compared with mathematical and logical science, for the senses and sense observation; the feeling that knowledge is high and worthy in the degree in which it deals with ideal symbols instead of with the concrete; the scorn of particulars except as they are deductively brought under a universal; the disregard for the body; the depreciation of arts and crafts as intellectual instrumentalities, all sought shelter and found sanction under this estimate of the respective values of experience and reason — or, what came to the same thing, of the practical and the intellectual. Medieval philosophy continued and reinforced the tradition. To know reality meant to be in relation to the supreme reality, or God, and to enjoy the eternal bliss of that relation. Contemplation of supreme reality was the ultimate end of man to which action is subordinate. Experience had to do with mundane, profane, and secular affairs, practically necessary indeed, but of little import in comparison with supernatural objects of knowledge. When we add to this motive the force derived from the literary character of the Roman education and the Greek philosophic tradition, and conjoin to them the preference for studies which obviously demarcated the aristocratic class from the lower classes, we can readily understand the tremendous power exercised by the persistent preference of the "intellectual" over the "practical" not simply in educational philosophies but in the higher schools.

2. The Modern Theory of Experience and Knowledge.

As we shall see later, the development of experimentation as a method of knowledge makes possible and necessitates a radical transformation of the view just set forth. But before coming to that, we have to note the theory of experience and knowledge developed in the seventeenth and eighteenth centuries. In general, it presents us with an almost complete reversal of the classic doctrine of the relations of experience and reason. To Plato experience meant habituation, or the conservation of the net product of a lot of past chance trials. Reason meant the principle of reform, of progress, of increase of control. Devotion to the cause of reason meant breaking through the limitations of custom and getting at things as they really were. To the modern reformers, the situation was the other way around. Reason, universal principles, a priori notions, meant either blank forms which had to be filled in by experience, by sense observations, in order to get significance and validity; or else were mere indurated prejudices, dogmas imposed by authority, which masqueraded and found protection under august names. The great need was to break way from captivity to conceptions which, as Bacon put it, "anticipated nature" and imposed merely human opinions upon her, and to resort to experience to find out what nature was like. Appeal to experience marked the breach with authority. It meant openness to new impressions; eagerness in discovery and invention instead of absorption in tabulating and systematizing received ideas and "proving" them by means of the relations they sustained to one another. It was the irruption into the mind of the things as they really were, free from the veil cast over them by preconceived ideas.

The change was twofold. Experience lost the practical meaning which it had borne from the time of Plato. It ceased to mean ways of doing and being done to, and became a name for something intellectual and cognitive. It meant the apprehension of material which should ballast and check the exercise of reasoning. By the modern philosophic empiricist and by his opponent, experience has been looked upon just as a way of knowing. The only question was how good a way it is. The result was an even greater "intellectualism" than is found in ancient philosophy, if that word be used to designate an emphatic and almost exclusive interest in knowledge in its isolation. Practice was not so much subordinated to knowledge as treated as a kind of tag-end or aftermath of knowledge. The educational result was only to confirm the exclusion of active pursuits from the school, save as they might be brought in for purely utilitarian ends — the acquisition by drill of certain habits. In the second place, the interest in experience as a means of basing truth upon objects, upon nature, led to looking at the mind as purely receptive. The more passive the mind is, the more truly objects will impress themselves upon it. For the mind to take a hand, so to speak, would be for it in the very process of knowing to vitiate true knowledge — to defeat its own purpose. The ideal was a maximum of receptivity. Since the impressions made upon the mind by objects were generally termed sensations, empiricism thus became a doctrine of sensationalism — that is to say, a doctrine which identified knowledge with the reception and association of sensory impressions. In John Locke, the most influential of the empiricists, we find this sensationalism mitigated by a recognition of certain mental faculties, like discernment or discrimination, comparison, abstraction, and generalization which work up the material of sense into definite and organized forms and which even evolve new ideas on their own account, such as the fundamental conceptions of morals and mathematics. (See ante, p. 61.) But some of his successors, especially in France in the latter part of the eighteenth century, carried his doctrine to the limit; they regarded discernment and judgment as peculiar sensations made in us by the conjoint presence of other sensations. Locke had held that the mind is a blank piece of paper, or a wax tablet with nothing engraved on it at birth (a tabula rasa) so far as any contents of ideas were concerned, but had endowed it with activities to be exercised upon the material received. His French successors razed away the powers and derived them also from impressions received.

As we have earlier noted, this notion was fostered by the new interest in education as method of social reform. (See ante, p. 93.) The emptier the mind to begin with, the more it may be made anything we wish by bringing the right influences to bear upon it. Thus Helvetius, perhaps the most extreme and consistent sensationalist, proclaimed that education could do anything—that it was omnipotent. Within the sphere of school instruction, empiricism found its directly beneficial office in protesting against mere book learning. If knowledge comes from the impressions made upon us by natural objects, it is impossible to procure knowledge without the use of objects which impress the mind. Words, all kinds of linguistic symbols, in the lack of prior presentations of objects with which they may be associated, convey nothing but sensations of their own shape and color — certainly not a very instructive kind of knowledge. Sensationalism was an extremely handy weapon with which to combat doctrines and opinions resting wholly upon tradition and authority. With respect to all of them, it set up a test: Where are the real objects from which these ideas and beliefs are received? If such objects could not be produced, ideas were explained as the result of false associations and combinations. Empiricism also insisted upon a first-hand element. The impression must be made upon me, upon my mind. The further we get away from this direct, first-hand source of knowledge, the more numerous the sources of error, and the vaguer the resulting idea.

As might be expected, however, the philosophy was weak upon the positive side. Of course, the value of natural objects and firsthand acquaintance was not dependent upon the truth of the theory. Introduced into the schools they would do their work, even if the sensational theory about the way in which they did it was quite wrong. So far, there is nothing to complain of. But the emphasis upon sensationalism also operated to influence the way in which natural objects were employed, and to prevent full good being got from them. "Object lessons" tended to isolate the mere sense-activity and make it an end in itself. The more isolated the object, the more isolated the sensory quality, the more distinct the sense-impression as a unit of knowledge. The theory worked not only in the direction of this mechanical isolation, which tended to reduce instruction to a kind of physical gymnastic of the sense-organs (good like any gymnastic of bodily organs, but not more so), but also to the neglect of thinking. According to the theory there was no need of thinking in connection with sense-observation; in fact, in strict theory such thinking would be impossible till afterwards, for thinking consisted simply in combining and separating sensory units which had been received without any participation of judgment.

As a matter of fact, accordingly, practically no scheme of education upon a purely sensory basis has ever been systematically tried, at least after the early years of infancy. Its obvious deficiencies have caused it to be resorted to simply for filling in "rationalistic" knowledge (that is to say, knowledge of definitions, rules, classifications, and modes of application conveyed through symbols), and as a device for lending greater "interest" to barren symbols. There are at least three serious defects of sensationalistic empiricism as an educational philosophy of knowledge.

(a) the historical value of the theory was critical; it was a dissolvent of current beliefs about the world and political institutions. It was a destructive organ of criticism of hard and fast dogmas. But the work of education is constructive, not critical. It assumes not old beliefs to be eliminated and revised, but the need of building up new experience into intellectual habitudes as correct as possible from the start. Sensationalism is highly unfitted for this constructive task. Mind, understanding, denotes responsiveness to meanings (ante, p. 29), not response to direct physical stimuli. And meaning exists only with reference to a context, which is excluded by any scheme which identifies knowledge with a combination of sense-impressions. The theory, so far as educationally applied, led either to a magnification of mere physical excitations or else to a mere heaping up of isolated objects and qualities.

(b) While direct impression has the advantage of being first hand, it also has the disadvantage of being limited in range. Direct acquaintance with the natural surroundings of the home environment so as to give reality to ideas about portions of the earth beyond the reach of the senses, and as a means of arousing intellectual curiosity, is one thing. As an end-all and be-all of geographical knowledge it is fatally restricted. In precisely analogous fashion, beans, shoe pegs, and counters may be helpful aids to a realization of numerical relations, but when employed except as aids to thought — the apprehension of meaning—they become an obstacle to the growth of arithmetical understanding. They arrest growth on a low plane, the plane of specific physical symbols. Just as the race developed especial symbols as tools of calculation and mathematical reasonings, because the use of the fingers as numerical symbols got in the way, so the individual must progress from concrete to abstract symbols — that is, symbols whose meaning is realized only through conceptual thinking. And undue absorption at the outset in the physical object of sense hampers this growth.

(c) A thoroughly false psychology of mental development underlay sensationalistic empiricism. Experience is in truth a matter of activities, instinctive and impulsive, in their interactions with things. What even an infant "experiences" is not a passively received quality impressed by an object, but the effect which some activity of handling, throwing, pounding, tearing, etc., has upon an object, and the consequent effect of the object upon the direction of activities. (See ante,.) Fundamentally (as we shall see in more detail), the ancient notion of experience as a practical matter is truer to fact that the modern notion of it as a mode of knowing by means of sensations. The neglect of the deep-seated active and motor factors of experience is a fatal defect of the traditional empirical philosophy. Nothing is more uninteresting and mechanical than a scheme of object lessons which ignores and as far as may be excludes the natural tendency to learn about the qualities of objects by the uses to which they are put through trying to do something with them.

It is obvious, accordingly, that even if the philosophy of experience represented by modern empiricism had received more general theoretical assent than has been accorded to it, it could not have furnished a satisfactory philosophy of the learning process. Its educational influence was confined to injecting a new factor into the older curriculum, with incidental modifications of the older studies and methods. It introduced greater regard for observation of things directly and through pictures and graphic descriptions, and it reduced the importance attached to verbal symbolization. But its own scope was so meager that it required supplementation by information concerning matters outside of sense-perception and by matters which appealed more directly to thought. Consequently it left unimpaired the scope of informational and abstract, or "rationalistic" studies.

3. Experience as Experimentation.

It has already been intimated that sensational empiricism represents neither the idea of experience justified by modern psychology nor the idea of knowledge suggested by modern scientific procedure. With respect to the former, it omits the primary position of active response which puts things to use and which learns about them through discovering the consequences that result from use. It would seem as if five minutes' unprejudiced observation of the way an infant gains knowledge would have sufficed to overthrow the notion that he is passively engaged in receiving impressions of isolated ready-made qualities of sound, color, hardness, etc. For it would be seen that the infant reacts to stimuli by activities of handling, reaching, etc., in order to see what results follow upon motor response to a sensory stimulation; it would be seen that what is learned are not isolated qualities, but the behavior which may be expected from a thing, and the changes in things and persons which an activity may be expected to produce. In other words, what he learns are connections. Even such qualities as red color, sound of a high pitch, have to be discriminated and identified on the basis of the activities they call forth and the consequences these activities effect. We learn what things are hard and what are soft by finding out through active experimentation what they respectively will do and what can be done and what

cannot be done with them. In like fashion, children learn about persons by finding out what responsive activities these persons exact and what these persons will do in reply to the children's activities. And the combination of what things do to us (not in impressing qualities on a passive mind) in modifying our actions, furthering some of them and resisting and checking others, and what we can do to them in producing new changes constitutes experience. The methods of science by which the revolution in our knowledge of the world dating from the seventeenth century, was brought about, teach the same lesson. For these methods are nothing but experimentation carried out under conditions of deliberate control. To the Greek, it seemed absurd that such an activity as, say, the cobbler punching holes in leather, or using wax and needle and thread, could give an adequate knowledge of the world. It seemed almost axiomatic that for true knowledge we must have recourse to concepts coming from a reason above experience. But the introduction of the experimental method signified precisely that such operations, carried on under conditions of control, are just the ways in which fruitful ideas about nature are obtained and tested. In other words, it is only needed to conduct such an operation as the pouring of an acid on a metal for the purpose of getting knowledge instead of for the purpose of getting a trade result, in order to lay hold of the principle upon which the science of nature was henceforth to depend. Sense perceptions were indeed indispensable, but there was less reliance upon sense perceptions in their natural or customary form than in the older science. They were no longer regarded as containing within themselves some "form" or "species" of universal kind in a disguised mask of sense which could be stripped off by rational thought. On the contrary, the first thing was to alter and extend the data of sense perception: to act upon the given objects of sense by the lens of the telescope and microscope, and by all sorts of experimental devices. To accomplish this in a way which would arouse new ideas (hypotheses, theories) required even more general ideas (like those of mathematics) than were at the command of ancient science. But these general conceptions were no longer taken to give knowledge in themselves. They were implements for instituting, conducting, interpreting experimental inquiries and formulating their results.

The logical outcome is a new philosophy of experience and knowledge, a philosophy which no longer puts experience in opposition to rational knowledge and explanation. Experience is no longer a mere summarizing of what has been done in a more or less chance way in the past; it is a deliberate control of what is done with reference to making what happens to us and what we do to things as fertile as possible of suggestions (of suggested meanings) and a means for trying out the validity of the suggestions. When trying, or experimenting, ceases to be blinded by impulse or custom, when it is guided by an aim and conducted by measure and method, it becomes reasonable — rational. When what we suffer from things, what we undergo at their hands, ceases to be a matter of chance circumstance, when it is transformed into a consequence of our own prior purposive endeavors, it becomes rationally significant — enlightening and instructive. The antithesis of empiricism and rationalism loses the support of the human situation which once gave it meaning and relative justification.

The bearing of this change upon the opposition of purely practical and purely intellectual studies is self-evident. The distinction is not intrinsic but is dependent upon conditions, and upon conditions which can be regulated. Practical activities may be intellectually narrow and trivial; they will be so in so far as they are routine, carried on under the dictates of authority, and having in view merely some external result. But childhood and youth, the period of schooling, is just the time when it is possible to carry them on in a different spirit. It is inexpedient to repeat the discussions of our previous chapters on thinking and on the evolution of educative subject matter from childlike work and play to logically organized subject matter. The discussions of this chapter and the prior one should, however, give an added meaning to those results.

(i) Experience itself primarily consists of the active relations subsisting between a human being and his natural and social surroundings. In some cases, the initiative in activity is on the side of the environment; the human being undergoes or suffers certain checkings and deflections of endeavors. In other cases, the behavior of surrounding things and persons carries to a successful issue the active tendencies of the individual, so that in the end what the individual undergoes are consequences which he has himself tried to produce. In just the degree in which connections are established between what happens to a person and what he does in response, and between what he does to his environment and what it does in response to him, his acts and the things about him acquire meaning. He learns to understand both himself and the world of men and things. Purposive education or schooling should present such an environment that this interaction will effect acquisition of those meanings which are so important that they become, in turn, instruments of further learnings. (ante, Ch. XI.) As has been repeatedly pointed out, activity out of school is carried on under conditions which have not been deliberately adapted to promoting the function of understanding and formation of effective intellectual dispositions. The results are vital and genuine as far as they go, but they are limited by all kinds of circumstances. Some powers are left quite undeveloped and undirected; others get only occasional and whimsical stimulations; others are formed into habits of a routine skill at the expense of aims and resourceful initiative and inventiveness. It is not the business of the school to transport youth from an environment of activity into one of cramped study of the records of other men's learning; but to transport them from an environment of relatively chance activities (accidental in the relation they bear to insight and thought) into one of activities selected with reference to guidance of learning. A slight inspection of the improved methods which have already shown themselves effective in education will reveal that they have laid hold, more or less consciously, upon the fact that "intellectual" studies instead of being opposed to active pursuits represent an intellectualizing of practical pursuits. It remains to grasp the principle with greater firmness.

(ii) The changes which are taking place in the content of social life tremendously facilitate selection of the sort of activities which will intellectualize the play and work of the school. When one bears in mind the social environment of the Greeks and the people of the Middle Ages, where such practical activities as could be successfully carried on were mostly of a routine and external sort and even servile in nature, one is not surprised that educators turned their backs upon them as unfitted to cultivate intelligence. But now that even the occupations of the household, agriculture, and manufacturing as well as transportation and intercourse are instinct with applied science, the case stands otherwise. It is true that many of those who now engage in them are not aware of the intellectual content upon which their personal actions depend. But this fact only gives an added reason why schooling should use these pursuits so as to enable the coming generation to acquire a comprehension now too generally lacking, and thus enable persons to carry on their pursuits intelligently instead of blindly. (iii) The most direct blow at the traditional separation of doing and knowing and at the traditional prestige of purely "intellectual" studies, however, has been given by the progress of experimental science. If this progress has demonstrated anything, it is that there is no such thing as genuine knowledge and fruitful understanding except as the offspring of doing. The analysis and rearrangement of facts which is indispensable to the growth of knowledge and power of explanation and right classification cannot be attained purely mentally — just inside the head. Men have to do something to the things when they wish to find out something; they have to alter conditions. This is the lesson of the laboratory method, and the lesson which all education has to learn. The laboratory is a discovery of the condition under which labor may become intellectually fruitful and not merely externally productive. If, in too many cases at present, it results only in the acquisition of an additional mode of technical skill, that is because it still remains too largely but an isolated resource, not resorted to until pupils are mostly too old to get the full advantage of it, and even then is surrounded by other studies where traditional methods isolate intellect from activity.

Summary.

The Greeks were induced to philosophize by the increasing failure of their traditional customs and beliefs to regulate life. Thus they were led to criticize custom adversely and to look for some other source of authority in life and belief. Since they desired a rational standard for the latter, and had identified with experience the customs which had proved unsatisfactory supports, they were led to a flat opposition of reason and experience. The more the former was exalted, the more the latter was depreciated. Since experience was identified with what men do and suffer in particular and changing situations of life, doing shared in the philosophic depreciation. This influence fell in with many others to magnify, in higher education, all the methods and topics which involved the least use of sense-observation and bodily activity. The modern age began with a revolt against this point of view, with an appeal to experience, and an attack upon so-called purely rational concepts on the ground that they either needed to be ballasted by the results of concrete experiences, or else were mere expressions of prejudice and institutionalized class interest, calling themselves rational for protection. But various circumstances led to considering experience as pure cognition, leaving out of account its intrinsic active and emotional phases, and to identifying it with a passive reception of isolated "sensations." Hence the education reform effected by the new theory was confined mainly to doing away with some of the bookishness of prior methods; it did not accomplish a consistent reorganization.

Meantime, the advance of psychology, of industrial methods, and of the experimental method in science makes another conception of experience explicitly desirable and possible. This theory reinstates the idea of the ancients that experience is primarily practical, not cognitive — a matter of doing and undergoing the consequences of doing. But the ancient theory is transformed by realizing that doing may be directed so as to take up into its own content all which thought suggests, and so as to result in securely tested knowledge. "Experience" then ceases to be empirical and becomes experimental. Reason ceases to be a remote and ideal faculty, and signifies all the resources by which activity is made fruitful in meaning. Educationally, this change denotes such a plan for the studies and method of instruction as has been developed in the previous chapters.

Chapter Twenty-one:

Physical and Social Studies: Naturalism and Humanism

ALLUSION has already been made to the conflict of natural science with literary studies for a place in the curriculum. The solution thus far reached consists essentially in a somewhat mechanical compromise whereby the field is divided between studies having nature and studies having man as their theme. The situation thus presents us with another instance of the external adjustment of educational values, and focuses attention upon the philosophy of the connection of nature with human affairs. In general, it may be said that the educational division finds a reflection in the dualistic philosophies. Mind and the world are regarded as two independent realms of existence having certain points of contact with each other. From this point of view it is natural that each sphere of existence should have its own separate group of studies connected with it; it is even natural that the growth of scientific studies should be viewed with suspicion as marking a tendency of materialistic philosophy to encroach upon the domain of spirit. Any theory of education which contemplates a more unified scheme of education than now exists is under the necessity of facing the question of the relation of man to nature.

1. The Historic Background of Humanistic Study.

It is noteworthy that classic Greek philosophy does not present the problem in its modern form. Socrates indeed appears to have thought that science of nature was not attainable and not very important. The chief thing to know is the nature and end of man. Upon that knowledge hangs all that is of deep significance—all moral and social achievement. Plato, however, makes right knowledge of man and society depend upon knowledge of the essential features of nature. His chief treatise, entitled the Republic, is at once a treatise on morals, on social organization, and on the metaphysics and science of nature. Since he accepts the Socratic doctrine that right achievement in the former depends upon rational knowledge, he is compelled to discuss the nature of knowledge. Since he accepts the idea that the ultimate object of knowledge is the discovery of the good or end of man, and is discontented with the Socratic conviction that all we know is our own ignorance, he connects the discussion of the good of man with consideration of the essential good or end of nature itself. To attempt to determine the end of man apart from a knowledge of the ruling end which gives law and unity to nature is impossible. It is thus quite consistent with his philosophy that he subordinates literary studies (under the name of music) to mathematics and to physics as well as to logic and metaphysics. But on the other hand, knowledge of nature is not an end in itself; it is a necessary stage in bringing the mind to a realization of the supreme purpose of existence as the law of human action, corporate and individual. To use the modern phraseology, naturalistic studies are indispensable, but they are in the interests of humanistic and ideal ends.

Aristotle goes even farther, if anything, in the direction of naturalistic studies. He subordinates (ante, p. 254) civic relations to the purely cognitive life. The highest end of man is not human but divine — participation in pure knowing which constitutes the divine life. Such knowing deals with what is universal and necessary, and finds, therefore, a more adequate subject matter in nature at its best than in the transient things of man. If we take what the philosophers stood for in Greek life, rather than the details of what they say, we might summarize by saying that the Greeks were too much interested in free inquiry into natural fact and in the aesthetic enjoyment of nature, and were too deeply conscious of the extent in which society is rooted in nature and subject to its laws, to think of bringing man and nature into conflict. Two factors conspire in the later period of ancient life, however, to exalt literary and humanistic studies. One is the increasingly reminiscent and borrowed character of culture; the other is the political and rhetorical bent of Roman life.

Greek achievement in civilization was native; the civilization of the Alexandrians and Romans was inherited from alien sources. Consequently it looked back to the records upon which it drew, instead of looking out directly upon nature and society, for material and inspiration. We cannot do better than quote the words of Hatch to indicate the consequences for educational theory and practice. "Greece on one hand had lost political power, and on the other possessed in her splendid literature an inalienable heritage. It was natural that she should turn to letters. It was natural also that the study of letters should be reflected upon speech. The mass of men in the Greek world tended to lay stress on that acquaintance with the literature of bygone generations, and that habit of cultivated speech, which has ever since been commonly spoken of as education. Our own comes by direct tradition from it. It set a fashion which until recently has uniformly prevailed over the entire civilized world. We study literature rather than nature because the Greeks did so, and because when the Romans and the Roman provincials resolved to educate their sons, they employed Greek teachers and followed in Greek paths." [2]

The so-called practical bent of the Romans worked in the same direction. In falling back upon the recorded ideas of the Greeks, they not only took the short path to attaining a cultural development, but they procured just the kind of material and method suited to their administrative talents. For their practical genius was not directed to the conquest and control of nature but to the conquest and control of men.

Mr. Hatch, in the passage quoted, takes a good deal of history for granted in saying that we have studied literature rather than nature because the Greeks, and the Romans whom they taught, did so. What is the link that spans the intervening centuries? The question suggests that barbarian Europe but repeated on a larger scale and with increased intensity the Roman situation. It had to go

---

[2] The Influence of Greek Ideas and Usages upon the Christian Church. pp. 43-44.

to school to Greco-Roman civilization; it also borrowed rather than evolved its culture. Not merely for its general ideas and their artistic presentation but for its models of law it went to the records of alien peoples. And its dependence upon tradition was increased by the dominant theological interests of the period. For the authorities to which the Church appealed were literatures composed in foreign tongues. Everything converged to identify learning with linguistic training and to make the language of the learned a literary language instead of the mother speech.

The full scope of this fact escapes us, moreover, until we recognize that this subject matter compelled recourse to a dialectical method. Scholasticism frequently has been used since the time of the revival of learning as a term of reproach. But all that it means is the method of The Schools, or of the School Men. In its essence, it is nothing but a highly effective systematization of the methods of teaching and learning which are appropriate to transmit an authoritative body of truths. Where literature rather than contemporary nature and society furnishes material of study, methods must be adapted to defining, expounding, and interpreting the received material, rather than to inquiry, discovery, and invention. And at bottom what is called Scholasticism is the whole-hearted and consistent formulation and application of the methods which are suited to instruction when the material of instruction is taken ready-made, rather than as something which students are to find out for themselves. So far as schools still teach from textbooks and rely upon the principle of authority and acquisition rather than upon that of discovery and inquiry, their methods are Scholastic — minus the logical accuracy and system of Scholasticism at its best. Aside from laxity of method and statement, the only difference is that geographies and histories and botanies and astronomies are now part of the authoritative literature which is to be mastered.

As a consequence, the Greek tradition was lost in which a humanistic interest was used as a basis of interest in nature, and a knowledge of nature used to support the distinctively human aims of man. Life found its support in authority, not in nature. The latter was moreover an object of considerable suspicion. Contemplation of it was dangerous, for it tended to draw man away from reliance upon the documents in which the rules of living were already contained. Moreover nature could be known only through observation; it appealed to the senses — which were merely material as opposed to a purely immaterial mind. Furthermore, the utilities of a knowledge of nature were purely physical and secular; they connected with the bodily and temporal welfare of man, while the literary tradition concerned his spiritual and eternal well-being.

2. The Modern Scientific Interest in Nature.

The movement of the fifteenth century which is variously termed the revival of learning and the renascence was characterized by a new interest in man's present life, and accordingly by a new interest in his relationships with nature. It was naturalistic, in the sense that it turned against the dominant supernaturalistic interest. It is possible that the influence of a return to classic Greek pagan literature in bringing about this changed mind has been overestimated.

Undoubtedly the change was mainly a product of contemporary conditions. But there can be no doubt that educated men, filled with the new point of view, turned eagerly to Greek literature for congenial sustenance and reinforcement. And to a considerable extent, this interest in Greek thought was not in literature for its own sake, but in the spirit it expressed. The mental freedom, the sense of the order and beauty of nature, which animated Greek expression, aroused men to think and observe in a similar untrammeled fashion. The history of science in the sixteenth century shows that the dawning sciences of physical nature largely borrowed their points of departure from the new interest in Greek literature. As Windelband has said, the new science of nature was the daughter of humanism. The favorite notion of the time was that man was in microcosm that which the universe was in macrocosm.

This fact raises anew the question of how it was that nature and man were later separated and a sharp division made between language and literature and the physical sciences. Four reasons may be suggested.

(a) The old tradition was firmly entrenched in institutions. Politics, law, and diplomacy remained of necessity branches of authoritative literature, for the social sciences did not develop until the methods of the sciences of physics and chemistry, to say nothing of biology, were much further advanced. The same is largely true of history. Moreover, the methods used for effective teaching of the languages were well developed; the inertia of academic custom was on their side. Just as the new interest in literature, especially Greek, had not been allowed at first to find lodgment in the scholastically organized universities, so when it found its way into them it joined hands with the older learning to minimize the influence of experimental science. The men who taught were rarely trained in science; the men who were scientifically competent worked in private laboratories and through the medium of academies which promoted research, but which were not organized as teaching bodies. Finally, the aristocratic tradition which looked down upon material things and upon the senses and the hands was still mighty.

(b) The Protestant revolt brought with it an immense increase of interest in theological discussion and controversies. The appeal on both sides was to literary documents. Each side had to train men in ability to study and expound the records which were relied upon. The demand for training men who could defend the chosen faith against the other side, who were able to propagandize and to prevent the encroachments of the other side, was such that it is not too much to say that by the middle of the seventeenth century the linguistic training of gymnasia and universities had been captured by the revived theological interest, and used as a tool of religious education and ecclesiastical controversy. Thus the educational descent of the languages as they are found in education to-day is not direct from the revival of learning, but from its adaptation to theological ends.

(c) The natural sciences were themselves conceived in a way which sharpened the opposition of man and nature. Francis Bacon presents an almost perfect example of the union of naturalistic and humanistic interest. Science, adopting the methods of observation and experimentation, was to give up the attempt to "anticipate" nature — to impose preconceived notions upon her — and was to become her humble interpreter. In obeying nature intellectually, man would learn to command her practically. "Knowledge is power." This aphorism meant that through science man is to control nature and turn her energies to the execution of his own ends. Bacon attacked the old learning and logic as purely controversial, having to do with victory in argument, not with discovery of the unknown. Through the new method of thought which was set forth in his new logic an era of expansive discoveries was to emerge, and these discoveries were to bear fruit in inventions for the service of man. Men were to give up their futile, never-finished effort to dominate one another to engage in the cooperative task of dominating nature in the interests of humanity.

In the main, Bacon prophesied the direction of subsequent progress. But he "anticipated" the advance. He did not see that the new science was for a long time to be worked in the interest of old ends of human exploitation. He thought that it would rapidly give man new ends. Instead, it put at the disposal of a class the means to secure their old ends of aggrandizement at the expense of another class. The industrial revolution followed, as he foresaw, upon a revolution in scientific method. But it is taking the revolution many centuries to produce a new mind. Feudalism was doomed by the applications of the new science, for they transferred power from the landed nobility to the manufacturing centers. But capitalism rather than a social humanism took its place. Production and commerce were carried on as if the new science had no moral lesson, but only technical lessons as to economies in production and utilization of saving in self-interest. Naturally, this application of physical science (which was the most conspicuously perceptible one) strengthened the claims of professed humanists that science was materialistic in its tendencies. It left a void as to man's distinctively human interests which go beyond making, saving, and expending money; and languages and literature put in their claim to represent the moral and ideal interests of humanity.

(d) Moreover, the philosophy which professed itself based upon science, which gave itself out as the accredited representative of the net significance of science, was either dualistic in character, marked by a sharp division between mind (characterizing man) and matter, constituting nature; or else it was openly mechanical, reducing the signal features of human life to illusion. In the former case, it allowed the claims of certain studies to be peculiar consignees of mental values, and indirectly strengthened their claim to superiority, since human beings would incline to regard human affairs as of chief importance at least to themselves. In the latter case, it called out a reaction which threw doubt and suspicion upon the value of physical science, giving occasion for treating it as an enemy to man's higher interests.

Greek and medieval knowledge accepted the world in its qualitative variety, and regarded nature's processes as having ends, or in technical phrase as teleological. New science was expounded so as to deny the reality of all qualities in real, or objective, existence. Sounds, colors, ends, as well as goods and bads, were regarded as purely subjective — as mere impressions in the mind. Objective existence was then treated as having only quantitative aspects — as so much mass in motion, its only differences being that at one point in space there was a larger aggregate mass than at another, and that in some spots there were greater rates of motion than at others. Lacking qualitative distinctions, nature lacked significant variety. Uniformities were emphasized, not diversities; the ideal was supposed to be the discovery of a single mathematical formula applying to the whole universe at once from which all the seeming variety of phenomena could be derived. This is what a mechanical philosophy means.

Such a philosophy does not represent the genuine purport of science. It takes the technique for the thing itself; the apparatus and the terminology for reality, the method for its subject matter. Science does confine its statements to conditions which enable us to predict and control the happening of events, ignoring the qualities of the events. Hence its mechanical and quantitative character. But in leaving them out of account, it does not exclude them from reality, nor relegate them to a purely mental region; it only furnishes means utilizable for ends. Thus while in fact the progress of science was increasing man's power over nature, enabling him to place his cherished ends on a firmer basis than ever before, and also to diversify his activities almost at will, the philosophy which professed to formulate its accomplishments reduced the world to a barren and monotonous redistribution of matter in space. Thus the immediate effect of modern science was to accentuate the dualism of matter and mind, and thereby to establish the physical and the humanistic studies as two disconnected groups. Since the difference between better and worse is bound up with the qualities of experience, any philosophy of science which excludes them from the genuine content of reality is bound to leave out what is most interesting and most important to mankind.

3. The Present Educational Problem.

In truth, experience knows no division between human concerns and a purely mechanical physical world. Man's home is nature; his purposes and aims are dependent for execution upon natural conditions. Separated from such conditions they become empty dreams and idle indulgences of fancy. From the standpoint of human experience, and hence of educational endeavor, any distinction which can be justly made between nature and man is a distinction between the conditions which have to be reckoned with in the formation and execution of our practical aims, and the aims themselves. This philosophy is vouched for by the doctrine of biological development which shows that man is continuous with nature, not an alien entering her processes from without. It is reinforced by the experimental method of science which shows that knowledge accrues in virtue of an attempt to direct physical energies in accord with ideas suggested in dealing with natural objects in behalf of social uses. Every step forward in the social sciences — the studies termed history, economics, politics, sociology — shows that social questions are capable of being intelligently coped with only in the degree in which we employ the method of collected data, forming hypotheses, and testing them in action which is characteristic of natural science, and in the degree in which we utilize in behalf of the promotion of social welfare the technical knowledge ascertained by physics and chemistry. Advanced methods of dealing with such perplexing problems as insanity, intemperance, poverty, public sanitation, city planning, the conservation of natural resources, the constructive use of governmental agencies for furthering the public good without weakening personal initiative, all illustrate the direct dependence of our important social concerns upon the methods and results of natural science.

With respect then to both humanistic and naturalistic studies, education should take its departure from this close interdependence. It should aim not at keeping science as a study of nature apart from literature as a record of human interests, but at cross-fertilizing both the natural sciences and the various human disciplines such as history, literature, economics, and politics. Pedagogically, the problem is simpler than the attempt to teach the sciences as mere technical bodies of information and technical forms of physical manipulation, on one side; and to teach humanistic studies as isolated subjects, on the other. For the latter procedure institutes an artificial separation in the pupils' experience. Outside of school pupils meet with natural facts and principles in connection with various modes of human action. (See ante, p. 30.) In all the social activities in which they have shared they have had to understand the material and processes involved. To start them in school with a rupture of this intimate association breaks the continuity of mental development, makes the student feel an indescribable unreality in his studies, and deprives him of the normal motive for interest in them.

There is no doubt, of course, that the opportunities of education should be such that all should have a chance who have the disposition to advance to specialized ability in science, and thus devote themselves to its pursuit as their particular occupation in life. But at present, the pupil too often has a choice only between beginning with a study of the results of prior specialization where the material is isolated from his daily experiences, or with miscellaneous nature study, where material is presented at haphazard and does not lead anywhere in particular. The habit of introducing college pupils into segregated scientific subject matter, such as is appropriate to the man who wishes to become an expert in a given field, is carried back into the high schools. Pupils in the latter simply get a more elementary treatment of the same thing, with difficulties smoothed over and topics reduced to the level of their supposed ability. The cause of this procedure lies in following tradition, rather than in conscious adherence to a dualistic philosophy. But the effect is the same as if the purpose were to inculcate an idea that the sciences which deal with nature have nothing to do with man, and vice versa. A large part of the comparative ineffectiveness of the teaching of the sciences, for those who never become scientific specialists, is the result of a separation which is unavoidable when one begins with technically organized subject matter. Even if all students were embryonic scientific specialists, it is questionable whether this is the most effective procedure. Considering that the great majority are concerned with the study of sciences only for its effect upon their mental habits — in making them more alert, more open-minded, more inclined to tentative acceptance and to testing of ideas propounded or suggested, — and for achieving a better understanding of their daily environment, it is certainly ill-advised. Too often the pupil comes out with a smattering which is too superficial to be scientific and too technical to be applicable to ordinary affairs.

The utilization of ordinary experience to secure an advance into scientific material and method, while keeping the latter connected with familiar human interests, is easier to-day than it ever was before. The usual experience of all persons in civilized communities to-day is intimately associated with industrial processes and results. These in turn are so many cases of science in action. The stationary and traction steam engine, gasoline engine, automobile, telegraph and telephone, the electric motor enter directly into the lives of most individuals. Pupils at an early age are practically acquainted with these things. Not only does the business occupation of their parents depend upon scientific applications, but household pursuits, the maintenance of health, the sights seen upon the streets, embody scientific achievements and stimulate interest in the connected scientific principles. The obvious pedagogical starting point of scientific instruction is not to teach things labeled science, but to utilize the familiar occupations and appliances to direct observation and experiment, until pupils have arrived at a knowledge of some fundamental principles by understanding them in their familiar practical workings.

The opinion sometimes advanced that it is a derogation from the "purity" of science to study it in its active incarnation, instead of in theoretical abstraction, rests upon a misunderstanding. AS matter of fact, any subject is cultural in the degree in which it is apprehended in its widest possible range of meanings. Perception of meanings depends upon perception of connections, of context. To see a scientific fact or law in its human as well as in its physical and technical context is to enlarge its significance and give it increased cultural value. Its direct economic application, if by economic is meant something having money worth, is incidental and secondary, but a part of its actual connections. The important thing is that the fact be grasped in its social connections — its function in life.

On the other hand, "humanism" means at bottom being imbued with an intelligent sense of human interests. The social interest, identical in its deepest meaning with a moral interest, is necessarily supreme with man. Knowledge about man, information as to his past, familiarity with his documented records of literature, may be as technical a possession as the accumulation of physical details. Men may keep busy in a variety of ways, making money, acquiring facility in laboratory manipulation, or in amassing a store of facts about linguistic matters, or the chronology of literary productions. Unless such activity reacts to enlarge the imaginative vision of life, it is on a level with the busy work of children. It has the letter without the spirit of activity. It readily degenerates itself into a miser's accumulation, and a man prides himself on what he has, and not on the meaning he finds in the affairs of life. Any study so pursued that it increases concern for the values of life, any study producing greater sensitiveness to social well-being and greater ability to promote that well-being is humane study. The humanistic spirit of the Greeks was native and intense but it was narrow in scope. Everybody outside the Hellenic circle was a barbarian, and negligible save as a possible enemy. Acute as were the social observations and speculations of Greek thinkers, there is not a word in their writings to indicate that Greek civilization was not self-inclosed and self-sufficient. There was, apparently, no suspicion that its future was at the mercy of the despised outsider. Within the Greek community, the intense social spirit was limited by the fact that higher culture was based on a substratum of slavery and economic serfdom—classes necessary to the existence of the state, as Aristotle declared, and yet not genuine parts of it. The development of science has produced an industrial revolution which has brought different peoples in such close contact with one another through colonization and commerce that no matter how some nations may still look down upon others, no country can harbor the illusion that its career is decided wholly within itself. The same revolution has abolished agricultural serfdom, and created a class of more or less organized factory laborers with recognized political rights, and who make claims for a responsible role in the control of industry—claims which receive sympathetic attention from many among the well-to- do, since they have been brought into closer connections with the less fortunate classes through the breaking down of class barriers.

This state of affairs may be formulated by saying that the older humanism omitted economic and industrial conditions from its purview. Consequently, it was one sided. Culture, under such circumstances, inevitably represented the intellectual and moral outlook of the class which was in direct social control. Such a tradition as to culture is, as we have seen (ante, p. 260), aristocratic; it emphasizes what marks off one class from another, rather than fundamental common interests. Its standards are in the past; for the aim is to preserve what has been gained rather than widely to extend the range of culture.

The modifications which spring from taking greater account of industry and of whatever has to do with making a living are frequently condemned as attacks upon the culture derived from the past. But a wider educational outlook would conceive industrial activities as agencies for making intellectual resources more accessible to the masses, and giving greater solidity to the culture of those having superior resources. In short, when we consider the close connection between science and industrial development on the one hand, and between literary and aesthetic cultivation and an aristocratic social organization on the other, we get light on the opposition between technical scientific studies and refining literary studies. We have before us the need of overcoming this separation in education if society is to be truly democratic.

Summary.
The philosophic dualism between man and nature is reflected in the division of studies between the naturalistic and the humanistic with a tendency to reduce the latter to the literary records of the past. This dualism is not characteristic (as were the others which we have noted) of Greek thought. It arose partly because

of the fact that the culture of Rome and of barbarian Europe was not a native product, being borrowed directly or indirectly from Greece, and partly because political and ecclesiastic conditions emphasized dependence upon the authority of past knowledge as that was transmitted in literary documents.

At the outset, the rise of modern science prophesied a restoration of the intimate connection of nature and humanity, for it viewed knowledge of nature as the means of securing human progress and well-being. But the more immediate applications of science were in the interests of a class rather than of men in common; and the received philosophic formulations of scientific doctrine tended either to mark it off as merely material from man as spiritual and immaterial, or else to reduce mind to a subjective illusion. In education, accordingly, the tendency was to treat the sciences as a separate body of studies, consisting of technical information regarding the physical world, and to reserve the older literary studies as distinctively humanistic. The account previously given of the evolution of knowledge, and of the educational scheme of studies based upon it, are designed to overcome the separation, and to secure recognition of the place occupied by the subject matter of the natural sciences in human affairs.

Chapter Twenty-two:

The Individual and the World

1. Mind as Purely Individual.

We have been concerned with the influences which have effected a division between work and leisure, knowing and doing, man and nature. These influences have resulted in splitting up the subject matter of education into separate studies. They have also found formulation in various philosophies which have opposed to each other body and mind, theoretical knowledge and practice, physical mechanism and ideal purpose. Upon the philosophical side, these various dualisms culminate in a sharp demarcation of individual minds from the world, and hence from one another. While the connection of this philosophical position with educational procedure is not so obvious as is that of the points considered in the last three chapters, there are certain educational considerations which correspond to it; such as the antithesis supposed to exist between subject matter (the counterpart of the world) and method (the counterpart of mind); such as the tendency to treat interest as something purely private, without intrinsic connection with the material studied. Aside from incidental educational bearings, it will be shown in this chapter that the dualistic philosophy of mind and the world implies an erroneous conception of the relationship between knowledge and social interests, and between individuality or freedom, and social control and authority. The identification of the mind with the individual self and of the latter with a private psychic consciousness is comparatively modern. In both the Greek and medieval periods, the rule was to regard the individual as a channel through which a universal and divine intelligence operated. The individual was in no true sense the knower; the knower was the "Reason" which operated through him. The individual interfered at his peril, and only to the detriment of the truth. In the degree in which the individual rather than reason "knew," conceit, error, and opinion were substituted for true knowledge. In Greek life, observation was acute and alert; and thinking was free almost to the point of irresponsible speculations. Accordingly the consequences of the theory were only such as were consequent upon the lack of an experimental method. Without such a method individuals could not engage in knowing, and be checked up by the results of the inquiries of others. Without such liability to test by others, the minds of men could not be intellectually responsible; results were to be accepted because of their aesthetic consistency, agreeable quality, or the prestige of their authors. In the barbarian period, individuals were in a still more humble attitude to truth; important knowledge was supposed to be divinely revealed, and nothing remained for the minds of individuals except to work it over after it had been received on authority. Aside from the more consciously philosophic aspects of these movements, it never occurs to any one to identify mind and the personal self wherever beliefs are transmitted by custom.

In the medieval period there was a religious individualism. The deepest concern of life was the salvation of the individual soul. In the later Middle Ages, this latent individualism found conscious formulation in the nominalistic philosophies, which treated the structure of knowledge as something built up within the individual through his own acts, and mental states. With the rise of economic and political individualism after the sixteenth century, and with the development of Protestantism, the times were ripe for an emphasis upon the rights and duties of the individual in achieving knowledge for himself. This led to the view that knowledge is won wholly through personal and private experiences. As a consequence, mind, the source and possessor of knowledge, was thought of as wholly individual. Thus upon the educational side, we find educational reformers, like Montaigne, Bacon, Locke, henceforth vehemently denouncing all learning which is acquired on hearsay, and asserting that even if beliefs happen to be true, they do not constitute knowledge unless they have grown up in and been tested by personal experience. The reaction against authority in all spheres of life, and the intensity of the struggle, against great odds, for freedom of action and inquiry, led to such an emphasis upon personal observations and ideas as in effect to isolate mind, and set it apart from the world to be known.

This isolation is reflected in the great development of that branch of philosophy known as epistemology—the theory of knowledge. The identification of mind with the self, and the setting up of the self as something independent and self-sufficient, created such a gulf between the knowing mind and the world that it became a question how knowledge was possible at all. Given a subject - - the knower—and an object—the thing to be known—wholly separate from one another, it is necessary to frame a theory to explain how they get into connection with each other so that valid knowledge may result. This problem, with the allied one of the possibility of the world acting upon the mind and the mind acting upon the world, became almost the exclusive preoccupation of philosophic thought.

The theories that we cannot know the world as it really is but only the impressions made upon the mind, or that there is no world beyond the individual mind, or that knowledge is only a certain association of the mind's own states, were products of this preoccupation. We are not directly concerned with their truth; but the fact that such desperate solutions were widely accepted is evidence of the extent to which mind had been set over the world of realities. The increasing use of the term "consciousness" as an equivalent for mind, in the supposition that there is an inner world of conscious states and processes, independent of any relationship to nature and society, an inner world more truly and immediately known than anything else, is evidence of the same fact. In short, practical individualism, or struggle for greater freedom of thought in action, was translated into philosophic subjectivism.

2. Individual Mind as the Agent of Reorganization.

It should be obvious that this philosophic movement misconceived the significance of the practical movement. Instead of being its transcript, it was a perversion. Men were not actually engaged in the absurdity of striving to be free from connection with nature and one another. They were striving for greater freedom in nature and society. They wanted greater power to initiate changes in the world of things and fellow beings; greater scope of movement and consequently greater freedom in observations and ideas implied in movement. They wanted not isolation from the world, but a more intimate connection with it. They wanted to form their beliefs about it at first hand, instead of through tradition. They wanted closer union with their fellows so that they might influence one another more effectively and might combine their respective actions for mutual aims.

So far as their beliefs were concerned, they felt that a great deal which passed for knowledge was merely the accumulated opinions of the past, much of it absurd and its correct portions not understood when accepted on authority. Men must observe for themselves, and form their own theories and personally test them. Such a method was the only alternative to the imposition of dogma as truth, a procedure which reduced mind to the formal act of acquiescing in truth. Such is the meaning of what is sometimes called the substitution of inductive experimental methods of knowing for deductive. In some sense, men had always used an inductive method in dealing with their immediate practical concerns. Architecture, agriculture, manufacture, etc., had to be based upon observation of the activities of natural objects, and ideas about such affairs had to be checked, to some extent, by results. But even in such things there was an undue reliance upon mere custom, followed blindly rather than understandingly. And this observational-experimental method was restricted to these "practical" matters, and a sharp distinction maintained between practice and theoretical knowledge or truth. (See Ch. XX.) The rise of free cities, the development of travel, exploration, and commerce, the evolution of new methods of producing commodities and doing business, threw men definitely upon their own resources. The reformers of science like Galileo, Descartes, and their successors, carried analogous methods into ascertaining the facts about nature. An interest in discovery took the place of an interest in systematizing and "proving" received beliefs.

A just philosophic interpretation of these movements would, indeed, have emphasized the rights and responsibilities of the individual in gaining knowledge and personally testing beliefs, no matter by what authorities they were vouched for. But it would not have isolated the individual from the world, and consequently isolated individuals—in theory—from one another. It would have perceived that such disconnection, such rupture of continuity, denied in advance the possibility of success in their endeavors. As matter of fact every individual has grown up, and always must grow up, in a social medium. His responses grow intelligent, or gain meaning, simply because he lives and acts in a medium of accepted meanings and values. (See ante, p. 30.) Through social intercourse, through sharing in the activities embodying beliefs, he gradually acquires a mind of his own. The conception of mind as a purely isolated possession of the self is at the very antipodes of the truth. The self achieves mind in the degree in which knowledge of things is incarnate in the life about him; the self is not a separate mind building up knowledge anew on its own account.

Yet there is a valid distinction between knowledge which is objective and impersonal, and thinking which is subjective and personal. In one sense, knowledge is that which we take for granted. It is that which is settled, disposed of, established, under control. What we fully know, we do not need to think about. In common phrase, it is certain, assured. And this does not mean a mere feeling of certainty. It denotes not a sentiment, but a practical attitude, a readiness to act without reserve or quibble. Of course we may be mistaken. What is taken for knowledge—for fact and truth—at a given time may not be such. But everything which is assumed without question, which is taken for granted in our intercourse with one another and nature is what, at the given time, is called knowledge. Thinking on the contrary, starts, as we have seen, from doubt or uncertainty. It marks an inquiring, hunting, searching attitude, instead of one of mastery and possession. Through its critical process true knowledge is revised and extended, and our convictions as to the state of things reorganized. Clearly the last few centuries have been typically a period of revision and reorganization of beliefs. Men did not really throw away all transmitted beliefs concerning the realities of existence, and start afresh upon the basis of their private, exclusive sensations and ideas. They could not have done so if they had wished to, and if it had been possible general imbecility would have been the only outcome. Men set out from what had passed as knowledge, and critically investigated the grounds upon which it rested; they noted exceptions; they used new mechanical appliances to bring to light data inconsistent with what had been believed; they used their imaginations to conceive a world different from that in which their forefathers had put their trust. The work was a piecemeal, a retail, business. One problem was tackled at a time. The net results of all the revisions amounted, however, to a revolution of prior conceptions of the world. What occurred was a reorganization of prior intellectual habitudes, infinitely more efficient than a cutting loose from all connections would have been.

This state of affairs suggests a definition of the role of the individual, or the self, in knowledge; namely, the redirection, or reconstruction of accepted beliefs. Every new idea, every conception of things differing from that authorized by current belief, must have its origin in an individual. New ideas are doubtless always sprouting, but a society governed by custom does not encourage their development. On the contrary, it tends to suppress them, just because they are deviations from what is current. The man who looks at things differently from others is in such a community a suspect character; for him to persist is generally fatal. Even when social censorship of beliefs is not so strict, social conditions may fail to provide the appliances which are requisite if new ideas are to be adequately elaborated; or they may fail to provide any material support and reward to those who entertain them. Hence they remain mere fancies, romantic castles in the air, or aimless speculations. The freedom of observation and imagination involved in the modern scientific revolution were not easily secured; they had to be fought for; many suffered for their intellectual independence. But, upon the whole, modern European society first permitted, and then, in some fields at least, deliberately encouraged the individual reactions which deviate from what custom prescribes. Discovery, research, inquiry in new lines, inventions, finally came to be either the social fashion, or in some degree tolerable. However, as we have already noted, philosophic theories of knowledge were not content to conceive mind in the individual as the pivot upon which reconstruction of beliefs turned, thus maintaining the continuity of the individual with the world of nature and fellow men. They regarded the individual mind as a separate entity, complete in each person, and isolated from nature and hence from other minds. Thus a legitimate intellectual individualism, the attitude of critical revision of former beliefs which is indispensable to progress, was explicitly formulated as a moral and social individualism. When the activities of mind set out from customary beliefs and strive to effect transformations of them which will in turn win general conviction, there is no opposition between the individual and the social. The intellectual variations of the individual in observation, imagination, judgment, and invention are simply the agencies of social progress, just as conformity to habit is the agency of social conservation. But when knowledge is regarded as originating and developing within an individual, the ties which bind the mental life of one to that of his fellows are ignored and denied.

When the social quality of individualized mental operations is denied, it becomes a problem to find connections which will unite an individual with his fellows. Moral individualism is set up by the conscious separation of different centers of life. It has its roots in the notion that the consciousness of each person is wholly private, a self-inclosed continent, intrinsically independent of the ideas, wishes, purposes of everybody else. But when men act, they act in a common and public world. This is the problem to which the theory of isolated and independent conscious minds gave rise: Given feelings, ideas, desires, which have nothing to do with one another, how can actions proceeding from them be controlled in a social or public interest? Given an egoistic consciousness, how can action which has regard for others take place?

Moral philosophies which have started from such premises have developed four typical ways of dealing with the question.

(i) One method represents the survival of the older authoritative position, with such concessions and compromises as the progress of events has made absolutely inevitable. The deviations and departures characterizing an individual are still looked upon with suspicion; in principle they are evidences of the disturbances, revolts, and corruptions inhering in an individual apart from external authoritative guidance. In fact, as distinct from principle, intellectual individualism is tolerated in certain technical regions — in subjects like mathematics and physics and astronomy, and in the technical inventions resulting therefrom. But the applicability of a similar method to morals, social, legal, and political matters, is denied. In such matters, dogma is still to be supreme; certain eternal truths made known by revelation, intuition, or the wisdom of our forefathers set unpassable limits to individual observation and speculation. The evils from which society suffers are set down to the efforts of misguided individuals to transgress these boundaries. Between the physical and the moral sciences, lie intermediate sciences of life, where the territory is only grudgingly yielded to freedom of inquiry under the pressure of accomplished fact. Although past history has demonstrated that the possibilities of human good are widened and made more secure by trusting to a responsibility built up within the very process of inquiry, the "authority" theory sets apart a sacred domain of truth which must be protected from the inroads of variation of beliefs. Educationally, emphasis may not be put on eternal truth, but it is put on the authority of book and teacher, and individual variation is discouraged.

(ii) Another method is sometimes termed rationalism or abstract intellectualism. A formal logical faculty is set up in distinction from tradition and history and all concrete subject matter. This faculty of reason is endowed with power to influence conduct directly. Since it deals wholly with general and impersonal forms, when different persons act in accord with logical findings, their activities will be externally consistent. There is no doubt of the services rendered by this philosophy. It was a powerful factor in the negative and dissolving criticism of doctrines having nothing but tradition and class interest behind them; it accustomed men to freedom of discussion and to the notion that beliefs had to be submitted to criteria of reasonableness. It undermined the power of prejudice, superstition, and brute force, by habituating men to reliance upon argument, discussion, and persuasion. It made for clarity and order of exposition. But its influence was greater in destruction of old falsities than in the construction of new ties and associations among men. Its formal and empty nature, due to conceiving reason as something complete in itself apart from subject matter, its hostile attitude toward historical institutions, its disregard of the influence of habit, instinct, and emotion, as operative factors in life, left it impotent in the suggestion of specific aims and methods. Bare logic, however important in arranging and criticizing existing subject matter, cannot spin new subject matter out of itself. In education, the correlative is trust in general ready-made rules and principles to secure agreement, irrespective of seeing to it that the pupil's ideas really agree with one another.

(iii) While this rationalistic philosophy was developing in France, English thought appealed to the intelligent self-interest of individuals in order to secure outer unity in the acts which issued from isolated streams of consciousness. Legal arrangements, especially penal administration, and governmental regulations, were to be such as to prevent the acts which proceeded from regard for one's own private sensations from interfering with the feelings of others. Education was to instill in individuals a sense that non-interference with others and some degree of positive regard for their welfare were necessary for security in the pursuit of one's own happiness. Chief emphasis was put, however, upon trade as a means of bringing the conduct of one into harmony with that of others. In commerce, each aims at the satisfaction of his own wants, but can gain his own profit only by furnishing some commodity or service to another. Thus in aiming at the increase of his own private pleasurable states of consciousness, he contributes to the consciousness of others. Again there is no doubt that this view expressed and furthered a heightened perception of the values of conscious life, and a recognition that institutional arrangements are ultimately to be judged by the contributions which they make to intensifying and enlarging the scope of conscious experience. It also did much to rescue work, industry, and mechanical devices from the contempt in which they had been held in communities founded upon the control of a leisure class. In both ways, this philosophy promoted a wider and more democratic social concern. But it was tainted by the narrowness of its fundamental premise: the doctrine that every individual acts only from regard for his own pleasures and pains, and that so-called generous and sympathetic acts are only indirect ways of procuring and assuring one's own comfort. In other words, it made explicit the consequences inhering in any doctrine which makes mental life a self-inclosed thing, instead of an attempt to redirect and readapt common concerns. It made union among men a matter of calculation of externals. It lent itself to the contemptuous assertions of Carlyle that it was a doctrine of anarchy plus a constable, and recognized only a "cash nexus" among men. The educational equivalents of this doctrine in the uses made of pleasurable rewards and painful penalties are only too obvious.

(iv) Typical German philosophy followed another path. It started from what was essentially the rationalistic philosophy of Descartes and his French successors. But while French thought upon the whole developed the idea of reason in opposition to the religious conception of a divine mind residing in individuals, German thought (as in Hegel) made a synthesis of the two. Reason is absolute. Nature is incarnate reason. History is reason in its progressive unfolding in man. An individual becomes rational only as he absorbs into himself the content of rationality in nature and in social institutions. For an absolute reason is not, like the reason of rationalism, purely formal and empty; as absolute it must include all content within itself. Thus the real problem is not that of controlling individual freedom so that some measure of social order and concord may result, but of achieving individual freedom through developing individual convictions in accord with the universal law found in the organization of the state as objective Reason. While this philosophy is usually termed absolute or objective idealism, it might better be termed, for educational purposes at least, institutional idealism. (See ante,.) It idealized historical institutions by conceiving them as incarnations of an immanent absolute mind. There can be no doubt that this philosophy was a powerful influence in rescuing philosophy in the beginning of the nineteenth century from the isolated individualism into which it had fallen in France and England. It served also to make the organization of the state more constructively interested in matters of public concern. It left less to chance, less to mere individual logical conviction, less to the workings of private self-interest. It brought intelligence to bear upon the conduct of affairs; it accentuated the need of nationally organized education in the interests of the corporate state. It sanctioned and promoted freedom of inquiry in all technical details of natural and historical phenomena. But in all ultimate moral matters, it tended to reinstate the principle of authority. It made for efficiency of organization more than did any of the types of philosophy previously mentioned, but it made no provision for free experimental modification of this organization. Political democracy, with its belief in the right of individual desire and purpose to take part in readapting even the fundamental constitution of society, was foreign to it.

3. Educational Equivalents.

It is not necessary to consider in detail the educational counterparts of the various defects found in these various types of philosophy. It suffices to say that in general the school has been the institution which exhibited with greatest clearness the assumed antithesis between purely individualistic methods of learning and social action, and between freedom and social control. The antithesis is reflected in the absence of a social atmosphere and motive for learning, and the consequent separation, in the conduct of the school, between method of instruction and methods of government; and in the slight opportunity afforded individual variations. When learning is a phase of active undertakings which involve mutual exchange, social control enters into the very process of learning. When the social factor is absent, learning becomes a carrying over of some presented material into a purely individual consciousness, and there is no inherent reason why it should give a more socialized direction to mental and emotional disposition. There is tendency on the part of both the upholders and the opponents of freedom in school to identify it with absence of social direction, or, sometimes, with merely physical unconstraint of movement. But the essence of the demand for freedom is the need of conditions which will enable an individual to make his own special contribution to a group interest, and to partake of its activities in such ways that social guidance shall be a matter of his own mental attitude, and not a mere authoritative dictation of his acts. Because what is often called discipline and "government" has to do with the external side of conduct alone, a similar meaning is attached, by reaction, to freedom. But when it is perceived that each idea signifies the quality of mind expressed in action, the supposed opposition between them falls away. Freedom means essentially the part played by thinking — which is personal — in learning: — it means intellectual initiative, independence in observation, judicious invention, foresight of consequences, and ingenuity of adaptation to them.

But because these are the mental phase of behavior, the needed play of individuality — or freedom — cannot be separated from opportunity for free play of physical movements. Enforced physical quietude may be unfavorable to realization of a problem, to undertaking the observations needed to define it, and to performance of the experiments which test the ideas suggested. Much has been said about the importance of "self-activity" in education, but the conception has too frequently been restricted to something merely internal — something excluding the free use of sensory and motor organs. Those who are at the stage of learning from symbols, or who are engaged in elaborating the implications of a problem or idea preliminary to more carefully thought-out activity, may need little perceptible overt activity. But the whole cycle of self-activity demands an opportunity for investigation and experimentation, for trying out one's ideas upon things, discovering what can be done with materials and appliances. And this is incompatible with closely restricted physical activity. Individual activity has sometimes been taken as meaning leaving a pupil to work by himself or alone. Relief from need of attending to what any one else is doing is truly required to secure calm and concentration. Children, like grown persons, require a judicious amount of being let alone. But the time, place, and amount of such separate work is a matter of detail, not of principle. There is no inherent opposition between working with others and working as an individual. On the contrary, certain capacities of an individual are not brought out except under the stimulus of associating with others. That a child must work alone and not engage in group activities in order to be free and let his individuality develop, is a notion which measures individuality by spatial distance and makes a physical thing of it.

Individuality as a factor to be respected in education has a double meaning. In the first place, one is mentally an individual only as he has his own purpose and problem, and does his own thinking. The phrase "think for one's self" is a pleonasm. Unless one does it for one's self, it isn't thinking. Only by a pupil's own observations, reflections, framing and testing of suggestions can what he already knows be amplified and rectified. Thinking is as much an individual matter as is the digestion of food. In the second place, there are variations of point of view, of appeal of objects, and of mode of attack, from person to person. When these variations are suppressed in the alleged interests of uniformity, and an attempt is made to have a single mold of method of study and recitation, mental confusion and artificiality inevitably result. Originality is gradually destroyed, confidence in one's own quality of mental operation is undermined, and a docile subjection to the opinion of others is inculcated, or else ideas run wild. The harm is greater now than when the whole community was governed by customary beliefs, because the contrast between methods of learning in school and those relied upon outside the school is greater. That systematic advance in scientific discovery began when individuals were allowed, and then encouraged, to utilize their own peculiarities of response to subject matter, no one will deny. If it is said in objection, that pupils in school are not capable of any such originality, and hence must be confined to appropriating and reproducing things already known by the better informed, the reply is twofold.

(i) We are concerned with originality of attitude which is equivalent to the unforced response of one's own individuality, not with originality as measured by product. No one expects the young to make original discoveries of just the same facts and principles as are embodied in the sciences of nature and man. But it is not unreasonable to expect that learning may take place under such conditions that from the standpoint of the learner there is genuine discovery. While immature students will not make discoveries from the standpoint of advanced students, they make them from their own standpoint, whenever there is genuine learning.

(ii) In the normal process of becoming acquainted with subject matter already known to others, even young pupils react in unexpected ways. There is something fresh, something not capable of being fully anticipated by even the most experienced teacher, in the ways they go at the topic, and in the particular ways in which things strike them. Too often all this is brushed aside as irrelevant; pupils are deliberately held to rehearsing material in the exact form in which the older person conceives it. The result is that what is instinctively original in individuality, that which marks off one from another, goes unused and undirected. Teaching then ceases to be an educative process for the teacher. At most he learns simply to improve his existing technique; he does not get new points of view; he fails to experience any intellectual companionship. Hence both teaching and learning tend to become conventional and mechanical with all the nervous strain on both sides therein implied.

As maturity increases and as the student has a greater background of familiarity upon which a new topic is projected, the scope of more or less random physical experimentation is reduced. Activity is defined or specialized in certain channels. To the eyes of others, the student may be in a position of complete physical quietude, because his energies are confined to nerve channels and to the connected apparatus of the eyes and vocal organs. But because this attitude is evidence of intense mental concentration on the part of the trained person, it does not follow that it should be set up as a model for students who still have to find their intellectual way about. And even with the adult, it does not cover the whole circuit of mental energy. It marks an intermediate period, capable of being lengthened with increased mastery of a subject, but always coming between an earlier period of more general and conspicuous organic action and a later time of putting to use what has been apprehended.

When, however, education takes cognizance of the union of mind and body in acquiring knowledge, we are not obliged to insist upon the need of obvious, or external, freedom. It is enough to identify the freedom which is involved in teaching and studying with the thinking by which what a person already knows and believes is enlarged and refined. If attention is centered upon the conditions which have to be met in order to secure a situation favorable to effective thinking, freedom will take care of itself. The individual who has a question which being really a question to him instigates his curiosity, which feeds his eagerness for information that will help him cope with it, and who has at command an equipment which will permit these interests to take effect, is intellectually free. Whatever initiative and imaginative vision he possesses will be called into play and control his impulses and habits. His own purposes will direct his actions. Otherwise, his seeming attention, his docility, his memorizings and reproductions, will partake of intellectual servility. Such a condition of intellectual subjection is needed for fitting the masses into a society where the many are not expected to have aims or ideas of their own, but to take orders from the few set in authority. It is not adapted to a society which intends to be democratic.

Summary.

True individualism is a product of the relaxation of the grip of the authority of custom and traditions as standards of belief. Aside from sporadic instances, like the height of Greek thought, it is a comparatively modern manifestation.

Not but that there have always been individual diversities, but that a society dominated by conservative custom represses them or at least does not utilize them and promote them. For various reasons, however, the new individualism was interpreted philosophically not as meaning development of agencies for revising and transforming previously accepted beliefs, but as an assertion that each individual's mind was complete in isolation from everything else. In the theoretical phase of philosophy, this produced the epistemological problem: the question as to the possibility of any cognitive relationship of the individual to the world. In its practical phase, it generated the problem of the possibility of a purely individual consciousness acting on behalf of general or social interests, — the problem of social direction. While the philosophies which have been elaborated to deal with these questions have not affected education directly, the assumptions underlying them have found expression in the separation frequently made between study and government and between freedom of individuality and control by others. Regarding freedom, the important thing to bear in mind is that it designates a mental attitude rather than external unconstraint of movements, but that this quality of mind cannot develop without a fair leeway of movements in exploration, experimentation, application, etc. A society based on custom will utilize individual variations only up to a limit of conformity with usage; uniformity is the chief ideal within each class. A progressive society counts individual variations as precious since it finds in them the means of its own growth. Hence a democratic society must, in consistency with its ideal, allow for intellectual freedom and the play of diverse gifts and interests in its educational measures.

Chapter Twenty-Three:

Vocational Aspects of Education

1. The Meaning of Vocation.

At the present time the conflict of philosophic theories focuses in discussion of the proper place and function of vocational factors in education. The bald statement that significant differences in fundamental philosophical conceptions find their chief issue in connection with this point may arouse incredulity: there seems to be too great a gap between the remote and general terms in which philosophic ideas are formulated and the practical and concrete details of vocational education. But a mental review of the intellectual presuppositions underlying the oppositions in education of labor and leisure, theory and practice, body and mind, mental states and the world, will show that they culminate in the antithesis of vocational and cultural education. Traditionally, liberal culture has been linked to the notions of leisure, purely contemplative knowledge and a spiritual activity not involving the active use of bodily organs. Culture has also tended, latterly, to be associated with a purely private refinement, a cultivation of certain states and attitudes of consciousness, separate from either social direction or service. It has been an escape from the former, and a solace for the necessity of the latter.

So deeply entangled are these philosophic dualisms with the whole subject of vocational education, that it is necessary to define the meaning of vocation with some fullness in order to avoid the impression that an education which centers about it is narrowly practical, if not merely pecuniary. A vocation means nothing but such a direction of life activities as renders them perceptibly significant to a person, because of the consequences they accomplish, and also useful to his associates. The opposite of a career is neither leisure nor culture, but aimlessness, capriciousness, the absence of cumulative achievement in experience, on the personal side, and idle display, parasitic dependence upon the others, on the social side. Occupation is a concrete term for continuity. It includes the development of artistic capacity of any kind, of special scientific ability, of effective citizenship, as well as professional and business occupations, to say nothing of mechanical labor or engagement in gainful pursuits.

We must avoid not only limitation of conception of vocation to the occupations where immediately tangible commodities are produced, but also the notion that vocations are distributed in an exclusive way, one and only one to each person. Such restricted specialism is impossible; nothing could be more absurd than to try to educate individuals with an eye to only one line of activity. In the first place, each individual has of necessity a variety of callings, in each of which he should be intelligently effective; and in the second place any one occupation loses its meaning and becomes a routine keeping busy at something in the degree in which it is isolated from other interests.

(i) No one is just an artist and nothing else, and in so far as one approximates that condition, he is so much the less developed human being; he is a kind of monstrosity. He must, at some period of his life, be a member of a family; he must have friends and companions; he must either support himself or be supported by others, and thus he has a business career. He is a member of some organized political unit, and so on. We naturally name his vocation from that one of the callings which distinguishes him, rather than from those which he has in common with all others. But we should not allow ourselves to be so subject to words as to ignore and virtually deny his other callings when it comes to a consideration of the vocational phases of education.

(ii) As a man's vocation as artist is but the emphatically specialized phase of his diverse and variegated vocational activities, so his efficiency in it, in the humane sense of efficiency, is determined by its association with other callings. A person must have experience, he must live, if his artistry is to be more than a technical accomplishment. He cannot find the subject matter of his artistic activity within his art; this must be an expression of what he suffers and enjoys in other relationships — a thing which depends in turn upon the alertness and sympathy of his interests. What is true of an artist is true of any other special calling. There is doubtless—in general accord with the principle of habit — a tendency for every distinctive vocation to become too dominant, too exclusive and absorbing in its specialized aspect. This means emphasis upon skill or technical method at the expense of meaning. Hence it is not the business of education to foster this tendency, but rather to safeguard against it, so that the scientific inquirer shall not be merely the scientist, the teacher merely the pedagogue, the clergyman merely one who wears the cloth, and so on.

2. The Place of Vocational Aims in Education.

Bearing in mind the varied and connected content of the vocation, and the broad background upon which a particular calling is projected, we shall now consider education for the more distinctive activity of an individual.

1. An occupation is the only thing which balances the distinctive capacity of an individual with his social service. To find out what one is fitted to do and to secure an opportunity to do it is the key to happiness. Nothing is more tragic than failure to discover one's true business in life, or to find that one has drifted or been forced by circumstance into an uncongenial calling. A right occupation means simply that the aptitudes of a person are in adequate play, working with the minimum of friction and the maximum of satisfaction. With reference to other members of a community, this adequacy of action signifies, of course, that they are getting the best service the person can render. It is generally believed, for example, that slave labor was ultimately wasteful even from the purely economic point of view — that there was not sufficient stimulus to direct the energies of slaves, and that there was consequent wastage. Moreover, since slaves were confined to certain prescribed callings, much talent must have remained unavailable to the community, and hence there was a dead loss. Slavery only illustrates on an obvious scale what happens in some degree whenever an individual does not find himself in his work. And he cannot completely find himself when vocations are looked upon with contempt, and a conventional ideal of a culture which is essentially the same for all is maintained. Plato laid

down the fundamental principle of a philosophy of education when he asserted that it was the business of education to discover what each person is good for, and to train him to mastery of that mode of excellence, because such development would also secure the fulfillment of social needs in the most harmonious way. His error was not in qualitative principle, but in his limited conception of the scope of vocations socially needed; a limitation of vision which reacted to obscure his perception of the infinite variety of capacities found in different individuals.

2. An occupation is a continuous activity having a purpose. Education through occupations consequently combines within itself more of the factors conducive to learning than any other method. It calls instincts and habits into play; it is a foe to passive receptivity. It has an end in view; results are to be accomplished. Hence it appeals to thought; it demands that an idea of an end be steadily maintained, so that activity cannot be either routine or capricious. Since the movement of activity must be progressive, leading from one stage to another, observation and ingenuity are required at each stage to overcome obstacles and to discover and readapt means of execution. In short, an occupation, pursued under conditions where the realization of the activity rather than merely the external product is the aim, fulfills the requirements which were laid down earlier in connection with the discussion of aims, interest, and thinking. (See Chapters VIII, X, XII.)

A calling is also of necessity an organizing principle for information and ideas; for knowledge and intellectual growth. It provides an axis which runs through an immense diversity of detail; it causes different experiences, facts, items of information to fall into order with one another. The lawyer, the physician, the laboratory investigator in some branch of chemistry, the parent, the citizen interested in his own locality, has a constant working stimulus to note and relate whatever has to do with his concern. He unconsciously, from the motivation of his occupation, reaches out for all relevant information, and holds to it. The vocation acts as both magnet to attract and as glue to hold. Such organization of knowledge is vital, because it has reference to needs; it is so expressed and readjusted in action that it never becomes stagnant. No classification, no selection and arrangement of facts, which is consciously worked out for purely abstract ends, can ever compare in solidity or effectiveness with that knit under the stress of an occupation; in comparison the former sort is formal, superficial, and cold.

3. The only adequate training for occupations is training through occupations. The principle stated early in this book (see Chapter VI) that the educative process is its own end, and that the only sufficient preparation for later responsibilities comes by making the most of immediately present life, applies in full force to the vocational phases of education. The dominant vocation of all human beings at all times is living — intellectual and moral growth. In childhood and youth, with their relative freedom from economic stress, this fact is naked and unconcealed. To predetermine some future occupation for which education is to be a strict preparation is to injure the

possibilities of present development and thereby to reduce the adequacy of preparation for a future right employment. To repeat the principle we have had occasion to appeal to so often, such training may develop a machine-like skill in routine lines (it is far from being sure to do so, since it may develop distaste, aversion, and carelessness), but it will be at the expense of those qualities of alert observation and coherent and ingenious planning which make an occupation intellectually rewarding. In an autocratically managed society, it is often a conscious object to prevent the development of freedom and responsibility, a few do the planning and ordering, the others follow directions and are deliberately confined to narrow and prescribed channels of endeavor. However much such a scheme may inure to the prestige and profit of a class, it is evident that it limits the development of the subject class; hardens and confines the opportunities for learning through experience of the master class, and in both ways hampers the life of the society as a whole. (See ante.)

The only alternative is that all the earlier preparation for vocations be indirect rather than direct; namely, through engaging in those active occupations which are indicated by the needs and interests of the pupil at the time. Only in this way can there be on the part of the educator and of the one educated a genuine discovery of personal aptitudes so that the proper choice of a specialized pursuit in later life may be indicated. Moreover, the discovery of capacity and aptitude will be a constant process as long as growth continues. It is a conventional and arbitrary view which assumes that discovery of the work to be chosen for adult life is made once for all at some particular date. One has discovered in himself, say, an interest, intellectual and social, in the things which have to do with engineering and has decided to make that his calling. At most, this only blocks out in outline the field in which further growth is to be directed. It is a sort of rough sketch for use in direction of further activities. It is the discovery of a profession in the sense in which Columbus discovered America when he touched its shores. Future explorations of an indefinitely more detailed and extensive sort remain to be made. When educators conceive vocational guidance as something which leads up to a definitive, irretrievable, and complete choice, both education and the chosen vocation are likely to be rigid, hampering further growth. In so far, the calling chosen will be such as to leave the person concerned in a permanently subordinate position, executing the intelligence of others who have a calling which permits more flexible play and readjustment. And while ordinary usages of language may not justify terming a flexible attitude of readjustment a choice of a new and further calling, it is such in effect. If even adults have to be on the lookout to see that their calling does not shut down on them and fossilize them, educators must certainly be careful that the vocational preparation of youth is such as to engage them in a continuous reorganization of aims and methods.

3. Present Opportunities and Dangers.

In the past, education has been much more vocational in fact than in name.

(i) The education of the masses was distinctly utilitarian. It was called apprenticeship rather than education, or else just learning from experience. The schools devoted themselves to the three R's in the degree in which ability to go through the forms of reading, writing, and figuring were common elements in all kinds of labor. Taking part in some special line of work, under the direction of others, was the out-of-school phase of this education. The two supplemented each other; the school work in its narrow and formal character was as much a part of apprenticeship to a calling as that explicitly so termed.

(ii) To a considerable extent, the education of the dominant classes was essentially vocational — it only happened that their pursuits of ruling and of enjoying were not called professions. For only those things were named vocations or employments which involved manual labor, laboring for a reward in keep, or its commuted money equivalent, or the rendering of personal services to specific persons. For a long time, for example, the profession of the surgeon and physician ranked almost with that of the valet or barber — partly because it had so much to do with the body, and partly because it involved rendering direct service for pay to some definite person. But if we go behind words, the business of directing social concerns, whether politically or economically, whether in war or peace, is as much a calling as anything else; and where education has not been completely under the thumb of tradition, higher schools in the past have been upon the whole calculated to give preparation for this business. Moreover, display, the adornment of person, the kind of social companionship and entertainment which give prestige, and the spending of money, have been made into definite callings. Unconsciously to themselves the higher institutions of learning have been made to contribute to preparation for these employments. Even at present, what is called higher education is for a certain class (much smaller than it once was) mainly preparation for engaging effectively in these pursuits.

In other respects, it is largely, especially in the most advanced work, training for the calling of teaching and special research. By a peculiar superstition, education which has to do chiefly with preparation for the pursuit of conspicuous idleness, for teaching, and for literary callings, and for leadership, has been regarded as non-vocational and even as peculiarly cultural. The literary training which indirectly fits for authorship, whether of books, newspaper editorials, or magazine articles, is especially subject to this superstition: many a teacher and author writes and argues in behalf of a cultural and humane education against the encroachments of a specialized practical education, without recognizing that his own education, which he calls liberal, has been mainly training for his own particular calling. He has simply got into the habit of regarding his own business as essentially cultural and of overlooking the cultural possibilities of other employments. At the bottom of these distinctions is undoubtedly the tradition which recognizes as employment only those pursuits where one is responsible for his work to a specific employer, rather than to the ultimate employer, the community.

There are, however, obvious causes for the present conscious emphasis upon vocational education — for the disposition to make explicit and deliberate vocational implications previously tacit.

(i) In the first place, there is an increased esteem, in democratic communities, of whatever has to do with manual labor, commercial occupations, and the rendering of tangible services to society. In theory, men and women are now expected to do something in return for their support — intellectual and economic — by society. Labor is extolled; service is a much-lauded moral ideal. While there is still much admiration and envy of those who can pursue lives of idle conspicuous display, better moral sentiment condemns such lives. Social responsibility for the use of time and personal capacity is more generally recognized than it used to be.

(ii) In the second place, those vocations which are specifically industrial have gained tremendously in importance in the last century and a half. Manufacturing and commerce are no longer domestic and local, and consequently more or less incidental, but are world-wide. They engage the best energies of an increasingly large number of persons. The manufacturer, banker, and captain of industry have practically displaced a hereditary landed gentry as the immediate directors of social affairs. The problem of social readjustment is openly industrial, having to do with the relations of capital and labor. The great increase in the social importance of conspicuous industrial processes has inevitably brought to the front questions having to do with the relationship of schooling to industrial life. No such vast social readjustment could occur without offering a challenge to an education inherited from different social conditions, and without putting up to education new problems.

(iii) In the third place, there is the fact already repeatedly mentioned: Industry has ceased to be essentially an empirical, rule-of-thumb procedure, handed down by custom. Its technique is now technological: that is to say, based upon machinery resulting from discoveries in mathematics, physics, chemistry, bacteriology, etc. The economic revolution has stimulated science by setting problems for solution, by producing greater intellectual respect for mechanical appliances. And industry received back payment from science with compound interest. As a consequence, industrial occupations have infinitely greater intellectual content and infinitely larger cultural possibilities than they used to possess. The demand for such education as will acquaint workers with the scientific and social bases and bearings of their pursuits becomes imperative, since those who are without it inevitably sink to the role of appendages to the machines they operate. Under the old regime all workers in a craft were approximately equals in their knowledge and outlook. Personal knowledge and ingenuity were developed within at least a narrow range, because work was done with tools under the direct command of the worker. Now the operator has to adjust himself to his machine, instead of his tool to his own purposes. While the intellectual possibilities of industry have multiplied, industrial conditions tend to make industry, for great masses, less of an educative resource than it was in the days of hand production for local markets. The burden of realizing the intellectual possibilities inhering in work is thus thrown back on the school.

(iv) In the fourth place, the pursuit of knowledge has become, in science, more experimental, less dependent upon literary tradition, and less associated with dialectical methods of reasoning, and with symbols. As a result, the subject matter of industrial occupation presents not only more of the content of science than it used to, but greater opportunity for familiarity with the method by which knowledge is made. The ordinary worker in the factory is of course under too immediate economic pressure to have a chance to produce a knowledge like that of the worker in the laboratory. But in schools, association with machines and industrial processes may be had under conditions where the chief conscious concern of the students is insight. The separation of shop and laboratory, where these conditions are fulfilled, is largely conventional, the laboratory having the advantage of permitting the following up of any intellectual interest a problem may suggest; the shop the advantage of emphasizing the social bearings of the scientific principle, as well as, with many pupils, of stimulating a livelier interest.

(v) Finally, the advances which have been made in the psychology of learning in general and of childhood in particular fall into line with the increased importance of industry in life. For modern psychology emphasizes the radical importance of primitive unlearned instincts of exploring, experimentation, and "trying on." It reveals that learning is not the work of something ready-made called mind, but that mind itself is an organization of original capacities into activities having significance. As we have already seen (ante, p. 204), in older pupils work is to educative development of raw native activities what play is for younger pupils. Moreover, the passage from play to work should be gradual, not involving a radical change of attitude but carrying into work the elements of play, plus continuous reorganization in behalf of greater control. The reader will remark that these five points practically resume the main contentions of the previous part of the work. Both practically and philosophically, the key to the present educational situation lies in a gradual reconstruction of school materials and methods so as to utilize various forms of occupation typifying social callings, and to bring out their intellectual and moral content. This reconstruction must relegate purely literary methods — including textbooks— and dialectical methods to the position of necessary auxiliary tools in the intelligent development of consecutive and cumulative activities.

But our discussion has emphasized the fact that this educational reorganization cannot be accomplished by merely trying to give a technical preparation for industries and professions as they now operate, much less by merely reproducing existing industrial conditions in the school. The problem is not that of making the schools an adjunct to manufacture and commerce, but of utilizing the factors of industry to make school life more active, more full of immediate meaning, more connected with out-of-school experience. The problem is not easy of solution. There is a standing danger that education will perpetuate the older traditions for a select few, and effect its adjustment to the newer economic conditions more or less on the basis of acquiescence in the untransformed, unrationalized, and unsocialized phases of our defective industrial regime. Put in concrete terms, there is danger that vocational education will be interpreted in theory and practice as trade education: as a means of securing technical efficiency in specialized future pursuits. Education would then become an instrument of perpetuating unchanged the existing industrial order of society, instead of operating as a means of its transformation. The desired transformation is not difficult to define in a formal way. It signifies a society in which every person shall be occupied in something which makes the lives of others better worth living, and which accordingly makes the ties which bind persons together more perceptible — which breaks down the barriers of distance between them. It denotes a state of affairs in which the interest of each in his work is uncoerced and intelligent: based upon its congeniality to his own aptitudes. It goes without saying that we are far from such a social state; in a literal and quantitative sense, we may never arrive at it. But in principle, the quality of social changes already accomplished lies in this direction. There are more ample resources for its achievement now than ever there have been before. No insuperable obstacles, given the intelligent will for its realization, stand in the way.

Success or failure in its realization depends more upon the adoption of educational methods calculated to effect the change than upon anything else. For the change is essentially a change in the quality of mental disposition — an educative change. This does not mean that we can change character and mind by direct instruction and exhortation, apart from a change in industrial and political conditions. Such a conception contradicts our basic idea that character and mind are attitudes of participative response in social affairs. But it does mean that we may produce in schools a projection in type of the society we should like to realize, and by forming minds in accord with it gradually modify the larger and more recalcitrant features of adult society. Sentimentally, it may seem harsh to say that the greatest evil of the present regime is not found in poverty and in the suffering which it entails, but in the fact that so many persons have callings which make no appeal to them, which are pursued simply for the money reward that accrues. For such callings constantly provoke one to aversion, ill will, and a desire to slight and evade. Neither men's hearts nor their minds are in their work. On the other hand, those who are not only much better off in worldly goods, but who are in excessive, if not monopolistic, control of the activities of the many are shut off from equality and generality of social intercourse. They are stimulated to pursuits of indulgence and display; they try to make up for the distance which separates them from others by the impression of force and superior possession and enjoyment which they can make upon others.

It would be quite possible for a narrowly conceived scheme of vocational education to perpetuate this division in a hardened form. Taking its stand upon a dogma of social predestination, it would assume that some are to continue to be wage earners under economic conditions like the present, and would aim simply to give them what is termed a trade education — that is, greater technical efficiency. Technical proficiency is often sadly lacking, and is surely desirable on all accounts — not merely for the sake of the production of better goods at less cost, but for the greater happiness found in work. For no one cares for what one cannot half do. But there is a great difference between a proficiency limited to immediate work, and a competency extended to insight into its social bearings;

between efficiency in carrying out the plans of others and in one forming one's own. At present, intellectual and emotional limitation characterizes both the employing and the employed class. While the latter often have no concern with their occupation beyond the money return it brings, the former's outlook may be confined to profit and power. The latter interest generally involves much greater intellectual initiation and larger survey of conditions. For it involves the direction and combination of a large number of diverse factors, while the interest in wages is restricted to certain direct muscular movements. But none the less there is a limitation of intelligence to technical and non- humane, non-liberal channels, so far as the work does not take in its social bearings. And when the animating motive is desire for private profit or personal power, this limitation is inevitable. In fact, the advantage in immediate social sympathy and humane disposition often lies with the economically unfortunate, who have not experienced the hardening effects of a one-sided control of the affairs of others.

Any scheme for vocational education which takes its point of departure from the industrial regime that now exists, is likely to assume and to perpetuate its divisions and weaknesses, and thus to become an instrument in accomplishing the feudal dogma of social predestination. Those who are in a position to make their wishes good, will demand a liberal, a cultural occupation, and one which fits for directive power the youth in whom they are directly interested. To split the system, and give to others, less fortunately situated, an education conceived mainly as specific trade preparation, is to treat the schools as an agency for transferring the older division of labor and leisure, culture and service, mind and body, directed and directive class, into a society nominally democratic. Such a vocational education inevitably discounts the scientific and historic human connections of the materials and processes dealt with. To include such things in narrow trade education would be to waste time; concern for them would not be "practical." They are reserved for those who have leisure at command—the leisure due to superior economic resources. Such things might even be dangerous to the interests of the controlling class, arousing discontent or ambitions "beyond the station" of those working under the direction of others. But an education which acknowledges the full intellectual and social meaning of a vocation would include instruction in the historic background of present conditions; training in science to give intelligence and initiative in dealing with material and agencies of production; and study of economics, civics, and politics, to bring the future worker into touch with the problems of the day and the various methods proposed for its improvement. Above all, it would train power of readaptation to changing conditions so that future workers would not become blindly subject to a fate imposed upon them. This ideal has to contend not only with the inertia of existing educational traditions, but also with the opposition of those who are entrenched in command of the industrial machinery, and who realize that such an educational system if made general would threaten their ability to use others for their own ends. But this very fact is the presage of a more equitable and enlightened social order, for it gives evidence of the dependence of social reorganization upon educational reconstruction. It is accordingly an encouragement to those believing in a better order to undertake the promotion of a vocational education which does not subject youth to the demands and standards of the present system, but which utilizes its scientific and social factors to develop a courageous intelligence, and to make intelligence practical and executive.

Summary.

A vocation signifies any form of continuous activity which renders service to others and engages personal powers in behalf of the accomplishment of results. The question of the relation of vocation to education brings to a focus the various problems previously discussed regarding the connection of thought with bodily activity; of individual conscious development with associated life; of theoretical culture with practical behavior having definite results; of making a livelihood with the worthy enjoyment of leisure. In general, the opposition to recognition of the vocational phases of life in education (except for the utilitarian three R's in elementary schooling) accompanies the conservation of aristocratic ideals of the past. But, at the present juncture, there is a movement in behalf of something called vocational training which, if carried into effect, would harden these ideas into a form adapted to the existing industrial regime. This movement would continue the traditional liberal or cultural education for the few economically able to enjoy it, and would give to the masses a narrow technical trade education for specialized callings, carried on under the control of others. This scheme denotes, of course, simply a perpetuation of the older social division, with its counterpart intellectual and moral dualisms. But it means its continuation under conditions where it has much less justification for existence. For industrial life is now so dependent upon science and so intimately affects all forms of social intercourse, that there is an opportunity to utilize it for development of mind and character. Moreover, a right educational use of it would react upon intelligence and interest so as to modify, in connection with legislation and administration, the socially obnoxious features of the present industrial and commercial order. It would turn the increasing fund of social sympathy to constructive account, instead of leaving it a somewhat blind philanthropic sentiment.

It would give those who engage in industrial callings desire and ability to share in social control, and ability to become masters of their industrial fate. It would enable them to saturate with meaning the technical and mechanical features which are so marked a feature of our machine system of production and distribution. So much for those who now have the poorer economic opportunities. With the representatives of the more privileged portion of the community, it would increase sympathy for labor, create a disposition of mind which can discover the culturing elements in useful activity, and increase a sense of social responsibility. The crucial position of the question of vocational education at present is due, in other words, to the fact that it concentrates in a specific issue two fundamental questions: — Whether intelligence is best exercised apart from or within activity which puts nature to human use, and whether individual culture is best secured under egoistic or social conditions. No discussion of details is undertaken in this chapter, because this conclusion but summarizes the discussion of the previous chapters, XV to XXII, inclusive.

Chapter Twenty-four:

Philosophy of Education

1. A Critical Review.

Although we are dealing with the philosophy of education, DO definition of philosophy has yet been given; nor has there been an explicit consideration of the nature of a philosophy of education. This topic is now introduced by a summary account of the logical order implied in the previous discussions, for the purpose of bringing out the philosophic issues involved. Afterwards we shall undertake a brief discussion, in more specifically philosophical terms, of the theories of knowledge and of morals implied in different educational ideals as they operate in practice. The prior chapters fall logically into three parts.

I. The first chapters deal with education as a social need and function. Their purpose is to outline the general features of education as the process by which social groups maintain their continuous existence. Education was shown to be a process of renewal of the meanings of experience through a process of transmission, partly incidental to the ordinary companionship or intercourse of adults and youth, partly deliberately instituted to effect social continuity. This process was seen to involve control and growth of both the immature individual and the group in which he lives.

This consideration was formal in that it took no specific account of the quality of the social group concerned—the kind of society aiming at its own perpetuation through education. The general discussion was then specified by application to social groups which are intentionally progressive, and which aim at a greater variety of mutually shared interests in distinction from those which aim simply at the preservation of established customs. Such societies were found to be democratic in quality, because of the greater freedom allowed the constituent members, and the conscious need of securing in individuals a consciously socialized interest, instead of trusting mainly to the force of customs operating under the control of a superior class. The sort of education appropriate to the development of a democratic community was then explicitly taken as the criterion of the further, more detailed analysis of education.

II. This analysis, based upon the democratic criterion, was seen to imply the ideal of a continuous reconstruction or reorganizing of experience, of such a nature as to increase its recognized meaning or social content, and as to increase the capacity of individuals to act as directive guardians of this reorganization. (See Chapters VI-VII.) This distinction was then used to outline the respective characters of subject matter and method. It also defined their unity, since method in study and learning upon this basis is just the consciously directed movement of reorganization of the subject matter of experience. From this point of view the main principles of method and subject matter of learning were developed (Chapters XIII-XIV.)

III. Save for incidental criticisms designed to illustrate principles by force of contrast, this phase of the discussion took for granted the democratic criterion and its application in present social life. In the subsequent chapters (XVIII-XXII) we considered the present limitation of its actual realization. They were found to spring from the notion that experience consists of a variety of segregated domains, or interests, each having its own independent value, material, and method, each checking every other, and, when each is kept properly bounded by the others, forming a kind of "balance of powers" in education. We then proceeded to an analysis of the various assumptions underlying this segregation. On the practical side, they were found to have their cause in the divisions of society into more or less rigidly marked-off classes and groups — in other words, in obstruction to full and flexible social interaction and intercourse. These social ruptures of continuity were seen to have their intellectual formulation in various dualisms or antitheses — such as that of labor and leisure, practical and intellectual activity, man and nature, individuality and association, culture and vocation. In this discussion, we found that these different issues have their counterparts in formulations which have been made in classic philosophic systems; and that they involve the chief problems of philosophy — such as mind (or spirit) and matter, body and mind, the mind and the world, the individual and his relationships to others, etc. Underlying these various separations we found the fundamental assumption to be an isolation of mind from activity involving physical conditions, bodily organs, material appliances, and natural objects. Consequently, there was indicated a philosophy which recognizes the origin, place, and function of mind in an activity which controls the environment. Thus we have completed the circuit and returned to the conceptions of the first portion of this book: such as the biological continuity of human impulses and instincts with natural energies; the dependence of the growth of mind upon participation in conjoint activities having a common purpose; the influence of the physical environment through the uses made of it in the social medium; the necessity of utilization of individual variations in desire and thinking for a progressively developing society; the essential unity of method and subject matter; the intrinsic continuity of ends and means; the recognition of mind as thinking which perceives and tests the meanings of behavior. These conceptions are consistent with the philosophy which sees intelligence to be the purposive reorganization, through action, of the material of experience; and they are inconsistent with each of the dualistic philosophies mentioned.

2. The Nature of Philosophy.

Our further task is to extract and make explicit the idea of philosophy implicit in these considerations. We have already virtually described, though not defined, philosophy in terms of the problems with which it deals: and that thing nor even to the aggregate of known things, but to the considerations which govern conduct.

Hence philosophy cannot be defined simply from the side of subject matter. For this reason, the definition of such conceptions as generality, totality, and ultimateness is most readily reached from the side of the disposition toward the world which they connote. In any literal and quantitative sense, these terms do not apply to the subject matter of knowledge, for completeness and finality are out of the question. The very nature of experience as an ongoing, changing process forbids. In a less rigid sense, they apply to science rather than to philosophy. For obviously it is to mathematics, physics, chemistry, biology, anthropology, history, etc. that we must go, not to philosophy, to find out the facts of the world. It is for the sciences to say what generalizations are tenable about the world and what they specifically are. But when we ask what sort of permanent disposition of action toward the world the scientific disclosures exact of us we are raising a philosophic question.

From this point of view, "totality" does not mean the hopeless task of a quantitative summation. It means rather consistency of mode of response in reference to the plurality of events which occur. Consistency does not mean literal identity; for since the same thing does not happen twice, an exact repetition of a reaction involves some maladjustment. Totality means continuity — the carrying on of a former habit of action with the readaptation necessary to keep it alive and growing. Instead of signifying a ready-made complete scheme of action, it means keeping the balance in a multitude of diverse actions, so that each borrows and gives significance to every other. Any person who is open-minded and sensitive to new perceptions, and who has concentration and responsibility in connecting them has, in so far, a philosophic disposition. One of the popular senses of philosophy is calm and endurance in the face of difficulty and loss; it is even supposed to be a power to bear pain without complaint. This meaning is a tribute to the influence of the Stoic philosophy rather than an attribute of philosophy in general. But in so far as it suggests that the wholeness characteristic of philosophy is a power to learn, or to extract meaning, from even the unpleasant vicissitudes of experience and to embody what is learned in an ability to go on learning, it is justified in any scheme. An analogous interpretation applies to the generality and ultimateness of philosophy. Taken literally, they are absurd pretensions; they indicate insanity. Finality does not mean, however, that experience is ended and exhausted, but means the disposition to penetrate to deeper levels of meaning — to go below the surface and find out the connections of any event or object, and to keep at it. In like manner the philosophic attitude is general in the sense that it is averse to taking anything as isolated; it tries to place an act in its context — which constitutes its significance. It is of assistance to connect philosophy with thinking in its distinction from knowledge. Knowledge, grounded knowledge, is science; it represents objects which have been settled, ordered, disposed of rationally. Thinking, on the other hand, is prospective in reference. It is occasioned by an unsettlement and it aims at overcoming a disturbance. Philosophy is thinking what the known demands of us — what responsive attitude it exacts. It is an idea of what is possible, not a record of accomplished fact. Hence it is hypothetical, like all thinking. It presents an assignment of something to be done — something to be tried. Its value lies not in furnishing solutions (which can be achieved only in action) but in defining difficulties and suggesting methods for dealing with them. Philosophy might almost be described as thinking which has become conscious of itself — which has generalized its place, function, and value in experience.

More specifically, the demand for a "total" attitude arises because there is the need of integration in action of the conflicting various interests in life. Where interests are so superficial that they glide readily into one another, or where they are not sufficiently organized to come into conflict with one another, the need for philosophy is not perceptible. But when the scientific interest conflicts with, say, the religious, or the economic with the scientific or aesthetic, or when the conservative concern for order is at odds with the progressive interest in freedom, or when institutionalism clashes with individuality, there is a stimulus to discover some more comprehensive point of view from which the divergencies may be brought together, and consistency or continuity of experience recovered. Often these clashes may be settled by an individual for himself; the area of the struggle of aims is limited and a person works out his own rough accommodations. Such homespun philosophies are genuine and often adequate. But they do not result in systems of philosophy. These arise when the discrepant claims of different ideals of conduct affect the community as a whole, and the need for readjustment is general. These traits explain some things which are often brought as objections against philosophies, such as the part played in them by individual speculation, and their controversial diversity, as well as the fact that philosophy seems to be repeatedly occupied with much the same questions differently stated. Without doubt, all these things characterize historic philosophies more or less. But they are not objections to philosophy so much as they are to human nature, and even to the world in which human nature is set. If there are genuine uncertainties in life, philosophies must reflect that uncertainty. If there are different diagnoses of the cause of a difficulty, and different proposals for dealing with it; if, that is, the conflict of interests is more or less embodied in different sets of persons, there must be divergent competing philosophies. With respect to what has happened, sufficient evidence is all that is needed to bring agreement and certainty. The thing itself is sure. But with reference to what it is wise to do in a complicated situation, discussion is inevitable precisely because the thing itself is still indeterminate. One would not expect a ruling class living at ease to have the same philosophy of life as those who were having a hard struggle for existence. If the possessing and the dispossessed had the same fundamental disposition toward the world, it would argue either insincerity or lack of seriousness. A community devoted to industrial pursuits, active in business and commerce, is not likely to see the needs and possibilities of life in the same way as a country with high aesthetic culture and little enterprise in turning the energies of nature to mechanical account. A social group with a fairly continuous history will respond mentally to a crisis in a very different way from one which has felt the shock of abrupt breaks. Even if the same data were present, they would be evaluated differently. But the different sorts of experience attending different types of life prevent just the same data from presenting themselves, as well as lead to a different scheme of values. As for the similarity of problems, this is often more a matter of appearance than of fact, due to old discussions being translated into the terms of contemporary perplexities. But in certain fundamental respects the same predicaments of life recur from time to time with only such changes as are due to change of social context, including the growth of the sciences.

The fact that philosophic problems arise because of widespread and widely felt difficulties in social practice is disguised because philosophers become a specialized class which uses a technical language, unlike the vocabulary in which the direct difficulties are stated. But where a system becomes influential, its connection with a conflict of interests calling for some program of social adjustment may always be discovered. At this point, the intimate connection between philosophy and education appears. In fact, education offers a vantage ground from which to penetrate to the human, as distinct from the technical, significance of philosophic discussions. The student of philosophy "in itself" is always in danger of taking it as so much nimble or severe intellectual exercise — as something said by philosophers and concerning them alone. But when philosophic issues are approached from the side of the kind of mental disposition to which they correspond, or the differences in educational practice they make when acted upon, the life-situations which they formulate can never be far from view. If a theory makes no difference in educational endeavor, it must be artificial. The educational point of view enables one to envisage the philosophic problems where they arise and thrive, where they are at home, and where acceptance or rejection makes a difference in practice. If we are willing to conceive education as the process of forming fundamental dispositions, intellectual and emotional, toward nature and fellow men, philosophy may even be defined as the general theory of education. Unless a philosophy is to remain symbolic — or verbal — or a sentimental indulgence for a few, or else mere arbitrary dogma, its auditing of past experience and its program of values must take effect in conduct. Public agitation, propaganda, legislative and administrative action are effective in producing the change of disposition which a philosophy indicates as desirable, but only in the degree in which they are educative — that is to say, in the degree in which they modify mental and moral attitudes. And at the best, such methods are compromised by the fact they are used with those whose habits are already largely set, while education of youth has a fairer and freer field of operation. On the other side, the business of schooling tends to become a routine empirical affair unless its aims and methods are animated by such a broad and sympathetic survey of its place in contemporary life as it is the business of philosophy to provide. Positive science always implies practically the ends which the community is concerned to achieve. Isolated from such ends, it is matter of indifference whether its disclosures are used to cure disease or to spread it; to increase the means of sustenance of life or to manufacture war material to wipe life out. If society is interested in one of these things rather than another, science shows the way of attainment. Philosophy thus has a double task: that of criticizing existing aims with respect to the existing state of science, pointing out values which have become obsolete with the command of new resources, showing what values are merely sentimental because there are no means for their realization; and also that of interpreting the results of specialized science in their bearing on future social endeavor. It is impossible that it should have any success in these tasks without educational equivalents as to what to do and what not to do. For philosophic theory has no Aladdin's lamp to summon into immediate existence the values which it intellectually constructs. In the mechanical arts, the sciences become methods of managing things so as to utilize their energies for recognized aims. By the educative arts philosophy may generate methods of utilizing the energies of human beings in accord with serious and thoughtful conceptions of life. Education is the laboratory in which philosophic distinctions become concrete and are tested.

It is suggestive that European philosophy originated (among the Athenians) under the direct pressure of educational questions. The earlier history of philosophy, developed by the Greeks in Asia Minor and Italy, so far as its range of topics is concerned, is mainly a chapter in the history of science rather than of philosophy as that word is understood to-day. It had nature for its subject, and speculated as to how things are made and changed. Later the traveling teachers, known as the Sophists, began to apply the results and the methods of the natural philosophers to human conduct.

When the Sophists, the first body of professional educators in Europe, instructed the youth in virtue, the political arts, and the management of city and household, philosophy began to deal with the relation of the individual to the universal, to some comprehensive class, or to some group; the relation of man and nature, of tradition and reflection, of knowledge and action. Can virtue, approved excellence in any line, be learned, they asked? What is learning? It has to do with knowledge. What, then, is knowledge? How is it achieved? Through the senses, or by apprenticeship in some form of doing, or by reason that has undergone a preliminary logical discipline? Since learning is coming to know, it involves a passage from ignorance to wisdom, from privation to fullness from defect to perfection, from non-being to being, in the Greek way of putting it. How is such a transition possible? Is change, becoming, development really possible and if so, how? And supposing such questions answered, what is the relation of instruction, of knowledge, to virtue? This last question led to opening the problem of the relation of reason to action, of theory to practice, since virtue clearly dwelt in action. Was not knowing, the activity of reason, the noblest attribute of man? And consequently was not purely intellectual activity itself the highest of all excellences, compared with which the virtues of neighborliness and the citizen's life were secondary? Or, on the other hand, was the vaunted intellectual knowledge more than empty and vain pretense, demoralizing to character and destructive of the social ties that bound men together in their community life? Was not the only true, because the only moral, life gained through obedient habituation to the customary practices of the community? And was not the new education an enemy to good citizenship, because it set up a rival standard to the established traditions of the community?

In the course of two or three generations such questions were cut loose from their original practical bearing upon education and were discussed on their own account; that is, as matters of philosophy as an independent branch of inquiry. But the fact that the stream of European philosophical thought arose as a theory of educational procedure remains an eloquent witness to the intimate connection of philosophy and education. "Philosophy of education" is not an external application of ready-made ideas to a system of practice having a radically different origin and purpose: it is only an explicit formulation of the problems of the formation of right mental and moral habitudes in respect to the difficulties of contemporary social life. The most penetrating definition of philosophy which can be given is, then, that it is the theory of education in its most general phases.

The reconstruction of philosophy, of education, and of social ideals and methods thus go hand in hand. If there is especial need of educational reconstruction at the present time, if this need makes urgent a reconsideration of the basic ideas of traditional philosophic systems, it is because of the thoroughgoing change in social life accompanying the advance of science, the industrial revolution, and the development of democracy. Such practical changes cannot take place without demanding an educational reformation to meet them, and without leading men to ask what ideas and ideals are implicit in these social changes, and what revisions they require of the ideas and ideals which are inherited from older and unlike cultures. Incidentally throughout the whole book, explicitly in the last few chapters, we have been dealing with just these questions as they affect the relationship of mind and body, theory and practice, man and nature, the individual and social, etc. In our concluding chapters we shall sum up the prior discussions with respect first to the philosophy of knowledge, and then to the philosophy of morals.

Summary.

After a review designed to bring out the philosophic issues implicit in the previous discussions, philosophy was defined as the generalized theory of education. Philosophy was stated to be a form of thinking, which, like all thinking, finds its origin in what is uncertain in the subject matter of experience, which aims to locate the nature of the perplexity and to frame hypotheses for its clearing up to be tested in action. Philosophic thinking has for its differentia the fact that the uncertainties with which it deals are found in widespread social conditions and aims, consisting in a conflict of organized interests and institutional claims. Since the only way of bringing about a harmonious readjustment of the opposed tendencies is through a modification of emotional and intellectual disposition, philosophy is at once an explicit formulation of the various interests of life and a propounding of points of view and methods through which a better balance of interests may be effected. Since education is the process through which the needed transformation may be accomplished and not remain a mere hypothesis as to what is desirable, we reach a justification of the statement that philosophy is the theory of education as a deliberately conducted practice.

Chapter Twenty-five:

Theories of Knowledge

1. Continuity versus Dualism.

A number of theories of knowing have been criticized in the previous pages. In spite of their differences from one another, they all agree in one fundamental respect which contrasts with the theory which has been positively advanced. The latter assumes continuity; the former state or imply certain basic divisions, separations, or antitheses, technically called dualisms. The origin of these divisions we have found in the hard and fast walls which mark off social groups and classes within a group: like those between rich and poor, men and women, noble and baseborn, ruler and ruled. These barriers mean absence of fluent and free intercourse. This absence is equivalent to the setting up of different types of life-experience, each with isolated subject matter, aim, and standard of values. Every such social condition must be formulated in a dualistic philosophy, if philosophy is to be a sincere account of experience. When it gets beyond dualism — as many philosophies do in form — it can only be by appeal to something higher than anything found in experience, by a flight to some transcendental realm. And in denying duality in name such theories restore it in fact, for they end in a division between things of this world as mere appearances and an inaccessible essence of reality.

So far as these divisions persist and others are added to them, each leaves its mark upon the educational system, until the scheme of education, taken as a whole, is a deposit of various purposes and procedures. The outcome is that kind of check and balance of segregated factors and values which has been described. (See Chapter XVIII.) The present discussion is simply a formulation, in the terminology of philosophy, of various antithetical conceptions involved in the theory of knowing. In the first place, there is the opposition of empirical and higher rational knowing. The first is connected with everyday affairs, serves the purposes of the ordinary individual who has no specialized intellectual pursuit, and brings his wants into some kind of working connection with the immediate environment. Such knowing is depreciated, if not despised, as purely utilitarian, lacking in cultural significance. Rational knowledge is supposed to be something which touches reality in ultimate, intellectual fashion; to be pursued for its own sake and properly to terminate in purely theoretical insight, not debased by application in behavior. Socially, the distinction corresponds to that of the intelligence used by the working classes and that used by a learned class remote from concern with the means of living. Philosophically, the difference turns about the distinction of the particular and universal. Experience is an aggregate of more or less isolated particulars, acquaintance with each of which must be separately made. Reason deals with universals, with general principles, with laws, which lie above the welter of concrete details. In the educational precipitate, the pupil is supposed to have to learn, on one hand, a lot of items of specific information, each standing by itself, and upon the other hand, to become familiar with a certain number of laws and general relationships. Geography, as often taught, illustrates the former; mathematics, beyond the rudiments of figuring, the latter. For all practical purposes, they represent two independent worlds.

Another antithesis is suggested by the two senses of the word "learning." On the one hand, learning is the sum total of what is known, as that is handed down by books and learned men. It is something external, an accumulation of cognitions as one might store material commodities in a warehouse. Truth exists ready-made somewhere. Study is then the process by which an individual draws on what is in storage. On the other hand, learning means something which the individual does when he studies. It is an active, personally conducted affair. The dualism here is between knowledge as something external, or, as it is often called, objective, and knowing as something purely internal, subjective, psychical. There is, on one side, a body of truth, ready-made, and, on the other, a ready-made mind equipped with a faculty of knowing — if it only wills to exercise it, which it is often strangely loath to do. The separation, often touched upon, between subject matter and method is the educational equivalent of this dualism. Socially the distinction has to do with the part of life which is dependent upon authority and that where individuals are free to advance. Another dualism is that of activity and passivity in knowing. Purely empirical and physical things are often supposed to be known by receiving impressions. Physical things somehow stamp themselves upon the mind or convey themselves into consciousness by means of the sense organs. Rational knowledge and knowledge of spiritual things is supposed, on the contrary, to spring from activity initiated within the mind, an activity carried on better if it is kept remote from all sullying touch of the senses and external objects. The distinction between sense training and object lessons and laboratory exercises, and pure ideas contained in books, and appropriated — so it is thought — by some miraculous output of mental energy, is a fair expression in education of this distinction. Socially, it reflects a division between those who are controlled by direct concern with things and those who are free to cultivate themselves.

Another current opposition is that said to exist between the intellect and the emotions. The emotions are conceived to be purely private and personal, having nothing to do with the work of pure intelligence in apprehending facts and truths, — except perhaps the single emotion of intellectual curiosity. The intellect is a pure light; the emotions are a disturbing heat. The mind turns outward to truth; the emotions turn inward to considerations of personal advantage and loss. Thus in education we have that systematic depreciation of interest which has been noted, plus the necessity in practice, with most pupils, of recourse to extraneous and irrelevant rewards and penalties in order to induce the person who has a mind (much as his clothes have a pocket) to apply that mind to the truths to be known. Thus we have the spectacle of professional educators decrying appeal to interest while they uphold with great dignity the need of reliance upon examinations, marks, promotions and emotions, prizes, and the time-honored paraphernalia of rewards and punishments. The effect of this situation in crippling the teacher's sense of humor has not received the attention which it deserves.

All of these separations culminate in one between knowing and doing, theory and practice, between mind as the end and spirit of action and the body as its organ and means. We shall not repeat what has been said about the source of this dualism in the division of society into a class laboring with their muscles for material sustenance and a class which, relieved from economic pressure, devotes itself to the arts of expression and social direction. Nor is it necessary to speak again of the educational evils which spring from the separation. We shall be content to summarize the forces which tend to make the untenability of this conception obvious and to replace it by the idea of continuity.

(i) The advance of physiology and the psychology associated with it have shown the connection of mental activity with that of the nervous system. Too often recognition of connection has stopped short at this point; the older dualism of soul and body has been replaced by that of the brain and the rest of the body. But in fact the nervous system is only a specialized mechanism for keeping all bodily activities working together. Instead of being isolated from them, as an organ of knowing from organs of motor response, it is the organ by which they interact responsively with one another. The brain is essentially an organ for effecting the reciprocal adjustment to each other of the stimuli received from the environment and responses directed upon it. Note that the adjusting is reciprocal; the brain not only enables organic activity to be brought to bear upon any object of the environment in response to a sensory stimulation, but this response also determines what the next stimulus will be. See what happens, for example, when a carpenter is at work upon a board, or an etcher upon his plate — or in any case of a consecutive activity. While each motor response is adjusted to the state of affairs indicated through the sense organs, that motor response shapes the next sensory stimulus. Generalizing this illustration, the brain is the machinery for a constant reorganizing of activity so as to maintain its continuity; that is to say, to make such modifications in future action as are required because of what has already been done. The continuity of the work of the carpenter distinguishes it from a routine repetition of identically the same motion, and from a random activity where there is nothing cumulative. What makes it continuous, consecutive, or concentrated is that each earlier act prepares the way for later acts, while these take account of or reckon with the results already attained — the basis of all responsibility. No one who has realized the full force of the facts of the connection of knowing with the nervous system and of the nervous system with the readjusting of activity continuously to meet new conditions, will doubt that knowing has to do with reorganizing activity, instead of being something isolated from all activity, complete on its own account.

(ii) The development of biology clinches this lesson, with its discovery of evolution. For the philosophic significance of the doctrine of evolution lies precisely in its emphasis upon continuity of simpler and more complex organic forms until we reach man. The development of organic forms begins with structures where the adjustment of environment and organism is obvious, and where anything which can be called mind is at a minimum. As activity becomes more complex, coordinating a greater number of factors in space and time, intelligence plays a more and more marked role, for it has a larger span of the future to forecast and plan for. The effect upon the theory of knowing is to displace the notion that it is the activity of a mere onlooker or spectator of the world, the notion which goes with the idea of knowing as something complete in itself. For the doctrine of organic development means that the living creature is a part of the world, sharing its vicissitudes and fortunes, and making itself secure in its precarious dependence only as it intellectually identifies itself with the things about it, and, forecasting the future consequences of what is going on, shapes its own activities accordingly. If the living, experiencing being is an intimate participant in the activities of the world to which it belongs, then knowledge is a mode of participation, valuable in the degree in which it is effective. It cannot be the idle view of an unconcerned spectator.

(iii) The development of the experimental method as the method of getting knowledge and of making sure it is knowledge, and not mere opinion — the method of both discovery and proof — is the remaining great force in bringing about a transformation in the theory of knowledge. The experimental method has two sides. (i) On one hand, it means that we have no right to call anything knowledge except where our activity has actually produced certain physical changes in things, which agree with and confirm the conception entertained. Short of such specific changes, our beliefs are only hypotheses, theories, suggestions, guesses, and are to be entertained tentatively and to be utilized as indications of experiments to be tried. (ii) On the other hand, the experimental method of thinking signifies that thinking is of avail; that it is of avail in just the degree in which the anticipation of future consequences is made on the basis of thorough observation of present conditions. Experimentation, in other words, is not equivalent to blind reacting. Such surplus activity — a surplus with reference to what has been observed and is now anticipated — is indeed an unescapable factor in all our behavior, but it is not experiment save as consequences are noted and are used to make predictions and plans in similar situations in the future. The more the meaning of the experimental method is perceived, the more our trying out of a certain way of treating the material resources and obstacles which confront us embodies a prior use of intelligence. What we call magic was with respect to many things the experimental method of the savage; but for him to try was to try his luck, not his ideas. The scientific experimental method is, on the contrary, a trial of ideas; hence even when practically — or immediately — unsuccessful, it is intellectual, fruitful; for we learn from our failures when our endeavors are seriously thoughtful.

The experimental method is new as a scientific resource—as a systematized means of making knowledge, though as old as life as a practical device. Hence it is not surprising that men have not recognized its full scope. For the most part, its significance is regarded as belonging to certain technical and merely physical matters. It will doubtless take a long time to secure the perception that it holds equally as to the forming and testing of ideas in social and moral matters. Men still want the crutch of dogma, of beliefs fixed by authority, to relieve them of the trouble of thinking and the responsibility of directing their activity by thought. They tend to confine their own thinking to a consideration of which one among the rival systems of dogma they will accept. Hence the schools are better adapted, as John Stuart Mill said, to make disciples than inquirers. But every advance in the influence of the experimental method is sure to aid in outlawing the literary, dialectic, and authoritative methods of forming beliefs which have governed the schools of the past, and to transfer their prestige to methods which will procure an active concern with things and persons, directed by aims of increasing temporal reach and deploying greater range of things in space. In time the theory of knowing must be derived from the practice which is most successful in making knowledge; and then that theory will be employed to improve the methods which are less successful.

2. Schools of Method.

There are various systems of philosophy with characteristically different conceptions of the method of knowing. Some of them are named scholasticism, sensationalism, rationalism, idealism, realism, empiricism, transcendentalism, pragmatism, etc. Many of them have been criticized in connection with the discussion of some educational problem. We are here concerned with them as involving deviations from that method which has proved most effective in achieving knowledge, for a consideration of the deviations may render clearer the true place of knowledge in experience. In brief, the function of knowledge is to make one experience freely available in other experiences. The word "freely" marks the difference between the principle of knowledge and that of habit. Habit means that an individual undergoes a modification through an experience, which modification forms a predisposition to easier and more effective action in a like direction in the future. Thus it also has the function of making one experience available in subsequent experiences. Within certain limits, it performs this function successfully. But habit, apart from knowledge, does not make allowance for change of conditions, for novelty. Prevision of change is not part of its scope, for habit assumes the essential likeness of the new situation with the old. Consequently it often leads astray, or comes between a person and the successful performance of his task, just as the skill, based on habit alone, of the mechanic will desert him when something unexpected occurs in the running of the machine. But a man who understands the machine is the man who knows what he is about. He knows the conditions under which a given habit works, and is in a position to introduce the changes which will readapt it to new conditions.

In other words, knowledge is a perception of those connections of an object which determine its applicability in a given situation. To take an extreme example; savages react to a flaming comet as they are accustomed to react to other events which threaten the security of their life. Since they try to frighten wild animals or their enemies by shrieks, beating of gongs, brandishing of weapons, etc., they use the same methods to scare away the comet. To us, the method is plainly absurd — so absurd that we fail to note that savages are simply falling back upon habit in a way which exhibits its limitations. The only reason we do not act in some analogous fashion is because we do not take the comet as an isolated, disconnected event, but apprehend it in its connections with other events. We place it, as we say, in the astronomical system. We respond to its connections and not simply to the immediate occurrence. Thus our attitude to it is much freer. We may approach it, so to speak, from any one of the angles provided by its connections. We can bring into play, as we deem wise, any one of the habits appropriate to any one of the connected objects. Thus we get at a new event indirectly instead of immediately — by invention, ingenuity, resourcefulness. An ideally perfect knowledge would represent such a network of interconnections that any past experience would offer a point of advantage from which to get at the problem presented in a new experience. In fine, while a habit apart from knowledge supplies us with a single fixed method of attack, knowledge means that selection may be made from a much wider range of habits.

Two aspects of this more general and freer availability of former experiences for subsequent ones may be distinguished. (See ante, p. 77.) (i) One, the more tangible, is increased power of control. What cannot be managed directly may be handled indirectly; or we can interpose barriers between us and undesirable consequences; or we may evade them if we cannot overcome them. Genuine knowledge has all the practical value attaching to efficient habits in any case. (ii) But it also increases the meaning, the experienced significance, attaching to an experience. A situation to which we respond capriciously or by routine has only a minimum of conscious significance; we get nothing mentally from it. But wherever knowledge comes into play in determining a new experience there is mental reward; even if we fail practically in getting the needed control we have the satisfaction of experiencing a meaning instead of merely reacting physically.

While the content of knowledge is what has happened, what is taken as finished and hence settled and sure, the reference of knowledge is future or prospective. For knowledge furnishes the means of understanding or giving meaning to what is still going on and what is to be done. The knowledge of a physician is what he has found out by personal acquaintance and by study of what others have ascertained and recorded. But it is knowledge to him because it supplies the resources by which he interprets the unknown things which confront him, fills out the partial obvious facts with connected suggested phenomena, foresees their probable future, and makes plans accordingly. When knowledge is cut off from use in giving meaning to what is blind and baffling, it drops out of consciousness entirely or else becomes an object of aesthetic contemplation. There is much emotional satisfaction to be had from a survey of the symmetry and order of possessed knowledge, and the satisfaction is a legitimate one. But this contemplative attitude is aesthetic, not intellectual. It is the same sort of joy that comes from viewing a finished picture or a well composed landscape. It would make no difference if the subject matter were totally different, provided it had the same harmonious organization. Indeed, it would make no difference if it were wholly invented, a play of fancy. Applicability to the world means not applicability to what is past and gone — that is out of the question by the nature of the case; it means applicability to what is still going on, what is still unsettled, in the moving scene in which we are implicated. The very fact that we so easily overlook this trait, and regard statements of what is past and out of reach as knowledge is because we assume the continuity of past and future. We cannot entertain the conception of a world in which knowledge of its past would not be helpful in forecasting and giving meaning to its future. We ignore the prospective reference just because it is so irretrievably implied.

Yet many of the philosophic schools of method which have been mentioned transform the ignoring into a virtual denial. They regard knowledge as something complete in itself irrespective of its availability in dealing with what is yet to be. And it is this omission which vitiates them and which makes them stand as sponsors for educational methods which an adequate conception of knowledge condemns. For one has only to call to mind what is sometimes treated in schools as acquisition of knowledge to realize how lacking it is in any fruitful connection with the ongoing experience of the students — how largely it seems to be believed that the mere appropriation of subject matter which happens to be stored in books constitutes knowledge. No matter how true what is learned to those who found it out and in whose experience it functioned, there is nothing which makes it knowledge to the pupils. It might as well be something about Mars or about some fanciful country unless it fructifies in the individual's own life.

At the time when scholastic method developed, it had relevancy to social conditions. It was a method for systematizing and lending rational sanction to material accepted on authority. This subject matter meant so much that it vitalized the defining and systematizing brought to bear upon it. Under present conditions the scholastic method, for most persons, means a form of knowing which has no especial connection with any particular subject matter. It includes making distinctions, definitions, divisions, and classifications for the mere sake of making them — with no objective in experience. The view of thought as a purely physical activity having its own forms, which are applied to any material as a seal may be stamped on any plastic stuff, the view which underlies what is termed formal logic is essentially the scholastic method generalized. The doctrine of formal discipline in education is the natural counterpart of the scholastic method.

The contrasting theories of the method of knowledge which go by the name of sensationalism and rationalism correspond to an exclusive emphasis upon the particular and the general respectively — or upon bare facts on one side and bare relations on the other. In real knowledge, there is a particularizing and a generalizing function working together. So far as a situation is confused, it has to be cleared up; it has to be resolved into details, as sharply defined as possible. Specified facts and qualities constitute the elements of the problem to be dealt with, and it is through our sense organs that they are specified. As setting forth the problem, they may well be termed particulars, for they are fragmentary. Since our task is to discover their connections and to recombine them, for us at the time they are partial. They are to be given meaning; hence, just as they stand, they lack it. Anything which is to be known, whose meaning has still to be made out, offers itself as particular. But what is already known, if it has been worked over with a view to making it applicable to intellectually mastering new particulars, is general in function. Its function of introducing connection into what is otherwise unconnected constitutes its generality. Any fact is general if we use it to give meaning to the elements of a new experience. "Reason" is just the ability to bring the subject matter of prior experience to bear to perceive the significance of the subject matter of a new experience. A person is reasonable in the degree in which he is habitually open to seeing an event which immediately strikes his senses not as an isolated thing but in its connection with the common experience of mankind.

Without the particulars as they are discriminated by the active responses of sense organs, there is no material for knowing and no intellectual growth. Without placing these particulars in the context of the meanings wrought out in the larger experience of the past — without the use of reason or thought — particulars are mere excitations or irritations. The mistake alike of the sensational and the rationalistic schools is that each fails to see that the function of sensory stimulation and thought is relative to reorganizing experience in applying the old to the new, thereby maintaining the continuity or consistency of life. The theory of the method of knowing which is advanced in these pages may be termed pragmatic. Its essential feature is to maintain the continuity of knowing with an activity which purposely modifies the environment. It holds that knowledge in its strict sense of something possessed consists of our intellectual resources — of all the habits that render our action intelligent. Only that which has been organized into our disposition so as to enable us to adapt the environment to our needs and to adapt our aims and desires to the situation in which we live is really knowledge. Knowledge is not just something which we are now conscious of, but consists of the dispositions we consciously use in understanding what now happens. Knowledge as an act is bringing some of our dispositions to consciousness with a view to straightening out a perplexity, by conceiving the connection between ourselves and the world in which we live.

Summary.

Such social divisions as interfere with free and full intercourse react to make the intelligence and knowing of members of the separated classes one-sided. Those whose experience has to do with utilities cut off from the larger end they subserve are practical empiricists; those who enjoy the contemplation of a realm of meanings in whose active production they have had no share are practical rationalists. Those who come in direct contact with things and have to adapt their activities to them immediately are, in effect, realists; those who isolate the meanings of these things and put them in a religious or so-called spiritual world aloof from things are, in effect, idealists. Those concerned with progress, who are striving to change received beliefs, emphasize the individual factor in knowing; those whose chief business it is to withstand change and conserve received truth emphasize the universal and the fixed — and so on. Philosophic systems in their opposed theories of knowledge present an explicit formulation of the traits characteristic of these cut-off and one-sided segments of experience — one-sided because barriers to intercourse prevent the experience of one from being enriched and supplemented by that of others who are differently situated.

In an analogous way, since democracy stands in principle for free interchange, for social continuity, it must develop a theory of knowledge which sees in knowledge the method by which one experience is made available in giving direction and meaning to another. The recent advances in physiology, biology, and the logic of the experimental sciences supply the specific intellectual instrumentalities demanded to work out and formulate such a theory. Their educational equivalent is the connection of the acquisition of knowledge in the schools with activities, or occupations, carried on in a medium of associated life.

Chapter Twenty-six:

Theories of Morals

1. The Inner and the Outer.

Since morality is concerned with conduct, any dualisms which are set up between mind and activity must reflect themselves in the theory of morals. Since the formulations of the separation in the philosophic theory of morals are used to justify and idealize the practices employed in moral training, a brief critical discussion is in place. It is a commonplace of educational theory that the establishing of character is a comprehensive aim of school instruction and discipline. Hence it is important that we should be on our guard against a conception of the relations of intelligence to character which hampers the realization of the aim, and on the look-out for the conditions which have to be provided in order that the aim may be successfully acted upon. The first obstruction which meets us is the currency of moral ideas which split the course of activity into two opposed factors, often named respectively the inner and outer, or the spiritual and the physical. This division is a culmination of the dualism of mind and the world, soul and body, end and means, which we have so frequently noted. In morals it takes the form of a sharp demarcation of the motive of action from its consequences, and of character from conduct. Motive and character are regarded as something purely "inner," existing exclusively in consciousness, while consequences and conduct are regarded as outside of mind, conduct having to do simply with the movements which carry out motives; consequences with what happens as a result. Different schools identify morality with either the inner state of mind or the outer act and results, each in separation from the other. Action with a purpose is deliberate; it involves a consciously foreseen end and a mental weighing of considerations pro and eon. It also involves a conscious state of longing or desire for the end. The deliberate choice of an aim and of a settled disposition of desire takes time. During this time complete overt action is suspended. A person who does not have his mind made up, does not know what to do. Consequently he postpones definite action so far as possible. His position may be compared to that of a man considering jumping across a ditch. If he were sure he could or could not make it, definite activity in some direction would occur. But if he considers, he is in doubt; he hesitates. During the time in which a single overt line of action is in suspense, his activities are confined to such redistributions of energy within the organism as will prepare a determinate course of action. He measures the ditch with his eyes; he brings himself taut to get a feel of the energy at his disposal; he looks about for other ways across, he reflects upon the importance of getting across. All this means an accentuation of consciousness; it means a turning in upon the individual's own attitudes, powers, wishes, etc.

Obviously, however, this surging up of personal factors into conscious recognition is a part of the whole activity in its temporal development. There is not first a purely psychical process, followed abruptly by a radically different physical one. There is one continuous behavior, proceeding from a more uncertain, divided, hesitating state to a more overt, determinate, or complete state. The activity at first consists mainly of certain tensions and adjustments within the organism; as these are coordinated into a unified attitude, the organism as a whole acts — some definite act is undertaken. We may distinguish, of course, the more explicitly conscious phase of the continuous activity as mental or psychical. But that only identifies the mental or psychical to mean the indeterminate, formative state of an activity which in its fullness involves putting forth of overt energy to modify the environment.

Our conscious thoughts, observations, wishes, aversions are important, because they represent inchoate, nascent activities. They fulfill their destiny in issuing, later on, into specific and perceptible acts. And these inchoate, budding organic readjustments are important because they are our sole escape from the dominion of routine habits and blind impulse. They are activities having a new meaning in process of development. Hence, normally, there is an accentuation of personal consciousness whenever our instincts and ready formed habits find themselves blocked by novel conditions. Then we are thrown back upon ourselves to reorganize our own attitude before proceeding to a definite and irretrievable course of action. Unless we try to drive our way through by sheer brute force, we must modify our organic resources to adapt them to the specific features of the situation in which we find ourselves. The conscious deliberating and desiring which precede overt action are, then, the methodic personal readjustment implied in activity in uncertain situations. This role of mind in continuous activity is not always maintained, however. Desires for something different, aversion to the given state of things caused by the blocking of successful activity, stimulates the imagination. The picture of a different state of things does not always function to aid ingenious observation and recollection to find a way out and on. Except where there is a disciplined disposition, the tendency is for the imagination to run loose. Instead of its objects being checked up by conditions with reference to their practicability in execution, they are allowed to develop because of the immediate emotional satisfaction which they yield. When we find the successful display of our energies checked by uncongenial surroundings, natural and social, the easiest way out is to build castles in the air and let them be a substitute for an actual achievement which involves the pains of thought. So in overt action we acquiesce, and build up an imaginary world in, mind. This break between thought and conduct is reflected in those theories which make a sharp separation between mind as inner and conduct and consequences as merely outer.

For the split may be more than an incident of a particular individual's experience. The social situation may be such as to throw the class given to articulate reflection back into their own thoughts and desires without providing the means by which these ideas and aspirations can be used to reorganize the environment. Under such conditions, men take revenge, as it were, upon the alien and hostile environment by cultivating contempt for it, by giving it a bad name. They seek refuge and consolation within their own states of mind, their own imaginings and wishes, which they compliment by calling both more real and more ideal than the despised outer world. Such periods have recurred in history. In the early centuries of the Christian era, the influential moral systems of Stoicism, of monastic and popular Christianity and other religious movements of the day, took shape under the influence of such conditions. The more action which might express prevailing ideals was checked, the more the inner possession and cultivation of ideals was regarded as self-sufficient — as the essence of morality. The external world in which activity belongs was thought of as morally indifferent. Everything lay in having the right motive, even though that motive was not a moving force in the world. Much the same sort of situation recurred in Germany in the later eighteenth and early nineteenth centuries; it led to the Kantian insistence upon the good will as the sole moral good, the will being regarded as something complete in itself, apart from action and from the changes or consequences effected in the world. Later it led to any idealization of existing institutions as themselves the embodiment of reason.

The purely internal morality of "meaning well," of having a good disposition regardless of what comes of it, naturally led to a reaction. This is generally known as either hedonism or utilitarianism. It was said in effect that the important thing morally is not what a man is inside of his own consciousness, but what he does — the consequences which issue, the charges he actually effects. Inner morality was attacked as sentimental, arbitrary, dogmatic, subjective — as giving men leave to dignify and shield any dogma congenial to their self-interest or any caprice occurring to imagination by calling it an intuition or an ideal of conscience. Results, conduct, are what counts; they afford the sole measure of morality. Ordinary morality, and hence that of the schoolroom, is likely to be an inconsistent compromise of both views. On one hand, certain states of feeling are made much of; the individual must "mean well," and if his intentions are good, if he had the right sort of emotional consciousness, he may be relieved of responsibility for full results in conduct. But since, on the other hand, certain things have to be done to meet the convenience and the requirements of others, and of social order in general, there is great insistence upon the doing of certain things, irrespective of whether the individual has any concern or intelligence in their doing. He must toe the mark; he must have his nose held to the grindstone; he must obey; he must form useful habits; he must learn self-control, — all of these precepts being understood in a way which emphasizes simply the immediate thing tangibly done, irrespective of the spirit of thought and desire in which it is done, and irrespective therefore of its effect upon other less obvious doings.

It is hoped that the prior discussion has sufficiently elaborated the method by which both of these evils are avoided. One or both of these evils must result wherever individuals, whether young or old, cannot engage in a progressively cumulative undertaking under conditions which engage their interest and require their reflection. For only in such cases is it possible that the disposition of desire and thinking should be an organic factor in overt and obvious conduct. Given a consecutive activity embodying the student's own interest, where a definite result

256

is to be obtained, and where neither routine habit nor the following of dictated directions nor capricious improvising will suffice, and there the rise of conscious purpose, conscious desire, and deliberate reflection are inevitable. They are inevitable as the spirit and quality of an activity having specific consequences, not as forming an isolated realm of inner consciousness.

2. The Opposition of Duty and Interest.

Probably there is no antithesis more often set up in moral discussion than that between acting from "principle" and from "interest." To act on principle is to act disinterestedly, according to a general law, which is above all personal considerations. To act according to interest is, so the allegation runs, to act selfishly, with one's own personal profit in view. It substitutes the changing expediency of the moment for devotion to unswerving moral law. The false idea of interest underlying this opposition has already been criticized (See Chapter X), but some moral aspects of the question will now be considered. A clew to the matter may be found in the fact that the supporters of the "interest" side of the controversy habitually use the term "self-interest." Starting from the premises that unless there is interest in an object or idea, there is no motive force, they end with the conclusion that even when a person claims to be acting from principle or from a sense of duty, he really acts as he does because there "is something in it" for himself. The premise is sound; the conclusion false. In reply the other school argues that since man is capable of generous self-forgetting and even self-sacrificing action, he is capable of acting without interest. Again the premise is sound, and the conclusion false. The error on both sides lies in a false notion of the relation of interest and the self.

Both sides assume that the self is a fixed and hence isolated quantity. As a consequence, there is a rigid dilemma between acting for an interest of the self and without interest. If the self is something fixed antecedent to action, then acting from interest means trying to get more in the way of possessions for the self — whether in the way of fame, approval of others, power over others, pecuniary profit, or pleasure. Then the reaction from this view as a cynical depreciation of human nature leads to the view that men who act nobly act with no interest at all. Yet to an unbiased judgment it would appear plain that a man must be interested in what he is doing or he would not do it. A physician who continues to serve the sick in a plague at almost certain danger to his own life must be interested in the efficient performance of his profession — more interested in that than in the safety of his own bodily life. But it is distorting facts to say that this interest is merely a mask for an interest in something else which he gets by continuing his customary services — such as money or good repute or virtue; that it is only a means to an ulterior selfish end. The moment we recognize that the self is not something ready-made, but something in continuous formation through choice of action, the whole situation clears up. A man's interest in keeping at his work in spite of danger to life means that his self is found in that work; if he finally gave up, and preferred his personal safety or comfort, it would mean that he preferred to be that kind of a self. The mistake lies in making a separation between interest and self, and supposing that the latter is the end to which interest in objects and acts and others is a mere means. In fact, self and interest are two names for the same fact; the kind and amount of interest actively taken in a thing reveals and measures the quality of selfhood which exists. Bear in mind that interest means the active or moving identity of the self with a certain object, and the whole alleged dilemma falls to the ground.

Unselfishness, for example, signifies neither lack of interest in what is done (that would mean only machine-like indifference) nor selflessness—which would mean absence of virility and character. As employed everywhere outside of this particular theoretical controversy, the term "unselfishness" refers to the kind of aims and objects which habitually interest a man. And if we make a mental survey of the kind of interests which evoke the use of this epithet, we shall see that they have two intimately associated features. (i) The generous self consciously identifies itself with the full range of relationships implied in its activity, instead of drawing a sharp line between itself and considerations which are excluded as alien or indifferent; (ii) it readjusts and expands its past ideas of itself to take in new consequences as they become perceptible. When the physician began his career he may not have thought of a pestilence; he may not have consciously identified himself with service under such conditions. But, if he has a normally growing or active self, when he finds that his vocation involves such risks, he willingly adopts them as integral portions of his activity. The wider or larger self which means inclusion instead of denial of relationships is identical with a self which enlarges in order to assume previously unforeseen ties.

In such crises of readjustment — and the crisis may be slight as well as great — there may be a transitional conflict of "principle" with "interest." It is the nature of a habit to involve ease in the accustomed line of activity. It is the nature of a readjusting of habit to involve an effort which is disagreeable — something to which a man has deliberately to hold himself. In other words, there is a tendency to identify the self — or take interest — in what one has got used to, and to turn away the mind with aversion or irritation when an unexpected thing which involves an unpleasant modification of habit comes up. Since in the past one has done one's duty without having to face such a disagreeable circumstance, why not go on as one has been? To yield to this temptation means to narrow and isolate the thought of the self — to treat it as complete. Any habit, no matter how efficient in the past, which has become set, may at any time bring this temptation with it. To act from principle in such an emergency is not to act on some abstract principle, or duty at large; it is to act upon the principle of a course of action, instead of upon the circumstances which have attended it. The principle of a physician's conduct is its animating aim and spirit — the care for the diseased. The principle is not what justifies an activity, for the principle is but another name for the continuity of the activity. If the activity as manifested in its consequences is undesirable, to act upon principle is to accentuate its evil. And a man who prides himself upon acting upon principle is likely to be a man who insists upon having his own way without learning from experience what is the better way. He fancies that some abstract principle justifies his course of action without recognizing that his principle needs justification.

Assuming, however, that school conditions are such as to provide desirable occupations, it is interest in the occupation as a whole — that is, in its continuous development — which keeps a pupil at his work in spite of temporary diversions and unpleasant obstacles. Where there is no activity having a growing significance, appeal to principle is either purely verbal, or a form of obstinate pride or an appeal to extraneous considerations clothed with a dignified title. Undoubtedly there are junctures where momentary interest ceases and attention flags, and where reinforcement is needed. But what carries a person over these hard stretches is not loyalty to duty in the abstract, but interest in his occupation. Duties are "offices" — they are the specific acts needed for the fulfilling of a function — or, in homely language — doing one's job. And the man who is genuinely interested in his job is the man who is able to stand temporary discouragement, to persist in the face of obstacles, to take the lean with the fat: he makes an interest out of meeting and overcoming difficulties and distraction.

3. Intelligence and Character.

A noteworthy paradox often accompanies discussions of morals. On the one hand, there is an identification of the moral with the rational. Reason is set up as a faculty from which proceed ultimate moral intuitions, and sometimes, as in the Kantian theory, it is said to supply the only proper moral motive. On the other hand, the value of concrete, everyday intelligence is constantly underestimated, and even deliberately depreciated. Morals is often thought to be an affair with which ordinary knowledge has nothing to do. Moral knowledge is thought to be a thing apart, and conscience is thought of as something radically different from consciousness. This separation, if valid, is of especial significance for education. Moral education in school is practically hopeless when we set up the development of character as a supreme end, and at the same time treat the acquiring of knowledge and the development of understanding, which of necessity occupy the chief part of school time, as having nothing to do with character. On such a basis, moral education is inevitably reduced to some kind of catechetical instruction, or lessons about morals. Lessons "about morals" signify as matter of course lessons in what other people think about virtues and duties. It amounts to something only in the degree in which pupils happen to be already animated by a sympathetic and dignified regard for the sentiments of others. Without such a regard, it has no more influence on character than information about the mountains of Asia; with a servile regard, it increases dependence upon others, and throws upon those in authority the responsibility for conduct. As a matter of fact, direct instruction in morals has been effective only in social groups where it was a part of the authoritative control of the many by the few. Not the teaching as such but the reinforcement of it by the whole regime of which it was an incident made it effective. To attempt to get similar results from lessons about morals in a democratic society is to rely upon sentimental magic.

At the other end of the scale stands the Socratic-Platonic teaching which identifies knowledge and virtue—which holds that no man does evil knowingly but only because of ignorance of the good. This doctrine is commonly attacked on the ground that nothing is more common than for a man to know the good and yet do the bad: not knowledge, but habituation or practice, and motive are what is required. Aristotle, in fact, at once attacked the Platonic teaching on the ground that moral virtue is like an art, such as medicine; the experienced practitioner is better than a man who has theoretical knowledge but no practical experience of disease and remedies. The issue turns, however, upon what is meant by knowledge. Aristotle's objection ignored the gist of Plato's teaching to the effect that man could not attain a theoretical insight into the good except as he had passed through years of practical habituation and strenuous discipline. Knowledge of the good was not a thing to be got either from books or from others, but was achieved through a prolonged education. It was the final and culminating grace of a mature experience of life. Irrespective of Plato's position, it is easy to perceive that the term knowledge is used to denote things as far apart as intimate and vital personal realization, — a conviction gained and tested in experience, — and a second- handed, largely symbolic, recognition that persons in general believe so and so — a devitalized remote information. That the latter does not guarantee conduct, that it does not profoundly affect character, goes without saying. But if knowledge means something of the same sort as our conviction gained by trying and testing that sugar is sweet and quinine bitter, the case stands otherwise. Every time a man sits on a chair rather than on a stove, carries an umbrella when it rains, consults a doctor when ill — or in short performs any of the thousand acts which make up his daily life, he proves that knowledge of a certain kind finds direct issue in conduct. There is every reason to suppose that the same sort of knowledge of good has a like expression; in fact "good" is an empty term unless it includes the satisfactions experienced in such situations as those mentioned. Knowledge that other persons are supposed to know something might lead one to act so as to win the approbation others attach to certain actions, or at least so as to give others the impression that one agrees with them; there is no reason why it should lead to personal initiative and loyalty in behalf of the beliefs attributed to them.

It is not necessary, accordingly, to dispute about the proper meaning of the term knowledge. It is enough for educational purposes to note the different qualities covered by the one name, to realize that it is knowledge gained at first hand through the exigencies of experience which affects conduct in significant ways. If a pupil learns things from books simply in connection with school lessons and for the sake of reciting what he has learned when called upon, then knowledge will have effect upon some conduct — namely upon that of reproducing statements at the demand of others. There is nothing surprising that such "knowledge" should not have much influence in the life out of school. But this is not a reason for making a divorce between knowledge and conduct, but for holding in low esteem this kind of knowledge. The same thing may be said of knowledge which relates merely to an isolated and technical specialty; it modifies action but only in its own narrow line. In truth, the problem of moral education in the schools is one with the problem of securing knowledge — the knowledge connected with the system of impulses and habits. For the use to which any known fact is put depends upon its connections. The knowledge of dynamite of a safecracker may be identical in verbal form with that of a chemist; in fact, it is different, for it is knit into connection with different aims and habits, and thus has a different import.

Our prior discussion of subject-matter as proceeding from direct activity having an immediate aim, to the enlargement of meaning found in geography and history, and then to scientifically organized knowledge, was based upon the idea of maintaining a vital connection between knowledge and activity. What is learned and employed in an occupation having an aim and involving cooperation with others is moral knowledge, whether consciously so regarded or not. For it builds up a social interest and confers the intelligence needed to make that interest effective in practice. Just because the studies of the curriculum represent standard factors in social life, they are organs of initiation into social values. As mere school studies, their acquisition has only a technical worth. Acquired under conditions where their social significance is realized, they feed moral interest and develop moral insight. Moreover, the qualities of mind discussed under the topic of method of learning are all of them intrinsically moral qualities. Open-mindedness, single-mindedness, sincerity, breadth of outlook, thoroughness, assumption of responsibility for developing the consequences of ideas which are accepted, are moral traits. The habit of identifying moral characteristics with external conformity to authoritative prescriptions may lead us to ignore the ethical value of these intellectual attitudes, but the same habit tends to reduce morals to a dead and machinelike routine. Consequently while such an attitude has moral results, the results are morally undesirable — above all in a democratic society where so much depends upon personal disposition.

4. The Social and the Moral. All of the separations which we have been criticizing — and which the idea of education set forth in the previous chapters is designed to avoid — spring from taking morals too narrowly, — giving them, on one side, a sentimental goody-goody turn without reference to effective ability to do what is socially needed, and, on the other side, overemphasizing convention and tradition so as to limit morals to a list of definitely stated acts. As a matter of fact, morals are as broad as acts which concern our relationships with others. And potentially this includes all our acts, even though their social bearing may not be thought of at the time of performance. For every act, by the principle of habit, modifies disposition — it sets up a certain kind of inclination and desire. And it is impossible to tell when the habit thus strengthened may have a direct and perceptible influence on our association with others. Certain traits of character have such an obvious connection with our social relationships that we call them "moral" in an emphatic sense — truthfulness, honesty, chastity, amiability, etc. But this only means that they are, as compared with some other attitudes, central: — that they carry other attitudes with them. They are moral in an emphatic sense not because they are isolated and exclusive, but

because they are so intimately connected with thousands of other attitudes which we do not explicitly recognize — which perhaps we have not even names for. To call them virtues in their isolation is like taking the skeleton for the living body. The bones are certainly important, but their importance lies in the fact that they support other organs of the body in such a way as to make them capable of integrated effective activity. And the same is true of the qualities of character which we specifically designate virtues. Morals concern nothing less than the whole character, and the whole character is identical with the man in all his concrete make-up and manifestations. To possess virtue does not signify to have cultivated a few namable and exclusive traits; it means to be fully and adequately what one is capable of becoming through association with others in all the offices of life.

The moral and the social quality of conduct are, in the last analysis, identical with each other. It is then but to restate explicitly the import of our earlier chapters regarding the social function of education to say that the measure of the worth of the administration, curriculum, and methods of instruction of the school is the extent to which they are animated by a social spirit. And the great danger which threatens school work is the absence of conditions which make possible a permeating social spirit; this is the great enemy of effective moral training. For this spirit can be actively present only when certain conditions are met.

(i) In the first place, the school must itself be a community life in all which that implies. Social perceptions and interests can be developed only in a genuinely social medium—one where there is give and take in the building up of a common experience. Informational statements about things can be acquired in relative isolation by any one who previously has had enough intercourse with others to have learned language. But realization of the meaning of the linguistic signs is quite another matter. That involves a context of work and play in association with others. The plea which has been made for education through continued constructive activities in this book rests upon the fact they afford an opportunity for a social atmosphere. In place of a school set apart from life as a place for learning lessons, we have a miniature social group in which study and growth are incidents of present shared experience. Playgrounds, shops, workrooms, laboratories not only direct the natural active tendencies of youth, but they involve intercourse, communication, and cooperation, — all extending the perception of connections.

(ii) The learning in school should be continuous with that out of school. There should be a free interplay between the two. This is possible only when there are numerous points of contact between the social interests of the one and of the other. A school is conceivable in which there should be a spirit of companionship and shared activity, but where its social life would no more represent or typify that of the world beyond the school walls than that of a monastery. Social concern and understanding would be developed, but they would not be available outside; they would not carry over. The proverbial separation of town and gown, the cultivation of academic seclusion, operate in this direction. So does such adherence to the culture of the past as generates a reminiscent social spirit, for this makes an individual feel more at home in the life of other days than in his own. A professedly cultural education is peculiarly exposed to this danger. An idealized past becomes the refuge and solace of the spirit; present-day concerns are found sordid, and unworthy of attention. But as a rule, the absence of a social environment in connection with which learning is a need and a reward is the chief reason for the isolation of the school; and this isolation renders school knowledge inapplicable to life and so infertile in character.

A narrow and moralistic view of morals is responsible for the failure to recognize that all the aims and values which are desirable in education are themselves moral. Discipline, natural development, culture, social efficiency, are moral traits — marks of a person who is a worthy member of that society which it is the business of education to further. There is an old saying to the effect that it is not enough for a man to be good; he must be good for something. The something for which a man must be good is capacity to live as a social member so that what he gets from living with others balances with what he contributes. What he gets and gives as a human being, a being with desires, emotions, and ideas, is not external possessions, but a widening and deepening of conscious life — a more intense, disciplined, and expanding realization of meanings. What he materially receives and gives is at most opportunities and means for the evolution of conscious life. Otherwise, it is neither giving nor taking, but a shifting about of the position of things in space, like the stirring of water and sand with a stick. Discipline, culture, social efficiency, personal refinement, improvement of character are but phases of the growth of capacity nobly to share in such a balanced experience. And education is not a mere means to such a life. Education is such a life. To maintain capacity for such education is the essence of morals. For conscious life is a continual beginning afresh.

Summary. The most important problem of moral education in the school concerns the relationship of knowledge and conduct. For unless the learning which accrues in the regular course of study affects character, it is futile to conceive the moral end as the unifying and culminating end of education. When there is no intimate organic connection between the methods and materials of knowledge and moral growth, particular lessons and modes of discipline have to be resorted to: knowledge is not integrated into the usual springs of action and the outlook on life, while morals become moralistic — a scheme of separate virtues.

The two theories chiefly associated with the separation of learning from activity, and hence from morals, are those which cut off inner disposition and motive — the conscious personal factor — and deeds as purely physical and outer; and which set action from interest in opposition to that from principle. Both of these separations are overcome in an educational scheme where learning is the accompaniment of continuous activities or occupations which have a social aim and utilize the materials of typical social situations. For under such conditions, the school becomes itself a form of social life, a miniature community and one in close interaction with other modes of associated experience beyond school walls. All education which develops power to share effectively in social life is moral. It forms a character which not only does the particular deed socially necessary but one which is interested in that continuous readjustment which is essential to growth. Interest in learning from all the contacts of life is the essential moral interest.

FREEDOM and CULTURE

Contents

CHAPTER ONE

The Problem of Freedom

WHAT is freedom and why is it prized? Is desire for freedom inherent in human nature or is it a product of special circumstances? Is it wanted as an end or as a means of getting other things? Does its possession entail responsibilities, and are these responsibilities so onerous that the mass of men will readily surrender liberty for the sake of greater ease? Is the struggle for liberty so arduous that most men are easily distracted from the endeavor to achieve and maintain it? Does freedom in itself and in the things it brings with it seem as important as security of livelihood; as food, shelter, clothing, or even as having a good time? Did man ever care as much for it as we in this country have been taught to believe? Is there any truth in the old notion that the driving force in political history has been the effort of the common man to achieve freedom? Was our own struggle for political independence in any genuine sense animated by desire for freedom, or were there a number of discomforts that our ancestors wanted to get rid of, things having nothing in common save that they were felt to be troublesome?

Is love of liberty ever anything more than a desire to be liberated from some special restriction? And when it is got rid of does the desire for liberty die down until something

3

else feels intolerable? Again, how does the desire for freedom compare in intensity with the desire to feel equal with others, especially with those who have previously been called superiors? How do the fruits of liberty compare with the enjoyments that spring from a feeling of union, of solidarity, with others? Will men surrender their liberties if they believe that by so doing they will obtain the satisfaction that comes from a sense of fusion with others and that respect by others which is the product of the strength furnished by solidarity?

The present state of the world is putting questions like these to citizens of all democratic countries. It is putting them with special force to us in a country where democratic institutions have been bound up with a certain tradition, the "ideology" of which the Declaration of Independence is the classic expression. This tradition has taught us that attainment of freedom is the goal of political history; that self-government is the inherent right of free men and is that which, when it is achieved, men prize above all else. Yet as we look at the world we see supposedly free institutions in many countries not so much overthrown as abandoned willingly, apparently with enthusiasm. We may infer that what has happened is proof they never existed in reality but only in name. Or we may console ourselves with a belief that unusual conditions, such as national frustration and humiliation, have led men to welcome any kind of government that promised to restore national self-respect. But conditions in our country as well as the eclipse of democracy in other countries compel us to ask questions about the career and fate of free societies, even our own.

There perhaps was a time when the questions asked

4

would have seemed to be mainly or exclusively political. Now we know better. For we know that a large part of the causes which have produced the conditions that are expressed in the questions is the dependence of politics upon other forces, notably the economic. The problem of the constitution of human nature is involved, since it is part of our tradition that love of freedom is inherent in its make-up. Is the popular psychology of democracy a myth? The old doctrine about human nature was also tied up with the ethical belief that political democracy is a moral right and that the laws upon which it is based are fundamental moral laws which every form of social organization should obey. If belief in natural rights and natural laws as the foundation of free government is surrendered, does the latter have any other moral basis? For while it would be foolish to believe that the American colonies fought the battles that secured their independence and that they built their government consciously and deliberately upon a foundation of psychological and moral theories, yet the democratic tradition, call it dream or call it penetrating vision, was so closely allied with beliefs about human nature and about the moral ends which political institutions should serve, that a rude shock occurs when these affiliations break down. Is there anything to take their place, anything that will give the kind of support they once gave?

The problems behind the questions asked, the forces which give the questions their urgency, go beyond the particular beliefs which formed the early psychological and moral foundation of democracy. After retiring from public office, Thomas Jefferson in his old age carried on a friendly philosophical correspondence with John Adams. In one of his letters he made a statement about existing American conditions and expressed a hope about their future estate: "The advance of liberalism encourages a hope that the human mind will some day get back to the freedom it enjoyed two thousand years ago. This country, which has given to the world the example of physical liberty, owes to it that of moral emancipation also, for as yet it is but nominal with us. The inquisition of public opinion overwhelms in practice the freedom asserted by the laws in theory." The situation that has developed since his time may well lead us to reverse the ideas he expressed, and inquire whether political freedom can be maintained without that freedom of culture which he expected to be the final result of political freedom. It is no longer easy to entertain the hope that given political freedom as the one thing necessary all other things will in time be added to it—and so to us. For we now know that the relations which exist between persons, outside of political institutions, relations of industry, of communication, of science, art and religion, affect daily associations, and thereby deeply affect the attitudes and habits expressed in government and rules of law. If it is true that the political and legal react to shape the other things, it is even more true that political institutions are an effect, not a cause.

It is this knowledge that sets the theme to be discussed. For this complex of conditions which taxes the terms upon which human beings associate and live together is summed up in the word *Culture*. The problem is to know what kind of culture is so free in itself that it conceives and begets political freedom as its accompaniment and consequence. What about the state of science and knowledge; of the arts,

6

fine and technological; of friendships and family life; of business and finance; of the attitudes and dispositions created in the give and take of ordinary day by day associations? No matter what is the native make-up of human nature, its working activities, those which respond to institutions and rules and which finally shape the pattern of the latter, are created by the whole body of occupations, interests, skills, beliefs that constitute a given culture. As the latter changes, especially as it grows complex and intricate in the way in which American life has changed since our political organization took shape, new problems take the place of those governing the earlier formation and distribution of political powers. The view that love of freedom is so inherent in man that, if it only has a chance given it by abolition of oppressions exercised by church and state, it will produce and maintain free institutions is no longer adequate. The idea naturally arose when settlers in a new country felt that the distance they had put between themselves and the forces that oppressed them effectively symbolized everything that stood between them and permanent achievement of freedom. We are now forced to see that positive conditions, forming the prevailing state of culture, are required. Release from oppressions and repressions which previously existed marked a necessary transition, but transitions are but bridges to something different.

Early republicans were obliged even in their own time to note that general conditions, such as are summed up under the name of culture, had a good deal to do with political institutions. For they held that oppressions of state and church had exercised a corrupting influence upon human nature, so that the original impulse to liberty had either been lost or warped out of shape. This was a virtual admission that surrounding conditions may be stronger than native tendencies. It proved a degree of plasticity in human nature that required exercise of continual solicitude —expressed in the saying that eternal vigilance is the price of liberty. The Founding Fathers were aware that love of power is a trait of human nature, so strong a one that definite barriers had to be erected to keep persons who get into positions of official authority from encroachments that undermine· free institutions. Admission that men may be brought by long habit to hug their chains implies a belief that second or acquired nature is stronger than original nature.

Jefferson at least went further than this. For his fear of the growth of manufacturing and trade and his preference for agrarian pursuits amounted to acceptance of the idea that interests bred by certain pursuits may fundamentally alter original human nature and the institutions that are congenial to it. That the development Jefferson dreaded has come about and to a much greater degree than he could have anticipated is an obvious fact. We face today the consequences of the fact that an agricultural and rural people has become an urban industrial population.

Proof is decisive that economic factors are an intrinsic part of the culture that determines the actual turn taken by political measures and rules, no matter what verbal beliefs are held. Although it later became the fashion to blur the connection which exists between economics and politics, and even to reprove those who called attention to it, Madison as well as Jefferson was quite aware of the connection and of its bearing upon democracy. Knowledge

8

that the connection demanded a general distribution of property and the prevention of rise of the extremely poor and the extremely rich, was however different from explicit recognition of a relation between culture and nature so intimate that the former may shape the patterns of thought and action.

Economic relations and habits cannot be set apart in isolation any more than political institutions can be. The state of knowledge of nature, that is, of physical science, is a phase of culture upon which industry and commerce, the production and distribution of goods and the regulation of services directly depend. Unless we take into account the rise of the new science of nature in the seventeenth century and its growth to its present state, our economic agencies of production and distribution and ultimately of consumption cannot be understood. The connection of the events of the industrial revolution with those of the advancing scientific revolution is an incontrovertible witness.

It has not been customary to include the arts, the fine arts, as an important part of the social conditions that bear upon democratic institutions and personal freedom. Even after the influence of the state of industry and of natural science has been admitted, we still tend to draw the line at the idea that literature, music, painting, the drama, architecture, have any intimate connection with the cultural bases of democracy. Even those who call themselves good democrats are often content to look upon the fruits of these arts as adornments of culture rather than as things in whose enjoyment all should partake, if democracy is to be a reality. The state of things in totalitarian countries may induce us to revise this opinion. For it proves that no mat-

9

ter what may be the case with the impulses and powers
that lead the creative artist to do his work, works of art
once brought into existence are the most compelling of
the means of communication by which emotions are stirred
and opinions formed. The theater, the movie and music
hall, even the picture gallery, eloquence, popular parades,
common sports and recreative agencies, have all been
brought under regulation as part of the propaganda agencies by which dictatorship is kept in power without being
regarded by the masses as oppressive. We are beginning to
realize that emotions and imagination are more potent in
shaping public sentiment and opinion than information and
reason.

Indeed, long before the present crisis came into being
there was a saying that if one could control the songs of a
nation, one need not care who made its laws. And historical study shows that primitive religions owe their
power in determining belief and action to their ability to
reach emotions and imagination by rites and ceremonies,
by legend and folklore, all clothed with the traits that
mark works of art. The Church that has had by far the
greatest influence in the modern world took over their
agencies of esthetic appeal and incorporated them into its
own structure, after adapting them to its own purpose, in
winning and holding the allegiance of the masses.

A totalitarian regime is committed to control of the
whole life of all its subjects by its hold over feelings, desires, emotions, as well as opinions. This indeed is a mere
truism, since a totalitarian state has to be total. But save as
we take it into account we shall not appreciate the intensity
of the revival of the warfare between state and church

that exists in Germany and Russia. The conflict is not the expression of the whim of a leader. It is inherent in any regime that demands the *total* allegiance of all its subjects. It must first of all, and most enduringly of all, if it is to be permanent, command the imagination, with all the impulses and motives we have been accustomed to call *inner*. Religious organizations are those which rule by use of these means, and for that reason are an inherent competitor with any political state that sets out on the totalitarian road. Thus it is that the very things that seem to us in democratic countries the most obnoxious features of the totalitarian state are the very things for which its advocates recommend it. They are the things for whose absence they denounce democratic countries. For they say that failure to enlist the whole make-up of citizens, emotional as well as ideological, condemns democratic states to employ merely external and mechanical devices to hold the loyal support of its citizens. We may regard all this as a symptom of a collective hallucination, such as at times seems to have captured whole populations. But even so, we must recognize the influence of this factor if we are ourselves to escape collective delusion—that totalitarianism rests upon external coercion alone.

Finally, the moral factor is an intrinsic part of the complex of social forces called culture. For no matter whether or not one shares the view, now held on different grounds by different groups, that there is no scientific ground or warrant for moral conviction and judgments—it is certain that human beings hold some things dearer than they do others, and that they struggle for the things they prize, spending time and energy in their behalf: doing so indeed to such an extent that the best measure we have of what is valued is the effort spent in its behalf. Not only so, but for a number of persons to form anything that can be called a community in its pregnant sense there must be values prized in common. Without them, any so-called social group, class, people, nation, tends to fall apart into molecules having but mechanically enforced connections with one another. For the present at least we do not have to ask whether values are moral, having a kind of life and potency of their own, or are but by-products of the working of other conditions, biological, economic or whatever.

The qualification will indeed seem quite superfluous to most, so habituated have most persons become to believing, at least nominally, that moral forces are the ultimate determinants of the rise and fall of all human societies—while religion has taught many to believe that cosmic as well as social forces are regulated in behalf of moral ends. The qualification is introduced, nevertheless, because of the existence of a school of philosophy holding that opinions about the values which move conduct are lacking in any scientific standing, since (according to them) the only things that can be *known* are physical events. The denial that values have any influence in the long run course of events is also characteristic of the Marxist belief that forces of production ultimately control every human relationship. The idea of the impossibility of intellectual regulation of ideas and judgments about values is shared by a number of intellectuals who have been dazzled by the success of mathematical and physical science. These last remarks suggest that there is at least one other factor in culture which needs some attention:—namely, the exist-

ence of schools of social philosophy, of competing ide-
ologies.

The intent of the previous discussion should be obvious.
The problem of freedom and of democratic institutions is
tied up with the question of what kind of culture exists;
with the necessity of free culture for free political institutions. The import of this conclusion extends far beyond its
contrast with the simpler faith of those who formulated
the democratic tradition. The question of human psychology, of the make-up of human nature in its original
state, is involved. It is involved not just in a general way
but with respect to its special constituents and their significance in their relations to one another. For every social
and political philosophy currently professed will be found
upon examination to involve a certain view about the constitution of human nature: in itself and in its relation to
physical nature. What is true of this factor is true of every
factor in culture, so that they need not here be listed again,
although it is necessary to bear them all in mind if we are
to appreciate the variety of factors involved in the problem of human freedom.

Running through the problem of the relation of this and
that constituent of culture to social institutions in general
and political democracy in particular is a question rarely
asked. Yet it so underlies any critical consideration of the
principles of each of them that some conclusion on the
matter ultimately decides the position taken on each special issue. The question is whether any one of the factors
is so predominant that it is *the* causal force, so that other
factors are secondary and derived effects. Some kind of

answer in what philosophers call a *monistic* direction has been usually given. The most obvious present example is the belief that economic conditions are ultimately the controlling forces in human relationships. It is perhaps significant that this view is comparatively recent. At the height of the eighteenth century, Enlightenment, the prevailing view, gave final supremacy to reason, to the advance of science and to education. Even during the last century, a view was held which is expressed in the motto of a certain school of historians: "History is past politics and politics is present history."

Because of the present fashion of economic explanation, this political view may now seem to have been the crotchet of a particular set of historical scholars. But, after all, it only formulated an idea consistently acted upon during the period of the formation of national states. It is possible to regard the present emphasis upon economic factors as a sort of intellectual revenge taken upon its earlier all but total neglect. The very word "political economy" suggests how completely economic considerations were once subordinated to political. The book that was influential in putting an end to this subjection, Adam Smith's *Wealth of Nations*, continued in its title, though not its contents, the older tradition. In the Greek period, we find that Aristotle makes the political factor so controlling that all normal economic activities are relegated to the household, so that all morally justifiable economic practice is literally domestic economy. And in spite of the recent vogue of the Marxist theory, Oppenheim has produced a considerable body of evidence in support of the thesis that political states are the result of military conquests in which defeated people have become subjects of their conquerors, who, by assuming rule over the conquered, begot the first political states.

The rise of totalitarian states cannot, because of the bare fact of their totalitarianism, be regarded as mere reversions to the earlier theory of supremacy of the political institutional factor. Yet as compared with theories that had subordinated the political to the economic, whether in the Marxist form or in that of the British classical school, it marks reversion to ideas and still more to practices which it was supposed had disappeared forever from the conduct of any modern state. And the practices have been revived and extended with the benefit of scientific technique of control of industry, finance and commerce in ways which show the earlier governmental officials who adopted "mercantile" economics in the interest of government were the veriest bunglers at their professed job.

The idea that morals ought to be, even if it is not, the supreme regulator of social affairs is not so widely entertained as it once was, and there are circumstances which support the conclusion that when moral forces were as influential as they were supposed to be it was because morals were identical with customs which happened in fact to regulate the relations of human beings with one another. However, the idea is still advanced by sermons from the pulpit and editorials from the press that adoption of say the Golden Rule would speedily do away with all social discord and trouble; and as I write the newspapers report the progress of a campaign for something called "moral re-armament." Upon a deeper level, the point made about the alleged identity of ethics with established customs

15

raises the question whether the effect of the disintegration of customs that for a long time held men together in social groups can be overcome save by development of new generally accepted traditions and customs. This development, upon this view, would be equivalent to the creation of a new ethics.

However, such questions are here brought up for the sake of the emphasis they place upon the question already raised: Is there any one factor or phase of culture which is dominant, or which tends to produce and regulate others, or are economics, morals, art, science, and so on only so many aspects of the interaction of a number of factors, each of which acts upon and is acted upon by the others? In the professional language of philosophy: shall our point of view be monistic or pluralistic? The same question recurs moreover about each one of the factors listed: —about economics, about politics, about science, about art. I shall here illustrate the point by reference not to any of these things but to theories that have at various times been influential about the make-up of human nature. For these psychological theories have been marked by serious attempts to make some one constituent of human nature *the* source of motivation of action; or at least to reduce all conduct to the action of a small number of alleged native "forces." A comparatively recent example was the adoption by the classic school of economic theory of self-interest as the main motivating force of human behavior; an idea linked up on its technical side with the notion that pleasure and pain are the causes and the ends-in-view of all conscious human conduct, in desire to obtain one and avoid the other. Then there was a view that self-interest and sympathy are the two components of human nature, as opposed and balanced centrifugal and centripetal tendencies are the moving forces of celestial nature.

Just now the favorite ideological psychological candidate for control of human activity is love of power. Reasons for its selection are not far to seek. Success of search for economic profit turned out to be largely conditioned in fact upon possession of superior power while success reacted to increase power. Then the rise of national states has been attended by such vast and flagrant organization of military and naval force that politics have become more and more markedly power-politics, leading to the conclusion that there is not any other kind, although in the past the power-element has been more decently and decorously covered up. One interpretation of the Darwinian struggle for existence and survival of the fittest was used as ideological support; and some writers, notably Nietzsche (though not in the crude form often alleged), proposed an ethics of power in opposition to the supposed Christian ethics of sacrifice.

Because human nature is the factor which in one way or another is always interacting with environing conditions in production of culture, the theme receives special attention later. But the shift that has occurred from time to time in theories that have gained currency about the "ruling motive" in human nature suggests a question which is seldom asked. It is the question whether these psychologies have not in fact taken the cart to be the horse. Have they not gathered their notion as to the ruling element in human nature from observation of tendencies that are marked in contemporary collective life, and then bunched these tendencies together in some alleged psychological "force" as their cause? It is significant that human nature was taken to be strongly moved by an inherent love of freedom at the time when there was a struggle for representative government; that the motive of self-interest appeared when conditions in England enlarged the role of money, because of new methods of industrial production; that the growth of organized philanthropic activities brought sympathy into the psychological picture, and that events today are readily converted into love of power as the mainspring of human action.

In any case, the idea of culture that has been made familiar by the work of anthropological students points to the conclusion that whatever are the native constituents of human nature, the culture of a period and group is the determining influence in their arrangement; it is that which determines the patterns of behavior that mark out the activities of any group, family, clan, people, sect, faction, class. It is at least as true that the state of culture determines the order and arrangement of native tendencies as that human nature produces any particular set or system of social phenomena so as to obtain satisfaction for itself. The problem is to find out the way in which the elements of a culture interact with each other and the way in which the elements of human nature are caused to interact with one another under conditions set by their interaction with the existing environment. For example, if our American culture is largely a pecuniary culture, it is not because the original or innate structure of human nature tends of itself to obtaining pecuniary profit. It is rather that a certain complex culture stimulates, promotes and consolidates na-

tive tendencies so as to produce a certain pattern of desires and purposes. If we take all the communities, peoples,
classes, tribes and nations that ever existed, we may be sure
that since human nature in its native constitution is the
relative constant, it cannot be appealed to, in isolation, to
account for the multitude of diversities presented by different forms of association.

Primitive peoples for reasons that are now pretty evident attribute magical qualities to blood. Popular beliefs
about race and inherent race differences have virtually perpetuated the older superstitions. Anthropologists are
practically all agreed that the differences we find in different "races" are not due to anything in inherent physiological structure but to the effects exercised upon members of
various groups by the cultural conditions under which they
are reared; conditions that act upon raw or original human
nature unremittingly from the very moment of birth. It has
always been known that infants, born without ability in
any language, come to speak the language, whatever it may
be, of the community in which they were born. Like most
uniform phenomena the fact aroused no curiosity and led
to no generalization about the influence of cultural conditions. It was taken for granted; as a matter of course it was
so "natural" as to appear inevitable. Only since the rise of
systematic inquiries carried on by anthropological students has it been noted that the conditions of culture which
bring about the common language of a given group produce other traits they have in common;—traits which like
the mother tongue differentiate one group or society from
others.

Culture as a complex body of customs tends to maintain

19

itself. It can reproduce itself only through effecting certain differential changes in the original or native constitutions of its members. Each culture has its own pattern, its own characteristic arrangement of its constituent energies. By the mere force of its existence as well as by deliberately adopted methods systematically pursued, it perpetuates itself through transformation of the raw or original human nature of those born immature.

These statements do not signify that biological heredity and native individual differences are of no importance. They signify that as they operate within a given social form, they are shaped and take effect *within* that particular form. They are not indigenous traits that mark off one people, one group, one class, from another, but mark differences in every group. Whatever the "white man's burden," it was not imposed by heredity.

We have traveled a seemingly long way from the questions with which we set out, so that it may appear that they had been forgotten on the journey. But the journey was undertaken for the sake of finding out something about the nature of the problem that is expressed in the questions asked. The maintenance of democratic institutions is not such a simple matter as was supposed by some of the Founding Fathers—although the wiser among them realized how immensely the new political experiment was favored by external circumstances—like the ocean that separated settlers from the governments that had an interest in using the colonists for their own purposes; the fact that feudal institutions had been left behind; that so many of the settlers had come here to escape restrictions upon religious beliefs and form of worship; and especially the existence of a vast territory with free land and immense unappropriated natural resources.

The function of culture in determining what elements of human nature are dominant and their pattern or arrangement in connection with one another goes beyond any special point to which attention is called. It affects the very idea of individuality. The idea that human nature is inherently and exclusively individual is itself a product of a cultural individualistic movement. The idea that mind and consciousness are intrinsically individual did not even occur to any one for much the greater part of human history. It would have been rejected as the inevitable source of disorder and chaos if it had occurred to anyone to suggest it:—not that their ideas of human nature on that account were any better than later ones but that they also were functions of culture. All that we can safely say is that human nature, like other forms of life, tends to differentiation, and this moves in the direction of the distinctively individual, and that it also tends toward combination, association. In the lower animals, physical-biological factors determine which tendency is dominant in a given animal or plant species and the ratio existing between the two factors—whether, for example, insects are what students call "solitary" or "social." With human beings, cultural conditions replace strictly physical ones. In the earlier periods of human history they acted almost like physiological conditions as far as deliberate intention was concerned. They were taken to be "natural" and change in them to be unnatural. At a later period the cultural conditions were seen to be subject in some degree to deliberate formation. For a time radicals then identified their policies with the belief that if only artificial social conditions could be got rid of human nature would produce almost automatically a certain kind of social arrangements, those which would give it free scope in its supposed exclusively individual character.

Tendencies toward sociality, such as sympathy, were admitted. But they were taken to be traits of an individual isolated by nature, quite as much as, say, a tendency to combine with others in order to get protection against something threatening one's own private self. Whether complete identification of human nature with individuality would be desirable or undesirable if it existed is an idle academic question. For it does not exist. Some cultural conditions develop the psychological constituents that lead toward differentiation; others stimulate those which lead in the direction of the solidarity of the beehive or anthill. The human problem is that of securing the development of each constituent so that it serves to release and mature the other. Cooperation—called fraternity in the classic French formula—is as much a part of the democratic ideal as is personal initiative. That cultural conditions were allowed to develop (markedly so in the economic phase) which subordinated cooperativeness to liberty and equality serves to explain the decline in the two latter. Indirectly, this decline is responsible for the present tendency to give a bad name to the very word *individualism* and to make *sociality* a term of moral honor beyond criticism. But that association of nullities on even the largest scale would constitute a realization of human nature is as absurd as to suppose that the latter can take place in beings whose only relations to one another are those entered into in behalf of exclusive private advantage.

The problem of freedom of cooperative individualities is then a problem to be viewed in the context of culture. The state of culture is a state of interaction of many factors, the chief of which are law and politics, industry and commerce, science and technology, the arts of expression and communication, and of morals, or the values men prize and the ways in which they evaluate them; and finally, though indirectly, the system of general ideas used by men to justify and to criticize the fundamental conditions under which they live, their social philosophy. We are concerned with the problem of freedom rather than with solutions: in the conviction that solutions are idle until the problem has been placed in the context of the elements that constitute culture as they interact with elements of native human nature. The fundamental postulate of the discussion is that isolation of any one factor, no matter how strong its workings at a given time, is fatal to understanding and to intelligent action. Isolations have abounded, both on the side of taking some one thing in human nature to be a supreme "motive" and in taking some one form of social activity to be supreme. Since the problem is here thought of as that of the ways in which a great number of factors within and without human nature interact, our next task is to ask concerning the reciprocal connections raw human nature and culture bear to one another.

Culture and Human Nature

IN the American as in the English liberal tradition, the idea of freedom has been connected with the idea of individuality, of *the* individual. The connection has been so close and so often reiterated that it has come to seem inherent. Many persons will be surprised if they hear that freedom has ever been supposed to have another source and foundation than the very nature of individuality. Yet in the continental European tradition the affiliation of the idea of freedom is with the idea of rationality. Those are free who govern themselves by the dictates of reason; those who follow the promptings of appetite and sense are so ruled by them as to be unfree. Thus it was that Hegel at the very time he was glorifying the State wrote a philosophy of history according to which the movement of historical events was from the despotic state of the Oriental World in which only one was free to the era dawning in Germany in the Western World in which *all* are free. The same difference in contexts that give freedom its meaning is found when representatives of totalitarian Germany at the present time claim their regime is giving the subjects of their state a "higher" freedom than can be found in democratic states, individuals in the latter being unfree because their lives are chaotic and undisciplined. The aroma of the continental tradition hangs about the sayings of those who settle so many social problems to their own satisfaction by invoking a distinction between liberty and license, identifying the former with "liberty under law"—for in the classic tradition law and reason are related as child and parent. So far as the saying assigns to law an origin and authority having nothing to do with freedom, so far, that is, as it affirms the impossibility of free conditions determining their own law, it points directly, even if unintentionally, to the totalitarian state.

We do not, however, have to go as far abroad as the European continent to note that freedom has had its practical significance fixed in different ways in different cultural contexts. For in the early nineteenth century there was a great practical difference between the English and the American theories, although both associated freedom with qualities that cause human beings to be *individuals* in the distinctive sense of that word. The contrast is so flat that it would be amusing if it were not so instructive. Jefferson, who was the original and systematic promulgator of the doctrine of free, self-governing institutions, found that the properties of individuals with which these institutions were most closely associated were traits found in the farming class. In his more pessimistic moments he even went so far as to anticipate that the development of manufacturing and commerce would produce a state of affairs in which persons in this country "would eat one another" as they did in Europe. In England, on the other hand, landed proprietors were the great enemy of the new freedom, which was connected in its social and political manifestations with the activities and aims of the manufacturing class.

It is not, of course, the bare fact of contrast which is instructive but the causes for its existence. They are not far to seek. Landed proprietors formed the aristocracy in Great Britain. The hold landed interests had over law-making bodies due to feudalism was hostile to the development of manufacturing and commerce. In the United States traces of feudalism were so faint that laws against primogeniture were about all that was needed to erase them. It was easy in this country to idealize the farmers as the sturdy yeomanry who embodied all the virtues associated with the original Anglo-Saxon love of liberty, the Magna Charta, and the struggle against the despotism of the Stuarts. Farmers were the independent self-supporting class that had no favors to ask from anybody, since they were not dependent for their livelihood nor their ideas upon others, owning and managing their own farms. It is a history that again would be amusing, were it not instructive, to find that as this country changed from an agrarian one to an urban industrial one, the qualities of initiative, invention, vigor and intrinsic contribution to progress which British *laissez-faire* liberalism had associated with manufacturing pursuits were transferred by American Courts and by the political representatives of business and finance from Jeffersonian individuals and given to the entrepreneurs who were individuals in the British sense.

In such considerations as these—which would be reinforced by an extensive survey of the history of the meaning given to freedom under different conditions—we have one instance and an important one of the relation of culture to the whole problem of freedom. The facts fall directly in line with the conclusion of the previous chapter: —a conclusion summed up in saying that the idea of Culture, which has become a central idea of anthropology, has such a wide sociological application that it puts a new face upon the old, old problem of the relation of the individual and the social. The idea of culture even outlaws the very terms in which the problem has been conceived, independently of its effect upon solutions proposed. For most statements of the problem have been posed as if there were some inherent difference amounting to opposition between what is called the individual and the social. As a consequence there was a tendency for those who were interested in theory to line up in two parties, which at the poles were so far apart that one denied whatever the other asserted. One party held that social conventions, traditions, institutions, rules are maintained only by some form of coercion, overt or covert, which encroaches upon the natural freedom of individuals; while the other school held that individuals are such by nature that the one standing social problem is the agencies by which recalcitrant individuals are brought under social control or "socialized." The term of honor of one school has been that of reproach of the other. The two extremes serve to define the terms in which the problem was put. Most persons occupy an intermediate and compromise position, one whose classic expression is that the basic problem of law and politics is to find the line which separates legitimate liberty from the proper exercise of law and political authority, so that each can maintain its own province under its own jurisdiction; law operating only when liberty oversteps its proper bounds, an operation supposed, during the heights of *laissez-faire* liberalism, to be legitimate only when police action was required to keep the peace.

Few persons today hold the extreme view of Hobbes, according to which human nature is so inherently anti-social that only experiences of the evil consequences of the war of all against all, reigning when human nature has free play, leads men, in connection with the motive of fear, to submit to authority—human nature even then remaining so intractable that the only assurance of safety against its marauding instincts is subjection to sovereignty. But in reading books on sociology it is still not uncommon to find the basic problem stated as if it were to list and analyze agencies by which individuals are tamed or "socialized." The chief difference of these writers from Hobbes consists in the fact that much less emphasis is laid upon merely political pressure, while it is recognized that there are tendencies in original human nature which render it amenable to social rules and regulations. As a result of the successful struggle of the new industrial class in England against the restrictions which existed even after the disappearance of feudalism in its grosser obvious forms, the favorite formula weighted the scales on the side of liberty, holding that each person was free as long as his actions did not restrict the freedom of others. The latter question, moreover, was never decided by going into the concrete consequences produced by the action of one person upon other persons. It was settled by a formal legal principle such as the equal right of every sane individual of a certain age to enter into contractual relations with others—no matter whether actual conditions gave equally free scope of action on both sides or made "free" contract a jug-handled affair.

However, the purpose is not to thrash over the old straw of these issues or similar issues on the moral side such as the respective parts of altruistic and egoistic tendencies in human nature. The point concerns the situation in which the problems were envisaged; the context of ideas in which as problems they were placed irrespective of the solution reached. With the intellectual resources now available, we can see that such opinions about the inherent make-up of human nature neglected the fundamental question of how its constituents are stimulated and inhibited, intensified and weakened; how their pattern is determined by interaction with cultural conditions. In consequence of this failure the views held regarding human nature were those appropriate to the purposes and policies a given group wanted to carry through. Those who wished to justify the exercise of authority over others took a pessimistic view of the constitution of human nature; those who wanted relief from something oppressive discovered qualities of great promise in its native makeup. There is here a field which has hardly been entered by intellectual explorers:— the story of the way in which ideas put forth about the makeup of human nature, ideas supposed to be the results of psychological inquiry, have been in fact only reflections of practical measures that different groups, classes, factions wished to see continued in existence or newly adopted, so that what passed as psychology was a branch of political doctrine.

We are thus brought back to the earlier statement of principle. The primary trouble has been that issues have been formulated as if they were matters of the structure of human beings on one side and of the very nature of social rules and authority on the other side, when in reality the underlying issue is that of the relation of the "natural" and the "cultural." Rousseau's attack upon the arts and sciences (as well as upon existing law and government) shocked his eighteenth century contemporaries, since the things he claimed to be operating to corrupt human nature, by creating inequality, were the very things they relied upon to generate unending human progress. Nevertheless, he stated, in a way, the problem of culture versus nature; putting, himself, all emphasis upon and giving all advantage to human nature; since to him, in spite of its raw unrefined condition, it retained its natural goodness as long as loss of original equality had not produced conditions that corrupted it. Kant and his German successors took up the challenge presented in the unpopular paradoxes of Rousseau. They tried to reverse his position; they interpreted all history as the continuing process of culture by which the original animal nature of man becomes refined and is transformed from the animal into the distinctively human.

But Rousseau and his opponents carried over into their discussion of the problem in its new form many of the elements derived from the traditional way of putting it. In German philosophy, the issue was further complicated by the rise of Nationalism which followed the encroachments of Napoleon. Though the Germans were defeated in war, in culture they were to be superior—an idea that still persists in the use of *Kultur* in German nationalistic propaganda, since superiority in culture gives the kind of rightful authority over peoples of less culture that the human

30

has over the animal. The French Revolution, as well as the writings of Rousseau, had the effect, in addition, of identifying in the minds of German thinkers the cause of culture with that of law and authority. The individual freedom, which was the "natural right" of mankind according to the philosophers of the Revolution, was to the German philosophers of the reaction but the freedom of primitive sensuous animality. A period of subjection to universal law, expressing the higher non-natural essence of humanity, was required to bring about a condition of "higher" and true freedom. Events in Germany, including the rise of totalitarianism, since the time this view was formulated, have borne the stamp of this idea. Anticipation of the existence of some ultimate and a final social state, different from original "natural" freedom and from present subordination, has played a role in all social philosophies—like the Marxist —framed under German intellectual influences. It has had the function once exercised by the idea of the Second Coming.

In no case, however, could the problem have taken its new form without the material made available by anthropological research. For what has been disclosed about the immense variety of cultures shows that the problem of the relation of individuals and their freedom to social convention, custom, tradition and rules has been stated in a wholesale form, and hence not capable of intelligent and scientific attack. Judged by the methods of the natural sciences, the procedure in the social field has been pre-scientific and anti-scientific. For science has developed by analytic observation, and by interpretations of observed facts on the basis of their relations to one another. Social theory has operated on the basis of general "forces," whether those of inherent natural "motives" or those alleged to be social.

Were it not for the inertia of habit (which applies to opinion as well as to overt acts) it would be astonishing to find today writers who are well acquainted with the procedure of physical science and yet appeal to "forces" in explanation of human and social phenomena. For in the former case, they are aware that electricity, heat, light, etc., are names for ways in which definite observable concrete phenomena behave in relation to one another, and that all description and explanation have to be made in terms of verifiable relations of observed singular events. They know that reference to electricity or heat, etc., is but a shorthand reference to relations between events which have been established by investigation of actual occurrences. But in the field of social phenomena they do not hesitate to explain concrete phenomena by reference to motives as forces (such as love of power), although these so-called forces are but reduplication, in the medium of abstract words, of the very phenomena to be explained.

Statement in terms of the relations of culture and nature to one another takes us away from vague abstractions and glittering generalities. Approach in its terms compels attention to go to the variety of cultures that exist and to the variety of constituents of human nature, including native differences between one human being and another—differences which are not just differences in quantity. The business of inquiry is with the ways in which specified constituents of human nature, native or already modified, *interact* with specified definite constituents of a given culture; conflicts and agreements between human nature on one side and social customs and rules on the other being *products* of specifiable modes of interaction. In a given community some individuals are in practical agreement with its existing institutions and others are in revolt—varying from a condition of moderate irritation and discontent to one of violent rebellion. The resulting differences when they are sufficiently marked to be labelled are the sources of the names conservative and radical, forward-looking or progressive and reactionary, etc. They cut across economic classes. For even revolutionaries have to admit that part of their problem is to create in an oppressed class consciousness of their servitude so as to arouse active protest.

This fact, so patent to even superficial observation, is sufficient disproof of the notion that the problem can be stated as one of the relation of *the* individual and *the* social, as if these names stood for any actual existences. It indicates that *ways of interaction* between human nature and cultural conditions are the first and the fundamental thing to be examined, and that the problem is to ascertain the effects of interactions between different components of different human beings and different customs, rules, traditions, institutions—the things called "social." A fallacy has controlled the traditional statement of the problem. It took results, good or bad—or both—of specific interactions as if they were original causes, on one side or the other, of what existed or else of what should exist.

It is just as certain, for example, that slaves have at times been contented with their estate of servitude as that a slave class has existed. It is certain that persons who have personally experienced no discomfort—except that commonly called moral—from existing conditions of oppression and injustice have been leaders in campaigns for equality and freedom. It is just as certain that inherent so-called social "instincts" have led men to form criminal gangs marked by certain mutual loyalties as that they have led men to co-operative activities. Now analytic observation of actual interactions to determine the elements operative on each side and their consequences is not easy in any case to execute. But recognition of its necessity is the condition of adequate judgment of actual events. Estimate of the value of any proposed policy is held back by taking the problem as if it were one of individual "forces" on one side and of social forces on the other, the nature of the forces being known in advance. We must start from another set of premises if we are to put the problem of freedom in the context where it belongs.

The questions which are asked at the beginning of the last chapter are genuine questions. But they are not questions in the abstract and cannot be discussed in a wholesale way. They are questions that demand discussion of cultural conditions, conditions of science, art, morals, religion, education and industry, so as to discover which of them in actuality promote and which retard the development of the native constituents of human nature. If we want individuals to be free we must see to it that suitable conditions exist:—a truism which at least indicates the direction in which to look and move.

It tells us among other things to get rid of the ideas that lead us to believe that democratic conditions automatically maintain themselves, or that they can be identified with fulfillment of prescriptions laid down in a constitution. Beliefs of this sort merely divert attention from what is going on, just as the patter of the prestidigitator enables him to do things that are not noticed by those whom he is engaged in fooling. For what is actually going on may be the formation of conditions that are hostile to any kind of democratic liberties. This would be too trite to repeat were it not that so many persons in the high places of business talk as if they believed or could get others to believe that the observance of formulae that have become ritualistic are effective safeguards of our democratic heritage. The same principle warns us to beware of supposing that totalitarian states are brought about by factors so foreign to us that "It can't happen here";—to beware especially of the belief that these states rest only upon unmitigated coercion and intimidation. For in spite of the wide use of purges, executions, concentration camps, deprivation of property and of means of livelihood, no regime can endure long in a country where a scientific spirit has once existed unless it has the support of so-called idealistic elements in the human constitution. There is a tendency in some quarters to treat remarks of this sort as if they were a sort of apology or justification of dictatorships and totalitarian states. This way of reacting to an attempt to find out what it is that commends, at least for a time, totalitarian conditions to persons otherwise intelligent and honorable, is dangerous. It puts hate in place of attempt at understanding; hate once aroused can be directed by skillful manipulation against other objects than those which first aroused it. It also leads us to think that we are immune from the disease to which others have given way so long as the evil things we see in totalitarianism are not known to be developing among us. The belief that only such things operate to harm democracy keeps us from being on our guard against the causes that may be at work undermining the values we nominally prize. It even leads us to ignore beams in our own eyes such as our own racial prejudices.

It is extremely difficult at a distance to judge just what are the appeals made to better elements in human nature by, say, such policies as form the Nazi faith. We may believe that aside from appeal to fear; from desire to escape responsibilities imposed by free citizenship; from impulses to submission strengthened by habits of obedience bred in the past; from desire for compensation for past humiliations, and from the action of nationalistic sentiments growing in intensity for over a century (and not in Germany alone), there is also love for novelty which in this particular case has taken the form of idealistic faith, among the youth in particular, of being engaged in creating a pattern for new institutions which the whole world will in time adopt. For one of the elements of human nature that is often discounted in both idea and practice is the satisfaction derived from a sense of sharing in creative activities; the satisfaction increasing in direct ratio to the scope of the constructive work engaged in.

Other causes may be mentioned, though with the admission that it is quite possible in good faith to doubt or deny their operation. There is the satisfaction that comes from a sense of union with others, a feeling capable of being intensified till it becomes a mystical sense of fusion with others and being mistaken for love on a high level of manifestation. The satisfaction obtained by the sentiment of communion with others, of the breaking down of barriers, will be intense in the degree in which it has previously been denied opportunity to manifest itself. The comparative ease with which provincial loyalties, which in Germany had been at least as intense and as influential as state-rights sentiments ever were in this country, were broken down; the similar ease, though less in degree, with which habitual religious beliefs and practices were subordinated to a feeling of racial and social union, would seem to testify that underneath there was yearning for emotional fusion. Something of this kind showed itself in most countries when they were engaged in the World War. For the time being it seemed as if barriers that separated individuals from one another had been swept away. Submission to abolition of political parties and to abolition of labor unions which had had great power would hardly have come about so readily had there not been some kind of a void which the new regime promised to fill. Just how far the fact of uniformity is accompanied by a sense of equality in a nation where class distinctions had been rigid, one can only guess at. But there is considerable ground for believing that it has been a strong factor in reconciling "humbler" folk to enforced deprivation of material benefits, so that, at least for a time, a sense of honorable equality more than compensates for less to eat, harder and longer hours of work—since it is psychologically true that man does not live by bread alone.

It might seem as if belief in operation of "idealistic" factors was contradicted by the cruel persecutions that have taken place, things indicative of a reign of sadism rather than of desire for union with others irrespective of birth and locale. But history shows that more than once social unity has been promoted by the presence, real or alleged, of some hostile group. It has long been a part of the technique of politicians who wish to maintain themselves in power to foster the idea that the alternative is the danger of being conquered by an enemy. Nor does what has been suggested slur over in any way the effect of powerful and unremitting propaganda. For the intention has been to indicate some of the conditions whose interaction produces the social spectacle. Other powerful factors in the interaction are those technologies produced by modern science which have multiplied the means of modifying the dispositions of the mass of the population; and which, in conjunction with economic centralization, have enabled mass opinion to become like physical goods a matter of mass production. Here also is both a warning and a suggestion to those concerned with cultural conditions which will maintain democratic freedom. The warning is obvious as to the role of propaganda, which now operates with us in channels less direct and less official. The suggestion is that the printing press and radio have made the problem of the intelligent and honest use of means of communication in behalf of openly declared public ends a matter of fundamental concern.

What has been said is stated by way of illustration, and it may, if any one desires, be treated as hypothetical. For even so, the suggestions serve to enforce the point that a social regime can come into enduring existence only as it satisfies some elements of human nature not previously afforded expression. On the other hand getting relief from saturation of elements that have become stale makes almost anything welcome if only it is different. The general principle holds even if the elements that are provided a

38

new outlet are the baser things in human nature: fear, suspicion, jealousy, inferiority complexes; factors that were excited by earlier conditions but that are now given channels of fuller expression. Common observation, especially of the young, shows that nothing is more exasperating and more resented than stirring up certain impulses and tendencies and then checking their manifestation. We should also note that a period of uncertainty and insecurity, accompanied as it is by more or less unsettlement and disturbance, creates a feeling that anything would be better than what exists, together with desire for order and stability upon almost any terms—the latter being a reason why revolutions are so regularly followed by reaction, and explain the fact that Lenin expressed by saying revolutions are authoritative, though not for the reason he gave.

Just which of these factors are involved in our own maintenance of democratic conditions or whether any of them are so involved is, at this juncture, not so pertinent as is the principle they illustrate. Negatively speaking, we have to get away from the influence of belief in bald single forces, whether they are thought of as intrinsically psychological or sociological. This includes getting away from mere hatred of abominable things, and it also means refusing to fall back on such a generalized statement as that Fascist institutions are expressions of the sort of thing to be expected in a stage of contracting capitalism, since they are a kind of final spasm of protest against approaching dissolution. We cannot reject out of hand any cause assigned; it may have some truth. But the primary need is to escape from wholesale reasons, as totalitarian as are the states

39

ruled by dictators. We have to analyze conditions by observations, which are as discriminating as they are extensive,
until we discover specific interactions that are taking place,
and learn to think in terms of interactions instead of force.
We are led to search even for the conditions which have
given the interacting factors the power they possess.

The lesson is far from being entirely new. The founders
of American political democracy were not so naively devoted to pure theory that they were unaware of the necessity of cultural conditions for the successful working of
democratic forms. I could easily fill pages from Thomas
Jefferson in which he insists upon the necessity of a free
press, general schooling and local neighborhood groups
carrying on, through intimate meetings and discussions, the
management of their own affairs, if political democracy
was to be made secure. These sayings could be backed up
by almost equally numerous expressions of his fears for
the success of republican institutions in South American
countries that had thrown off the Spanish yoke.

He expressly set forth his fear that their traditions were
such that domestic military despotisms would be substituted
for foreign subjugations. A background of "ignorance,
bigotry and superstition" was not a good omen. On one
occasion he even went so far as to suggest that the best
thing that could happen would be for the South American
states to remain under the nominal supremacy of Spain,
under the collective guarantee of France, Russia, Holland
and the United States, until experience in self-government
prepared them for complete independence.

The real source of the weakness that has developed later
in the position of our democratic progenitors is not that

they isolated the problem of freedom from the positive conditions that would nourish it, but that they did not—and in their time could not—carry their analysis far enough. The outstanding examples of this inability are their faith in the public press and in schooling. They certainly were not wrong in emphasizing the need of a free press and of common public schools to provide conditions favorable to democracy. But to them the enemy of freedom of the press was official governmental censorship and control; they did not foresee the non-political causes that might restrict its freedom, nor the economic factors that would put a heavy premium on centralization. And they failed to see how education in literacy could become a weapon in the hands of an oppressive government, nor that the chief cause for promotion of elementary education in Europe would be increase of military power.

The inefficacy of education in general, that is, apart from constant attention to all the elements of its constitution, is illustrated in Germany itself. Its schools were so efficient that the country had the lowest rate of illiteracy in the world, the scholarship and scientific researches of its universities were known throughout the civilized globe. In fact it was not so many years ago that a distinguished American educator held them up as models to be followed in this country if the weaknesses of our higher institutions were to be remedied. Nevertheless German lower schools furnished the intellectual fodder for totalitarian propaganda, and the higher schools were the centers of reaction against the German Republic.

The illustrations are simple, and perhaps too familiar to carry much force. Nevertheless they proclaim that while free institutions over a wide territory are not possible without a mechanism, like the press, for quick and extensive communication of ideas and information, and without general literacy to take advantage of the mechanism, yet these very factors create a problem for a democracy instead of providing a final solution. Aside from the fact that the press may distract with trivialities or be an agent of a faction, or be an instrument of inculcating ideas in support of the hidden interest of a group or class (all in the name of public interest), the wide-world present scene is such that individuals are overwhelmed and emotionally confused by publicized reverberation of isolated events. And after a century of belief that the Common School system was bound by the very nature of its work to be what its earlier apostles called a "pillar of the republic," we are learning that everything about the public schools, its official agencies of control, organization and administration, the status of teachers, the subjects taught and methods of teaching them, the prevailing modes of discipline, set *problems;* and that the problems have been largely ignored as far as the relation of schools to democratic institutions is concerned. In fact the attention these things have received from various technical standpoints has been one reason why the central question has been obscured.

After many centuries of struggle and following of false gods, the natural sciences now possess methods by which particular facts and general ideas are brought into effective cooperation with one another. But with respect to means for understanding social events, we are still living in the pre-scientific epoch, although the events to be understood are the consequences of application of scientific knowledge to a degree unprecedented in history. With respect to information and understanding of social events, our state is that on one side of an immense number of undigested and unrelated facts, reported in isolation (and hence easily colored by some twist of interest) and large untested generalizations on the other side.

The generalizations are so general in the sense of remoteness from the events to which they are supposed to apply that they are matters of opinion, and frequently the rallying cries and slogans of factions and classes. They are often expressions of partisan desire clothed in the language of intellect. As matters of opinion, they are batted hither and yon in controversy and are subject to changes of popular fashion. They differ at practically every point from scientific generalizations, since the latter express the relations of facts to one another and, as they are employed to bring together more facts, are tested by the material to which they are applied.

If a glance at an editorial page of a newspaper shows what is meant by untested opinions put forth in the garb of the general principles of sound judgment, the items of the news columns illustrate what is meant by a multitude of diverse unrelated facts. The popular idea of "sensational," as it is derived from the daily press, is more instructive as to meaning of *sensations* than is the treatment accorded that subject in books on psychology. Events are sensational in the degree in which they make a strong impact in isolation from the relations to other events that give them their significance. They appeal to those who like things raw. Ordinary reports of murders, love nests, etc., are of this sort, with an artificial intensity supplied by un-

43

usual size or color of type. To say that a response is intellectual, not sensational, in the degree in which its significance is supplied by relations to other things is to state a truism. They are two sets of words used to describe the same thing.

One effect of literacy under existing conditions has been to create in a large number of persons an appetite for the momentary "thrills" caused by impacts that stimulate nerve endings but whose connections with cerebral functions are broken. Then stimulation and excitation are not so ordered that intelligence is produced. At the same time the habit of using judgment is weakened by the habit of depending on external stimuli. Upon the whole it is probably a tribute to the powers of endurance of human nature that the consequences are not more serious than they are.

The new mechanisms resulting from application of scientific discoveries have, of course, immensely extended the range and variety of particular events, or "news items" which are brought to bear upon the senses and the emotions connected with them. The telegraph, telephone, and radio report events going on over the whole face of the globe. They are for the most part events about which the individuals who are told of them can do nothing, except to react with a passing emotional excitation. For, because of lack of relation and organization in reference to one another, no imaginative reproduction of the situation is possible, such as might make up for the absence of personal response. Before we engage in too much pity for the inhabitants of our rural regions before the days of invention of modern devices for circulation of information, we should recall that they knew more about the things that

44

affected their own lives than the city dweller of today is likely to know about the causes of his affairs. They did not possess nearly as many separate items of information, but they were compelled to know, in the sense of *understanding*, the conditions that bore upon the conduct of their own affairs. Today the influences that affect the actions performed by individuals are so remote as to be unknown. We are at the mercy of events acting upon us in unexpected, abrupt, and violent ways.

The bearing of these considerations upon the cultural conditions involved in maintenance of freedom is not far to seek. It is very directly connected with what now seems to us the over-simplification of the democratic idea indulged in by the authors of our republican government. They had in mind persons whose daily occupations stimulated initiative and vigor, and who possessed information which even if narrow in scope, bore pretty directly upon what they had to do, while its sources were pretty much within their control. Their judgment was exercised upon things within the range of their activities and their contacts. The press, the telegraph, the telephone and radio have broadened indefinitely the range of information at the disposal of the average person. It would be foolish to deny that a certain quickening of sluggish minds has resulted. But quite aside from having opened avenues through which organized propaganda may operate continuously to stir emotion and to leave behind a deposit of opinion, there is much information about which judgment is not called upon to respond, and where even if it wanted to, it cannot act effectively so dispersive is the material about which it is called upon to exert itself. The average person is surrounded today by readymade intellectual goods as he is by readymade foods, articles, and all kinds of gadgets. He has not the personal share in making either intellectual or material goods that his pioneer ancestors had. Consequently they knew better what they themselves were about, though they knew infinitely less concerning what the world at large was doing.

Self-government of the town-meeting type is adequate for management of local affairs, such as school buildings, district revenues, school local roads and local taxation. Participation in these forms of self-government was a good preparation for self-government on a larger scale. But such matters as roads and schools under existing conditions have more than local import even in country districts; and while participation in town meetings is good as far as it arouses public spirit, it cannot provide the information that enables a citizen to be an intelligent judge of national affairs—now also affected by world conditions. Schooling in literacy is no substitute for the dispositions which were formerly provided by direct experiences of an educative quality. The void created by lack of relevant personal experiences combines with the confusion produced by impact of multitudes of unrelated incidents to create attitudes which are responsive to organized propaganda, hammering in day after day the same few and relatively simple beliefs asseverated to be "truths" essential to national welfare. In short, we have to take into account the attitudes of human nature that have been created by the immense development in mechanical instrumentalities if we are to understand the present power of organized propaganda.

The effect of the increase in number and diversity of unrelated facts that now play pretty continuously upon

46

the average person is more easily grasped than is the influence of popular generalities, not checked by observed facts, over the interpretation put upon practical events, one that provokes acquiescence rather than critical inquiry. One chief reason for underestimation of the influence of generalities or "principles" is that they are so embodied in habits that those actuated by them are hardly aware of their existence. Or, if they are aware of them, they take them to be self-evident truths of common sense. When habits are so ingrained as to be second nature, they seem to have all of the inevitability that belongs to the movement of the fixed stars. The "principles" and standards which are stated in words and which circulate widely at a given time are usually only formulations of things which men do not so much believe in the intellectual sense of belief as live by unconsciously. Then when men who have lived under different conditions and have formed different life habits put forth different "principles," the latter are rejected as sources of some contagion introduced by foreigners hostile to our institutions.

Opinions are at once the most superficial and the most steel-plated of all human affairs. This difference between them is due to connection or lack of connection with habits that operate all but unconsciously. Verbal habits also exist and have power. Men continue to give assent to formulae after they have ceased to be more than linguistic rituals. Even lip-service has practical effect, that of creating intellectual and emotional divisions. The latter may not be deliberate hypocrisy. But they constitute that kind of insincerity, that incompatibility of actions with professions, which startles us in those cases in which it is clear that a person "believes" what he says in the sense that he is not even aware of its inconsistency with what he does. These gaps, these insincerities, become deeper and wider in times like the present when great change in events and practical affairs is attended with marked cultural lags in verbal formulations. And the persons who have first deceived themselves are most effective in misleading others. One of the most perplexing of human phenomena is the case of persons who do "in good faith" the sort of things which logical demonstration can easily prove to be incompatible with good faith.

Insincerities of this sort are much more frequent than deliberate hypocrisies and more injurious. They exist on a wide scale when there has been a period of rapid change in environment accompanied by change in what men do in response and by a change in overt habits, but without corresponding readjustment of the basic emotional and moral attitudes formed in the period prior to change of environment. This "cultural lag" is everywhere in evidence at the present time. The rate of change in conditions has been so much greater than anything the world has known before that it is estimated that the last century has seen more changes in the conditions under which people live and associate than occurred in thousands of previous years. The pace has been so swift that it was practically impossible for underlying traditions and beliefs to keep step. Not merely individuals here and there but large numbers of people habitually respond to conditions about them by means of actions having no connection with their familiar verbal responses. And yet the latter express dispositions saturated with emotions that find an outlet in words but not in acts.

No estim ite of the effects of culture upon the elements that now r ake up freedom begins to be adequate that does not take i ito account the moral and religious splits that are found in our very make-up as persons. The problem of creation of genuine democracy cannot be successfully dealt with in theory or in practice save as we create intellectual and moral integration out of present disordered conditions. Splits, divisions, between attitudes emotionally and congenially attuned to the past and habits that are forced into existence because of the necessity of dealing with present conditions are a chief cause of continued profession of devotion to democracy by those who do not think nor act day by day in accord with the moral demands of the profession. The consequence is a further weakening of the environing conditions upon which genuine democracy occurs, whether the division is found in business men, in clergymen, in educators or in politicians. The serious threat to our democracy is not the existence of foreign totalitarian states. It is the existence within our own personal attitudes and within our own institutions of conditions similar to those which have given a victory to external authority, discipline, uniformity and dependence upon The Leader in foreign countries. The battlefield is also accordingly here—within ourselves and our institutions.

The American Background

WHILE the sudden appearance of dictatorships and totalitarian states in Europe has raised such questions as have been asked, events in our country have put similar questions directly to ourselves. There is now raised the question of what was actually back of the formulation of the democratic faith a century and a half ago. Historians of the events that led up to the Declaration of Independence, the creation of the Confederation, and the adoption of the Federal Constitution tell us that what actually moved the leaders of the Rebellion against Great Britain were specific restrictions placed on industry and trade, together with levying of obnoxious taxes; and that what figured in doctrinal formulation as limitations upon inherent rights to freedom were in fact burdens imposed upon industrial pursuits from which persons of prestige and influence suffered economic losses.

Historians do not draw from their report of the concrete conditions, which, according to them, brought about the Revolution, the cynical conclusion that the ideas put forth about freedom, self-government and republican institutions were deliberate insincerities, intended to gull those who might otherwise have been indifferent in the struggle. It was rather that leaders generalized the particular restrictions from which they suffered into the general idea of oppression; and in similar fashion extended their efforts to get liberation from specific troubles into a struggle for liberty as a single all-embracing political ideal.

The distance, the physical distance, between American settlers and British officials was so generalized that it became a symbol of the idea that all government not self-imposed is foreign to human nature and to human rights. In the language of modern psychology, a local struggle of a group to obtain release from certain specific abuses was "rationalized" into a universal struggle of humanity to obtain freedom in the abstract; a rationalization which, like other idealizations springing up in times of crisis, enabled men better to endure hardship and summon up energy for a struggle continued long enough to get rid of immediate abuses. They do not, as historians, draw the inference that anything that goes by the name of an active love for liberty is in fact but an effort to get liberation from some specific evil; and that when that evil is got rid of, men turn from love of liberty to enjoyment of the specific goods they happen to possess. But their account of facts suggests a conclusion of this sort.

Nor have these historians drawn the conclusion that economic forces are the only forces that move men to collective action, and that the state of forces of production is the ultimate factor in determining social relations. Historians have not ventured so far afield into broad generalizations. But in their capacity as historians they have pointed out the effect of specific economic factors in producing the Revolution; and of changed economic conditions, after the confusion of the period of the Confederation, in producing special provisions of the Constitution. They have called attention to the enduring influence upon political events of conflict of interests between farmers and traders. They show, for example, that the difference in the policies advocated by the Republican and Federal parties respectively during the first thirty or forty years of the Republic represent a difference in the interests of agricultural and commercial sections and groups: conflicts reflected in the party attitudes toward centralized and decentralized government, the power of the judiciary, especially of the supreme court, free trade and protective tariff, foreign policies with regard to France and Great Britain, etc.

The striking differences in temper between the Declaration of Independence and the Constitution are cited. That the first should be much the more radical in tone is easily explicable by the fact that it was written by the man who was the firmest and most explicit of all the leaders of the movement in faith in democracy. Conditions conspired to make him the spokesman at this juncture as changed conditions brought others to the front in the Constitutional Convention while he was absent in France. In one case, it was necessary to rally all the forces in the country in the name of freedom against a foreign foe. In the other case, the most urgent need of men of established position seemed to be protection of established economic interests against onslaughts of a populace using liberty as a cloak for an attack upon order and stability. There was also need of compromise to unite various sections in a single federal government. Even during his own lifetime the author of the Declaration of Independence feared lest monarchical and oligarchical tendencies should undermine republic institutions.

Marxist social philosophy has made a sweeping generalization where historians have been content to point out specific economic conditions operating in specific emergencies. The Marxist has laid down a generalization that is supposed to state the law governing the movement and final outcome of all the social changes with which historians are occupied in detail. The generalization to which historians have pointed is rather a practical maxim: If you wish to secure a certain political result, you must see to it that economic conditions are such as to tend to produce that result. If you wish to establish and maintain political self-government, you must see to it that conditions in industry and finance are not such as to militate automatically against your political aim.

This position leaves room for a great variety of shades of political opinion and practical policies, all the way from political action to curb tendencies toward monopolies when the latter gain undue strength to attempts to "socialize" industry and finance. The Marxist position, on the other hand, lays down a universal law claimed to be scientific. It derives its practical policies from adherence, actual or alleged, to the "law" which is formulated.

Whether the effect of the economic factor upon political conditions is taken in its moderate or its extreme form, the facts involved tremendously complicate the problem of democratic freedom as it existed when the Union was formed. The original democratic theory was simple in its formulation because the conditions under which it took effect were simple. As theory, it postulated a widespread desire in human nature for personal freedom, for release from dominion over personal beliefs and conduct that is exercised from sources external to the individual. Combined with belief in this desire was the belief, generated by the conditions that had provoked the struggle for independence, that the chief enemy to realization of the desire was the tendency of government officials to extend their power without limit. Guarantees against this abuse were then supposed to be enough to establish republican government.

The latter belief was a manifestation of the existing struggle to obtain independence from British rule. It was strengthened by memories of conditions which had induced many persons to emigrate from the old country. In the case of Jefferson, the most intellectual and the most definitely explicit of all the American leaders, it was strengthened by what he personally observed during his residence in France. What he experienced there led him to give unqualified support to the saying that in a country with an oppressive government everyone is either hammer or anvil. The doctrine received negative support, if I may put the matter in that way, from the fact that there was in the late eighteenth century no other organized foe to freedom visible above the horizon—although Jefferson anticipated with dread the rise of such an enemy in the growth of manufacturing and commerce and the growth of cities of large populations.

In any event, the heart of the doctrine as a theory was a virtual identification of freedom with the very state of being an individual; and the extent of freedom that existed was taken to be the measure of the degree in which indi-

54

viduality was realized. It is possible to interpret this attitude and faith in two different ways. According to one view, it was an expression of pioneer conditions; it was appropriate to those conditions but was thoroughly naïve as a universal truth about the individual and about government. According to the other view, while the idea had some of the qualities of a dream, yet it expresses a principle to be maintained by deliberative effort if mankind is to have a truly human career. Call it dream or call it vision, it has been interwoven in a tradition that has had an immense effect upon American life.

However, the influence of tradition is two-fold. On the one hand, it leads to effort to perpetuate and strengthen the conditions which brought it into existence. But, on the other hand, a tradition may result in habits that obstruct observation of what is actually going on; a mirage may be created in which republican institutions are seen as if they were in full vigor after they have gone into a decline. There are now persons who think that the anti-democratic effect of economic development has so far destroyed essential democracy that only by the democratization or "socialization" of industry and finance can political democracy be restored. Whatever be thought of this view, its existence marks an immense change in conditions. To the Founding Fathers control of production and distribution of commodities and services by means of any political agency whatsoever would have seemed the complete nullification of all they were fighting for. A similar belief is still put forward with especial strength when a movement, even a moderate one, is made toward social control of business by political action—which is then denounced as the destruction of "Americanism." No matter which side (if either) is right, the division is not helpful to the democratic cause.

We are not concerned to decide which one of the different schools of social theory is correct. We are not even concerned at this point to judge whether governmental action is necessarily hostile to the maintenance of personal freedom or whether the latter becomes an empty shell if it is without organized political backing. The point is the complication of the earlier situation regarding freedom which is made evident when it is possible for men to urge that preservation of democratic institutions requires just that extension of governmental functions which to the authors of our tradition was the enemy to be fought. Whatever school of social philosophy be right, the situation has been transformed since the day when the problem of freedom and democracy presented itself as essentially a *personal* problem capable of being decided by strictly personal choice and action. For, according to the earlier idea, about all that was needed was to keep alive a desire for freedom, which is inherent in the very constitution of individuals, and jealously to watch the actions of governmental officials. Given these basic conditions, the means required for perpetuation of self-government were simple. They were exhausted in personal responsibility of officials to the citizens for whom they are but delegates; general suffrage; frequent elections so that officials would have to give frequent accounts of the way they had used their powers; majority rule; and keeping the units of government as small as possible so that people would know what their representatives were up to. These measures, combined with complete abolition of whatever traces of the feudal system had been

56

brought over from England, were sufficient, provided only a Bill of Rights was adopted and kept in force. For the Bill of Rights gave guarantees against certain specific encroachments of governmental officials upon personal freedom—such as arbitrary arrest. It instituted the moral and psychological conditions of self-government by securing the rights of free speech, free press, free assembly, free choice of creed. Given the maintenance of these rights, the few and simple governmental mechanisms mentioned would make secure the cause of free institutions.

That the conditions which influence the working of governmental mechanisms and the maintenance of the liberties constituting the Bill of Rights are infinitely more complex than they were a century and a half ago is evident beyond need for argument. Whether one is a believer in the necessity for increased social control of economic activities or in allowing the maximum possible of private initiative in industry and exchange, both sides must admit that impersonal forces have been set in motion on a scale undreamed of in the early days of the Republic.

Whatever else is reasonably settled or is unsettled, it is certain that the ratio of impersonal to personal activities in determining the course of events has enormously increased. The machine as compared with the hand tool is an impersonal agency. Free land and an abundance of unappropriated and unused natural resources—things which brought men in face-to-face personal connection with Nature and which also kept individual persons in pretty close contact with one another—have been replaced by impersonal forces working on a vast scale, with causes and effects so remote as not to be perceptible. A symbolic example is the change

57

in production between the day when a comparatively small number of "hired hands" worked side by side with their employer in a shop, and modern factories with hundreds or thousands of laborers who never see the owners (who moreover, as scattered shareholders, do not even know one another); and who come in contact with those immediately responsible for the conduct of the work only through delegates. Need for large capital to carry on mass production has also separated even personal financial liability from ownership. The whole significance of property has changed. "Private" property, in its old sense, has disappeared. Or, if another illustration is needed, there is the replacement of village life where everyone knew everybody else's character by congested cities in which persons do not know the persons who live on the same floor with them; and where, on the political side, they are called upon to vote for a large number of persons many of whom they cannot identify even by name.

The point is the intervention of an indefinite number of indefinitely ramifying conditions between what a person does and the consequences of his actions, including even the consequences which return upon him. The intervals in time and space are so extensive that the larger number of factors that decide the final outcome cannot be foreseen. Even when they can be anticipated, the results are produced by factors over which the average person has hardly any more control than he has over those which produce earthquakes. The recurrence of large-scale unemployment with sharp curtailment of production and the consequent instability of the conditions of both employer and employed is a convincing example. When all allowance is made for shiftlessness and incompetency of employees and for recklessness on the part of the employer, the recurrence of these crises cannot be understood save as evidence of the working of forces operating beyond the possibility of personal control. The current proposal to take away the vote from persons on relief, if it were supplemented by a proposal to deprive of suffrage all employers who are not paying their debts, would carry out the Biblical remark about taking away from those who have not even that which they seem to have.

When conditions that make for unemployment are as extensively ramified as they are at present, political action assumes an importance for workers, employed and unemployed, that it does not have when conditions are settled and opportunity for employment is fairly general and secure. There are movements in all industrialized countries to provide work by governmental projects; there are schemes for offsetting, by doles and official relief, evils that have resulted from the failure of industrialists and financial captains to provide the means of livelihood. The chiefly palliative nature of these measures is an evidence that symptoms rather than causes are dealt with; and this fact is in turn further proof that fundamental economic conditions are so far out of control that emergency measures are resorted to. The fact that evils are not remedied and in some respects are aggravated calls out a reaction in favor of return to individual initiative—that is, leaving the course of events to determination by those who have a store of resources in reserve.

There is little to prevent this reaction from making temporary headway. For the chief phenomenon in American

59

politics at the present time is that voters are moved primarily by the ills which are easily seen to be those from which they and the country at large are suffering. Since the evils are attributed more or less to the action of the party in power, there is a succession of swings back and forward as the relative impotency of this and that party and of this and that line of policy to regulate economic conditions, sufficiently to prevent widespread disaster, becomes clear. This impotency of existing political forms to direct the working and the social effects of modern industry has operated to generate distrust of the working of parliamentary institutions and all forms of popular government. It explains why democracy is now under attack from both the right and the left. There is no reason to suppose that a country as highly industrialized as the United States is immune.

While the possessing class is relatively more secure, yet its members are also profoundly unsettled by recurring cyclic depression. Emergence in political life of populist movements, square deals, new deals, accompanies depressions on the part of those most directly affected—farmers, factory laborers, etc., who are kept from uniting politically by divergence of immediate interests. But it would be foolish to suppose that the well-to-do class, the class of employers and investors, is not unsettled in a way that stirs it to political action to strengthen its hold on the agencies of political action. As the activities increase of the groups which are radical from the standpoint of the possessing class, and especially as they fail to effect a fundamental remedy of the situation, the activities of the favored economic class increase. When disorders appear on any considerable scale, the adherence of the middle class to the side of "law and order" is won. Ironically enough, the desire for security which proceeds from the two groups of very different economic status combines to increase readiness to surrender democratic forms of action. The coalescence of desire for security from two opposite sources has been a factor in the substitution of dictators for parliaments in European countries. The danger of the rise of an American Fascist movement in this country comes from a similar source. It is absurd to suppose that the class having relatively the superior economic status can promote a dictatorship unless it has strong popular support—which means the support of those relatively at a disadvantage. "Security" is a word covering a great diversity of interests, and all of them have a bearing upon the conditions required for maintenance of democracy.

In brief, economic developments which could not possibly have been anticipated when our political forms took shape have created confusion and uncertainty in the working of the agencies of popular government, and thereby have subjected the idea of democracy to basic strain. The change in conditions goes far beyond the particular consequences which Jefferson feared as a result of growth of manufacturing and trade at the expense of agriculture. The strengthening of the political power of laborers that occurred in Great Britain as the consequence of industrialization, and the part played by this factor in the liberalization of government, were not anticipated by him. In so far, there is no special cause for surprise in the fact that the interests originally represented by Jefferson and Hamilton have now changed places with respect to exercise of federal political power. For Jeffersonian principles of self-government, of the prime authority of the people, of general happiness or welfare as the end of government, can be appealed to in support of policies that are opposite to those urged by Jefferson in his day.

The real problem is deeper. There is no well-defined continuity of political movement because of the confusion that exists in general social movements. That the general trend is toward increase of public control of private industry and finance in the United States as in other countries is undeniable. But the movement is not clear-cut in theory nor are its consequences consistent in practice. In fact, there is one thesis of Herbert Spencer that could now be revived with a good deal of evidence in its support: namely, the economic situation is so complex, so intricate in the interdependence of delicately balanced factors, that planned policies initiated by public authority are sure to have consequences totally unforeseeable,—often the contrary of what was intended—as has happened in this country rather notably in connection with some of the measures undertaken for control of agricultural production.

So far I have been speaking of the fairly direct impact of economic conditions upon democratic political habits and beliefs. The mining and sapping have not begun to go so far in this country as in European countries which have adopted some form of National Socialism. But uncertainty and confusion and increasing scepticism about the relevancy of political democracy to present conditions, have been created. In this connection another effect of change from conditions which relatively were capable of being seen and regulated by personal skill and personal insight must be noted. The comparative helplessness of persons in their strictly singular capacities to influence the course of events expresses itself in formation of combinations in order to secure protection from too destructive impact of impersonal forces. That groups now occupy much the same place that was occupied earlier by individuals is almost a commonplace of writers on sociology. For example, trades unions for collective bargaining in regulation of wages, hours and physical conditions of work are produced on one side; pools, mergers, syndicates, trusts and employers' associations, often with command of armed strike-breakers, are generated on the other side. The theory of the self-actuated and self-governing individual receives a rude shock when massed activity has a potency which individual effort can no longer claim.

The growth of organized combinations has had an effect on that part of democratic doctrine which held that all men should be free as well as equal. The doctrine of equality never meant what some of its critics supposed it to mean. It never asserted equality of natural gifts. It was a moral, a political and legal principle, not a psychological one. Thomas Jefferson believed as truly in a "natural aristocracy" as did John Adams. The existence of marked psychological inequalities was indeed one of the reasons why it was considered so important to establish political and legal equality. For otherwise those of superior endowment might, whether intentionally or without deliberation, reduce those of inferior capacity to a condition of virtual servitude. The words "nature" and "natural" are among the most ambiguous of all the words used to justify courses of action. Their very ambiguity is one source of their use in defense of any measure and end regarded as desirable. The words

63

mean what is native, what is original or innate, what exists at birth in distinction from what is acquired by cultivation and as a consequence of experience. But it also means that which men have got used to, inured to by custom, that imagination can hardly conceive of anything different. Habit is second nature and second nature under ordinary circumstances as potent and urgent as first nature. Again, nature has a definitely moral import; that which is *normal* and hence is right; that which should be.

The assertion that men are free and equal by nature unconsciously, possibly deliberately, took advantage of the prestige possessed by what is "natural" in the first two senses to reinforce the moral force of the word. That "naturalness" in the moral sense provided the imperative ethical foundation of politics and law was, however, the axiomatic premise of democratic theory. Exercise of a liberty which was taken to be a moral right has in the course of events, especially economic events, seriously threatened the moral right to legal and political equality. While we may not believe that the revolutionary effect of steam, electricity, etc., has nullified moral faith in equality, their operation has produced a new difficult problem. The effect of statutes, of administrative measures, of judicial decisions, upon the maintenance of equality and freedom cannot be estimated in terms of fairly direct personal consequences. We have first to estimate their effects upon complicated social conditions (largely a matter of guesswork), and then speculate what will be the effect of the new social conditions upon individual persons.

Even if everybody, no matter how unequal in other endowments, possessed in like measure the faculty of reason or of common sense with which the optimistic rationalism of the eighteenth century supposed men to be equipped, the faculty would not go far in judging causes and effects of political and legal action at the present time. What purports to be experiment in the social field is very different from experiment in natural science; it is rather a process of trial and error accompanied with some degree of hope and a great deal of talk. Legislation is a matter of more or less intelligent improvisation aiming at palliating conditions by means of patchwork policies. The apparent alternative seems to be a concentration of power that points toward ultimate dictatorship. Since at best legislation can only pass measures in general terms, which are not self-interpreting much less self-applying, and since it is a costly and uncertain process to wait upon decisions of the courts to ascertain what laws mean in the concrete, administrative bodies possessed of large powers are multiplied—in spite of their inconsistency with the doctrine of the three-fold division of powers that is still the nominal constitutional theory. Persons of a liberal outlook, captured by fear of dictatorship, join with persons whose special and anti-social interests are unfavorably affected by the action of these commissions and indulge in wholesale attack—failing to see that new administrative bodies are so imperatively needed that the real problem is that of building up an intelligent and capable civil-service under conditions that will operate against formation of rigid bureaucracies.

The point which is here pertinent is that early theory and practice assumed an inherent, and so to say pre-established, harmony between liberty and equality. As liberty has been practiced in industry and trade, the economic inequalities produced have reacted against the existence of equality of opportunity. Only those who have a special cause to plead will hold that even in the most democratic countries, under the most favorable conditions, have children of the poor the same chances as those of the well-to-do, even in a thing like schooling which is supported at public expense. And it is no consoling offset that the children of the rich often suffer because of the one-sided conditions under which they grow up.

The way in which the problem of the relation of liberty and equality was earlier conceived is perhaps most clearly exhibited in the pains taken in the French Revolution to prevent combinations and associations from growing up, even those of a voluntary sort; so convinced were the leaders of the revolutionary doctrine of Liberty, Equality and Fraternity that combinations are hostile to liberty. The laws against trade unions as conspiracies, which existed in England, had a very different source. But fear of combination and organization from whatever source it has emanated, liberal or reactionary, gives evidence of the existence of a problem. Even the late President Eliot voiced a not uncommon belief of a certain type of liberal in his jealous fear lest the growth of labor unions put restrictions upon the liberty of wage-earners to work when and where and how they individually liked, an attitude that still appears on a large scale when it is a question of the closed shop. Persons who are favorable "in principle" to collective bargaining shrink when the principle is systematically applied. Once more the point here pertinent is not who is right and who is wrong, but the fact that the conditions of industry and commerce produced by existing technologies have

66

created in a wholly unanticipated way the problem of the relation of organization and freedom—with what philosophers call an antinomy as a result.

For there are convincing arguments both that individuals can be free only in connection with large-scale organizations and that such organizations are limitations of freedom. In any case, the organized associations of wage-workers in labor unions and of capitalistic employers in pools, combines, mergers, trusts, syndicates, gentlemen's agreements, are two aspects of the same process; while that indefinite amorphous thing called the consuming public tends by turns to be about equally suspicious of both, according to which one seems most active at a given time in producing a visible inconvenience. Just how mass-production and mass-distribution together with elimination of spatial barriers by speedy transportation and communication could have come into existence without consolidation and concentration on a large scale it is impossible to explain. And yet many who adhere to the letter rather than to the spirit of the early formulation of democratic faith will be found deploring or denouncing one or the other of the two forms of organizations that had come into existence as destructive of the ideals of liberty and equality—a fact which proves that a new type of problem has come into existence, whatever be its solution.

Growing distrust of the efficacy of parliamentary bodies is, as has been intimated, a result of the increased complexity of events. How can a collection of men, selected chiefly upon grounds of party availability, have either the knowledge or the skill required to cope with such extensive interlocking conditions as now exist? Some measure of conflict between the legislative body and the executive is an old story in American life whenever the President has happened to have strong convictions of his own; and it is a fact of a wider history than the American that in the case of such a conflict the executive tends to set himself up as an agent of the masses and the legislative body to be so selected as to be close to special interests. Difficulties in the way of effective action by law-making bodies in meeting actual conditions are increased by the general belief that they, with the courts and with administrative bodies, are favorable to special interests, by association and by education and at times by corruption. Distrust gives both the rabble-rouser and the would-be dictator their opportunities. The former speaks in words for the oppressed mass against oppression; in historic fact he has usually been an agent, willing or unknowing, of a new form of oppression. As Huey Long is reported to have said, Fascism would come in this country under the name of protecting democracy from its enemies.

Any adequate discussion of the present relations of politics and economics would have to extend to conditions in village, city, country, state and nation, and its conclusions would fill volumes. Its conclusions would enforce in detail the thesis that the interconnections and interdependence of industry and government puts a radically new face upon the problem of democratic policies. I shall mention but one more fact of those that could be cited. Modern industry could not have reached its present development without legalization of the corporation. The corporation is a creature of the state: that is, of political action. It has no existence save by the action of legislatures and courts. Many of the

68

earlier arguments for limitation and extreme decentralization of political power were virtually outlawed when the first statute authorizing the formation of business corporations was passed. The bitter struggle in this country between business interests and governmental actions has been in large degree a struggle to see whether the child begot by the state or the progenitor should control the subsequent activities of the parent. Operation of the state-created corporation under the decisions of the courts is proof positive that the careers of politics and business cross and mix in intimate and manifold ways, all of them unforseeable when our governmental arrangements took shape. Epigrams about the difference between the day of the stagecoach and of the railway and airplane are at best only suggestions of the enormous change in human relationships that has been produced by change in the means by which industry is carried on. The new relations require a new determination of rights and duties. The determination of them made during the time when the chief problem was that of maintaining peaceful relations between persons as persons is not adequate to determine rights and obligations when large combinations have largely replaced individual persons as the units of effective action. The very necessity for change only makes urgent the question of whether the existing agencies of democracy are competent to effect the change.

This is the basic question pointed to by the considerations which have been barely sketched. It is the problem which has precedence over the various plans and policies that are urged from one quarter or another. Consider, as an example, the argument that since the *processes* of industry, on the side of both labor and capital, have become collective, ownership and control must also be collective, resulting in elimination of private income from rent, interest and dividends. From the standpoint of democracy, this end, which is put forward in the interest of maintenance of democracy, raises the problem of the possibility of its execution by democratic methods. Can the change be effected by democratic means? After it is effected, supposing that it is, can production and distribution of goods and services be effected except by a centralized power that is destructive of democracy? The first of these two questions finds a profound split existing among professed socialists. Some of them hold the transition can be effected by recognized democratic means. But a larger and at present more vigorous section holds that democratic states are inherently bound up with just the things to be eliminated. Hence it is absurd— or, worse, deliberate deception—to believe the change can be effected by any means save violent overthrow of existing political governments and transfer of power to representatives of workers, urban factory workers at that. According to this view, the political state always has been and by its very nature is an arm of the dominant political class, and as long as that class is bourgeois capitalism, it is axiomatic with them that change must proceed from its complete overthrow.

Suppose the great change has come about, whether by one procedure or the other, what then? Asking the question is almost equivalent to calling attention to the relatively slight attention the underlying issue has received. For the most part the answer is to the effect that sufficient to the day is the evil or the good thereof. Since it would be utopian to try to imagine the details of a social state such as has never existed, energies should be taken up either with bringing about the violent revolution or with the educative process required for a peaceful transition to a socialist society. Many socialists of the latter type remain within our democratic tradition in believing that the continued use of democratic methods will mature those methods so that they will be effective in dealing with special problems as the latter arise. Nevertheless, the fact that popular ideas about socialism identify it with state or government socialism, while democratic socialists are strongly opposed to the latter—unless perhaps as a transitional stage—shows that the problem has not had a great deal of attention, syndicalist socialists being the faction that has considered it most explicitly.

So far social control of industry has mostly taken the form of regulation or ownership exercised under governmental auspices by governmental officials. This is so in National Socialist, in Bolshevist Socialist countries, and in democratic countries. Neither theory nor practical experience has as yet shown that state socialism will be essentially different from state capitalism. Even if we are obliged to abandon permanently the earlier belief that governmental action is by its own momentum hostile to free self-government, we are far from having refuted the evidence of history that officials who have political power will use it arbitrarily. Belief in what is sometimes called taking industry out of private hands is naïve until it is shown that the new private—or personal—hands to which it is confided are so controlled that they are reasonably sure to work in behalf of public ends. I am not saying the problem cannot be solved democratically nor that "socialization" of industry is bound to be followed by the regimentation so freely predicted by adherents of *laissez-faire* individualism. What I am saying is that the issue of democracy has taken a new form, where not much experience is available about the relation of economic factors, as they now operate, to democratic ends and methods.

In the absence of adequate experience, the tendency is to set up wholesale theories in opposition to one another; the current statement of the human problem as individualism versus socialism being both a reflex expression of the divisions in the economic factors of present society, and an example of wholesale opposition. In such an opposition of ideas, each theory thrives on the weaknesses of the other one; confusion is thereby increased. If it is utopian to expect a new social order will be ushered in as soon as industry is "socialized"—with little idea of what that means save negatively, or abolition of private profit, interest, rent and returns from fixed investment—it is highly unrealistic to go on repeating phrases about the connection of industry with personal independence, initiative and other desirable qualities that had a meaning in agrarian pioneer conditions. The idea of a pre-established harmony between the existing so-called capitalistic regime and democracy is as absurd a piece of metaphysical speculation as human history has ever evolved.

The strife of interests, parties and factions is especially harmful since the problem is a common human one, the ways in which it is dealt with and their results affecting all alike. The first necessity is study of the scientifically co-operative type. It is theoretically conceivable that strife of interests might bring to clearer recognition the different interests that are involved and that have to be harmonized in any enduring solution. As long, however, as conflict is conducted on the assumption, upon each side, that there is already possession of the truth, a position that amounts to denial for the need of any scientific examination of conditions in order to determine the policies that should be undertaken, the rivalry of parties will be a source of division and confusion.

The discussion of this chapter has been one-sided in its emphasis upon the economic phase of our culture. But industrialization and commercialization play such a part in determining the qualities of present culture that the primary need for analysis of its conditions is made especially clear. The facts that justify economic emphasis do not prove, however, that the issue of co-operative democratic freedom can be settled by dealing directly and exclusively with the economic aspect, if only because command of the means which would be needed to effect desirable changes in industry and in the distribution of income can be achieved only by the aid of correlative changes in science, morals and other phases of our common experience. The facts bring out in sharp outline that as yet the full conditions, economic and legal, for a completely democratic experience have not existed. Upon both the negative and the positive side, the facts suggest the importance of critical examination of the theory that attaches supremacy to economic factors in isolation. The significance of interaction will appear more clearly in the contrast.

Totalitarian Economics and Democracy

SOCIAL movements that have a new direction are accompanied by simplifications. Imagination ignores things that might obscure singleness of vision; plans ignore whatever gets in the way of concentrated energy. Later on, the things that were left out of the reckoning are noted. They are then seen to be involved in the failure to realize the original program. Disappointment and frustration succeed a period of enthusiasms; hope is followed by sober and critical second thought. There is often discouragement as to the practical value of any large social outlook. What is thought to be hard realism and is certainly an emotional disillusionment comes after a period of romantic idealism. We were in that state to a considerable degree until the rise of totalitarian states issued a challenge that compels us to reconsider fundamental principles.

It is easy to overlook later advantages that were obtained by an earlier simplification. Benefits wrought and harm done are wrongly located both at the time of origin and of later criticism. Simplification is beneficial as far as it brings about clear recognition of some new operative tendency in human affairs, a fuller and freer operation of which would occasion enrichment of human life. The exaggeration tends to make the new factor stand out in relief; acknowledgment of it then becomes a positive influence in furthering it, so that it works deliberately instead of more or less unconsciously. Harm comes from the fact that the theory framed is stated in absolute terms, as one which applies at all places and times, instead of under the contemporary conditions and having definite limits. Later, when conditions have undergone such a change that the idea does not work, a reaction sets in which is equally wholesale. The original idea is dismissed as pure illusion; some newer movement, going contrary to the conditions which evoked the earlier idea, is then often given similar absoluteness.

Since the rise of natural science and its attendant technologies, simplifications on the side of theory have been of two general classes. Theories have simplified in exaggeration of either the human factor, the constituents derived from human nature, or the "external" environing factor. Popular ideas are usually a more or less confused and inconsistent compromise, drawing some elements from each point of view and combining them in a haphazard way. Clarification may, then, be had if in this chapter and the next, we consider two types of theory that carry one-sided simplifications to extremes, extremes which are logical, given the premises, but which mislead action because of the absolute quality of the premises. The kind of theory thus formed contrasts radically with the procedure in which social events are seen to be *interactions* of components of human nature on one side with cultural conditions on the other. Events are explained as if one factor or other in the interaction were the whole thing. In this chapter, I shall criticize the type of social theory which reduces the human factor as nearly as possible to zero; since it explains events

75

and frames policies exclusively in terms of conditions provided by the environment. Marxism is taken as the typical illustration of the absolutism which results when this factor in the interaction is isolated and made supreme. It provides a typical illustration both because of its present vogue, and because it claims to represent the only strictly scientific theory of social change and thereby the method by which to effect change in the future.

Since the theory is involved in practical and party controversies in which feelings are excited, it is almost useless to say that the theory is here discussed as an illustration of what may be called "objective" or "realistic" absolutism, and for the sake of the light which thereby is thrown upon the actual problems of the present. For its adherents, by reason of the very nature of the theory, readily become so absolutistic in their attitude that they can see only a display of class-bias, unconscious or deliberate, in any criticism of their theory—an attitude now summed up in calling any opposition pro-Fascist. With those not committed it may promote understanding if I say that the criticism is not aimed at denying the role of economic factors in society nor at denying the tendency of the present economic regime to produce consequences adverse to democratic freedom. These things are rather taken for granted. Criticism aims to show what happens when this undeniable factor is isolated and treated as *the* cause of *all* social change. One may hold that if there is to be genuine and adequate democracy there must be a radical transformation of the present controls of production and distribution of goods and services, and may nevertheless accept the criticisms to be made—indeed may make or accept the criticisms *because* one believes the transformation is required.

The Marxist isolation of one factor (one which actually operates only in interaction with another one) takes the form of holding that the state of the forces of economic productivity at a given time ultimately determines all forms of social activities and relations, political, legal, scientific, artistic, religious, moral. In its original formulation, there was an important qualification which later statements have tended to ignore. For it was admitted that when political relations, science, etc., are once produced, they operate as causes of subsequent events, and in this capacity are capable of modifying in some degree the operation of the forces which originally produced them.

The subsequent ignoring of this qualification, the relegation of it to a footnote, was not wholly accidental. For there were practical reasons for paying little attention to it. If the qualification be admitted, observation of existing conditions (not the theory in the abstract) can alone tell just what consequences at a given time are produced by secondary effects which have now themselves acquired the standing of causes. The only way to decide would be to investigate, and by investigation in the concrete decide just what effects are due, say, to science, and just what to the naked, so to say, forces of economic production. To adopt and pursue this method would be in effect to abandon the all-comprehensive character of economic determination. It would put us in the relativistic and pluralistic position of considering a number of interacting factors—of which a very important one is undoubtedly the economic.

Marx would have a distinguished historic position if the

77

qualification were admitted in even fuller extent than he allowed for. He would not have been the first by any means to recognize the importance of economic conditions in determination of political and legal forms. Their close connection was almost a commonplace of the political philosophy of Aristotle. It was restated in a different form by English writers who influenced the ideas of the founders of the American republic. The latter uniformly emphasized connection between a certain state of the distribution of property and secure maintenance of popular government. But Marx did go back of property relations to the working of the forces of production as no one before him had done. He also discriminated between the state of the forces of productivity and the actual state of production existing at a given time, pointing out the lag often found in the latter. He showed in considerable detail that the cause of the lag is subordination of productive forces to legal and political conditions holding over from a previous regime of production. Marx's criticism of the present state of affairs from this last point of view was penetrating and possessed of enduring value.

The great merit, however, of the Marxist simplification, for those who accept it in its extreme form, is the fact that it combines the romantic idealism of earlier social revolutionaries with what purports to be a thoroughly "objective" scientific analysis, expressed in formulation of a single all-embracing "law", a law which moreover sets forth the proper method to be followed by the oppressed economic class in achieving its final liberation. For the theory went far beyond presenting a point of view to be employed in historical and sociological investigations. It claimed to state the one and only law in accordance with which economic relations determine the course of social change. This law is that of the existence of classes which are economically determined, which are engaged in constant warfare with one another, the outcome of which is direction of social change toward the liberation of producers from the bonds which have kept them subjugated in the past. Final creation of a classless society is to be the outcome.

It is quite possible to accept the idea of some sort of economic determinism. But that acceptance does not constitute one a Marxian, since the essence of the latter is the view that class warfare is the channel through which economic forces operate to effect social change and progress. This "law" was not derived nor supposed to be derived from study of historical events. It was derived from Hegelian dialectical metaphysics. The method of its derivation is indicated by the saying of Marx that he stood Hegel on his head. Hegel's system is one of dialectic idealism, in which logical categories, through the movement inherent in any partial and incomplete formulation of the rational structure of the universe, generate their own opposites, while the union of these opposites constitutes a higher and more adequate grasp of the nature of things, until finally all possible points of view with all their seeming conflicts are "organic" constituents of one all-comprehensive system.

Marx converted dialectic idealism into dialectic materialism—where the dialectic of conflict as the means of ultimate union and harmony is preserved, while the moving forces are economic classes, not ideas. Its "materialism" is therefore as different from "vulgar" materialism, based solely on conclusions of physical science, as the ultimate socialism, or the final synthesis of classless society is different from the "utopian" socialism of earlier communists:—utopian because they gave power and impetus to human preferences of values, thereby assigning causal power to moral factors. To Marx the economic movement is necessarily as self-determined toward its ultimate goal as the movement of logical categories had been in the Hegelian system. Marxism thus not only dropped the idealistic rationalism of the Hegelian system and violently condemned it, but he also, in the name of science, denied moving power to human valuations.

In lieu of one type of romantic absolutism, it developed another type more in harmony with the prestige which science and scientific law were gaining. It was a wonderful intellectual achievement to formulate laws for all social phenomena; it was still more wonderful to set forth one law working with absolute necessity, grasp of which enabled men to observe the "contradictions" in existing bourgeois capitalism, while it indicated with certainty the goal to which the contradictions by their own dialectic were carrying society. The law of history became the law for revolutionary action:—and all was accomplished that can possibly be accomplished in behalf of a clear vision of a goal and the concentration of emotion and energy in its behalf.

The idea of causal necessity in social phenomena and of development or "evolution" were in the intellectual atmosphere a century ago, the latter anteceding the Darwinian notion of biological development. Kant had taught that the idea of causal necessity is a prerequisite for natural science; German scientists at least accepted the idea without question, especially as Kant also made a sharp division between the fields of science and that of morals where freedom reigned. Hume's criticism of the idea of necessity was unwelcome even when it was known, because of its association with scepticism. In any case Kant seemed to have made an adequate reply to Hume.

In almost every quarter attempts were made to create a science of social phenomena, for which undertaking the idea of necessary law was deemed indispensable. August Comte introduced the word *Sociology* as a name for a comprehensive synthesis, while he found its basis in the "law" of three necessary stages of development. At a later period, Herbert Spencer had no difficulty in finding a single formula to cover all phenomena, cosmic, biological, psychological, social. The earlier attempts at introducing scientific arrangement into human events made use of the principle of stages of necessary "evolution" in some form or other.

The forties of the last century were also the time of promising radical political movements, all of which had a marked economic slant, while some were avowedly social- istic and communistic, especially at that time in France. There was a period in Germany when Hegel's philosophy was so dominant that all important differences were those between wings of the Hegelian school. All of these cir- cumstances put together, it is not surprising that Marx saw in the Hegelian dialectic a principle which, when it was given economic interpretation, provided a sure basis for a science of social changes, while at the same time, it furnished the revolutionary movement a supreme directive for its practical activities.

As has been said, important social movements develop some sort of philosophy by which to guide, nominally, at least, their practical efforts and also to justify them *ex post facto*. German culture has been especially ardent and prolific in this direction, all attempts to deal with actual conditions on any other basis being regarded as proof that those engaged in them are mere "empiricists," a term of condemnation about equivalent to calling them quacks. In Marxism those who accepted any law except one having exclusively material support were utopian dreamers. The fact then that the dialectical formula was borrowed from the most metaphysical, in a non-scientific sense, of all modern philosophers was no deterrent to the vogue of the Marxist synthesis, since its practical character seemed to be vouched for not only by actual economic conditions and by Marx's predictions, but in particular by the increase in class conflict that was taking place.

The idea of class war took on a peculiarly timely quality because of its teaching that the then existing class struggle was that of bourgeoisie capitalists with the proletariat, the class of factory wage-workers having neither land nor any form of reserve capital. Moreover, Marx's study of the concrete facts of the factory system in Great Britain backed up his general theory with a considerable number of economic generalizations which proved sound on any theory: —such as the existence of economic cycles with crises of increasing severity, a tendency toward combination and concentration, etc. The simplified Romanticism of the principle of a negation of negations taught that class war would, through the mediation of a temporary dictatorship of the proletariat, finally usher in a classless society. In the latter the state as a political coercive power would wither away, all political agencies becoming organs of democratic administration of affairs of common interest. Even the anarchist with his opposition to all coercive power could find satisfaction in contemplation of this ultimate outcome.

Marxists object vigorously and naturally to any suggestion of an identification of their creed with theological systems of the past. But all absolutisms tend to assume a theological form and to arouse the kind of emotional ardor that has accompanied crusading religions in the past. The theological concerns and conflicts of the earlier centuries of our era involved, moreover, contemporary interests not now recoverable in imagination. That is, they were more "practical" in fact than they now appear in retrospect. Similarly the monolithic and in itself speculative Marxist doctrine took on immediate practical coloring in connection with existing economic conditions and new forms of oppressions they had produced. There is nothing novel or peculiar in a combination of theory and practice in which practical events give definite color to an abstract theory, while the theory serves as a fountainhead of inspiration to action, providing also rallying cries and slogans. Exegesis can always serve to bridge gaps and inconsistencies; and every absolutistic creed demonstrates that no limits can be put to exegetical ingenuity. What actually happens can, accordingly, be brought into harmony with dogma while the latter is covertly accommodated to events.

There is no need to go into the full scope of Marxist philosophy upon its theoretical side. What is of concern here is the support alleged to be given by it to a strictly *scientific* form of social development, one which is inevitable *because* scientific. As is said of literary products, Marxism is "dated" in the matter of its claims to be peculiarly scientific. For just as *necessity* and search for a *single* all-comprehensive law was typical of the intellectual atmosphere of the forties of the last century, so *probability* and *pluralism* are the characteristics of the present state of science. That the older interpretation of the idea of causal necessity has undergone a shock does not need to be told to those acquainted with recent developments. It is not necessary, however, to go to the point of throwing the idea entirely overboard to make the point which is significant for the present topic.

There is a worldwide difference between the idea that causal sequences will be found in any given set of events taken for investigation, and the idea that *all* sets of events are linked together into a *single* whole by *one* causal law. Even if it be admitted that the former principle is a necessary postulate of scientific inquiry, the latter notion is metaphysical and *extra*-scientific. When natural science was first struggling to achieve its independence, and later when an attempt was made to take social phenomena out of the domain of arbitrary free-will, those who wanted to promote the new struggles borrowed from dominant theology the idea which the latter had made familiar, that of a single all-embracing causal force. The nature of the force and the way it worked were radically altered in the new apologetics for science. But the requirements of habit were satisfied in maintaining the old forms of thought—just as the first "horseless carriages" kept the shape of the carriages they displaced. The void left by surrender first of a supernatural force, and then of Nature (which had replaced

84

Deity during the periods of deistic rationalism) are thus made good. Only gradually did the work of science and the specific conclusions it reached make it clear that science was not a competitor with theology for a single ultimate explanation, so that the justification was no longer resorted to.

The surrender does not mean that search for broad generalizations has been given up. It means that the nature and function of these generalizations have changed. They are now, in effect and function, formulae for effecting transformations from one field to another, the qualitative difference of the fields being maintained. The doctrine of the conservation of energy represents, for example, an exceedingly comprehensive generalization. In terms of the now discarded philosophy of science, it would be said to set up a force which is at once electrical, mechanical, thermal, etc., and yet none of them, but a kind of nondescript Thing-in-itself back of all of them. In actual scientific procedure, it is a formula for converting any one of these forms of energy into any other, provided certain conditions are satisfied.

The same principle holds good of the recently discovered transmutation of chemical elements. It does not wipe out the differences of quality that mark off phenomena from one another but sets forth the conditions under which one kind is changed into another kind. Differences in the practical operations that are based upon science correspond with the change that has come about in theory—as the techniques of modern chemical industry are different from the dreams of the alchemists. No one today would think of undertaking a definite invention, the heavier-than-air flying boat, the internal combustion engine, and so on, by setting out from an alleged universal law of the working of some single ultimate force. The inventor who translates an idea into a working technological device starts from examination of special materials and tries special methods for combining them.

The practical techniques derived from the Marxist single all-embracing law of a single causative force follow the pattern discarded in scientific inquiry and in scientific engineering. What is necessary according to it is to promote class war in as great a variety of ways and on as many occasions as possible. For the essence of the theory, according to the dialectical method, is not recognition of class conflicts as *facts*—in which respect it provided a needed correction of the early nineteenth century notion of universal harmony and universal interdependence. Its distinguishing trait is that social progress is made by intensifying the conflict between the capitalistic employing classes and the proletarian employed class, so that the supreme principle of morals is to strengthen the power of the latter class.

The physical analogy is about like this: suppose that there had once been a theory that "nature abhors friction." It is then discovered that no mechanical work is done without resistance, and that there is no resistance without friction. It is then concluded that by abolishing lubrication and magnifying friction, a state of universal friction will by its own inner dialectic result in an adjustment of energies to one another which will provide the best possible conditions for doing useful work. Society *is* marked by conflict and friction of interests; interests may by some stretching and more consolidation be used to define classes. It may also be admitted that the conflict between them has under certain conditions served as a stimulus to social progress; it might even be admitted that a society in which there was no opposition of interests would be sunk in a condition of hopeless lethargy. But the idea of obtaining universal harmony by the greatest possible intensification of conflicts would remain analogous to the physical illustration given. Persons who are not Marxists often identify the proposition that serious strife of economic interests exists with the genuine Marxist thesis that it is the sole agency by which social change is effected in the desirable direction of a classless society.

The criticism made is not directed then to any generalization made by Marx on the basis of observation of actual conditions. On the contrary, the implication of the criticism is the necessity for *continued* observation of actual conditions, with testing and revision of all earlier generalization on the basis of what is now observed. The inherent theoretical weakness of Marxism is that it supposed a generalization that was made at a particular date and place (and made even then only by bringing observed facts under a premise drawn from a metaphysical source) can obviate the need for continued resort to observation, and to continual revision of generalizations in their office of working hypotheses. In the name of science, a thoroughly antiscientific procedure was formulated, in accord with which a generalization is made having the nature of ultimate "truth," and hence holding good at all times and places.

Laissez-faire individualism indulged in the same kind of sweeping generalization but in the opposite direction. Doubtless, in accordance with the law of the union of

87

opposites, this background played its part in creating a cultural atmosphere favorable to Marxism. But two opposite errors do not constitute one truth, especially when both errors have the same root. With some disregard for historic facts, the Marxist doctrine might even be regarded as a generalized version of that aspect of classic economic theory which held that completely free competition in the open market would automatically produce universal harmony of persons and nations, Marx converting competition of individuals into war of classes.

Marxism has, then, been selected as an illustration of the monistic block-universe theory of social causation. A few years ago the laissez-faire view, developed out of ideas of Adam Smith when they were wedded to ideas of utilitarian morals and psychology, would have been appropriately taken. The Russian Revolution is chiefly accountable for having brought Marxism to the foreground. Being conducted in the name of Marx, it claimed to be a large scale demonstration of the validity of the Marxist theory. The Union of Socialist Soviet Republics has fastened attention upon the theory as no idea ever succeeds on its own account in obtaining notice. It caused Marxism to be a terrifying menace in some quarters while giving it enormous prestige in other quarters. It led to a disruption of old socialist parties, as the Russian Revolution was held up in other countries as proof of the Marxist theory of class war and the dictatorship of the proletariat. The issue raised by events in Russia gave actuality to Marxist doctrine in every country of the globe.

An event of this sort cannot occur without arousing intense feeling, and corresponding conflicts of interpretation. In the present case, the division extends not only to the theory but to the facts of the situation. One can find data, real or alleged, to support almost any view as to the actual situation in the U.S.S.R., according to the source one takes to be authoritative. Facts, including statistics, are cited to show that extraordinary progress has been made in industrialization of the country and mechanization of agricultural pursuits, with an immense gain in productivity, and, what is more important, in creation of a genuine workers' republic, attended with striking rise in the material and cultural standards of living of the great mass of the population. But one may also find evidence to support the view that the dictatorship of the proletariat became first that of a party over the proletariat and then the dictatorship of a small band of bureaucrats over the party, until the latter, to maintain power, has adopted, with greatly improved technical skill in execution, all the repressive measures of the overthrown Czarist despotism. One can find evidence that, under a regime of governmental, instead of social, control, economic classes marked by great inequality of income are growing up. Such questions of fact are not settled by argument. Hence though there is no doubt in my own mind as to the conclusion available evidence points to, I shall not here attempt to take a stand on the particular issues of fact which are involved.

Certain facts that are not denied suffice as far as the present topic and problem are concerned. A monistic theory is accompanied in its practical execution by one-party control of press, schools, radio, the theater and every means of communication, even to effective restrictions imposed on private gatherings and private conversations. One of the reasons for the great difference in opinion about the state of facts—the point just mentioned—is the fact that effective dictatorship (and an ineffective dictatorship is not a dictatorship at all) exercises complete command over the press, over travel, over letters and personal communications. In consequence, only a few have access to the sources of information about political methods, and that few is just the group with the greatest interest in preventing free inquiry and report.

This suppression of freedom of belief and of speech, press and assembly is not among the facts in dispute for it is of the essence of the dictatorship, which in turn is of the essence of the doctrine the Revolution claims to have put in force. Nor is ruthless persecution and punishment of all dissenters one of the disputed facts. A succession of trials has eliminated from life (as well as from political action) every one of the men and women who brought on the Revolution, save a few relatively minor characters. The *justification* of the action is one of the things in controversy, but not the fact of the exile, imprisonment or execution of every important earlier leader. As a criterion for judging the theory back of revolutionary method of class war, it would not seem to make a great deal of difference whether we decide these men were traitors to their own cause of the liberation of humanity, or are victims of the desire of a clique to keep in their hands a monopoly of all power—great as will be the difference in our judgment about the character of the persons involved.

Events not in dispute confirm the conclusion drawn from other historical instances that absolute principles are intolerant of dissent, for dissent from "The Truth" is more than an intellectual error. It is proof of an evil and dangerous will. When the dominant dogma is definitely theological, the evil will is described in one set of terms; when it is political, the phraseology is different, "counter-revolution" taking the place of "heresy."

The psychological and moral dispositions stimulated and the kind of activities in which they are expressed are extraordinarily similar. No general theory, moreover, is self-translating in application to particular events. Some body of persons must exist to state just what its significance is in its bearing upon this and that situation, and a body that merely interprets is impotent unless it has power to enforce decisions. The extreme danger of giving any body of persons power for whose exercise they are not accountable is a commonplace in a democracy. Arbitrary irresponsibility varies in direct ratio to the claim for absoluteness on the part of the principle in behalf of which power is exercised. To sustain the principle against heresy, or counter-revolutionary action, it finally becomes necessary to clothe the human officials that are supposed to represent the principle with the finality of the professed end. Divinity once hedged about kings. An earlier repudiation in Russia of glorification of individual persons, because of the immensely superior importance of collective action, gives way to Byzantine adulation of the Leader.

That the state, as governmental coercive power, is not withering away is another indisputable fact. Instead there has been an increase of the intensity and range of state action; the independent activity of factions within the party, of trade unions and of the original soviets is now judged to be, if not counter-revolutionary, at least hostile to the maintenance of the dictatorship of the proletariat. It is a part of original Marxist doctrine that no class having power surrenders it without being compelled to do so by superior force. The application of this particular phase of the doctrine to those who now wield power is one of the "contradictions" attending the dialectical theory. It might be worth while to ask whether the constant splintering of professed Marxists into factions that fight one another as bitterly as they fight their professed foe does not bear a similar relation to the doctrine of class war.

For while it was part of the original doctrine that personal hatred is outside the scope of the impersonal sweep of economic forces, it is doubtful if there is any case in history of *odium theologicum* that surpasses in intensity the venom displayed by convinced disciples of the orthodox Marxist creed toward dissenters, the venom being even greater against those who agree in some respects than towards professed representatives of capitalism. For the former are heretics, while the latter are simply believers in a faith that is natural to them. Like pagans, as distinct from heretics, they do not know any better. Verbal abuse in countries like the United States is the substitute for the physical power exerted where dictatorship exists, the mildest epithet being that of Fascist or friend of Fascism.

The large measure of sympathy shown by liberals in our own country toward Russian totalitarianism—to the extent of asserting the country is essentially a democracy with which common cause should be made against Fascist states—is not surprising. There are undoubted advances made in many directions in the U.S.S.R., since the overthrow of Czardom. They are visible and well-publicized, while the conduct of political affairs is a sealed book. More influential still is the fact that those persons who see the obstructive power of the existing economic system in our country are moved by the fact that one country has done something about overthrowing that system. Also we are not in the habit of taking social and political philosophies very seriously. We take them empirically and "pragmatically," as useful rallying-cries. We do not realize that continental Europeans, especially those educated under the influence of German ideas, have a still greater contempt for action which is "empirically" directed than we have for abstract theory. Again, when events occur that are obviously unfortunate, it is easy to explain them as a result of survival of tendencies bred in the earlier despotism or as expressions of a mentality which is still quasi-Asiatic—although in fact these are the attitudes which have made it possible for a monolithic theory of the Marxist type to flourish.

While nothing said discounts the effect of economic factors upon other components of culture (and certainly not upon political ones at the present time), nevertheless democratic methods are proved, even if they lack adequate substance, to be indispensable to effecting economic change in the interest of freedom. In common with many others, I have from time to time pointed out the harmful consequences the present regime of industry and finance has upon the reality of democratic ends and methods. I have nothing to retract. But conditions in totalitarian countries have brought home the fact, not sufficiently realized by critics, myself included, that the forms which still exist

93

encourage freedom of discussion, criticism and voluntary associations, and thereby set a gulf between a country having suffrage and popular representation and a country having dictatorships, whether of the right or left—the differences between the two latter growing continually less as they borrow each other's techniques.

The Marxist theory holds that government in so-called democratic states is only the organ of a capitalist class, using legislatures, courts, army and police to do its will and maintain its class supremacy. But the effect of constant criticism of governmental action; of more than one political party in formulating rival policies; of frequent elections; of the discussion and public education that attend majority rule, and above all the fact that political action is but one factor in the interplay of a number of cultural factors, have a value that critics of partial democracy have not realized. And this point is strengthened when we accept the criticism that much of our political democracy is more formal than substantial, provided it is placed in contrast with totalitarian political control. Subordination of the political to the economic has a meaning for those trained to take for granted the operation of an indefinite plurality of social tendencies, many of which are neither political nor economic, that it cannot possibly have in countries that are without the democratic tradition. It is difficult for even English people to understand why and how it is that politics are not the absorbing interest in this country they are in England. If the result with us is often looseness of cohesion and indefiniteness in direction of action, there is generated a certain balance of judgment and some sort of equilibrium in social affairs. We take for granted the action of a number of diverse factors in producing any social result. There are temporary waves of insistence upon this and that particular measure and aim. But there is at least enough democracy so that in time any one tendency gets averaged up in interplay with other tendencies. An average presents qualities that are open to easy criticism. But as compared with the fanaticism generated by monistic ideas when they are put into operation, the averaging of tendencies, a movement toward a mean, is an achievement of splendor. However, the habit of imagination that is bred makes it easier than it otherwise would be to idealize conditions in a country which, like Russia, aims at a monolithic structure. The "common man" may be common but for that reason he strikes a certain balance, and the balance struck is a greater safeguard of democracy than any particular law can be, even if written into the Constitution.

The moral is not unintelligent glorification of empirical, pluralistic, and pragmatic method. On the contrary, the lesson to be learned is the importance of ideas and of a plurality of ideas employed in experimental activity as working hypotheses. Thoughtless empiricism provides opportunity for secret manipulation behind the visible scene. When we assume that we are following common sense policies, in the most honorable sense of common sense, we may in fact, unless we direct observation of conditions by means of general ideas, be in process of being led around by the nose by agencies purporting to be democratic, but whose activities are subversive of freedom: a generalized warning which, when translated into concrete words, should make us wary toward those who talk glibly about the "American way of life," after they have identified Americanism with a partisan policy in behalf of concealed economic aims.

The experimental method of science is the exemplification of empirical method when experience has reached maturity. It is opposed equally to "vulgar" empiricism which recognizes only rule-of-thumb action, depending upon a succession of trial-and-error acts that are unregulated by connection with an idea which is both expressed and tested, and to that absolutism which insists there is but one Truth and that truth one already revealed and possessed by some group or party. Mr. John Strachey, an Englishman, not a Russian, may be quoted upon the extent to which present "Communist" thought is authoritarian and monistic—that is, ruled by an ideal of uniformity. For he says that communistic parties even outside of Russia, e. g., in this country, in "refusal to tolerate the existence of incompatible opinions ... are simply asserting the claim that Socialism is scientific." It would be difficult, probably impossible, to find a more direct and elegantly finished denial of all the qualities that make ideas and theories either scientific or democratic than is contained in this statement. It helps explain why literary persons have been chiefly the ones in this country who have fallen for Marxist theory, since they are the ones who, having the least amount of scientific attitude, swallow most readily the notion that "science" is a new kind of infallibility.

To repeat a statement already made in another connection, no generalization which, like Marxism, claims to state the final truth about changes (whether physical or social), can set forth the significance of the general idea that is

96

accepted in connection with actual events as they happen. For the purpose of day by day *action*, the sole value of a theory is the significance given to concrete events, when they are viewed in the light of the theory, in the concrete relations they sustain to one another. It is no accident that the final effect of uniformity of ideas is to set up some selected body of persons above the theoretical generalization. Those who determine what the theory signifies in terms of the one important thing—namely, *what should be done*—are supreme over the theory even when they claim to act in subjection to it. The demand for uniformity of opinion, "the refusal to tolerate the existence of incompatible opinions," demands first that there be a party and then a select council of persons within the party, to decide just what after all is The Truth with respect to events as they arise —together with a truly theological technique of exegesis to explain the perfect consistency existing among a succession of inconsistent policies. Thus there has been the change from the earlier denunciation of democracy as identical with middle class capitalism and the labeling of all other socialists as Social-Fascists, to the present policy of a Popular Front, and to the presentation of Bolshevism as twentieth century democracy. And, again, change from denunciation of Nazi Germany to the beginnings of a virtual alliance with it, but now in the wholly praiseworthy interest of world peace, following upon the former orthodox doctrine that only communism can institute peace after a succession of wars international and civil. Scientific method in operating with working hypotheses instead of with fixed and final Truth is not forced to have an Inner Council to declare just what is the Truth nor to develop

97

a system of exegesis which rivals the ancient theological way of explaining away apparent inconsistencies. It welcomes a clash of "incompatible opinions" as long as they can produce observed facts in their support.

Since Marxism has been taken as the example of a uniformitarian theory, basing itself upon "objective" factors of the environment in separation from their interaction with the factors of human nature, something will be said in closing about the ignoring of human qualities. For it contradicts the statement sometimes made that the essence of Marxism, at least as a practical doctrine, is appeal to the motive of self-interest. This statement is made as an accusation by non-Marxists, while it sometimes appears in what profess to be Marxist documents. But actually it comes close to reversing actual Marxist doctrine—the doctrine that the state of the forces of production is the sole causal force. For according to this view, all the factors of human nature are shaped from without by "materialistic," that is economic, forces. To give independent validity to any component of human nature would be, from the Marxist standpoint, a relapse into the "idealistic" type of theory that Marxism came to destroy.

A much juster criticism would be that Marxism systematically neglects everything on the side of human nature with respect to its being a factor having efficacy, save as it is previously determined by the state of the forces of production. In claiming to replace "Utopian" socialisms, Marxism throws out psychological as well as moral considerations. Whether the theory is in fact able to live up to this claim—without which its "materialism" is meaningless —is another matter. For it would seem as if certain organic needs and appetites at least were required to set the "forces of production" moving. But if this bio-psychological factor is admitted, then it must *interact* with "external" factors, and there is no particular point at which its operation can be said to cease.

The point involved has a practical as well as theoretical force. Take for example the matter of classes and of class-*consciousness*, the latter being an imperatively required condition in the Marxist theory. According to orthodox Marxism, the class consciousness of the proletariat is generated by the fact that the state of economic forces represented by large-scale factory production throws wage-workers closely together with little or no direct intercourse with employers—such as existed, for example, in shops where hand tools were used. Physical conditions thus demarcate economic classes, and throw into relief the conflict of interests between employers and employees, together with the community of interests, if only in misery, that bind together the latter. Now as an observation there is an undeniable element of truth in this position—especially in contrast with the favorite editorial exhortation that there can be no conflict between "Capital" and "Labor" since each depends on the other. But the facts involved in the observation are not compatible with the ultimate theory. The formation of a class, especially of class consciousness, depends upon the operation of psychological factors which are not mentioned—and which the theory rules out.

The fact is that Marx and every Marxist after him unconsciously assumes the existence and operation of factors in the constitution of human nature which must cooperate with "external" economic or "material" conditions in producing what actually happens. Explicit recognition of these factors would give the theory a different practical slant. It would have put the things emphasized by Marx in a different perspective. The fact seems to be that Marx himself unconsciously took over the current psychology of his time, standing also on *its* head the optimistic psychology of laissez-faire liberalism. Overt recognition of the psychological factors entails introduction of values and judgments of valuation into a theory of social movement—as is shown later.

Any monolithic theory of social action and social causation tends to have a ready-made answer for problems that present themselves. The wholesale character of this answer prevents critical examination and discrimination of the particular facts involved in the actual problem. In consequence, it dictates a kind of all-or-none practical activity, which in the end introduces new difficulties. I suggest as illustrations two sets of events that have played a great part in the history of the U.S.S.R. According to the theory, the members of the agricultural class, as far as they own land, belong to the bourgeoisie, although of the "petty" subdivision. Only factory workers, congregated in cities, belong to the proletariat. By theory then class war exists between city workers and most of the rural population. There is a genuine psychological and political problem involved in getting these two groups of human beings together for common social action. But the wholesale or monistic character of the theoretical premise prevents exploration of the problem *as* a problem. It is settled in advance that the class conflict is of such a nature that success of the revolutionary movement is bound up with domination of the urban wage worker over the rural population. Anybody who has followed Russian history knows that an already difficult problem has been tremendously exacerbated by acceptance of this absolute principle—in spite of considerable flexibility on Lenin's part in applying it.

The other example is the question of the possibility of building socialism in one country at a time when the state of forces of production is international. Here again there is a difficult problem with respect to the policies to be adopted in adjusting domestic and foreign relations. The all-or-none theory led in Russia to a complete political break-up in the formation of two completely hostile factions within the original Communist Party. Negotiations, compromise, working out of a policy on the basis of study of actual conditions was ruled out in advance. Even when the original orthodox Marxism was abandoned in favor of an effort to build socialism in one country—a policy for which on practical grounds a great deal could be said—it had to be proved that this policy was the one and the only one authorized by the all-or-none theory which cannot "tolerate incompatible opinions" because of the "scientific" character of the doctrine. The most effective way of proving the point was to behead all those who took a contrary view as traitors and counter-revolutionaries.

It is ironical that the theory which has made the most display and the greatest pretense of having a scientific foundation should be the one which has violated most systematically every principle of scientific method. What we may learn from the contradiction is the potential alliance between scientific and democratic method and the need of consummating this potentiality in the techniques of legislation and administration. It is of the nature of science not so much to tolerate as to welcome diversity of opinion, while it insists that inquiry brings the evidence of observed facts to bear to effect a consensus of conclusions —and even then to hold the conclusion subject to what is ascertained and made public in further new inquiries. I would not claim that any existing democracy has ever made complete or adequate use of scientific method in deciding upon its policies. But freedom of inquiry, toleration of diverse views, freedom of communication, the distribution of what is found out to every individual as the ultimate intellectual consumer, are involved in the democratic as in the scientific method. When democracy openly recognizes the existence of *problems* and the need for probing them *as* problems as its glory, it will relegate political groups that pride themselves upon refusing to admit incompatible opinions to the obscurity which already is the fate of similar groups in science.

CHAPTER FIVE

Democracy and Human Nature

IT is not accidental that the rise of interest in human nature coincided in time with the assertion in political
matters of the rights of the people as a whole, over
against the rights of a class supposedly ordained by God
or Nature to exercise rule. The full scope and depth of the
connection between assertion of democracy in government
and new consciousness of human nature cannot be presented without going into an opposite historic background,
in which social arrangements and political forms were
taken to be an expression of Nature—but most decidedly
not of *human* nature. There would be involved an account,
upon the side of theory, of the long history of the idea of
Laws of Nature from the time of Aristotle and the Stoics
to the formulators of modern jurisprudence in the sixteenth
and seventeenth centuries.

The story of this development and of the shift, in the
eighteenth century, from Natural Law to Natural Rights
is one of the most important chapters in the intellectual
and moral history of mankind. But to delve into it would
here take us too far away from the immediate theme. I
must content myself then with emphatic reassertion of the
statement that regard for *human* nature as the source of
legitimate political arrangements is comparatively late in

European history; that when it arose it marked an almost revolutionary departure from previous theories about the basis of political rule and citizenship and subjection—so much so that the fundamental difference between even ancient republican and modern democratic governments has its source in the substitution of human nature for cosmic nature as the foundation of politics. Finally changes and the need for further change in democratic theory are connected with an inadequate theory of the constitution of human nature and its component elements in their relation to social phenomena.

The subject matter which follows is that of a drama in three acts, of which the last is the unfinished one now being enacted in which we, now living, are the participants. The first act, as far as it is possible to tell its condensed story, is that of a one-sided simplification of human nature which was used to promote and justify the new political movement. The second act is that of the reaction against the theory and the practices connected with it, on the ground that it was the forerunner of moral and social anarchy, the cause of dissolution of the ties of cohesion that bind human beings together in organic union. The third act, now playing, is that of recovery of the moral significance of the connection of human nature and democracy, now stated in concrete terms of existing conditions and freed from the one-sided exaggerations of the earlier statement. I give this summary first because in what follows I have been compelled to go in some detail into matters that if pursued further are technically theoretical.

I begin by saying that the type of theory which isolated the "external" factor of interactions that produce social phenomena is paralleled by one which isolated the "internal" or human factor. Indeed, if I had followed the historic order the latter type of theory would have been discussed first. And this type of theory is still more widely and influentially held than we might suppose. For its vogue is not now adequately represented by those professional psychologists and sociologists who claim that all social phenomena are to be understood in terms of the mental operations of individuals, since society consists in the last analysis only of individual persons. The practically effective statement of the point of view is found in economic theory, where it furnished the backbone of laissez-faire economics; and in the British political liberalism which developed in combination with this economic doctrine. A particular view of human motives in relation to social events, as explanations of them and as the basis of all sound social policy, has not come to us labeled psychology. But as a theory about human nature it is essentially psychological. We still find a view put forth as to an intrinsic and necessary connection between democracy and capitalism which has a psychological foundation and temper. For it is only because of belief in a certain theory of human nature that the two are said to be Siamese twins, so that attack upon one is a threat directed at the life of the other.

The classic expression of the point of view which would explain social phenomena by means of psychological phenomena is that of John Stuart Mill in his *Logic*—a statement that probably appeared almost axiomatic when it was put forth. "All phenomena of society are phenomena of human nature . . . and if therefore the phenomena of human thought, feeling and action are subject to fixed laws, the phenomena of society cannot but conform to law." And again, "The laws of the phenomena of society are and can be nothing but the laws of the actions and passions of human beings united in the social state." And then, as if to state conclusively that being "united in the social state" makes no difference as to the laws of individuals and hence none in those of society, he adds, "Human beings in society have no properties but those which are derived from and may be resolved into the laws of the nature of individual man."

This reference to "individual man" discloses the nature of the particular simplification which controlled the views and the policies of this particular school. The men who expressed and entertained the type of philosophy whose method was summed up by Mill were in their time revolutionaries. They wished to liberate a certain group of individuals, those concerned in new forms of industry, commerce and finance, from shackles inherited from feudalism which were endeared by custom and interest to a powerful landed aristocracy. If they do not appear now to be revolutionary (operating to bring about social change by change in men's opinions not by force), it is because their views are now the philosophy of conservatives in every highly industrialized country.

They essayed an intellectual formulation of principles which would justify the success of the tendencies which present day revolutionaries call the bourgeois capitalism they are trying to overthrow. The psychology in question is not that of present textbooks. But it expressed the individualistic ideas that animated the economic and political theories of the radicals of the time. Its "individualism," supplied the background of a great deal of even the technical psychology of the present day—pretty much all of it, save that which has started on a new tack because of biological and anthropological considerations. At the time of its origin, it was not a bookish doctrine even when written down in books. The books were elaborations of ideas that were propounded in electoral campaigns and offered as laws to be adopted by parliament.

Before engaging in any detailed statements, I want to recall a statement made earlier; namely, that the popular view of the constitution of human nature at any given time is a reflex of social movements which have either become institutionalized or else are showing themselves against opposing social odds and hence need intellectual and moral formulation to increase their power. I may seem to be going far afield if I refer to Plato's statement of the way by which to determine the constituents of human nature. The proper method, he said, was to look at the version of human nature written in large and legible letters in the organization of classes in society, before trying to make it out in the dim petty edition found in individuals. And so on the basis of the social organization with which he was acquainted he found that since in society there was a laboring class toiling to find the means of satisfying the appetites, a citizen soldiery class loyal even to death to the laws of the state, and a legislative class, so the human soul must be composed of appetite at the base—in both significations of "base"—of generous spirited impulses which looked beyond personal enjoyment, while appetite was engaged only in taking in and absorbing for its own satisfaction, and finally reason, the legislative power.

Having found these three things in the composition of human nature, he had no difficulty in going back to social organization and proving that there was one class which had to be kept in order by rules and laws imposed from above, since otherwise its action was without limits, and would in the name of liberty destroy harmony and order; another class, whose inclinations were all towards obedience and loyalty to law, towards right beliefs, although itself incapable of discovering the ends from which laws are derived; and at the apex, in any well-ordered organization, the rule of those whose predominant natural qualities were reason, after that faculty had been suitably formed by education.

It would be hard to find a better illustration of the fact that any movement purporting to discover the psychological causes and sources of social phenomena is in fact a reverse movement, in which current social tendencies are read back into the structure of human nature; and are then used to explain the very things from which they are deduced. It was then "natural" for the men who reflected the new movement of industry and commerce to erect the appetites, treated by Plato as a kind of necessary evil, into the cornerstone of social well-being and progress. Something of the same kind exists at present when love of power is put forward to play the role taken a century ago by self-interest as the dominant "motive"—and if I put the word motive in quotations marks, it is for the reason just given. What are called motives turn out upon critical examination to be complex attitudes patterned under cultural conditions, rather than simple elements in human nature.

Even when we refer to tendencies and impulses that actually are genuine elements in human nature we find, unless we swallow whole some current opinion, that of themselves they explain nothing about social phenomena. For they produce consequences only as they are shaped into acquired dispositions by interaction with environing cultural conditions. Hobbes, who was the first of the moderns to identify the "state of nature" and its laws—the classic background of all political theories—with the raw uneducated state of human nature, may be called as witness. According to Hobbes, "In the nature of man we find three principal causes of quarrel. First competition, secondly diffidence, thirdly glory. The first maketh men invade for gain; the second for safety; and the third for reputation. The first use violence to make themselves the masters of other persons; the second to defend them; the third for trifles as a word, a smile, a different opinion or any other sign of undervalue, either direct in their persons or by reflection in their kindred, their friends, their nation."

That the qualities mentioned by Hobbes actually exist in human natue and that they may generate "quarrel," that is, conflict and war between states and civil war within a nation—the chronic state of affairs when Hobbes lived—is not denied. Insofar, Hobbes' account of the natural psychology which prevents the state of security which is a pre-requisite for civilized communities shows more insight than many attempts made today to list the traits of raw human nature that are supposed to cause social phenomena. Hobbes thought that the entire natural state of men in their relations to one another was a war of all against all, man being naturally to man "as a wolf." The intent of Hobbes was thus a glorification of deliberately instituted relations, authoritative laws and regulations which should rule not just overt actions, but the impulses and ideas which cause men to hold up certain things as ends or goods. Hobbes himself thought of this authority as a political sovereign. But it would be in the spirit of his treatment to regard it as glorification of culture over against raw human nature, and more than one writer has pointed out the likeness between his Leviathan and the Nazi totalitarian state.

There are more than one instructive parallelisms that may be drawn between the period in which Hobbes lived and the present time, especially as to insecurity and conflict between nations and classes. The point here pertinent, however, is that the qualities Hobbes selected as the causes of disorders making the life of mankind "brutish and nasty," are the very "motives" that have been selected by others as the cause of *beneficent* social effects; namely, harmony, prosperity, and indefinite progress. The position taken by Hobbes about competition as love of gain was completely reversed in the British social philosophy of the nineteenth century. Instead of being a source of war, it was taken to be the means by which individuals found the occupation for which they were best fitted; by which needed goods reached the consumer at least cost, and by which a state of ultimate harmonious interdependence would be produced—provided only competition were allowed to operate without "artificial" restriction. Even today one reads articles and hears speeches in which the cause of our present economic troubles is laid to political interference with the beneficent workings of private competitive effort for gain.

The object of alluding to these two very different conceptions of this component in human nature is not to decide or discuss which is right. The point is that both are guilty of the same fallacy. In itself, the impulse (or whatever name be given it) is neither socially maleficent nor beneficent. Its significance depends upon consequences actually produced; and these depend upon the conditions under which it operates and with which it interacts. The conditions are set by tradition, by custom, by law, by the kind of public approvals and disapprovals; by all conditions constituting the environment. These conditions are so pluralized even in one and the same country at the same period that love of gain (regarded as a trait of human nature) may be both socially useful and socially harmful. And, in spite of the tendency to set up cooperative impulses as thoroughly beneficial, the same thing is true of them—regarded simply as components of human nature. Neither competition nor cooperation can be judged as traits of human nature. They are names for certain relations among the actions of individuals as the relations actually obtain in a community.

This would be true even if there were tendencies in human nature so definitely marked off from one another as to merit the names given them and even if human nature were as fixed as it is sometimes said to be. For even in that case, human nature operates in a multitude of different environing conditions, and it is interaction with the latter that determines the consequences and the social significance and value, positive or negative, of the tendencies. The alleged fixity of the structure of human nature does not explain in the least the differences that mark off one tribe, family, people, from another—which is to say that in and of itself it explains no state of society whatever. It issues no advice as to what policies it is advantageous to follow. It does not even justify conservatism as against radicalism.

But the alleged unchangeableness of human nature cannot be admitted. For while certain needs in human nature are constant, the consequences they produce (because of the existing state of culture—of science, morals, religion, art, industry, legal rules) react back into the original components of human nature to shape them into new forms. The total pattern is thereby modified. The futility of exclusive appeal to psychological factors both to explain what takes place and to form policies as to what *should* take place, would be evident to everybody—had it not proved to be a convenient device for "rationalizing" policies that are urged on other grounds by some group or faction. While the case of "competition" urging men both to war and to beneficent social progress is most obviously instructive in this respect, examination of the other elements of Hobbes supports the same conclusion.

There have been communities, for example, in which regard for the honor of one's self, one's family, one's class, has been the chief conservator of all worth while social values. It has always been the chief virtue of an aristocratic class, civil or military. While its value has often been exaggerated, it is folly to deny that in interaction with certain cultural conditions, it has had valuable consequences. "Diffidence" or fear as a motive is an even more ambiguous and meaningless term as far as its consequences are concerned. It takes any form, from craven cowardice to prudence, caution, and the circumspection without which no intelligent foresight is possible. It may become reverence—which has been exaggerated in the abstract at times but which may be attached to the kind of objects which render it supremely desirable. "Love of power," to which it is now fashionable to appeal, has a meaning only when it applies to everything in general and hence explains nothing in particular.

Discussion up to this point has been intended to elicit two principles. One of them is that the views about human nature that are popular at a given time are usually derived from contemporary social currents; currents so conspicuous as to stand out or else less marked and less effective social movements which a special group believes *should* become dominant:—as for example, in the case of the legislative reason with Plato, and of competitive love of gain with classical economists. The other principle is that reference to components of original human nature, even if they actually exist, explains no social occurrence whatever and gives no advice or direction as to what policies it is better to adopt. This does not mean that reference to them must necessarily be of a "rationalizing" concealed apologetic type. It means that whenever it occurs with practical significance it has *moral* not psychological import. For, whether brought forward from the side of conserving what already exists or from that of producing change, it is an expression of valuation, and of purpose determined by estimate of values. When a trait of human nature is put forward on this basis, it is in its proper context and is subject to intelligent examination.

The prevailing habit, however, is to assume that a social issue does not concern values to be preferred and striven for, but rather something predetermined by the constitution of human nature. This assumption is the source of serious social ills. Intellectually it is a reversion to the type of explanation that governed physical science until say, the seventeenth century: a method now seen to have been the chief source of the long-continued retardation of natural science. For this type of theory consists of appeal to general forces to "explain" what happens.

Natural science began to progress steadily only when general forces were banished and inquiry was directed instead to ascertaining correlations that exist between observed changes. Popular appeal to, say, electricity, light or heat, etc., as a force to account for some particular event still exists, as to electricity to explain storms attended by thunder and lightning. Scientific men themselves often talk in similar words. But such general terms are in their case shorthand expressions. They stand for uniform relations between events that are observed to occur; they do not mark appeal to something behind what happens and which is supposed to produce it. If we take the case of the lightning flash and electricity, Franklin's identification of the former as of the electrical kind brought it into connection with things from which it had been formerly isolated, and knowledge about them was available in dealing with it. But instead of electricity being an explanatory force, knowledge that lightning is an electrical phenomenon opened a number of special problems, some of which are still unsolved.

If the analogy between the relatively sterile condition of natural science when this method prevailed and the present state of the social "sciences" is not convincing, the misdirection of inquiry that results may be cited in evidence. There is an illusion of understanding, when in reality there is only a general word that conceals lack of understanding. Social ideas are kept in the domain of glittering generalities. Opinion as distinct from knowledge breeds controversy. Since what is regarded as a cause is that which is used as an agency or instrumentality of production, there is no controlled method of bringing anything into existence and of preventing the occurrence of that not wanted, save as there is knowledge of the conditions of its occurrence. When men knew that a certain kind of friction produced fire, they had at command at least one means, rubbing of sticks together, for producing fire when they wanted it. And it goes without saying that greater acquaintance with causal conditions has multiplied men's practical ability to have fire when needed, and to use it for an increased number of ends. The principle applies to the relation of social theory and social action.

Finally theories supposed to explain the course of events are used to urge and justify certain practical policies. Marxism is, of course, a striking instance. But it is so far from being the only instance that non-Marxian and anti-Marxian social theories often exemplify the principle. Utilitarianism used the idea that pleasure and pain are the sole determinants of human action to advance a sweeping theory of legislation, judicial and penal procedure; namely, that they be directed to secure the greatest happiness of the greatest number. Explanation of events on the basis of free, unimpeded manifestation of wants was used on the practical side as active propaganda for an open-market economic regime with all political and legal measures adapted to it. Belief in the general character of the alleged "force" rendered it unnecessary to keep track of actual events so as to check the theory. If things happened that obviously went contrary to the creed, the inconsistency was not taken as a reason for examining it, but as the cue for alleging special reasons for the failure, so that the truth of the principle could be kept intact.

Mere general ideas can be argued for and against without the necessity of recourse to observation. The arguments are saved from being a mere matter of words only because there are certain emotional attitudes involved. When general ideas are not capable of being continuously checked and revised by observation of what actually takes place, they are, as a mere truism, in the field of opinion. Clash of opinions is in that case the occasion for controversy, not, as is now the case in natural science, a location of a problem and an occasion for making further observations. If any generalization can be safely laid down about intellectual matters and their consequences, it is that the reign of opinion, and of controversial conflicts, is a function of absence of methods of inquiry which bring new facts to light and by so doing establish the basis for consensus of beliefs.

Social events are sufficiently complex in any case so that the development of effective methods of observation, yielding generalization about correlation of events, is difficult. The prevailing type of theory adds the further handicap of making such observation unnecessary—save as this and that arbitrarily selected event is used in argumentative controversy. The prime necessity is to frame general ideas, first, to promote search for problems—as against the assumption of a ready-made solution in view of which there are no problems; and, secondly, to solve these problems by generalizations that state interactions between analytically observed events.

I return to the particular social philosophy which associates the economic regime actuated by effort to make private profit with the essential conditions of free and democratic institutions. It is not necessary to go back to the theory in its early English formulation at the hands of laissez-faire liberals. For in spite of the discrediting of the philosophy by events, efforts put forth in this country to establish so-called social control of business has led at present to its revival in an extremely naked form. One does not need to endorse the measures for control that are used to be aware of the fallacy of the theory upon which current objections to thèm are based. The theory is that capitalism, interpreted as the maximum range of free personal opportunity for production and exchange of goods and services is the Siamese twin of democracy. For the former is identical, so it is claimed, with the personal qualities of initiative, independence, vigor, that are the basic conditions of free political institutions. Hence, so it is argued, the check given to the operation of these personal qualities by governmental regulation of business activities is at the same time an attack upon the practical and moral conditions for the existence of political democracy.

I am not concerned here with the merits of the special arguments put forth in behalf and against the measures employed. The point is that appeal to certain alleged human motivations in a wholesale way, such as "initiative, independence, enterprise" at large, obscures the need for observation of events in the concrete. If and when special events are observed, interpretation of them is predestined instead of growing out of what is observed. By keeping the issues in the realm of opinion, appeal to equally general wholesale views on the other side is promoted. Then we get a kind of head-on conflict between something called "individualism" on one side and "socialism" on the other. Examination of concrete conditions might disclose certain specifiable conditions under which both of the methods vaguely pointed at by these words would operate to advantage.

The current use of the word *enterprise* as an honorific term is especially instructive with regard to the attempt to draw support for policies from a reference to general inherent traits of human nature. For the only legitimate signification of "enterprise" is a neutral one, an *undertaking* the desirability of which is a matter of actual results produced, which accordingly need to be studied in the concrete. But *enterprise* is given the significance of a certain desirable trait of human nature, so that the issue is taken out of the field of observation into that of opinion plus a eulogistic emotion. "Enterprise" like "initiative" and like "industry" can be exerted in behalf of an indefinite number of objects; the words may designate the activities of an Al Capone or a racketeering labor union as well as a socially useful industrial undertaking.

The case is cited in some detail because it provides a striking example, first, of the conversion of an existing mode of social behavior into a psychological property of human nature; and, secondly, conversion of an alleged matter of psychological fact into a principle of value—a moral matter. Social problems that are set by conditions having definite spatial and temporal boundaries—which have to be determined by observation—are made into matters capable of absolute determination without reference to conditions of place and date. Hence they become matters of opinion and controversial argument—and as the latter decides nothing, the final tendency is to appeal to force as the ultimate arbiter.

The theory of the components of human nature used by the intellectual radicals of Great Britain to justify popular government and freedom included more than the self-interest motivation. It was officially held that sympathy with the gains and losses, the pleasures and pains of others, is a native part of the human endowment. The two components, self-interest and sympathy, opposite in quality, were ingeniously linked together in the complete doctrine—occasionally with explicit reference to the supposedly analogous centripetal and centrifugal components of Newtonian celestial mechanics. The self-interest phase supplied the foundation of the theory of public and governmental action; the sympathetic phase took care of the relations of individuals to one another in their private capacities. The doctrine taught that if political institutons were reformed to do away with special privileges and unfair favoritisms, the sympathetic motive would have a vastly enlarged field of effective and successful operation, since bad institutions were the chief cause that led men to find their personal advantage in acts injurious to others.

The theory was even more important in the reaction it called out than in itself. For "organic idealistic" philosophies developed in Germany during the nineteenth century, and now form the theoretical background and justification of totalitarianism. They took their clew and point of departure from the weaknesses of the theories that based politics and morals, in theory and in practice, upon alleged components of human nature. An adequate account of the form and substance of the reaction would take us into matters which cannot be set forth without going into technicalities. But its basis is simple.

The attempt to locate the source of authority of politics and morals in human nature was regarded as the source of anarchy, disorder, and conflict;—an attempt to build social institutions and personal relationships upon the most unstable of shifting quicksands. At the same time, the philosophers who formulated the new view were Protestants and Northerners. Hence their reaction did not move them to urge acceptance of the doctrines of the Roman Church as the bulwark against the dissolving tendencies of ultra-individualistic ideas and policies.

The French Revolution, with its excesses, was uniformly regarded in German thought as the logical outcome of the attempt to locate authority where nothing binding could be found. It was thus taken to be a practical large scale demonstration of the weakness inherent in the position. The most that could be said for the doctrine was what could be said in defense of the French Revolution—it helped to get rid of abuses that had grown up. As a positive and constructive principle, it was a tragic delusion. The statement of the Rights of Man setting forth the official creed of the Revolution was said to be a summary of the false doctrines that had produced all the characteristic evils of the age. The protest, as just said, refused to accept the doctrines of the Church as the basis for its criticisms and for the constructive measures it proposed. It was itself too deeply influenced by the conditions which had produced the individualism against which it revolted. The extent of this influence is why the movement is criticized by representatives of the Hellenic-medieval ideas as itself intensely "subjectivistic." It found the way to "reconcile" freedom and authority, individuality and law, by setting up an Absolute Self, Mind, Spirit, of which human beings are individually partial manifestations, a "truer" and fuller manifestation being found in social institutions, the state and the course of history. Since history is the final court of judgment and since it represents the movement of absolute Spirit, appeal to force to settle issues between nations is not "really" an appeal to force, but rather to the ultimate logic of absolute reason. The individualistic movement was a necessary transitional movement to bring men to recognition of the primacy and ultimacy of Spirit and Personality in the constitution of nature, man, and society. German organic idealism was to save all that is true in the movement, while eliminating its errors and dangers by lifting it up to the plane of absolute Self and Spirit. There is much that is technical in the movement; much of its detail can be explained only on the ground of special intellectual events. But its heart and core is found in its attempt to find a "higher" justification for individuality and freedom where the latter are merged with law and authority, which *must* be rational since they are manifestations of Absolute Reason. Contemporary totalitarianism has no difficulty in discovering that the Germanic racial spirit embodied in the

German state is an adequate substitute, for all practical purposes, for the Hegelian Absolute Spirit.

Rousseau is usually, and in many respects properly, regarded as the prophet and intellectual progenitor of the French Revolution. But by one of those ironies with which history abounds he was also a step-father of the theory that came to full expression in Germany. He served in this capacity partly indirectly by his attack on culture which, as previously said, was the challenge that resulted in glorification of culture over against human nature. But he also acted positively and directly. For in his political writings he advanced the idea that a Common Will is the source of legitimate political institutions; that freedom and law are one and the same thing in the operations of the Common Will, for it must act for the Common Good and hence for the "real" or true Good of every individual.

If the latter set up their purely personal desires against the General Will, it was accordingly legitimate (indeed necessary) to "*force* them to be free." Rousseau intended his theory to state the foundation of self-governing institutions and majority rule. But his premise was employed to prove that the Common—or Universal—Will and Reason was embodied in the national state. Its most adequate incarnation was in those states in which the authority of law, order, and discipline had not been weakened by democratic heresies:—a view which was used in Germany after the Napoleonic conquest to create an aggressive national spirit in that country, one which provided the basis for systematic depreciation of French "materialistic" civilization as over against German *Kultur*—a depreciation later extended to condemnation of democratic institutions in any country.

While this brief exposition of the reaction against the individualistic theory of human nature suggests the ground pattern of National Socialism, it also throws some light upon the predicament in which democratic countries find themselves. The fact that the individualistic theory was used a century and more ago to justify political self-government and then aided promotion of its cause does not constitute the theory a present trustworthy guide of democratic action. It is profitable to read today the bitterly vivid denunciations of Carlyle on the theory as it was originally put forth. He denounced with equal fierceness the attempt to erect political authority upon the basis of self-interest and private morals upon the exercise of sympathy. The latter was sentimentalism run riot and the former was "Anarchy plus the Constable"—the latter being needed to preserve even a semblance of outward order. His plea for discipline and order included even a plea for leadership by select persons.

The present predicament may be stated as follows: Democracy does involve a belief that political institutions and law be such as to take fundamental account of human nature. They must give it freer play than any non-democratic institutions. At the same time, the theory, legalistic and moralistic, about human nature that has been used to expound and justify this reliance upon human nature has proved inadequate. Upon the legal and political side, during the nineteenth century it was progressively overloaded with ideas and practices which have more to do with business carried on for profit than with democracy. On the moralistic side, it has tended to substitute emotional exhortation to act in accord with the Golden Rule for the discipline and the control afforded by incorporation of democratic ideals into *all* the relations of life. Because of lack of an adequate theory of human nature in its relations to democracy, attachment to democratic ends and methods has tended to become a matter of tradition and habit—an excellent thing as far as it goes, but when it becomes routine is easily undermined when change of conditions changes other habits.

Were I to say that democracy needs a new psychology of human nature, one adequate to the heavy demands put upon it by foreign and domestic conditions, I might be taken to utter an academic irrelevancy. But if the remark is understood to mean that democracy has always been allied with humanism, with faith in the potentialities of human nature, and that the present need is vigorous reassertion of this faith, developed in relevant ideas and manifested in practical attitudes, it but continues the American tradition. For belief in the "common man" has no significance save as an expression of belief in the intimate and vital connection of democracy and human nature.

We cannot continue the idea that human nature when left to itself, when freed from external arbitrary restrictions, will tend to the production of democratic institutions that work successfully. We have now to state the issue from the other side. We have to see that democracy means the belief that humanistic culture *should* prevail; we should be frank and open in our recognition that the proposition is a moral one—like any idea that concerns what *should* be.

Strange as it seems to us, democracy is challenged by

totalitarian states of the Fascist variety on moral grounds just as it is challenged by totalitarianisms of the left on economic grounds. We may be able to defend democracy on the latter score, as far as comparative conditions are involved, since up to the present at least the Union of Socialist Republics has not "caught up" with us, much less "surpassed" us, in material affairs. But defense against the other type of totalitarianism (and perhaps in the end against also the Marxist type) requires a positive and courageous constructive awakening to the significance of faith in human nature for development of every phase of our culture:—science, art, education, morals and religion, as well as politics and economics. No matter how uniform and constant human nature is in the abstract, the conditions within which and upon which it operates have changed so greatly since political democracy was established among us, that democracy cannot now depend upon or be expressed in political institutions alone. We cannot even be certain that they and their legal accompaniments are actually democratic at the present time—for democracy is expressed in the attitudes of human beings and is measured by consequences produced in their lives.

The impact of the humanist view of democracy upon all forms of culture, upon education, science and art, morals and religion, as well as upon industry and politics, saves it from the criticism passed upon moralistic exhortation. For it tells us that we need to examine every one of the phases of human activity to ascertain what effects it has in release, maturing and fruition of the potentialities of human nature. It does not tell us to "re-arm morally" and all social problems will be solved. It says, Find out how all the constituents of our existing culture are operating and then see to it that whenever and wherever needed they be modified in order that their workings may release and fulfill the possibilities of human nature.

It used to be said (and the statement has not gone completely out of fashion) that democracy is a by-product of Christianity, since the latter teaches the infinite worth of the individual human soul. We are now told by some persons that since belief in the soul has been discredited by science, the moral basis for democracy supposed to exist must go into the discard. We are told that if there are reasons for preferring it to other arrangements of the relations of human beings to one another, they must be found in specialized external advantages which outweigh the advantages of other social forms. From a very different quarter, we are told that weakening of the older theological ·doctrine of the soul is one of the reasons for the eclipse of faith in democracy. These two views at opposite poles give depth and urgency to the question whether there are adequate grounds for faith in the potentialities of human nature and whether they can be accompanied by the intensity and ardor once awakened by religious ideas upon a theological basis. Is human nature intrinsically such a poor thing that the idea is *absurd?* I do not attempt to give any answer, but the word *faith* is intentionally used. For in the long run democracy will stand or fall with the possibility of maintaining the faith and justifying it by works.

Take, for example, the question of intolerance. Systematic hatred and suspicion of any human group, "racial," sectarian, political, denotes deep-seated scepticism about the qualities of human nature. From the standpoint of a faith in the possibilities of human nature possessing religious quality it is blasphemous. It may start by being directed at a particular group, and be supported in name by assigning special reasons why that group is not worthy of confidence, respect, and decent human treatment. But the underlying attitude is one of fundamental distrust of human nature. Hence it spreads from distrust and hatred of a particular group until it may undermine the conviction that any group of persons has any intrinsic right for esteem or recognition—which, then, if it be given, is for some special and external grounds, such as usefulness to our particular interests and ambitions. There is no physical acid which has the corrosive power possessed by intolerance directed against persons because they belong to a group that bears a certain name. Its corrosive potency gains with what it feeds on. An anti-humanist attitude is the essence of every form of intolerance. Movements that begin by stirring up hostility against a group of people end by denying to them all human qualities.

The case of intolerance is used as an illustration of the intrinsic connection between the prospects of democracy and belief in the potentialities of human nature—not for its own sake, important as it is on its own account. How much of our past tolerance was positive and how much of it a toleration equivalent to "standing" something we do not like, "putting up" with something because it involves too much trouble to try to change it? For a good deal of the present reaction against democracy is probably simply the disclosure of a weakness that was there before; one that was covered up or did not appear in its true light. Certainly racial prejudice against negroes, Catholics, and Jews is no new thing in our life. Its presence among us is an intrinsic weakness and a handle for the accusation that we do not act differently from Nazi Germany.

The greatest practical inconsistency that would be revealed by searching our own habitual attitudes is probably one between the democratic method of forming opinions in political matters and the methods in common use in forming beliefs in other subjects. In theory, the democratic method is persuasion through public discussion carried on not only in legislative halls but in the press, private conversations and public assemblies. The substitution of ballots for bullets, of the right to vote for the lash, is an expression of the will to substitute the method of discussion for the method of coercion. With all its defects and partialities in determination of political decisions, it has worked to keep factional disputes within bounds, to an extent that was incredible a century or more ago. While Carlyle could bring his gift of satire into play in ridiculing the notion that men by talking to and at each other in an assembly hall can settle what is true in social affairs any more than they can settle what is true in the multiplication table, he failed to see that if men had been using clubs to maim and kill one another to decide the product of 7 times 7, there would have been sound reasons for appealing to discussion and persuasion even in the latter case. The fundamental reply is that social "truths" are so unlike mathematical truths that unanimity of uniform belief is possible in respect to the former only when a dictator has the power to tell others what they must believe—or profess they believe. The adjustment of interests demands that diverse interests have a chance to articulate themselves.

The real trouble is that there is an intrinsic split in our habitual attitudes when we profess to depend upon discussion and persuasion in politics and then systematically depend upon other methods in reaching conclusions in matters of morals and religion, or in anything where we depend upon a person or group possessed of "authority." We do not have to go to theological matters to find examples. In homes and in schools, the places where the essentials of character are supposed to be formed, the usual procedure is settlement of issues, intellectual and moral, by appeal to the "authority" of parent, teacher, or textbook. Dispositions formed under such conditions are so inconsistent with the democratic method that in a crisis they may be aroused to act in positively anti-democratic ways for anti-democratic ends; just as resort to coercive force and suppression of civil liberties are readily palliated in nominally democratic communities when the cry is raised that "law and order" are threatened.

It is no easy matter to find adequate authority for action in the demand, characteristic of democracy, that conditions be such as will enable the potentialities of human nature to reach fruition. Because it is not easy the democratic road is the hard one to take. It is the road which places the greatest burden of responsibility upon the greatest number of human beings. Backsets and deviations occur and will continue to occur. But that which is its weakness at particular times is its strength in the long course of human history. Just because the cause of democratic freedom is the cause of the fullest possible realization of human potentialities, the latter when they are suppressed and oppressed will in time rebel and demand an opportunity for manifestation.

With the founders of American democracy, the claims of democracy were inherently one with the demands of a just and equal morality. We cannot now well use their vocabulary. Changes in knowledge have outlawed the significations of the words they commonly used. But in spite of the unsuitability of much of their language for present use, what they asserted was that self-governing institutions are the means by which human nature can sec..re its fullest realization in the greatest number of persons. The question of what is involved in self-governing methods is now much more complex. But for this very reason, the task of those who retain belief in democracy is to revive and maintain in full vigor the original conviction of the intrinsic moral nature of democracy, now stated in ways congruous with present conditions of culture. We have advanced far enough to say that democracy is a way of life. We have yet to realize that it is a way of personal life and one which provides a moral standard for personal conduct.

Science and Free Culture

I T is no longer possible to hold the simple faith of the Enlightenment that assured advance of science will produce free institutions by dispelling ignorance and superstition:—the sources of human servitude and the pillars of oppressive government. The progress of natural science has been even more rapid and extensive than could have been anticipated. But its technological application in mass production and distribution of goods has required concentration of capital; it has resulted in business corporations possessed of extensive legal rights and immunities; and, as is a commonplace, has created a vast and intricate set of new problems. It has put at the disposal of dictators means of controlling opinion and sentiment of a potency which reduces to a mere shadow all previous agencies at the command of despotic rulers. For negative censorship it has substituted means of propaganda of ideas and alleged information on a scale that reaches every individual, reiterated day after day by every organ of publicity and communication, old and new. In consequence, for practically the first time in human history, totalitarian states exist claiming to rest upon the active consent of the governed. While despotic governments are as old as political history, this particular phenomenon is as startlingly unexpected as it is powerful.

One of the earlier arguments for democracy is countered in the most disturbing way. Before the industrial revolution had made much headway it was a commonplace that oppressive governments had the support of only a relatively small class. Republican government, it was assumed, would have the broad support of the masses, so that the "people" who, as Rousseau expressed it, had been nothing would become everything. We are now told the contrary. Democracy is said to be but a numerical contrivance, resting upon shifting combinations of individuals who happen at a given time to make up a majority of voters. We are told that the moral consensus which exists only when there is unity of beliefs and aims, is conspicuously lacking in democracies, and is of the very essence of totalitarian states. The claim stands side by side with that of Marxist communists who say that since their views are inherently scientific, false opinions have no legitimate standing as against the authority of The Truth. But in a way the Fascist claim goes deeper since it pretends to extend below merely intellectual loyalties, to which science appeals, and lay hold of fundamental emotions and impulses.

There is an argument about science which so far has found comparatively little response in democratic countries, but which nevertheless puts a problem so basic that it will receive more and more attention as time goes by. It is said that the principles of laissez-faire individualism have governed the conduct of scientific inquiry; that the tastes and preferences of individual investigators have been allowed to regulate its course to such an extent that present intellectual confusion and moral chaos of the world exists because of tacit connivance of science with uncontrolled individualistic activity in industry.

The position is so extreme and goes so contrary to all we had come to believe that it is easily passed over as an aberration. But the view, because of its extreme character, may be taken to point to a genuine issue: just what are the social consequences of science? Are they not so important, because of technological applications, that the social interest is paramount over intellectual interest? Can the type of social control of industry urged by socialists be carried through without some kind of public regulation of the scientific investigations that are the source of the inventions determining the course of industry? And might not such regulation throttle the freedom of science? Those who say that the social effect of inventions (which exist only because of the findings of scientific inquiry) is so unsettling that the least which can be done is to declare a moratorium on science express the same problem with more moderation.

The claim is made in Russia that the direction taken by science has in the last hundred and fifty years been so determined by the interest of the dominant economic class, that science has been upon the whole an organ of bourgeois democracy:—not so consciously perhaps as in the case of government, the police and the army, but yet in substantial effect. Since it is impossible to draw any fixed line between the physical and the social sciences, and since the latter—both with respect to investigation and teaching —must be regulated in the interest of the politics of the new social order, it is impossible to allow the physical sciences to go their way apart without political regulation. Nazi Germany decrees what is scientific truth in anthropology regarding race, and Moscow determines that Mendelism is scientifically false, and dictates the course to be pursued by Genetics. Both countries look askance at the theory of Relativity, although on different grounds. Quite aside, however, from special cases, a general atmosphere of control of opinion cannot exist without reacting in pretty fundamental ways upon every form of intellectual activity—art too as well as science.

Even if we hold that extreme views are so extreme as to be distorted caricatures, there remains an actual problem. Can society, especially a democratic society, exist without a basic consensus and community of beliefs? If it cannot, can the required community be achieved without regulation of scientific pursuits exercised by a public authority in behalf of social unity?

In this connection the accusation of irresponsibility as to social consequences is brought against scientific men, and it is in this context that the underlying issue takes shape. It is argued (and some who take the position are themselves scientists) that the main directions of physical science during the past hundred years, increasingly so in the last half century, have been set, indirectly and directly, by the requirements of industry carried on for private profit. Consideration of the *problems* which have not received attention in comparison with those which have absorbed expenditure of intellectual energies will, it is said, prove the proposition.

Direct control has been exercised for the most part by

governments. They have subsidized the kind of investigations that promise increased national power, either by promoting manufacturing and commerce as against other national states, or by fostering researches that strengthen military prowess. Indirect control has been exercised in subtler ways. The place of industry is so central in modern life that quite apart from questions handed directly over to scientific laboratories by industrial enterprises, it is psychologically impossible for men engaged in scientific research not to be most sensitive and most responsive to the *type* of problems presented in practical effort to control natural energies;—which in the concrete means manufacturing and distributing goods. Moreover, a kind of positive halo surrounds scientific endeavors. For it has been held, not without grounds, that general social—or at least national—welfare is thereby promoted. Germany led other countries in physical research; and it was in Germany that scientific advances could be shown to have contributed most directly to national strength and prestige. It was thus possible for some intellectual observers, not particularly naïve, to hold up German universities as models to follow in our own country.

It is not implied that personal economic interest has played any important part in directing the researches of individual scientists. The contrary is notoriously the rule. But attention and interest are not freely ranging searchlights that can be directed at all parts of the natural universe with equal ease. They operate within certain channels, and the general state of culture determines what and where the channels are. The "climate of opinion" decides the direction taken by scientific activity as truly as physical climate decides what agricultural pursuits can be carried on. Social imagination comes to have a certain tone and color; intellectual immunity in one direction and intellectual sensitivity in other directions are the result. It has even been said, and with a good deal of evidence in its support, that the prevailing mechanistic creed of science during the nineteenth century was an indirect product of the importance assumed by the machine in industrial production, so that now, when machine-production is giving way to power-production, basic scientific "concepts" are also changing.

I referred above to the role of nationalism in deciding the direction taken by science. The striking instance is of course the organization of scientific men for aid to a nation in time of war. The instance brings to a head tendencies that are going on in less overt and more unconscious ways pretty much all the time, even in times of nominal peace. Increase of the scope of governmental activities in all industrialized countries, going on for some years at an accelerated pace, has reinforced the alliance between national interest and scientific inquiry. It is certainly arguable that when the choice at hand is between regulation of science by private economic interests and by nationalist interest, the latter should have preference. It may be inferred that the open control of science exercised in totalitarian states is but a culmination of tendencies that have been going on in more or less covert ways for some time—from which it follows that the problem presented extends beyond the borders of those particular states.

Strangely enough, at first sight, the demand for direct social control of scientific inquiries and conclusion is unwittingly reinforced by an attitude quite commonly taken by scientific men themselves. For it is commonly said and commonly believed that science is completely neutral and indifferent as to the ends and values which move men to act: that at most it only provides more efficient means for realization of ends that are and must be due to wants and desires completely independent of science. It is at this point that the present climate of opinion differs so widely from that which marked the optimistic faith of the Enlightenment; the faith that human science and freedom would advance hand in hand to usher in an era of indefinite human perfectibility.

That the popular esteem of science is largely due to the aid it has given to men for attainment of things they wanted independently of what they had learned from science is doubtless true. Russell has stated in a vivid way the sort of thing that has enabled science to displace beliefs that had previously been held: "The world ceased to believe that Joshua caused the sun to stand still, because Copernican astronomy was useful in navigation; it abandoned Aristotle's physics, because Galileo's theory of falling bodies made it possible to calculate the trajectory of a cannonball. It rejected the theory of the flood because geology is useful in mining and so on." * That the quotation expresses the sort of thing that gave the conclusions of the new science prestige and following at a time when it badly needed some outside aid in getting a hearing can hardly be doubted. As illustrative material it is especially impressive because of the enormous authority enjoyed by the doctrines of Aristotle and of the Church. If even in the

---

* Bertrand Russell, *Power*, p. 138.

137

case where all the advantage was on the side of old doctrines, the demonstrated serviceability of science gave it the victory, we can easily judge the enhancement of the esteem in which science was held in matters where it had no such powerful foe to contend with.

Quite apart from the antagonism to science displayed by entrenched institutional interests that had previously obtained a monopoly over beliefs in, say, astronomy, geology and some fields of history, history proves the existence of so much indifference on the part of mankind to the quality of its beliefs and such lethargy towards methods that disturb old beliefs, that we should be glad that the new science has had such powerful adventitious aid. But it leaves untouched the question as to whether scientific knowledge has power to modify the ends which men prize and strive to attain. Is it proved that the findings of science —the best authenticated knowledge we have—add only to our power to realize desires already in existence? Or is this view derived from some previous theory about the constitution of human nature? Can it be true that desires and knowledge exist in separate non-communicating compartments? Do the facts which can undoubtedly be cited as evidence, such as the use of scientific knowledge indifferently to heal disease and prolong human life and to provide the instruments for wholesale destruction of life, really prove the case? Or are they specially selected cases that support a doctrine that originated on other grounds than the evidence of facts? Is there such a complete separation of human ends from human beliefs as the theory assumes?

The shock given old ideas by the idea that knowledge

138

is incapable of modifying the quality of desires (and hence cannot affect the formation of ends and purposes) is not of course in itself a ground for denying it is sound. It may be that the old view is totally false. Nevertheless, the point is worth discussion. We do not have to refer to the theory of Plato that knowledge, or what passes as knowledge, is the sole final determinant of men's ideas of the Good and hence of their actions. Nor is it needful to refer to Bacon's vision of the organization of scientific knowledge as the prospective foundation of future social policies directed exclusively to the advance of human well-being. The simple fact is that all the deliberately liberal and progressive movements of modern times have based themselves on the idea that action is determined by ideas, up to the time when Hume said that reason was and should be the "slave of the passions"; or, in contemporary language, of the emotions and desires. Hume's voice was a lonely one when he uttered the remark. The idea is now echoed and re-echoed from almost every quarter. The classic economic school made wants the prime motors of human action, reducing reason to a power of calculating the means best fitted to satisfy the wants. The first effect of biology upon psychology was to emphasize the primacy of appetites and instincts. Psychiatrists have enforced the same conclusion by showing that intellectual disturbances originate in emotional maladjustments, and by exhibiting the extent of dictation of belief by desire.

It is one thing, however, to recognize that earlier theories neglected the importance of emotions and habits as determinants of conduct and exaggerated that of ideas and reason. It is quite another thing to hold that ideas (especially those warranted by competent inquiry) and emotions (with needs and desires) exist in separate compartments so that no interaction between them exists. When the view is as baldly stated it strikes one as highly improbable that there can be any such complete separation in the constitution of human nature. And while the idea must be accepted if the evidence points that way, no matter into what plight human affairs are forever plunged, the implications of the doctrine of complete separation of desire and knowledge must be noted. The assumption that desires are rigidly fixed is not one on its face consistent with the history of man's progress from savagery through barbarism to even the present defective state of civilization. If knowledge, even of the most authenticated kind, cannot influence desires and aims, if it cannot determine what is of value and what is not, the future outlook as to formation of desires is depressing. Denial that they can be influenced by knowledge points emphatically to the non-rational and anti-rational forces that will form them. One alternative to the power of ideas is habit or custom, and then when the rule of sheer habit breaks down—as it has done at the present time—all that is left is competition on the part of various bodies and interests to decide which shall come out ahead in a struggle, carried on by intimidation, coercion, bribery, and all sorts of propaganda, to shape the desires which shall predominantly control the ends of human action. The prospect is a black one. It leads one to consider the possibility that Bacon, Locke, and the leaders of the Enlightenment—typified by the act of Condorcet, writing, while imprisoned and waiting for death, about the role of science in the future liberation of mankind—were after all quite aware of the actual influence of appetite, habit, and blind desire upon action, but were engaged in holding up another and better way as the alternative to follow in the future.

That the course they anticipated has not come to fruition is obvious without argument. Bacon's action in using his own knowledge as a servant of the Crown in strengthening Great Britain in a military way against other nations now seems more prophetic of what has happened than what he put down in words. The power over Nature which he expected to follow the advance of science has come to pass. But in contradiction to his expectations, it has been largely used to increase, instead of reduce, the power of Man over Man. Shall we conclude that the early prophets were totally and intrinsically wrong? Or shall we conclude that they immensely underestimated the obduracy of institutions and customs antedating the appearance of science on the scene in shaping desires in their image? Have events after all but accentuated the problem of discovering the means by which authenticated beliefs shall influence desires, the formation of ends, and thereby the course of events? Is it possible to admit the power of propaganda to shape ends and deny that of science?

Looked at from one angle, the question brings us back to our fundamental issue: the relation of culture and human nature. For the fact which is decisive in answering the question whether verified knowledge is or is not capable of shaping desires and ends (as well as means) is whether the desires that are effective in settling the course of action are innate and fixed, or are themselves the product of a certain culture. If the latter is the case, the practical issue reduces itself to this: Is it possible for the scientific attitude to become such a weighty and widespread constituent of culture that, through the medium of culture, it may shape human desires and purposes?

To state the question is a long way from ability to answer it. But it is something to have the issue before us in its actual instead of in its factitious form. The issue ceases to be the indeterminate one of the relation of knowledge and desires in the native psychological constitution of man —indeterminate, among other reasons, because it is disputable whether there is any such thing as the latter apart from native biological constitution. It becomes the determinate one of the institution of the kind of culture in which scientific method and scientific conclusions are integrally incorporated.

The problem stated in this way puts in a different light the esteem gained by science because of its serviceability. That there are individuals here and there who have been influenced to esteem science because of some obvious contribution to satisfaction of their merely personal desires may well be a fact. That there are groups similarly influenced must be admitted. But the reasons why men have been willing to accept conclusions derived from science in lieu of older ideas are not exclusively or even mainly those of direct personal and class benefit. Improvements in navigation and mining have become part of the state of culture. It is in this capacity they have tended to displace beliefs that were congenial to an earlier state of culture. By and large the same thing is true of the application of physics and chemistry in more effective satisfaction of wants and in creation of new wants. While their application to produce increased efficiency in carrying on war has doubtlessly recommended those sciences to persons like rulers and generals, who otherwise would have been indifferent, the mass of persons have been moved to an attitude of favorable esteem by what has happened in the arts of peace. The decisive factor would seem to be whether the arts of war or of peace are to be in the future the ones that will control culture, a question that involves the need of discovering why war is such an important constituent of present culture.

I should be on controversial ground if I held up as evidence the belief that the technologies, which are the practical correlates of scientific theories, have now reached a point in which they can be used to create an era of abundance instead of the deficit-economies that existed before natural science developed, and that with an era of abundance and security the causes of conflict would be reduced. It may be mentioned as a hypothetical illustration. The kind of serviceability which is capable of generating high esteem for science *may* possibly be serviceability for general and shared, or "social", welfare. If the economic regime were so changed that the resources of science were employed to maintain security for all, the present view about the limitation of science might fade away. I imagine there are not many who will deny that esteem for science, even when placed upon the ground of serviceability alone, is produced at least in part by an admixture of general with private serviceability. If there is a skeptic let him consider the contribution made by science both actually and still more potentially to agriculture, and the social consequences of the change in production of foods and raw materials, thereby effected.

The other side of the ledger is marked by such a debit entry as the following from the English chemist Soddy: "So far the pearls of science have been cast before swine, who have given us in return millionaires and slums, armaments and the desolation of war." The contrast is real. If its existence seems to support the doctrine that science only supplies means for more efficient execution of already existing desires and purposes, it is because it points to the division which exists in our culture. The war that mobilizes science for wholesale destruction mobilizes it, also, for support of life and for healing the wounded. The desires and ends involved proceed not from native and naked human nature but from modifications it has undergone in interaction with a complex of cultural factors of which science is indeed one, but one which produces social consequences only as it is affected by economic and political traditions and customs formed before its rise.

For in any case, the influence of science on both means and ends is not exercised directly upon individuals but indirectly through incorporation within culture. In this function and capacity it is that scientific beliefs have replaced earlier unscientific beliefs. The position stated at its worst is that science operates as a part of folklore, not just as science. Even when put in this way, attention is invited to differences in folklore and to differences of the consequences that are produced by different folklores. And when it is admitted that the folklore may be one of aggressive nationalism, where the consequences of science as part of the prevailing folklore is war of the present destructive scope, we at least have the advantage of clear knowledge as to the location of the problem.

SCIENCE AND FREE CULTURE

We have been considering science as a body of conclusions. We have ignored science in its quality of an attitude embodied in habitual will to employ certain methods of observation, reflection, and test rather than others. When we look at science from this point of view, the significance of science as a constituent of culture takes on a new color. The great body of scientific inquirers would deny with indignation that they are actuated in *their* esteem for science by its material serviceability. If they use words sanctioned by long tradition, they say they are moved by love of the truth. If they use contemporary phraseology, less grandiloquent in sound but of equivalent meaning, they say they are moved by a controlling interest in inquiry, in discovery, in following where the evidence of discovered facts points. Above all they say that this kind of interest excludes interest in reaching any conclusion not warranted by evidence, no matter how personally congenial it may be.

In short, it is a fact that a certain group of men, perhaps relatively not very numerous, have a "disinterested" interest in scientific inquiry. This interest has developed a morale having its own distinctive features. Some of its obvious elements are willingness to hold belief in suspense, ability to doubt until evidence is obtained; willingness to go where evidence points instead of putting first a personally preferred conclusion; ability to hold ideas in solution and use them as hypotheses to be tested instead of as dogmas to be asserted; and (possibly the most distinctive of all) enjoyment of new fields for inquiry and of new problems.

145

Every one of these traits goes contrary to some human impulse that is naturally strong. Uncertainty is disagreeable to most persons; suspense is so hard to endure that assured expectation of an unfortunate outcome is usually preferred to a long-continued state of doubt. "Wishful thinking" is a comparatively modern phrase; but men upon the whole have usually believed what they wanted to believe, except as very convincing evidence made it impossible. Apart from a scientific attitude, guesses, with persons left to themselves, tend to become opinions and opinions dogmas. To hold theories and principles in solution, awaiting confirmation, goes contrary to the grain. Even today questioning a statement made by a person is often taken by him as a reflection upon his integrity, and is resented. For many millennia opposition to views widely held in a community was intolerable. It called down the wrath of the deities who are in charge of the group. Fear of the unknown, fear of change and novelty, tended, at all times before the rise of scientific attitude, to drive men into rigidity of beliefs and habits; they entered upon unaccustomed lines of behavior—even in matters of minor moment —with qualms which exacted rites of expiation. Exceptions to accepted rules have either been ignored or systematically explained away when they were too conspicuous to ignore. Baconian idols of the tribe, the cave, the theater, and den have caused men to rush to conclusions, and then to use all their powers to defend from criticism and change the conclusions arrived at. The connection of common law with custom and its resistance to change are familiar facts. Even religious beliefs and rites which were at first more or less heretical deviations harden into modes of action it

146

is impious to question, after once they have become part of the habits of a group.

If I mention such familiar considerations it is in part to suggest that we may well be grateful that science has had undeniable social serviceability, and that to some extent and in some places strong obstructions to adoption of changed beliefs have been overcome. But the chief reason for calling attention to them is the proof they furnish that in some persons and to some degree science has already created a new morale—which is equivalent to the creation of new desires and new ends. The existence of the scientific attitude and spirit, even upon a limited scale, is proof that science is capable of developing a distinctive type of disposition and purpose: a type that goes far beyond provision of more effective means for realizing desires which exist independently of any effect of science.

It is not becoming, to put it moderately, for those who are themselves animated by the scientific morale to assert that other persons are incapable of coming into possession of it and being moved by it.

Such an attitude is saved from being professional snobbery only when it is the result of sheer thoughtlessness. When one and the same representative of the intellectual class denounces any view that attaches inherent importance to the consequences of science, claiming the view is false to the spirit of science—and also holds that it is impossible for science to do anything to affect desires and ends, the inconsistency demands explanation.

A situation in which the fundamental dispositions and ends of a few are influenced by science while that of most persons and most groups is not so influenced proves that the issue is cultural. The difference sets a social problem: what are the causes for the existence of this great gap, especially since it has such serious consequences? If it is possible for persons to have their beliefs formed on the ground of evidence, procured by systematic and competent inquiry, nothing can be more disastrous socially than that the great majority of persons should have them formed by habit, accidents of circumstance, propaganda, personal and class bias. The existence, even on a relatively narrow scale, of a morale of fairmindedness, intellectual integrity, of will to subordinate personal preference to ascertained facts and to share with others what is found out, instead of using it for personal gain, is a challenge of the most searching kind. Why don't a great many more persons have this attitude?

The answer given to this challenge is bound up with the fate of democracy. The spread of literacy, the immense extension of the influence of the press in books, newspapers, periodicals, make the issue peculiarly urgent for a democracy. The very agencies that a century and a half ago were looked upon as those that were sure to advance the cause of democratic freedom, are those which now make it possible to create pseudo-public opinion and to undermine democracy from within. Callousness due to continuous reiteration may produce a certain immunity to the grosser kinds of propaganda. But in the long run negative measures afford no assurance. While it would be absurd to believe it desirable or possible for every one to become a scientist when science is defined from the side of subject matter, the future of democracy is allied with spread of the scientific attitude. It is the sole guarantee against wholesale misleading by propaganda. More important still, it is the only assurance of the possibility of a public opinion intelligent enough to meet present social problems.

To become aware of the problem is a condition of taking steps toward its solution. The problem is in part economic. The nature of control of the means of publicity enters directly; sheer financial control is not a favorable sign. The democratic belief in free speech, free press and free assembly is one of the things that exposes democratic institutions to attack. For representatives of totalitarian states, who are the first to deny such freedom when they are in power, shrewdly employ it in a democratic country to destroy the foundations of democracy. Backed with the necessary financial means, they are capable of carrying on a work of continuous sapping and mining. More dangerous, perhaps, in the end is the fact that all economic conditions tending toward centralization and concentration of the means of production and distribution affect the public press, whether individuals so desire or not. The causes which require large corporate capital to carry on modern business, naturally influence the publishing business.

The problem is also an educative one. A book instead of a paragraph could be given to this aspect of the topic. That the schools have mostly been given to imparting information ready-made, along with teaching the tools of literacy, cannot be denied. The methods used in acquiring such information are not those which develop skill in inquiry and in test of opinions. On the contrary, they are positively hostile to it. They tend to dull native curiosity, and to load powers of observation and experimentation with such a mass of unrelated material that they do not operate as effectively as they do in many an illiterate person. The problem of the common schools in a democracy has reached only its first stage when they are provided for everybody. Until what shall be taught and how it is taught is settled upon the basis of formation of the scientific attitude, the so-called educational work of schools is a dangerously hit-or-miss affair as far as democracy is concerned.

The problem—as was suggested earlier—is also one of art. It is difficult to write briefly on this aspect of the question without giving rise to false impressions. For of late there has been an active campaign, carried on in the name of the social function of art, for using the arts, the plastic arts as well as literature, in propaganda for special views which are dogmatically asserted to be socially necessary. In consequence, any reference to the topic may seem to have a flavor of commendation of something of the same kind, only exercised by way of a counter-campaign in behalf of democratic ideas. The point is different. It is a reminder that ideas are effective not as bare ideas but as they have imaginative content and emotional appeal. I have alluded to the extensive reaction that has set in against the earlier over-simplified rationalism. The reaction tended to go to an opposite extreme. In emphasizing the role of wants, impulse, habit, and emotion, it often denied any efficacy whatever to ideas, to intelligence. The problem is that of effecting the union of ideas and knowledge with the non-rational factors in the human make-up. Art is the name given to all the agencies by which this union is effected.

The problem is also a moral and religious one. That religions have operated most effectively in alliance with the fine arts was indicated earlier. Yet the historic influence of religions has often been to magnify doctrines that are not subject to critical inquiry and test. Their cumulative effect in producing habits of mind at odds with the attitudes required for maintenance of democracy is probably much greater than is usually recognized. Shrewd observers have said that one factor in the relatively easy victory of totalitarianism in Germany was the void left by decay of former theological beliefs. Those who had lost one external authority upon which they had depended were ready to turn to another one which was closer and more tangible.

To say that the issue is a moral one is to say that in the end it comes back to personal choice and action. From one point of view everything which has been said is a laboring of the commonplace that democratic government is a function of public opinion and public sentiment. But identification of its formation in the democratic direction with democratic extension of the scientific morale till it is part of the ordinary equipment of the ordinary individual indicates the issue is a moral one. It is individual persons who need to have this attitude substituted for pride and prejudice, for class and personal interest, for beliefs made dear by custom and early emotional associations. It is only by the choice and the active endeavor of many individuals that this result can be effected.

A former president of the United States once made a political stir by saying that "Public office is a public trust." The saying was a truism although one that needed emphasis. That possession of knowledge and special skill in intellectual methods is a public trust has not become a truism even in words. Scientific morale has developed in some persons to a point where it is a matter of course that what is found out is communicated to other persons who are also engaged in specialized research. But it has not developed to the point where wider responsibility for communication is acknowledged. Circumstances which have attended the historic growth of modern science explain why this is so, although they do not justify its continuance. Internal and external circumstances have brought about a social seclusion of science which from a certain standpoint is analogous to an earlier monastic seclusion.

The external circumstance was the opposition scientific men had to overcome before it was possible for them to carry on their work free from dictation or persecution. The internal circumstance was in part the need for extreme specialization of inquiries which necessarily accompanied the novelty of the new method; in part, it was a self-protective policy for maintaining the purity of a new, still immature and struggling attitude from contamination that proceeded from taking sides in practical affairs. This attitude had the blessing of the old and ingrained tradition of the "purity" of science as an exclusively theoretical subject; a subject aloof from practice, since reason and theory were so high above practice, which was, according to tradition, only material and utilitarian. The danger of loss of the impartiality of the scientific spirit through affiliation with some partisan and partial interest seemed to give significance to the established tradition about "purity," which, like traditional feminine chastity, needed all kinds of external safeguards to hedge it about. The need is not that scientific men become crusaders in special practical causes. Just as the problem with art is to unite the inherent in-

152

tegrity of the artist with imaginative and emotional appeal of ideas, so the present need is recognition by scientific men of social responsibility for contagious diffusion of the scientific attitude: a task not to be accomplished without abandoning once for all the belief that science is set apart from all other social interests as if possessed of a peculiar holiness.

Extension of the qualities that make up the scientific attitude is quite a different matter than dissemination of the results of physics, chemistry, biology and astronomy, valuable as the latter may be. The difference is the reason why the issue is a moral one. The question of whether science is capable of influencing the formation of ends for which men strive or is limited to increasing power of realizing those which are formed independently of it is the question whether science has intrinsic moral potentiality. Historically, the position that science is devoid of moral quality has been held by theologians and their metaphysical allies. For the position points unmistakably to the necessity for recourse to some other source of moral guidance. That a similar position is now taken in the name of science is either a sign of a confusion that permeates all aspects of culture, or is an omen of ill for democracy. If control of conduct amounts to conflict of desires with no possibility of determination of desire and purpose by scientifically warranted beliefs, then the practical alternative is competition and conflict between unintelligent forces for control of desire. The conclusion is so extreme as to suggest that denial in the name of science of the existence of any such things as moral facts may mark a transitional stage thoughtlessly taken to be final. It is quite true that science cannot affect moral values, ends, rules, principles as these were once thought of and believed in, namely, prior to the rise of science. But to say that that there are no such things as moral facts because desires control formation and valuation of ends is in truth but to point to desires and interests as themselves moral facts requiring control by intelligence equipped with knowledge. Science through its physical technological consequences is now determining the relations which human beings, severally and in groups, sustain to one another. If it is incapable of developing moral techniques which will also determine these relations, the split in modern culture goes so deep that not only democracy but all civilized values are doomed. Such at least is the problem. A culture which permits science to destroy traditional values but which distrusts its power to create new ones is a culture which is destroying itself. War is a symptom as well as a cause of the inner division.

Democracy and America

I MAKE no apology for linking what is said in this chapter with the name of Thomas Jefferson. For he was the first modern to state in human terms the principles of democracy. Were I to make an apology, it would be that in the past I have concerned myself unduly, if a comparison has to be made, with the English writers who have attempted to state the ideals of self-governing communities and the methods appropriate to their realization. If I now prefer to refer to Jefferson it is not, I hope, because of American, provincialism, even though I believe that only one who was attached to American soil and who took a consciously alert part in the struggles of the country to attain its independence, could possibly have stated as thoroughly and intimately as did Jefferson the aims embodied in the American tradition: "the definitions and axioms of a free government," as Lincoln called them. Nor is the chief reason for going to him, rather than to Locke or Bentham or Mill, his greater sobriety of judgment due to that constant tempering of theory with practical experience which also kept his democratic doctrine within human bounds.

The chief reason is that Jefferson's formulation is moral through and through: in its foundations, its methods, its ends. The heart of his faith is expressed in his words "Nothing is unchangeable but inherent and inalienable rights of man." The words in which he stated the moral basis of free institutions have gone out of vogue. We repeat the opening words of the Declaration of Independence, but unless we translate them they are couched in a language that, even when it comes readily to our tongue, does not penetrate today to the brain. He wrote: "These truths are self-evident: that all men are created equal; that they are endowed by their Creator with inherent and unalienable rights; that among these are life, liberty and the pursuit of happiness." Today we are wary of anything purporting to be self-evident truths; we are not given to associating politics with the plans of the Creator; the doctrine of natural rights which governed his style of expression has been weakened by historic and by philosophic criticism.

To put ourselves in touch with Jefferson's position we have therefore to translate the word "natural" into *moral*. Jefferson was under the influence of the Deism of his time. Nature and the plans of a benevolent and wise Creator were never far apart in his reflections. But his fundamental beliefs remain unchanged in substance if we forget all special associations with the word *Nature* and speak instead of ideal aims and values to be realized—aims which, although ideal, are not located in the clouds but are backed by something deep and indestructible in the needs and demands of humankind.

Were I to try to connect in any detail what I have to say with the details of Jefferson's speeches and letters—he wrote no theoretical treatises—I should probably seem to be engaged in a partisan undertaking; I should at times be compelled to indulge in verbal exegesis so as to attribute to him ideas not present in his mind. Nevertheless, there are three points contained in what has to be said about American democracy that I shall here explicitly connect with his name. In the first place, in the quotation made, it was the *ends* of democracy, the rights of *man*—not of men in the plural—which are unchangeable. It was not the forms and mechanisms through which inherent moral claims are realized that are to persist without change. Professed Jeffersonians have often not even followed the words of the one whose disciples they say they are, much less his spirit. For he said: "I know that laws and institutions must go hand in hand with the progress of the human mind.... As new discoveries are made, new truths disclosed, and manners and opinions change with the change of circumstances, institutions must change also and keep pace with the times. We might as well require a man to wear the coat which fitted him when a boy, as civilized society to remain ever under the regime of their barbarous ancestors."

Because of the last sentence his idea might be interpreted to be a justification of the particular change in government he was championing against earlier institutions. But he goes on to say: "Each generation has a right to choose for itself the form of government it believes the most promotive of its own happiness." Hence he also said: "The idea that institutions established for the use of a nation cannot be touched or modified, even to make them answer their end ... may perhaps be a salutary provision against the abuses of a monarch, but is most absurd against the nation itself." "A generation holds all the rights and powers their predecessors once held and may change their laws and institutions to suit themselves." He engaged in certain calculations based on Buffon, more ingenious than convincing, to settle upon a period of eighteen years and eight months that fixed the natural span of the life of a generation; thereby indicating the frequency with which it is desirable to overhaul "laws and institutions" to bring them into accord with "new discoveries, new truths, change of manners and opinions." The word *culture* is not used; Jefferson's statement would have been weakened by its use. But it is not only professed followers of Jefferson who have failed to act upon his teaching. It is true of all of us so far as we have set undue store by established mechanisms. The most flagrantly obvious violation of Jefferson's democratic point of view is found in the idolatry of the Constitution as it stands that has been sedulously cultivated. But it goes beyond this instance. As believers in democracy we have not only the right but the duty to question existing mechanisms of, say, suffrage and to inquire whether some functional organization would not serve to formulate and manifest public opinion better than the existing methods. It is not irrelevant to the point that a score of passages could be cited in which Jefferson refers to the American Government as an *experiment*.

The second point of which I would speak is closely bound up with an issue which has become controversial and partisan, namely, states rights versus federal power. There is no question of where Jefferson stood on that issue, nor as to his fear in general of governmental encroachment on liberty—inevitable in his case, since it was the cause of the Rebellion against British domination and was also the ground of his struggle against Hamiltonianism. But any one who stops with this particular aspect of Jefferson's doctrine misses an underlying principle of utmost importance. For while he stood for state action as a barrier against excessive power at Washington, and while on the *practical side* his concern with it was most direct, in his theoretical writings chief importance is attached to local self-governing units on something like the New England town-meeting plan. His project for general political organization on the basis of small units, small enough so that all its members could have direct communication with one another and take care of all community affairs was never acted upon. It never received much attention in the press of immediate practical problems.

But without forcing the significance of this plan, we may find in it an indication of one of the most serious of present problems regarding democracy. I spoke earlier of the way in which individuals at present find themselves in the grip of immense forces whose workings and consequences they have no power of affecting. The situation calls emphatic attention to the need for face-to-face associations, whose interactions with one another may offset if not control the dread impersonality of the sweep of present forces. There is a difference between a society, in the sense of an association, and a community. Electrons, atoms and molecules are in association with one another. Nothing exists in isolation anywhere throughout nature. Natural associations are conditions for the existence of a community, but a community adds the function of communication in which emotions and ideas are shared as well as joint undertakings engaged in. Economic forces have immensely widened the scope of associational activities. But it has done so largely at the expense of the intimacy and directness of communal group interests and activities. The American habit of "joining" is a tribute to the reality of the problem but has not gone far in solving it. The power of the rabblerouser, especially in the totalitarian direction, is mainly due to his power to create a factitious sense of direct union and communal solidarity—if only by arousing the emotion of common intolerance and hate.

I venture to quote words written some years ago: "Evils which are uncritically and indiscriminately laid at the door of industrialism and democracy might, with greater intelligence, be referred to the dislocation and unsettlement of local communities. Vital and thorough attachments are bred only in the intimacy of an intercourse which is of necessity restricted in range.... Is it possible to restore the reality of the less communal organizations and to penetrate and saturate their members with a sense of local community life? ... Democracy must begin at home, and its home is the neighborly community." * On account of the vast extension of the field of association, produced by elimination of distance and lengthening of temporal spans, it is obvious that social agencies, political and non-political, cannot be confined to localities. But the problem of harmonious adjustment between extensive activities, precluding direct contacts, and the intensive activities of community intercourse is a pressing one for democracy. It involves even more than apprenticeship in the practical processes of self-government, important as that is, which Jefferson had in mind. It involves development of local agencies of communication and cooperation, creating stable loyal attach-

* *The Public and its Problems*, pp. 212-13.

ments, to militate against the centrifugal forces of present culture, while at the same time they are of a kind to respond flexibly to the demands of the larger unseen and indefinite·public. To a very considerable extent, groups having a functional basis will probably have to replace those based on physical contiguity. In the family both factors combine.

The third point of which I would make express mention as to Jefferson and democracy has to do with his ideas about property. It would be absurd to hold that his personal views were "radical" beyond fear of concentrated wealth and a positive desire for general distribution of wealth without great extremes in either direction. However, it is sometimes suggested that his phrase "pursuit of happiness" stood for economic activity, so that life, liberty, and property were the rights he thought organized society should maintain. But just here is where he broke most completely with Locke. In connection with property, especially property in land, he makes his most positive statements about the inability of any generation to bind its successors. Jefferson held that property rights are created by the "social pact" instead of representing inherent individual moral claims which government is morally bound to maintain.

The right to pursue happiness stood with Jefferson for nothing less than the claim of every human being to choose his own career and to act upon his own choice and judgment free from restraints and constraints imposed by the arbitrary will of other human beings—whether these others are officials of government, of whom Jefferson was especially afraid, or are persons whose command of capital and control of the opportunities for engaging in useful work limits the ability of others to "pursue happiness." The Jeffersonian principle of equality of rights without special favor to any one justifies giving supremacy to personal rights when they come into conflict with property rights. While his views are properly enough cited against ill-considered attacks upon the economic relations that exist at a given time, it is sheer perversion to hold that there is anything in Jeffersonian democracy that forbids political action to bring about equalization of economic conditions in order that the equal right of all to free choice and free action be maintained.

I have referred with some particularity to Jefferson's ideas upon special points because of the proof they afford that the source of the American democratic tradition is moral—not technical, abstract, narrowly political nor materially utilitarian. It is moral because based on faith in the ability of human nature to achieve freedom for individuals accompanied with respect and regard for other persons and with social stability built on cohesion instead of coercion. Since the tradition is a moral one, attacks upon it, however they are made, wherever they come from, from within or from without, involve moral issues and can be settled only upon moral grounds. In as far as the democratic ideal has undergone eclipse among us, the obscuration is moral in source and effect. The dimming is both a product and a manifestation of the confusion that accompanies transition from an old order to a new one for the arrival of the latter was heralded only as conditions plunged it into an economic regime so novel that there was no adequate preparation for it and which dislocated the established relations of persons with one another.

Nothing is gained by attempts to minimize the novelty of the democratic order, nor the scope of the change it requires in old and long cherished traditions. We have not even as yet a common and accepted vocabulary in which to set forth the order of moral values involved in realization of democracy. The language of Natural Law was once all but universal in educated Christendom. The conditions which gave it force disappeared. Then there was an appeal to natural rights, supposed by some to center in isolated individuals—although not in the original American formulation. At present, appeal to the individual is dulled by our inability to locate the individual with any assurance. While we are compelled to note that his freedom can be maintained only through the working together toward a single end of a large number of different and complex factors, we do not know how to coordinate them on the basis of voluntary purpose.

The intimate association that was held to exist between individualism and business activity for private profit gave, on one side, a distorted meaning to individualism. Then the weakening, even among persons who nominally retain older theological beliefs, of the imaginative ideas and emotions connected with the sanctity of the individual, disturbed democratic individualism on the positive moral side. The moving energy once associated with things called spiritual has lessened; we use the word *ideal* reluctantly, and have difficulty in giving the word *moral* much force beyond, say, a limited field of mutually kindly relations

163

among individuals. That such a syllogism as the following once had a vital meaning to a man of affairs like Jefferson today seems almost incredible: "Man was created for social intercourse, but social intercourse cannot be maintained without a sense of justice; then man must have been created with a sense of justice."

Even if we have an abiding faith in democracy, we are not likely to express it as Jefferson expressed his faith: "I have no fear but that the result of our experiment will be that men may be trusted to govern themselves without a master. Could the contrary of this be proved, I should conclude either there is no God or that he is a malevolent being." The belief of Jefferson that the sole legitimate object of government among men "is to secure the greatest degree of happiness possible to the general mass of those associated under it" was connected with his belief that Nature—or God—benevolent in intent, had created men for happiness on condition they attained knowledge of natural order and observed the demands of that knowledge in their actions. The obsolescence of the language for many persons makes it the more imperative for all who would maintain and advance the ideals of democracy to face the issue of the moral ground of political institutions and the moral principles by which men acting together may attain freedom of individuals which will amount to fraternal associations with one another. The weaker our faith in Nature, in its laws and rights and its benevolent intentions for human welfare, the more urgent is the need for a faith based on ideas that are now intellectually credible and that are consonant with present economic conditions, which will inspire and direct action with something of the ardor once attached to things religious.

Human power over the physical energies of nature has immensely increased. In moral ideal, power of man over physical nature should be employed to reduce, to eliminate progressively, the power of man over man. By what means shall we prevent its use to effect new, more subtle, more powerful agencies of subjection of men to other men? Both the issue of war or peace between nations, and the future of economic relations for years and generations to come in contribution either to human freedom or human subjection are involved. An increase of power undreamed of a century ago, one to whose further increase no limits can be put as long as scientific inquiry goes on, is an established fact. The thing still uncertain is what we are going to do with it. That it is power signifies of itself it is electrical, thermic, chemical. What will be done with it is a moral issue.

Physical interdependence has increased beyond anything that could have been foreseen. Division of labor in industry was anticipated and was looked forward to with satisfaction. But it is relatively the least weighty phase of the present situation. The career of individuals, their lives and security as well as prosperity is now affected by events on the other side of the world. The forces back of these events he cannot touch or influence—save perhaps by joining in a war of nations against nations. For we seem to live in a world in which nations try to deal with the problems created by the new situation by drawing more and more into themselves, by more and more extreme assertions of independent nationalist sovereignty, while everything they do in the direction of autarchy leads to ever closer mixture with other nations—but in war.

War under existing conditions compels nations, even those professedly the most democratic, to turn authoritarian and totalitarian as the World War of 1914-18 resulted in Fascist totalitarianism in non-democratic Italy and Germany and in Bolshevist totalitarianism in non-democratic Russia, and promoted political, economic and intellectual reaction in this country. The necessity of transforming physical interdependence into moral—into human—interdependence is part of the democratic problem: and yet war is said even now to be the path of salvation for democratic countries!

Individuals can find the security and protection that are prerequisites for freedom only in association with others—and then the organization these associations take on, as a measure of securing their efficiency, limits the freedom of those who have entered into them. The importance of organization has increased so much in the last hundred years that the word is now quite commonly used as a synonym for association and society. Since at the very best organization is but the mechanism through which association operates, the identification is evidence of the extent in which a servant has become a master; in which means have usurped the place of the end for which they are called into existence. The predicament is that individuality demands association to develop and sustain it and association requires arrangement and coordination of its elements, or organization —since otherwise it is formless and void of power. But we have now a kind of molluscan organization, soft individuals within and a hard constrictive shell without. Individuals voluntarily enter associations which have become practically nothing but organizations; and then conditions under which they act take control of what they do whether they want it or not.

Persons acutely aware of the dangers of regimentation when it is imposed by government remain oblivious of the millions of persons whose behavior is regimented by an economic system through whose intervention alone they obtain a livelihood. The contradiction is the more striking because the new organizations were for the most part created in the name of freedom, and, at least at the outset, by exercise of voluntary choice. But the kind of working-together which has resulted is too much like that of the parts of a machine to represent a co-operation which expresses freedom and also contributes to it. No small part of the democratic problem is to achieve associations whose ordering of parts provides the strength that comes from stability, while they promote flexibility of response to change.

Lastly, in this brief survey, there is the problem of the relation of human nature and physical nature. The ancient world solved the problem, in abstract philosophical theory, by endowing all nature, in its cosmic scope, with the moral qualities of the highest and most ideal worth in humanity. The theology and rites of the Church gave this abstract theory direct significance in the lives of the peoples of the western world. For it provided practical agencies by means of which the operation of the power creating and maintaining the universe were supposed to come to the support of individuals in this world and the next. The rise of physical science rendered an ever increasing number of men skeptical of the intellectual foundation provided by the old theory. The unsettlement, going by the name of the conflict of science and religion, proves the existence of the division in the foundations upon which our culture rests, between ideas in the form of knowledge and ideas that are emotional and imaginative and that directly actuate conduct.

This disturbance on the moral side has been enormously aggravated by those who are remote from the unsettlement due to intellectual causes. It comes home to everyone by the effects of the practical application of the new physical science. For all the physical features of the present regime of production and distribution of goods and services are products of the new physical science, while the distinctively *human* consequences of science are still determined by habits and beliefs established before its origin. That democracy should not as yet have succeeded in healing the breach is no cause for discouragement: provided there is effected a union of human possibilities and ideals with the spirit and methods of science on one side and with the workings of the economic system on the other side. For a considerable period laissez-faire individualism prevented the problem from being even seen. It treated the new economic movement as if it were simply an expression of forces that were fundamental in the human constitution but were only recently released for free operation. It failed to see that the great expansion which was occurring was in fact due to release of *physical* energies; that as far as human action and human freedom is concerned, a problem, not a solution, was thereby instituted: the problem, namely, of management and direction of the new physical energies so they would contribute to realization of human possibilities.

The reaction that was created by the inevitable collapse of a movement that failed so disastrously in grasp of the problem has had diverse results, the diversity of which is part of the present confused state of our lives. Production of the material means of a secure and free life has been indefinitely increased and at an accelerated rate. It is not surprising that there is a large group which attributes the gains which have accrued, actually and potentially, to the economic regime under which they have occurred—instead of to the scientific knowledge which is the source of physical control of natural energies. The group is large. It is composed not only of the immediate beneficiaries of the system but also of the much larger number who hope that they, or at least their children, are to have full share in its benefits. Because of the opportunities furnished by free land, large unused natural resources and the absence of fixed class differences (which survive in European countries in spite of legal abolition of feudalism), this group is particularly large in this country. It is represented by those who point to the higher standard of living in this country and by those who have responded to the greater opportunities for advancement this country has afforded to them. In short, this group, in both categories of its constituents, is impressed by actual gains that have come about. They have a kind of blind and touching faith that improvement is going to continue in some more or less automatic way until it includes them and their offspring.

Then there is a much smaller group who are as sensitive, perhaps more so, to the immense possibilities represented by the physical means now potentially at our command, but who are acutely aware of our failure to realize them; who see instead the miseries, cruelties, oppressions and frustrations which exist. The weakness of this group has been that it has also failed to realize the involvement of the new scientific method in producing the existing state of affairs, and the need for its further extensive and unremitting application to determine analytically—in detail—the causes of present ills, and to project means for their elimination. In social affairs, the wholesale mental attitude that has been referred to persists with little change. It leads to formation of ambitious and sweeping beliefs and policies. The human *ideal* is indeed comprehensive. As a standpoint from which to view existing conditions and judge the direction change should take, it cannot be too inclusive. But the problem of production of change is one of infinite attention to means; and means can be determined only by definite analysis of the conditions of each problem as it presents itself. Health is a comprehsnsive, a "sweeping" ideal. But progress toward it has been made in the degree in which recourse to panaceas has been abandoned and inquiry has been directed to determinate disturbances and means for dealing with them. The group is represented at its extreme by those who believe there is a necessary historical law which governs the course of events so that all that is needed is deliberate acting in accord with it. The law by which class conflict produces by its own dialectic its complete opposite becomes then the supreme and sole regulator for determining policies and methods of action.

That more adequate knowledge of human nature is demanded if the release of physical powers is to serve human ends is undeniable. But it is a mistake to suppose that this knowledge of itself enables us to control human energies as physical science has enabled us to control physical energies. It suffers from the fallacy into which those have fallen who have supposed that physical energies put at our disposal by science are sure to produce human progress and prosperity. A more adequate science of human nature might conceivably only multiply the agencies by which some human beings manipulate other human beings for their own advantage. Failure to take account of the moral phase of the problem, the question of values and ends, marks, although from the opposite pole, a relapse into the fallacy of the theorists of a century ago who assumed that "free"—that is to say, politically unrestrained—manifestation of human wants and impulses would tend to bring about social prosperity, progress, and harmony. It is a counterpart fallacy to the Marxist notion that there is an economic or "materialistic," dialectic of history by which a certain desirable (and in that sense moral) end will be brought about with no intervention of choice of values and effort to realize them. As I wrote some years ago, "the assimilation of human science to physical science represents only another form of absolutistic logic, a kind of physical absolutism."

Social events will continue, in any case, to be products of interaction of human nature with cultural conditions. Hence the primary and fundamental question will always be what sort of social results we supremely want. Improved science of human nature would put at our disposal means, now lacking, for defining the problem and working effectively for its solution. But save as it should reinforce respect for the morale of science, and thereby extend and

171

deepen the incorporation of the attitudes which form the method of science into the disposition of individuals, it might add a complication similar to that introduced by improved physcal science. Anything that obscures the fundamentally moral nature of the social problem is harmful, no matter whether it proceeds from the side of physical or of psychological theory. Any doctrine that eliminates or even obscures the function of choice of values and enlistment of desires and emotions in behalf of those chosen weakens personal responsibility for judgment and for action. It thus helps create the attitudes that welcome and support the totalitarian state.

I have stated in bare outline some of the outstanding phases of the problem of culture in the service of democratic freedom. Difficulties and obstacles have been emphasized. This emphasis is a result of the fact that a *problem* is presented. Emphasis upon the problem is due to belief that many weaknesses which events have disclosed are connected with failure to see the immensity of the task involved in setting mankind upon the democratic road. That with a background of millennia of non-democratic societies behind them, the earlier advocates of democracy tremendously simplified the issue is natural. For a time the simplification was an undoubted asset. Too long continued it became a liability.

Recognition of the scope and depth of the problem is neither depressing nor discouraging when the democratic movement is placed in historic perspective. The ideas by which it formulated itself have a long history behind them. We can trace their source in Hellenic humanism and in

172

Christian beliefs; and we can also find recurrent efforts to realize this or that special aspect of these ideas in some special struggle against a particular form of oppression. By proper selection and arrangement, we can even make out a case for the idea that all past history has been a movement, at first unconscious and then conscious, to attain freedom. A more sober view of history discloses that it took a very fortunate conjunction of events to bring about the rapid spread and seemingly complete victory of democracy during the nineteenth century. The conclusion to be drawn is not the depressing one that it is now in danger of destruction because of an unfavorable conjunction of events. The conclusion is that what was won in a more or less external and accidental manner must now be achieved and sustained by deliberate and intelligent endeavor.

The contrast thus suggested calls attention to the fact that underlying persistent attitudes of human beings were formed by traditions, customs, institutions, which existed when there was no democracy—when in fact democratic ideas and aspirations tended to be strangled at birth. Persistence of these basic dispositions accounts, on one side, for the sudden attack upon democracy; it is a reversion to old emotional and intellectual habits; or rather it is not so much a reversion as it is a manifestation of attitudes that have been there all the time but have been more or less covered up. Their persistence also explains the depth and range of the present problem. The struggle for democracy has to be maintained on as many fronts as culture has aspects: political, economic, international, educational, scientific and artistic, religious. The fact that we now have to accomplish of set purpose what in an earlier period was

173

more or less a gift of grace renders the problem a moral one to be worked out on moral grounds.

Part of the fortunate conjunction of circumstances with respect to us who live here in the United States consists, as has been indicated, of the fact that our forefathers found themselves in a new land. The shock of physical dislocation effected a very considerable modification of old attitudes. Habits of thought and feeling which were the products of long centuries of acculturation were loosened. Less entrenched dispositions dropped off. The task of forming new institutions was thereby rendered immensely easier. The readjustment thus effected has been a chief factor in creating a general attitude of adaptability that has enabled us, save for the Civil War, to meet change with a minimum of external conflict and, in spite of an heritage of violence, with good nature. It is because of such consequences that the geographical New World may become a New World in a human sense. But, all the more on this account, the situation is such that most of the things about which we have been complacent and self-congratulatory now have to be won by thought and effort, instead of being results of evolution of a manifest destiny.

In the present state of affairs, a conflict of the moral Old and New Worlds is the essence of the struggle for democracy. It is not a question for us of isolationism, although the physical factors which make possible physical isolation from the warring ambitions of Europe are a factor to be cherished in an emergency. The conflict is not one waged with arms, although the question whether we again take up arms on European battlefields for ends that are foreign to the ends to which this country is dedicated will have weight in deciding whether we win or lose our own battle on our own ground. It is possible to stay out for reasons that have nothing to do with the maintenance of democracy, and a good deal to do with pecuniary profit, just as it is possible to be deluded into participation in the name of fighting for democracy.

The conflict as it concerns the democracy to which our history commits us is *within* our own institutions and attitudes. It can be won only by extending the application of democratic methods, methods of consultation, persuasion, negotiation, communication, co-operative intelligence, in the task of making our own politics, industry, education, our culture generally, a servant and an evolving manifestation of democratic ideas. Resort to military force is a first sure sign that we are giving up the struggle for the democratic way of life, and that the Old World has conquered morally as well as geographically—succeeding in imposing upon us its ideals and methods.

If there is one conclusion to which human experience unmistakably points it is that democratic ends demand democratic methods for their realization. Authoritarian methods now offer themselves to us in new guises. They come to us claiming to serve the ultimate ends of freedom and equity in a classless society. Or they recommend adoption of a totalitarian regime in order to fight totalitarianism. In whatever form they offer themselves, they owe their seductive power to their claim to serve ideal ends. Our first defense is to realize that democracy can be served only by the slow day by day adoption and contagious diffusion in every phase of our common life of methods that are identical with the ends to be reached and that recourse to monistic, wholesale, absolutist procedures is a betrayal of human freedom no matter in what guise it presents itself. An American democracy can serve the world only as it demonstrates in the conduct of its own life the efficacy of plural, partial, and experimental methods in securing and maintaining an ever-increasing release of the powers of human nature, in service of a freedom which is co-operative and a co-operation which is voluntary.

We have no right to appeal to time to justify complacency about the ultimate result. We have every right to point to the long non-democratic and anti-democratic course of human history and to the recentness of democracy in order to enforce the immensity of the task confronting us. The very novelty of the experiment explains the impossibility of restricting the problem to any one element, aspect, or phase of our common everyday life. We have every right to appeal to the long and slow process of time to protect ourselves from the pessimism that comes from taking a short-span temporal view of events—under one condition. We must know that the dependence of ends upon means is such that the only *ultimate* result is the result that is attained today, tomorrow, the next day, and day after day, in the succession of years and generations. Only thus can we be sure that we face our problems in detail one by one as they arise, with all the resources provided by collective intelligence operating in co-operative action. At the end as at the beginning the democratic method is as fundamentally simple and as immensely difficult as is the energetic, unflagging, unceasing creation of an ever-present new road upon which we can walk together.

BOOKS PUBLISHED
BY
FREDERICK ELLIS
(New Hardbacks)

Buy Direct - 25% Off
Free Shipping – Pay with PayPal

Contact - frederick659@yahoo.com

Author - Jack London

$43.75..,..........MARTIN EDEN

$36.75...........WAR OF THE CLASSES

$36.75...........JOHN BARLEYCORN

$33.75...........THE PEOPLE OF THE ABYSS

$34.75...........JACK LONDON ON THE ROAD

$35.75...........THE ASSASSINATION BUREAU, LTD.

$36.75...........THE IRON HEEL

Author – Bruno Traven

$32.75...........GENERAL FROM THE JUNGLE

$38.75...........THE DEATH SHIP

$35.75...........THE REBELLION OF THE HANGED

$34.75...........THE WHITE ROSE

$34.75...........THE BRIDGE IN THE JUNGLE

$34.75..............MARCH TO THE MONTERIA

$37.95..............THE TREASURE OF THE SIERRA MADRE

Author – Carl Frederick

$39.95..............est: PLAYING THE GAME THE NEW WAY

Authors - Frederick Ellis & Carl Frederick

$19.75..............THE OAKLAND STATEMENT (softcover)

Author – Mao Tsetung

$39.75..............QUOTATIONS FROM CHAIRMAN
MAO TSETUNG

Author – Upton Sinclair

$33.75..............OUR LADY

$44.75..............OIL

$39.75..............THE JUNGLE

$32.75..............THE FLIVVER KING: THE STORY OF
FORD-AMERICA

$35.75..............ONE HUNDRED PERCENT: THE STORY
OF A PATRIOT

$37,75..............WORLD'S END I

$42.75..............WORLD'S END II

$34.75..............THE SECRET LIFE OF JESUS

$34.75..............THE MONEYCHANGERS

$35.75...............MENTAL RADIO

$35.75...............THE MILLENIUM

$35.75...............A PERSONAL JESUS

$36.75...............PROFITS OF RELIGION

$34.95...............THEY CALL ME CARPENTER: A TALE
OF THE SECOND COMING

$45.75...............DRAGON'S TEETH

Author – Thomas Paine

$38.75...............COMMON SENSE & THE RIGHTS OF
MAN & THE AGE OF REASON

$33.75...............THE AMERICAN CRISIS

Author – Karl Marx

$39.75...............DAS KAPITAL

$33.75...............THE COMMUNIST MANIFESTO &
WAGES, PRICE AND PROFIT

$32.75...............WAGE-LABOUR AND CAPITAL
& VALUE, PRICE AND PROFIT

Author – W. E. B. Du Bois

$34.75...............THE SOULS OF BLACK FOLK

Author – Eugene Debs

$35.75...............WALLS AND BARS

Author – Jean-Jacques Rousseau

$34.75................THE SOCIAL CONTRACT

Author – John Reed

$37.75................TEN DAYS THAT SHOOK THE WORLD

$36.75................INSURGENT MEXICO

Author – Antonio Gramsci

$33.75................THE MODERN PRINCE AND
SELECTED WRITINGS

Author – V. I. Lenin

$35.75................THE STATE AND REVOLUTION

$36.95................FIGHT AGAINST STALINISM &
IMPERIALISM: THE HIGHEST
STAGE OF CAPITALISM

Author – John Dewey

$35.75................HOW WE THINK & EDUCATION
AND EXPERIENCE

$37.75................ INDIVIDUALISM OLD AND NEW &
LIBERALISM AND SOCIAL ACTION
& A COMMON FAITH

$39.75................DEMOCRACY AND EDUCATION &
FREEDOM AND CULTURE

Author – David Ricardo

$37.75....................PRINCIPLES OF POLITICAL
ECONOMY AND TAXATION

Author – Thomas Jefferson

$34.75................BIOGRAPHY OF THOMAS JEFFERSON &
THE LIFE AND MORALS OF JESUS OF
NAZARETH

Author – Emma Goldman

$35.95................ANARCHISM AND OTHER WRITINGS

Author – Rosa Luxemburg

$32.95.................REFORM OR REVOLUTION & THE
MASS STRIKE

Author – Leon Trotsky

$35.75.................THE REVOLUTION BETRAYED

Author – John Stuart Mill

$33.95..................ON SOCIALISM & THE SUBJECTION
OF WOMEN

Author – Friedrich Nietzsche

$34.75.................BEYOND GOOD AND EVIL

$40.75...................THE BIRTH OF TRAGEDY &
75 APHORISMS &
THE ANTI-CHRIST

Author – John Quincy Adams

$33.95................THE AMISTAD ARGUMENT &
                     THE STATE OF THE UNION
                     ADDRESSES

Authors – James Madison. Alexander Hamilton, John Jay

$40.75..................THE FEDERALIST PAPERS